URBAN ECONOMICS
AND
REAL ESTATE MARKETS

URBAN ECONOMICS AND REAL ESTATE MARKETS

DENISE DiPASQUALE
Harvard University

WILLIAM C. WHEATON
Massachusetts Institute of Technology

PRENTICE HALL, Englewood Cliffs, NJ 07632

Acquisitions editor   *Leah Jewell*
Production manager   *Maureen Wilson/Penny Linskey*
Assistant editor   *Teresa Cohan*
Buyer   *Marie McNamara*
Marketing manager   *Susan McLaughlin*
Cover designer   *Maureen Eide*

© 1996 by Prentice-Hall, Inc.
Englewood Cliffs, New Jersey 07632

All rights reserved. No part of this book may be
reproduced, in any form or by any means,
without permission in writing from the publisher.

Printed in the United States of America

10   9   8   7   6   5

ISBN 0-13-225244-9

Prentice-Hall International (UK) Limited, *London*
Prentice-Hall of Australia Pty. Limited, *Sydney*
Prentice-Hall Canada, Inc., *Toronto*
Prentice-Hall Hispanoamericana, S.A., *Mexico*
Prentice-Hall of India Private Limited, *New Delhi*
Prentice-Hall of Japan, Inc., *Tokyo*
Editora Prentice Hall do Brasil, Ltda., *Rio de Janeiro*

CONTENTS

Preface ix

SECTION ONE: INTRODUCTION TO REAL ESTATE MARKETS

Chapter 1: The Property and Capital Markets 1

THE SIZE AND CHARACTER OF U.S. REAL ESTATE 2
THE MARKETS FOR REAL ESTATE ASSETS AND REAL ESTATE USE 6
OWNER-OCCUPIED REAL ESTATE 10
REAL ESTATE AND THE NATIONAL ECONOMY 11
REAL ESTATE MARKETS AND PUBLIC POLICY 18
SUMMARY 20
REFERENCES AND ADDITIONAL READINGS 21

Chapter 2: The Operation of Property Markets: A Micro and Macro Approach 22

DEFINING MARKETS: PROPERTY TYPES 23
DEFINING MARKETS: AREAS 24
REAL ESTATE MICROECONOMICS: URBAN LAND AND LOCATION 25
REAL ESTATE MACROECONOMICS: MARKET GROWTH AND DYNAMICS 31
SUMMARY 34

SECTION TWO: MICROECONOMIC ANALYSIS OF PROPERTY MARKETS

Residential Real Estate

Chapter 3: The Urban Land Market: Rents and Prices 35

Urban Commuting and Ricardian Rent 36
Population, Land Supply, and Ricardian Rent 40
Competition and Spatial Separation 42
Growth and Rents 46
Growth and Prices 49
Housing Prices: Some Empirical Evidence 56
Summary 57
Appendix: Continuous Time Discounting 58
References and Additional Readings 59

Chapter 4: The Urban Housing Market: Structural Attributes and Density 60

Urban Density 61
Housing Attributes and Housing Preferences 65
Housing Attributes and New Construction 72
Residential Density, Land Value, and Highest Use 73
Location and Residential Density 79
Patterns of Urban Development and Redevelopment 81
Redevelopment, Occupancy, and Land-Use Succession 87
Summary 89
References and Additional Readings 90

Nonresidential Property Markets

Chapter 5: Firm Site Selection, Employment Decentralization, and Multicentered Cities 91

The Spatial Distribution of Employment 92
Land Markets with a Central Business District 97
Technology and the Decentralization of Manufacturers 100
Wages, the Labor Market, and Office Decentralization 102
Subcenters and Urban Agglomeration 109
Subcenters, Wages, and the Urban Land Market 111
Subcenters and Rents in Greater Boston 118
Subcenters, Local Governments, and Land-Use Restrictions 120

Contents

  Summary 122
  References and Additional Readings 122

Chapter 6: Retail Location and Market Competition 124

  Retail Location Patterns 125
  Store Frequency and Consumer Shopping Behavior 128
  Goods and Shopping Frequency 132
  Classical Retail Competition Theory 133
  Neoclassical Retailing: Joint Purchases and Centers 137
  Modeling Shopping Center Attraction 140
  Forecasting Shopping Behavior in Boston 143
  Markets and Retail Sales 146
  Summary 147
  References and Additional Readings 148

SECTION THREE: MACROECONOMIC ANALYSIS OF PROPERTY MARKETS

Chapter 7: Economic Growth and Metropolitan Real Estate Markets 149

  Regional Economies 150
  A Three-Sector Model of Metropolitan Economic Growth 155
  Demand-Induced Regional Growth 159
  Supply-Induced Regional Growth 162
  Regional Exports and Product Demand Shifts 165
  Regional Labor Supply: Migration and Demography 175
  Regional Competition, Wages, and Real Estate Markets 177
  Summary 179
  References and Additional Readings 180

Residential Real Estate

Chapter 8: The Market for Housing Units: Households, Prices, and Financing 182

  Household Formation and the Demand for Housing Units 183
  Tenure Choice 186
  The Price of Housing 189
  Financing Homeownership 193
  The U.S. Mortgage Market 199
  Federal Tax Policy and the Costs of Homeownership 202

FEDERAL TAX POLICY AND THE RETURN TO INVESTORS IN RENTAL HOUSING   206
SUMMARY   211
REFERENCES AND ADDITIONAL READINGS   212

Chapter 9: The Market for Housing Services: Moving, Sales, and Vacancy   216

HOUSEHOLDS AND THEIR HOUSING CONSUMPTION PATTERNS   217
INCOME AND HOUSING CONSUMPTION: THE ELASTICITY OF DEMAND   217
HOUSING CONSUMPTION AND LIFE CYCLE   220
HOUSEHOLD MOBILITY AND CHANGES IN HOUSING DEMAND   222
VACANCY, MOBILITY, AND HOUSING SALES   224
VACANCY, SALES TIME, PRICES, AND RENTS   227
VACANCY AND NEW CONSTRUCTION   229
VACANCY, SALES, AND PRICES: A SIMPLE MODEL   230
NEW CONSTRUCTION AND THE EVOLUTION OF THE HOUSING STOCK   235
SUMMARY   238
REFERENCES AND ADDITIONAL READINGS   239

Chapter 10: The Cyclical Behavior of Metropolitan Housing Markets   242

A HOUSING MARKET STOCK-FLOW MODEL   243
MARKET DYNAMICS WITH EXOGENOUS PRICE EXPECTATIONS   247
MARKET DYNAMICS WITH MYOPIC PRICE EXPECTATIONS   251
MARKET DYNAMICS WITH RATIONAL EXPECTATIONS   254
FORECASTING BOSTON HOUSE PRICES: AN APPLICATION   257
SUMMARY   266
REFERENCES AND ADDITIONAL READINGS   267

Nonresidential Property Markets

Chapter 11: The Operation of Nonresidential Property Markets   269

MARKET CONDITIONS AND THE INVESTMENT RETURNS TO REAL ESTATE   270
CONSTRUCTION CYCLES AND THE STOCK OF SPACE   273
THE DEMAND FOR PROPERTY: OWNERSHIP AND OCCUPANCY   277
LEASES, RENTS, AND VACANCY: THE COST OF SPACE TO USERS   285
SUMMARY   290
APPENDIX 11-A   291
REFERENCES AND ADDITIONAL READINGS   292

Chapter 12: Econometric Analysis of Metropolitan Office and Industrial Markets 293

THE MARKET FOR OFFICE SPACE IN SAN FRANCISCO 294
THE MARKET FOR INDUSTRIAL SPACE IN PHILADELPHIA 309
SUMMARY 317
REFERENCES AND ADDITIONAL READINGS 317

SECTION FOUR: THE IMPACT OF LOCAL GOVERNMENTS ON REAL ESTATE MARKETS

Chapter 13: Local Governments, Property Taxes, and Real Estate Markets 319

GOVERNMENTS AND PUBLIC SERVICES 321
LOCAL GOVERNMENTS AND PROPERTY TAXES IN METROPOLITAN AREAS 325
HOUSEHOLD LOCATION AND COMMUNITY STRATIFICATION 331
ZONING AND THE FISCAL IMPACTS OF RESIDENTIAL DEVELOPMENT 334
THE FISCAL COSTS AND BENEFITS OF NONRESIDENTIAL DEVELOPMENT 338
CAPITALIZATION AND THE INCIDENCE OF LOCAL TAXES AND SERVICES 342
SUBURBAN COMPETITION, TAXES, AND THE PLIGHT OF CENTRAL CITIES 344
SUMMARY 345
REFERENCES AND ADDITIONAL READINGS 346

Chapter 14: Public Goods, Externalities, and Development Regulation 348

PROPERTY VALUES AND PUBLIC AMENITIES 349
PUBLIC AMENITIES AND FREE RIDERS 350
EXTERNAL EFFECTS ACROSS PROPERTIES 354
CONTRACTS, COOPERATION, AND GOVERNMENT REGULATION 357
HISTORY, EXTERNALITIES, AND LAND-USE PATTERNS 360
CONGESTION EXTERNALITIES, REGIONAL PLANNING, AND THE LAND MARKET 363
SUMMARY 369
REFERENCES AND ADDITIONAL READINGS 369

Index 371

PREFACE

In today's world, real estate professionals, financial institutions, local planners, and government officials increasingly realize that a broad understanding of the economic forces affecting cities and urban development is crucial to making wise decisions. Our goal for this book is to contribute to that understanding and provide students with the tools and perspective required to operate effectively, in either the private or public sectors, to promote a better built environment. To accomplish this goal, we use basic economic models combined with real world data to build a sophisticated understanding of urban development and real estate markets. Our intent is to provide students with both a theoretical perspective as well as the tools and basic facts they need to analyze urban markets.

The conceptual foundations provided in this book largely build on an extensive urban economics literature developed over the last five decades. This literature provides valuable insights into the operation of urban land and housing markets, transportation systems, and the process of metropolitan growth and regional development. Throughout the book, we illustrate the power of using fairly simple economic models to understand and predict the operation of real estate markets, with a variety of real world applications.

We designed the book for use in advanced undergraduate courses in real estate or urban economics and in graduate level courses in business schools and schools of public policy and planning. We assume that students in these courses have taken at least one course in economic principles; students with intermediate economics will be able to move more quickly through the material. We also assume that students have a solid knowledge of high school mathematics; we use calculus only in footnotes to explain some of the more complex concepts. An introductory statistics course including regression analysis would also be useful because, throughout the book, we estimate statistical models to illustrate a variety of points.

PLAN OF BOOK

Section One of this book includes two introductory chapters. Chapter 1 defines real estate and examines its importance in the national economy. In addition, it provides a simple conceptual framework for analyzing real estate markets. Chapter 2 lays out the distinction between micro- and macroeconomic analysis as it applies to analyzing real estate markets. We use this distinction throughout the rest of the book.

In Section Two, we focus on the microeconomics of real estate markets. In Chapters 3 and 4, we study how residential land markets work, how house prices are determined across locations, and how patterns of urban density evolve over time in response to such prices. The objective is to build a broad understanding of urban land use and to apply this understanding in several practical ways. These include determining the best use for a site, the most profitable density for residential development, and the timing for when existing houses should be torn down for new construction.

In Chapters 5 and 6, we shift over to the microeconomic analysis of commercial property markets. Chapter 5 looks at the location decisions of commercial and industrial firms within metropolitan areas, establishing the strong link between the residential location of workers and the location of their workplaces. Tendencies toward spatial centralization or decentralization are carefully studied in these chapters. Chapter 6 continues the study of firm-household spatial connections, this time examining the location decisions of retailers. The decentralization of retail development is examined along with the emerging tendency toward large scale retail clustering.

Section Three of the book focuses on the macroeconomics of real estate markets. Chapter 7 examines metropolitan economic growth and its determinants. We consider the impacts of a region's industrial mix and competitiveness on its economic growth, as well as the impacts on growth of changes in the demand for a region's output versus changes in the region's supply of factors of production. National patterns in the formation of households and the construction of residential units are examined in Chapter 8, along with the various institutions that shape the financing of housing. Chapter 9 looks at household mobility, housing transactions, and the selection of unit type by different households. The central role that vacancy plays in this choice is carefully examined. In Chapter 10, we build a stock-flow model of the housing market that illustrates how expectations concerning the future of the market influence market outcomes. We conclude the chapter by empirically estimating a stock-flow model for the Boston single-family housing market.

Chapters 11 and 12 deal with the macroeconomic behavior of nonresidential property markets. In Chapter 11, aggregate data on office and industrial construction are examined, as well as information on rents and vacancy. In Chapter 12, we build forecasting models for the office space market in San Francisco and the industrial space market in Philadelphia.

Finally, in Section Four, we examine the impact of local government on real estate markets. A distinctive characteristic of real estate is the extensive government regulation of both land and structure. Chapter 13 looks at property taxation and the system of local government finance. Competition between local governments is shown to result in financial incentives for such governments to exclude certain uses and encourage others. Chapter 14 looks at the various ways that local governments regulate land development and examines the rationale for such controls. A system of competing local governments is shown to have profound effects on the metropolitan-wide pattern of land development.

ACKNOWLEDGMENTS

There are many people who contributed insight, time, and encouragement to us during the four years we worked on this project. During this time, we worked with three excellent editors at Prentice Hall: Whitney Blake who signed the book, Stephen Dietrich who patiently watched us miss deadlines but continued to be an enthusiastic cheerleader for us and the book, and Leah Jewell who impressively coached us through the final quarter. While three editors for one book certainly indicates that it took us a while to finish, it also provides some indication of the dynamic nature of the publishing business.

We want to thank our colleagues who reviewed the manuscript. We are particularly grateful to Tsur Somerville, University of British Columbia, who not only provided detailed comments on the manuscript but taught a number of the draft chapters and gave very useful feedback on how the material worked in his classes. We also thank Dennis Capozza, University of Michigan; Steven Grenadier, Stanford University; Edwin S. Mills, Northwestern University; and Susan Wachter, University of Pennsylvania, for their comments. As usual, we remain responsible for any errors that remain.

We gratefully acknowledge the Joint Center for Housing Studies of Harvard University, which provided significant funding and a gracious home for the first half of this project. The Taubman Center for State and Local Government at Harvard University's Kennedy School of Government provided the home base during the second half of the project. The MIT Center for Real Estate and Prentice Hall provided additional funding.

Providing empirical analysis of real estate markets was an important goal for us that we could not have accomplished in the chapters on nonresidential property markets without the generous provision of data by CB Commercial. We want to thank the research staff there, particularly Anne O'Donnell, Kathleen Shavel, and Jeff Torto.

This book grew out of our needs for materials for our own courses and over the past few years our students have made important contributions to this effort. They read early drafts, listened to us present various versions of this material, and provided important reactions ranging from suggestions on better ways to present a model to blank stares in class that indicated to us that it was time to return to the drawing board. We are very grateful for their patience and input. We also would like to thank our teaching fellows who provided important feedback on the book while teaching with us, particularly Guy Dumais and Ingrid Ellen. We thank John Cawley for his expert research assistance.

We are very grateful to Ken Caplan who provided excellent research assistance, extensive comments on a variety of chapters, and an undaunted spirit in conquering the gremlins in mapping software.

Our greatest debt and gratitude is to Jean L. Cummings, who worked on this project from beginning to end. She compiled most of the empirical evidence, read and commented on every chapter through what must have seemed like an endless succession of drafts, and suggested ways of improving the presentation of both models and data. Throughout this endeavor, Jean was our colleague, friend, sounding board, and, at times, referee. To the extent that the reader finds any glimmers of clarity in this book, it is safe to assume that Jean was involved.

DENISE DIPASQUALE
WILLIAM C. WHEATON

Section 1 Introduction to Real Estate Markets

CHAPTER 1

THE PROPERTY AND CAPITAL MARKETS

What is real estate? How big is the real estate sector? How does the market for the use of real estate differ from the market for real estate assets? In this chapter, our objectives are (1) to define *real estate,* (2) to describe how the real estate sector operates within the national economy, and (3) to distinguish between the market for real estate use (where space is rented or purchased for occupancy) and the market for real estate assets (where buildings are bought and sold as investments).

The most common definition of *real estate* is the national stock of buildings, the land on which they are built, and all vacant land. These buildings are used either by firms, government, nonprofit organizations, and so on, as workplaces, or by households as places of residence. When defined this way, the value of all real estate makes up the largest single component of national wealth.

The yearly value of new buildings put in place represents an annual investment in the nation's stock of capital. The dollar value of these new buildings also has been the largest single category of national investment in recent years. Investment in new buildings accounts for roughly 7 percent of gross domestic product (GDP). Of this 7 percent, about 60 percent is payments to the construction sector (for labor, construction equipment, etc.), with the remaining 40 percent going to the producers of building materials. It is important to note that land is not counted as part of investment or GDP since it is not a produced commodity. On the other hand, land is a national asset, and so the value of land beneath buildings should be counted as stock or wealth.

The distinction between real estate as space and real estate as an asset is most clear when buildings are not occupied by their owners. The needs of tenants and the type and quality of buildings available determine the rent for space in the market for property use. At the same time, buildings may be bought, sold, or exchanged between investors. These transactions occur in the capital market and determine the *asset* price of space. In this chapter, we present a simple analytic framework which illustrates the connections between the market for real estate space (the property market) and the market for real estate assets (the asset or capital market). As we will show later in this chapter, this same approach can be used for owner-occupied real estate where the user of space is also the investor in the asset.

Our view of the real estate market as actually two markets helps to clarify how different forces influence this important sector. If, for example, there is a sudden demand by foreign investors to purchase U.S. office buildings, the impact on rents is very different than if firms suddenly decide that they wish to rent more office space for their use. A reduction in long-term mortgage rates has just the opposite effect on house prices from that caused by a reduction in short-term rates for construction financing. Distinguishing between the property and capital markets provides a clearer understanding of how such forces operate in the real estate sector as a whole.

In addition, there is a methodological objective in this first chapter—to reacquaint the reader with simple supply and demand analysis. By considering how the markets for both real estate property and assets operate within a global economy, we recall the distinction between endogenous economic variables and exogenous economic forces.[1] Within the markets for real estate, economic variables like prices, sales, and output are all determined endogenously. The outcome of the market, however, may be strongly influenced by exogenous forces such as world trade, interest rates, or even climate. Studying how changes in exogenous forces affect endogenous variables is one of the most important and fundamental pursuits of economics. How this methodology is applied to the real estate markets is a major focus of this book.

THE SIZE AND CHARACTER OF U.S. REAL ESTATE

Private real estate is composed of all types of buildings as well as the land they sit on. Houses, office buildings, warehouses, and shopping centers all are clear examples of real estate. Other, less obvious examples include privately owned ice-skating rinks and aircraft hangars. These are the buildings that various service firms (e.g., recreation, lodging, and travel) need for their operations. Finally, petroleum refineries, steel mills, and utility power plants are partially real estate—some portion of these structures is considered industrial "plant," while the remainder is "equipment." Public real estate is composed of all government-owned office buildings, schools, firehouses, military barracks, and the like.

---

[1] By *exogenous forces* we mean factors that influence real estate market outcomes but are not influenced by the real estate market. For example, interest rates have profound impacts on real estate market outcomes, but the real estate market has very little if any impact on interest rates. *Endogenous variables* are measures of real estate market outcomes. Prices and rents are endogenous, which means that they are determined by the real estate market.

Chapter 1   The Property and Capital Markets

Like any economic variable, real estate can be measured both as a flow and as a stock. The *flow* of real estate is the value of new buildings put in place each year, less losses from the stock through depreciation or demolition. New completions represent an important component of national investment, which is also a flow variable. On the other hand, the total value of all existing buildings and the value of all land are *stock* variables, and are part of national wealth—also a stock variable. Since land is nonreproducible, it is always a stock variable and never a flow variable.

Table 1.1 breaks down the value of new construction put in place in 1990. Virtually all private construction was in the form of buildings and represented $301 billion (5.5

TABLE 1.1   Value of New Construction Put in Place, 1990

	$ (in billions)	% of GDP
Private Construction	338	6.1
Buildings	301	5.5
Residential Buildings	183	3.3
Nonresidential Buildings	118	2.1
Industrial	24	0.4
Office	29	0.5
Hotels/Motels	10	0.2
Other Commercial	34	0.6
All Other Nonresidential	21	0.4
Nonbuilding Construction	37	0.7
Public Utilities	31	0.6
All Other	6	0.1
Public Construction	109	2.0
Buildings	46	0.8
Housing and Development	4	0.1
Industrial	1	0.0
Other	41	0.7
Nonbuilding Construction	63	1.1
Infrastructure	55	1.0
All Other	8	0.1
Total New Construction	446	8.1
Total GDP:	5,514	100.0

Source: Current Construction Reports, Series C30, U.S. Bureau of the Census; gross domestic product, *Economic Report of the President 1992.*

percent of GDP). Residential buildings accounted for about 61 percent of the dollar value of private buildings constructed, with office, industrial and other commercial structures representing the remainder. In the public sector, buildings represented only about 42 percent of the $109 billion in public construction. The largest component of public construction was investment in infrastructure (roads, bridges, airports, etc.).

Total gross private domestic investment, which measures purchases of fixed capital goods including structures and equipment, was $803 billion in the U.S. in 1990. (Board of Governors 1991). In these figures, structures include purchases of new residential and nonresidential structures, as well as net purchases of existing structures. The structure component accounted for just over half of the nation's gross investment ($415 billion), while the remaining $388 billion was investment in machinery or equipment.

Over the years, government statistics have tracked the flow of gross investment into real estate (i.e., new building construction) with a high degree of accuracy. Valuing the total real estate stock at any point in time, however, is far more difficult. The Bureau of Economic Analysis (BEA) provides estimates of "fixed reproducible tangible wealth," which attempt to value the stock of both residential and nonresidential structures. Estimates of gross stock are calculated by summing investment flows and deducting the cumulated investment in structures that have been discarded. The investment flow data are from the national income and product accounts. Net capital stock is calculated by using a depreciation formula to write off the value over the life of the stock. The Federal Reserve uses the BEA estimates of net stock and adds their estimates of the value of land to provide balance sheet estimates of the value of U.S. real estate (Miles 1990).

An important problem with this approach to value is that the cumulated investment flow less demolition and depreciation may bear little resemblance to the actual market value of real estate. While the investment flow data may be a fairly accurate measure of the value of additions to the stock in the current year, changes in the value of those additions to the stock over time are a function of market forces that are unlikely to be captured even by the most sophisticated estimates of depreciation. In addition, it is difficult to estimate the value of the land on which those structures are built because most observed transactions provide a single purchase price for the existing building and the land, with no breakdown by the land and structure components.

A 1991 study made a gallant attempt at estimating the value of all U.S. real estate according to type of real estate (e.g., residential, office, and retail) and type of owner (e.g., individuals, corporations) by piecing together data from a variety of sources (IREM 1991). The study employed standard government statistics, such as the American Housing Survey (AHS) for residential units, and trade association data such as those collected by the International Council of Shopping Centers. In addition, it used state and county property tax records as a basis for regression models that estimate real estate value. Finally, the study relied on interviews with industry experts to augment their data.

In this study, total real estate in the U.S. for 1990 was estimated to be worth $8.8 trillion. As shown in Table 1.2, almost 70 percent of all U.S. real estate was residential, and almost 90 percent of the value of residential real estate was in the nation's stock of single-family homes. The 30 percent of U.S. real estate that was nonresidential was dominated by office and retail space—at least in dollar value. While estimates of total national

TABLE 1.2 Value of U.S. Real Estate, 1990

	$ (in billions)	% of Total
Residential	6,122	69.8
Single-Family Homes	5,419	61.7
Multifamily	552	6.3
Condominiums/Coops	96	1.1
Mobile Homes	55	0.6
Nonresidential	2,655	30.2
Retail	1,115	12.7
Office	1,009	11.5
Manufacturing	308	3.5
Warehouse	223	2.5
Total U.S. Real Estate	8,777	100.0

Source: Managing the Future: Real Estate in the 1990s (Chicago: IREM Foundation and Arthur Anderson, 1991), pp. 28, 31.

wealth often vary, the Federal Reserve estimates that national net worth was at $15.6 trillion in 1990. Thus, the figures in Table 1.2 suggest that real estate, valued at $8.8 trillion, constituted roughly 56 percent of the nation's wealth in 1990.[2]

Who owns American real estate? The legal ownership status of this wealth is shown in Table 1.3. In 1990, 83 percent of residential real estate was owned by individuals. It is important to remember that this figure covers not only individual ownership of personal residences but also sole-proprietor ownership of apartment buildings. Similarly, the 62 percent of nonresidential real estate that was owned by corporations consists of investment property as well as buildings occupied by their corporate owners. Partnerships own almost equal shares of residential and nonresidential property. Finally, the ownership of U.S. real estate by foreign entities is very small, despite considerable concern about this during the last few years.

In summary, U.S. real estate is the largest single component of national wealth and the largest component of annual net private investment. This huge base of assets, however, has been accumulated by devoting only about 5 to 7 percent of each year's GDP to the construction and renovation of that base. It is, of course, the durability of real estate that allows us to devote such a small fraction of GDP to the accumulation and maintenance of such a large share of our assets.

---

[2]The national net worth estimate is from *Balance Sheets for the U.S. Economy 1945–1990* (Washington, D.C.: Board of Governors of the Federal Reserve System, 1991). It should be noted that the Federal Reserve estimates the value of real estate at $10.7 trillion. Miles (1991:74) argues that the BEA/Federal Reserve estimates of the value of nonresidential real estate may be high because the data used for the stock estimates include special fixtures in manufacturing plants that are certainly part of the capital stock, but should not be included when measuring the value of real estate.

TABLE 1.3 Who Owns U.S. Real Estate, 1990

	All Real Estate		Residential Only		Nonresidential Only	
	$ (in billions)	%	$ (in billions)	%	$ (in billions)	%
Individuals	5,088	58.0	5,071	82.8	17	0.6
Corporations	1,699	19.4	66	1.1	1,633	61.5
Partnerships	1,011	11.5	673	11.0	338	12.7
Nonprofits	411	4.7	104	1.7	307	11.6
Government	234	2.6	173	2.8	61	2.3
Institutional Investors	128	1.5	14	0.2	114	4.3
Financial Institutions	114	1.3	13	0.2	101	3.8
Other (Includes Foreign)	92	1.0	8	0.1	84	3.2
Total:	8,777	100.0	6,122	100.0	2,655	100.0
% of All Real Estate:		100.0		69.8		30.2

Source: Managing the Future: Real Estate in the 1990s (Chicago: IREM Foundation and Arthur Anderson, 1991), pp. 29–33.

THE MARKETS FOR REAL ESTATE ASSETS AND REAL ESTATE USE

Since real estate is a durable capital good, its production and price are determined in an asset, or capital, market. In this market, the demand to own real estate assets must equal their supply. Thus, the price of houses in the U.S. largely depends on how many households wish to *own* units and how many units are available for ownership. Likewise, the value or price of shopping center space depends on how many investors wish to own such space and how many centers there are available to invest in. In both cases, all else being equal, an increase in the demand to own these assets will raise prices, while a greater supply of space will depress prices.

The supply of new real estate assets comes from the construction sector and depends on the price of those assets relative to the cost of replacing or constructing them. In the long run, the asset market should equate market prices with replacement costs that include the cost of land. In the short run, however, the two may diverge significantly because of the lags and delays that are inherent in the construction process. For example, if demand for the ownership of space suddenly rises, then, with a fixed supply of assets, prices will rise as well. With prices now above construction and land costs, new development takes place. As this space arrives on the market, demand is satisfied and prices begin to fall back towards the cost of replacement. A question to be addressed in future chapters is whether the cost of asset replacement is constant, varies with the level of development, or depends on the total stock of assets.

What would cause the demand for owning real estate assets to suddenly increase? More generally, are there other determinants of asset demand besides simply the price of these assets? The answer is yes, and the most important of these determinants is the rental income that real estate assets earn. To understand rent, it is necessary to consider the market for the *use* of real estate.

In the market for real estate use or space (referred to here as the property market), demand comes from the *occupiers* of space, whether they be tenants or owners, firms or households. For firms, space is one of many factors of production, and, like any other factor, its use will depend on firm output levels and the relative cost of space. Households likewise divide their income into the consumption of many commodities, only one of which is space. The household demand for space depends on income and the cost of occupying that space relative to the cost of other commodities, such as food, clothing, or entertainment. For firms or households, the cost of occupying space is the annual outlay necessary to obtain the use of real estate—its *rent*. For tenants, rent is simply specified in a lease agreement. For owners, rent is defined as the annualized cost associated with the ownership of property.

Rent is determined in the property market for space use, not in the asset market for ownership. In the property market, the supply of space is given (from the asset market). The demand for space depends on rent and other exogenous economic factors such as firm production levels, income levels, or the number of households. The task of the property market is to determine a rent level at which the demand for space use equals the supply of space. All else being equal, when the number of households increases or firms expand production, the demand for space *use* rises. With fixed supply, rents rise as well.

The link between the asset market and the property market occurs at two junctions. First, the rent levels determined in the property market are central in determining the demand for real estate assets. After all, in acquiring an asset, investors are really purchasing a current or future income stream. Thus, changes in rent occurring in the property market immediately affect the demand for ownership in the asset market. The second link between the two markets occurs through the construction or development sector. If construction increases and the supply of assets grows, not only are prices driven down in the asset market, but rents decline in the property market as well. These connections between the two markets are illustrated in the four-quadrant diagram in Figure 1.1.

In explaining Figure 1.1, it is useful to refer to quadrants by their compass designation. The two right-hand quadrants (northeast and southeast) represent the property market for the use of space, while the two left-hand quadrants (northwest and southwest) deal with the asset market for the ownership of real estate. Let's begin with the northeast quadrant, where rents are determined in the short run.

The northeast quadrant has two axes: rent (per unit of space) and the stock of space (also measured in units of space, such as square feet). The curve represents how the demand for space depends on rents, given the state of the economy. Movement along that curve depicts how much space would be demanded given a particular rent level on the vertical axis. If households or firms tend to demand the same amount of space regardless of rent levels (inelastic demand), then the curve is nearly vertical. If space usage is quite sensitive to rents (elastic demand), then the curve is more horizontal. If the economy changes, then the entire curve shifts. An upward shift occurs with an increase in firms or households (economic growth) and signifies that more space is demanded for the same rent. Economic decline causes a downward shift in the line, with the reverse implications.

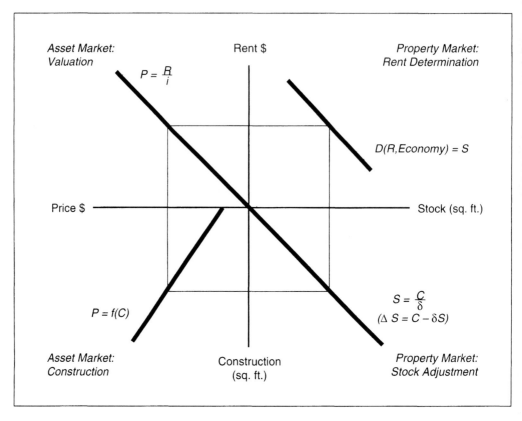

FIGURE 1.1 Real estate: the property and asset markets.

In equilibrium the demand for space, D, is equal to the stock of space, S. Thus, rent, R, must be determined so that demand is exactly equal to stock. Demand is a function of rent and conditions in the economy:

$$D(R, \text{Economy}) = S \tag{1.1}$$

Recall that in the property market the supply of stock is given from the asset market. In Figure 1.1, then, rent is determined by taking a level of stock of space on the horizontal axis, drawing a line up to the demand curve, and then over to the vertical axis. With this rent for the use of space, we then move to the asset market in the northwest quadrant.[3]

The northwest quadrant represents the first part of the asset market and has two axes: rent and price (per unit of space). The ray emanating from the origin represents the

---

[3]If we take the office market as an example, it would be reasonable to assume that the demand for office space use (in square feet), D, is equal to: $E(400 - 10R)$, where E is the number of office workers in the economy (in millions), and R is the annual rent per square foot. In the northeast quadrant, we equate this demand to the existing stock, S, solving for rent. Equation (1.1) can be rewritten as:

$$R = 40 - \frac{S}{10E}$$

capitalization rate for real estate assets: the ratio of rent-to-price. This is the current yield that investors demand in order to hold real estate assets. Generally, four considerations make up this capitalization rate: the long-term interest rate in the economy, the expected growth in rents, the risks associated with that rental income stream, and the treatment of real estate in the U.S. federal tax code. A higher capitalization rate is represented by a clockwise rotation in the ray, while a decline in the cap rate is represented by a counter-clockwise rotation. In this quadrant, the capitalization rate is taken as exogenous, based on interest rates and returns in the broader capital market for all assets (stocks, bonds, short-term deposits). Thus, the purpose of the northwest quadrant is to take the rent level, R, from the northeast quadrant and determine a price for real estate assets, P, using a capitalization rate, i:

$$P = \frac{R}{i} \quad (1.2)$$

This is done by moving from the rent level on the vertical axis in the northeast quadrant over to the ray in the northwest quadrant, and then down to the horizontal axis where asset price is given.

The next (southwest) quadrant is that portion of the asset market in which the creation of new assets is determined. Here, the curve $f(C)$ represents the replacement cost of real estate. In this version of the diagram, the cost of replacement through new construction is assumed to increase with greater building activity (C), and so the curve moves in a southwesterly direction. It intersects the price axis at that minimum dollar value (per unit of space) required to get some level of new development underway. If this construction can be supplied at any level with almost the same costs, then the ray will be close to vertical. Construction bottlenecks, scarce land, and other impediments to development lead to inelastic supply and a ray that is more horizontal. Given the price of real estate assets from the northwest quadrant, a line down to the replacement cost curve and then over to the vertical axis determines the level of new construction where replacement costs equal asset prices.[4] Lower levels of construction would lead to excess profits, whereas higher levels would be unprofitable. Hence, new construction occurs at that level, C, at which asset price, P, is equal to replacement costs, $f(C)$:

$$P = f(C) \quad (1.3)$$

In the southeast quadrant, the annual flow of new construction, C, is converted into a long-run stock of real estate space. The change in the stock, ΔS, in a given period is equal to new construction minus losses from the stock measured by the depreciation (removal) rate, δ:

$$\Delta S = C - \delta S \quad (1.4)$$

---

[4]For the office market example, a reasonable cost function (dollar per square foot) for the development of new office space would be: $200 + 5C$. The annual level of new construction, C, is in millions of square feet. If these costs are equated to the asset price (per square foot) of office space, Equation (1.3) can be rewritten to solve for the level of construction where costs equal asset prices:

$$C = \frac{P - 200}{5}$$

The ray emanating from the origin represents that level of stock (on the horizontal axis) that requires an annual level of construction for replacement just equal to that value on the vertical axis. At that level of stock and corresponding level of construction, the stock of space will be constant over time, since depreciation will equal new completions. Hence, ΔS is equal to 0 and $S = C/\delta$.[5] Future chapters will discuss this relationship in more detail; for now, it is important only to remember that the southeast quadrant assumes a certain level of construction and determines the level of stock that would result if that construction continued forever.

This completes a 360-degree rotation around the four-quadrant diagram. Starting with a level of stock, the property market determines rents, which are then translated into property prices by the asset market. These asset prices, in turn, generate new construction, which, back in the property market, eventually yields a new level of stock. The combined property and asset markets are in equilibrium when the starting and ending levels of stock are the same. If the ending stock differs from the starting stock, then the values of the four variables in the diagram (rent, prices, construction, and stock) are not in complete equilibrium. If the starting value exceeds the finishing value, then rents, prices, and construction must all rise to be in equilibrium. If the initial stock is less than the finishing stock, then rents, prices, and construction must be decreased to be in equilibrium. This journey around the four-quadrant diagram provides a simple, intuitive illustration of the solution to the simultaneous system of Equations (1.1)–(1.4).[6]

OWNER-OCCUPIED REAL ESTATE

A reasonable question is how all of this works in the case of real estate that is mainly occupied by its owner. In this case, the four quadrants still hold, but asset prices and rents are determined by the same market participants—the owner occupants. Consider for the

---

[5]The increase each year in the stock of office space is the difference between construction and depreciation. Assuming depreciation, δ, is 1 percent annually, then: $\Delta S = C - 0.01S$. Given a stable level of construction, the stock that will eventually emerge is: $S = C/0.01$. This is the steady-state version of Equation (1.4) and is the ray emanating out of the southeast quadrant.

[6]If the equations in footnotes 3–5 plus Equation (1.2) are successively substituted into each other, the result is:

$$S = \frac{800 - 2\frac{S}{E}}{i} - 4{,}000$$

Solving so that S is only on the left-hand side of the equation, we get the equilibrium stock level:

$$S = E\frac{[800 - 4{,}000i]}{iE + 2}$$

Thus, if there are 10 million office workers in the economy ($E = 10$) and the interest or capitalization rate is 5% ($i = 0.05$), the long-run stock of office space will be 240 square feet per worker, or 2,400 million square feet. This stock will require that 24 million square feet be constructed each year, and this will require that asset prices equal a replacement cost of $320 per square foot. Rents of $16 annually will sustain such asset prices with a 5% capitalization rate.

moment the market for owner-occupied housing. The demand for single-family homes depends on the number of households, their incomes, and the annual costs of owning a home. This annual cost is equivalent to rent. A rise in the number of households shifts the demand curve out. With greater demand and a fixed stock of housing units, the annual payment to occupy a house must rise. The northwest quadrant then translates this payment into the actual price that households are willing to pay for the home.

Lower interest rates, for example, imply that with the same annual payment (rent), households can afford to pay a higher purchase (asset) price. Hence, with owner-occupied real estate, decisions by the user-owner determine both rent (the annual payment) and price. These decisions, however, are influenced by the same economic and capital market conditions that influence rental properties. Thus, owner-occupiers have the same investment motives as the owners of rental property. Once the purchase price is determined, then new housing development and eventually a new equilibrium stock of space follow in the other two quadrants (southwest, southeast).

This same analysis can be applied to the case of corporate-owned and -occupied industrial or office space. The demand for this space is determined by the annual cost of owning it (rent) as well as the number and size of firms in the market. In equilibrium, the annual cost of owning (rent) equates demand with the fixed stock of office or industrial space. The cost of capital for the corporation (capitalization rate) converts this annual cost into the asset price that corporations are willing to pay for the space.

REAL ESTATE AND THE NATIONAL ECONOMY

Using Figure 1.1, we can trace the various impacts of the broader economy on the real estate market. The economy can grow or contract. Long-term interest rates or other factors can shift the demand for real estate assets. Changes in short-term credit availability or local regulations can alter the cost of supplying new space. Each has different repercussions, and these are easily determined by examining alternative solutions within the four-quadrant diagram. In each case, we can identify which quadrant is initially affected, trace the impacts through the other quadrants, and arrive at a new long-run equilibrium. This comparison of different long-run solutions (market equilibria) in a model is called "comparative static" analysis.

Economic Growth and the Demand for Real Estate Use

As the economy expands, the curve in the northeast quadrant shifts out to the northeast. This reflects a greater demand to use space at current (or other) rent levels, such as would occur with increases in production, household income, or the number of households. For a given level of real estate space, rents must therefore rise if the demand to use space is to equal available space. These higher rents then lead to greater asset prices in the northwest quadrant, which, in turn generate a higher level of new construction in the southwest quadrant. Eventually, this leads to a greater stock of space (southeast quadrant). As shown

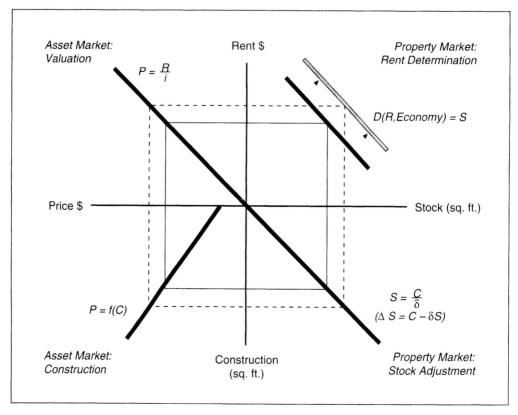

FIGURE 1.2 The property and asset markets: property demand shifts.

in Figure 1.2, the new market equilibrium involves a dashed box that in every direction lies outside of the box that connected the four curves in the original equilibrium.[7]

It should be clear that the equilibrium solution with an expanded economy must generate a box that lies outside of the original. Neither rents, prices, construction, nor stock can be less than in the initial equilibrium. The new solution, however, need not at all involve a proportional expansion of the original box. The shape of the new box depends on the slopes of the various curves. For example, if construction were very elastic with respect to asset prices (a nearly vertical curve in the southwest quadrant), then the new levels of prices and rents would be only slightly greater than before, whereas construction and stock would expand considerably.

---

[7] We can use growth in the number of office workers as an example of economic expansion. Returning to the equation in footnote 6, if the number of office workers increased from 10 million to 20 million, the long-run stock of space would increase to 4,000 million square feet, or just 200 square feet per worker. Rents would increase to $20 per square foot annually. Such rents would generate asset prices of $400 per square foot, which would just equal the replacement costs necessary to sustain the higher level of annual construction (40 million sq. ft.).

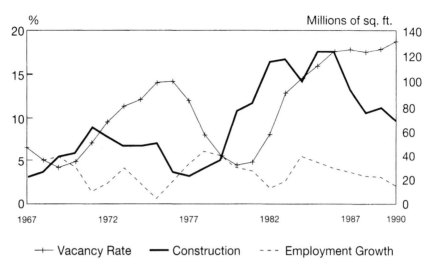

FIGURE 1.3 Office employment growth, vacancy rate, and construction, 1967–1990.

These data are aggregated from 30 metropolitan areas.

Source: Employment, adjusted U.S. government figures courtesy of Regional Financial Associates, Bala-Cynwyd, PA; vacancy and construction, CB Commercial.

Economic growth, then, increases all equilibrium variables in the real estate market(s), while economic contraction leads to decreases in all variables. Figure 1.3 compares the growth of total employment in the U.S. with construction of office space and the overall office vacancy rate. It is clear that the national office market moves with the economy: during recessions, vacancies tend to rise and construction falls, whereas the opposite occurs during recoveries.

Long-Term Interest Rates and the Demand for Real Estate Assets

If the demand to *own* real estate shifts, the impact on the combined markets is quite different than if the demand to *use* real estate changes. A number of factors can cause shifts in the demand to own real estate assets. If interest rates in the rest of the economy rise (fall), then the existing yield from real estate becomes low (high) relative to fixed income securities and investors will wish to shift their funds from (into) the real estate sector. Similarly, if the risk characteristics of real estate are perceived to have worsened (improved), then the existing yield from real estate may also become insufficient (more than necessary) to get investors to purchase real estate assets relative to other assets. Finally, changes in how real estate income is treated in the U.S. federal tax code can also greatly impact the demand to invest in real estate. As will be discussed in Chapter 8, if the depreciation allowance for real estate is increased, the same income stream generates a higher after-tax yield. This will increase the demand to hold real estate assets.

This book assumes that the capital market efficiently adjusts the prices of particular assets—so that each investment earns a common risk-adjusted, after-tax total rate of return. Thus, shifts in asset demand, such as described above, will alter the capitalization rate at which investors are willing to hold real estate. Reductions in long-term interest rates, decreases in the perceived risk of real estate, and generous depreciation or other favorable changes in the tax treatment of real estate all will reduce the yield that investors require from real estate. As shown in Figure 1.4 in the northwest quadrant, this has the effect of a counterclockwise rotation (the ray always goes through the origin) in the capitalization rate ray emanating from the origin, raising asset prices. Higher interest rates, greater perceived risk, and adverse tax changes rotate the ray in a clockwise manner, lowering asset prices.

Given a level of rent from the property market, a reduction in the current yield or capitalization rate for real estate raises asset prices, and in the southwest quadrant, this begins to expand construction. Eventually this increases the stock of space (in the southeast quadrant), which then lowers rents in the property market for space (northeast quadrant). A new equilibrium requires that the initial and finishing rent levels be equal. In

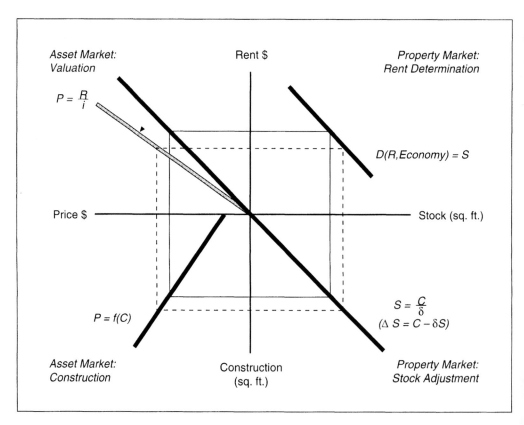

FIGURE 1.4 The property and asset markets: asset demand shifts.

Chapter 1   The Property and Capital Markets

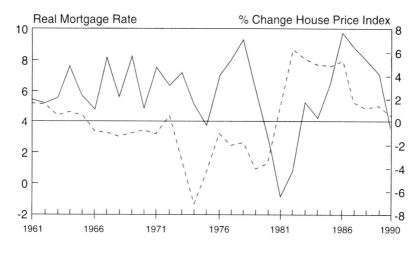

- - - Mortgage Rate (minus CPI inflation)   ——— % Change in House Price (1990 $s)

FIGURE 1.5 Change in house price versus mortgage rates (real), 1961–1990.

Source: Price index: 1960–69: Federal Housing Finance Board, *1990 Rates & Terms on Conventional Home Mortgages, Annual Summary.* 1970–90: Federal Home Loan Mortgage Corp., *Quality-Controlled Existing Home Price Index,* unpublished report. Mortgage rates: 1960–62: FHA insured rate plus .44 percentage points. 1963–90: Federal Housing Finance Board, *1990 Rates & Terms on Conventional Home Mortgages, Annual Summary.*

Figure 1.4, this new equilibrium results in a new solution box that is lower and more rectangular than the original.

It is important to be convinced that the new solution box is as portrayed in Figure 1.4. Asset prices must be higher and rents lower, while the long-term stock and its supporting level of construction must be greater. If rents were not lower, the stock would have to be the same (or lower), and this would be inconsistent with higher asset prices and greater construction. If asset prices were not higher, rents would be lower, which is inconsistent with the reduced stock (and less construction) generated by lower asset prices. A positive shift in asset demand, like a positive shift in space demand, will raise prices, construction, and the stock. It will, however, eventually lower—rather than raise—the level of rents. This inverse relationship between asset prices and long-term interest rates can be seen in Figure 1.5, which examines the historic movements in house prices (in 1990 dollars) and real mortgage rates (adjusted for inflation).

Credit, Construction Costs, and the Supply of New Space

The final exogenous change likely to impact the real estate market is a shift in the supply schedule for new construction. This can come about through several channels. Higher short-term interest rates and a general scarcity of construction financing will increase the costs of providing a given amount of new space, leading to less construction. Likewise, stricter local zoning or other building regulations will also add to development costs and (for a fixed level of asset prices) reduce the profitability of new construction. These kinds of negative supply changes have the effect of causing a westerly shift in the cost schedule of the southwest quadrant: for the same level of asset prices, construction will be less. Positive changes in the supply environment, such as the easy availability of construction financing or a relaxation of development regulations, move the curve in an easterly direction, and for the same asset price expand construction. Figure 1.6 shows the powerful inverse relationship that has existed historically between short-term real interest rates (inflation-adjusted) and new home construction.

Finally, Figure 1.7 traces the long-run implications of a negative supply change, such as would occur with higher short-term interest rates.[8] For a given level of asset prices, a negative shift in the new space supply schedule (southwest quadrant) will lower the level of construction and eventually lower the stock of space (southeast quadrant). With less space in the northeast quadrant, rent levels will have to rise, which will generate higher asset prices in the northwest quadrant. When starting and finishing asset prices

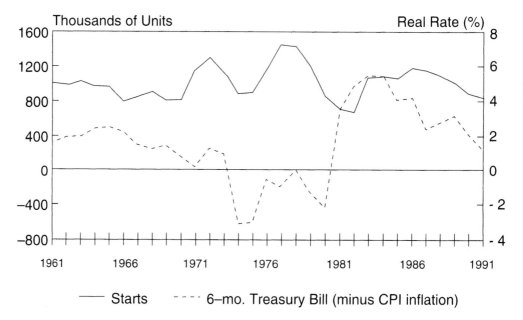

FIGURE 1.6 Single-family construction and real interest rates, 1961–1991.

Source: Construction, *Economic Report of the President 1992*; interest rates, The Federal Reserve.

---

[8]In Figure 1.7, this negative supply change is drawn as a shift in the cost curve, which means that the minimum level of asset price necessary to get construction going has increased. There may also be supply changes that leave this minimum asset price the same, but lower or raise the amount of construction resulting from increases in asset prices. Such changes would result in a pivot in the schedule, changing its slope (i.e., if the slope becomes flatter there is less construction with increases in asset prices; if the slope becomes steeper, there is more construction with increases in asset prices).

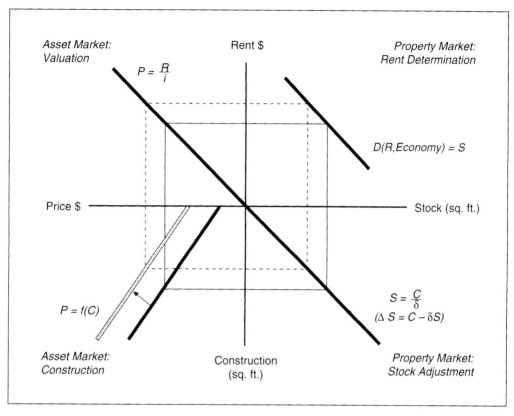

FIGURE 1.7 The property and asset markets: asset cost shifts.

are equal, the new solution box will lie strictly to the northwest of the original solution. Rents and asset prices will increase, whereas construction and stock levels will be less. The magnitude of these changes, of course, will depend on the slopes (or elasticities) of the various curves. For example, if the demand for space is very rent elastic (a nearly horizontal curve in the northeast quadrant), then the increase in rents will be slight. An inelastic (nearly vertical) demand curve will generate a larger increase in rents. It should be clear that if any of these variables moved in a different direction, the solution would be inconsistent—that is, not an equilibrium.

Occasionally, single, individual shifts, such as are portrayed in Figures 1.2, 1.4, and 1.7, do occur by themselves. For example, the Economic Recovery Tax Act of 1981 (ERTA), greatly shortened the depreciation period for rental housing. This generated a sharp reduction in the capitalization rate for this asset, and the ensuing construction boom and fall in rents are quite consistent with Figure 1.4. Some researchers are also convinced that much of the commercial building boom and eventual fall in office rents and asset prices during the 1980s was the result of deregulating the nation's thrift (savings and loan, or S&L) industry. Deregulation is argued to have resulted in a dramatic increase in the availability of cheap construction credit for new commercial development. As such, it would have caused a singular (easterly) shift in the construction cost schedule.

It is more likely the case that economic events cause several shifts to occur simultaneously. This is particularly true of movements in the nation's macroeconomy. As the national economy enters a slowdown, not only is there a contraction in output and employment (northeast quadrant), but there are usually increases in short-term interest rates as well (southwest quadrant). An economic expansion leads to the opposite combination. This combination of shifts can generate any pattern of new box solutions that lies between the two shown in Figures 1.2 and 1.7. Although the analysis gets more complicated in the case of multiple shifts, the net outcome is always some combination of the impacts from each individual change.

The simple framework represented by the four-quadrant diagram works well in illustrating the new equilibria that result as the exogenous environment changes. An important drawback of this framework is that it is not easy to trace the intermediate steps as the market moves to its new equilibrium. A dynamic system of equations is needed to depict the intermediate adjustments of the market, which significantly complicates our analysis. More complicated dynamic models will be developed in Chapters 10 and 12.

REAL ESTATE MARKETS AND PUBLIC POLICY

The real estate sector is affected by public policy changes at the federal, state, and local levels. However, the real estate sector may or may not be the primary target of a specific policy. For example, national monetary policy has several goals and implications. As a prime determinant of interest rate movements, monetary policy clearly affects the demand for real estate assets as well as the level of new construction. The four-quadrant diagrams presented in the previous section illustrate the impacts of such policy changes on the real estate markets. The public sector also creates policies that are aimed specifically at the real estate sector. In developing such policies, government decision makers must be able to anticipate the impacts of their actions on the broader real estate market. The framework represented by the four-quadrant diagram permits a useful analysis of the impacts of these policies. Consider the following examples of major public policies designed to impact the real estate markets directly.

Publicly Assisted Housing

Both federal and state governments provide a range of assistance programs to encourage the development of low- and moderate-income housing. Some programs directly build units for targeted groups, while other programs assist households in making rental payments. The construction of publicly owned units generally decreases the demand for privately owned rental units. This decrease in demand assumes that public units succeed in attracting tenants. This seems a safe assumption since public units generally carry subsidies, which mean that the units are offered at below market rents. In fact, in many urban areas in the U.S., there are long waiting lists for public housing units. This decrease in demand for private units results in an inward shift in the demand curve in the northeast quadrant which will, in turn, decrease rents, asset prices, construction and ultimately the stock of private units. Thus, building public housing produces a new equilibrium that is exactly the opposite of that illustrated in Figure 1.2, where demand is increasing. The reduction of private building activity due to public construction programs is sometimes referred to as public displacement of private construction.

Rental assistance programs, on the other hand, act to simulate housing demand in much the same way as an expansion in the economy. These programs will shift out the demand curve in the northeast quadrant, resulting in increases in rents, prices, construction, and the stock, as occurred in Figure 1.2. Proponents of rental assistance programs argue that such programs will encourage construction and have only a modest impact on rents. Hence, they argue that the net effect of such programs will be to expand the housing opportunities of low-income households. Opponents of such policies suggest that rental assistance only serves to increase rents in the market and has very little impact on construction. Hence, they argue that the main beneficiaries of the program are landlords. Clearly, the size of the impact on construction and rents depends on the relative elasticities of the curves presented in Figure 1.2.

Local Government Development Regulations

In the U.S., local governments exercise great control over the amount and type of development permitted on privately owned land. Such regulations often are in the public interest, but they do impose two additional costs on private development. First, they frequently extend the time necessary for completion of a project, since local governments require developers to apply for various permits in order to proceed. Second, they sometimes act to create a scarcity of sites. This can drive up land prices and add to site-acquisition costs. The more binding or restrictive such regulations become, the more they increase development costs. This increase in costs will shift the supply schedule in the southwest quadrant in a westerly direction, as occurred in Figure 1.7.

The Taxation of Real Estate

The federal tax code generally treats real estate favorably in several ways. Interest payments on real estate debt are fully tax deductible for both firms and households. Homeowners also are effectively exempt from the taxation of housing capital gains realized with the sale of their homes. For investors, generous depreciation deductions are allowed each year far in excess of actual economic obsolescence. Favorable provisions like these act to reduce the current yield necessary from real estate, as the tax advantage supplements property income. This will rotate the capitalization schedule of the northwest quadrant in a counterclockwise manner and lead to the higher asset prices and other impacts described in Figure 1.4.

At the local level, real estate is treated quite unfavorably, largely through the widespread use of property taxation. Most local governments finance their services with a flat tax rate on commercial, industrial, and residential property value. The effective rate of such taxation generally is in the 1 to 2 percent range, and this directly raises the capitalization rate necessary for real estate. Increased property taxation will rotate the capitalization ray clockwise, reducing asset prices, reducing construction, and raising rents.

Real Estate Financial Institutions and Regulations

In the U.S., the federal government has created a number of institutions whose purpose is to facilitate the financing of residential real estate. The system of S&L banks was established to channel local savings into mortgage lending, and the secondary market together with national mortgage insurance ensure that mortgages have almost instant liquidity. By facilitating the flow of investment funds into mortgage lending, such institutions have effectively reduced the cost of mortgage borrowing. This again will rotate the capitalization rate ray of the northwest quadrant in a counterclockwise manner, increasing asset prices and residential construction.

The federal government also regulates a number of financial institutions in ways that can increase or decrease the flows both of long-term investment funds and short-term construction lending to nonresidential real estate. For example, when the Employee Retirement Income Security Act of 1974 (ERISA) was passed by Congress, pension funds were required to increase diversification of their assets—a policy which many believe greatly increased the supply of funds for long-term commercial mortgages. In 1989, Congress enacted the Financial Institutions Reform, Recovery, and Enforcement Act (FIRREA) which was designed to deal with the S&L crisis. FIRREA increased the capital reserve requirements for loans that were viewed as risky, such as commercial mortgages and short-term construction loans. These requirements substantially decreased the willingness of lenders to originate and hold these loans. The history of the U.S. financial industry is full of many such examples, each of which has influenced the flow of funds into real estate. In our four-quadrant diagram, a decrease in the availability of long-term financing will shift the capitalization rate in the northwest quadrant; a decrease in the availability of short-term construction financing will shift the cost schedule in the southwest quadrant.

SUMMARY

In this chapter, we defined real estate and provided a simple analytic framework to examine the operation of this important market.

- Real estate is defined as the national stock of buildings, the land on which those buildings sit, and all vacant land. Real estate is a very important component of our nation's wealth; the total value of real estate was estimated at $8.8 trillion in 1990, representing 56 percent of the nation's net worth. Additions to the stock represent roughly 5 to 7 percent of annual GDP.
- The four-quadrant model divides the real estate market into the property market where space use is determined and the asset market where buildings are bought

and sold. There are two critical links between these markets. First, rents determined in the property market are translated into asset prices in the asset market. Second, asset prices determine the level of new construction, which determines the amount of stock available in the property market.

Exogenous shocks to the property market can have very different impacts on the operation on the real estate market than exogenous shocks to the asset market. In this chapter, we showed that:

- An increase in the demand for space in the property market shifts out the demand curve in the northeast quadrant, increasing rents, which, in turn, increases asset prices, construction, and the stock of space.
- A decrease in the capitalization rate in the asset market increases the demand for real estate assets, which increases asset prices. Increased asset prices in turn bring forth more construction, increasing the stock of space and decreasing rents.
- An increase in construction costs decreases construction levels, which, in turn, decreases the stock of space, driving up both rents and asset prices.

REFERENCES AND ADDITIONAL READINGS

Balance Sheets of the U.S. Economy: 1945–1990. Washington, D.C.: Board of Governors of the Federal Reserve System, September 1991.

BRUEGGEMAN, WILLIAM, J. FISHER, AND LEO STONE, *Real Estate Finance,* 8th ed. Homewood, Ill: Irwin, 1989.

Managing the Future: Real Estate in the 1990s. Chicago: IREM Foundation and Arthur Anderson, 1991.

MILES, MIKE E., "What Is the Value of All U.S. Real Estate?" *Real Estate Review* (1990), 20(2): 69–77.

CHAPTER 2

THE OPERATION OF PROPERTY MARKETS: A MICRO AND MACRO APPROACH

What is the fair market value of a specific house? How much rent can a property manager charge for his office space? Is now the best time to develop a site? What should the density and use be? Real estate decisions such as these must be based on an understanding of the economic environment of each parcel or property. This economic environment is constantly being changed by forces and events at two levels: the micro level and the macro level. Micro forces are those location-specific factors that influence the value or use of one particular site. Macro forces, on the other hand, are those broad economic factors that affect market timing and influence the profitability or use of all properties.

As a discipline, the study of economics is divided into two broad fields with a similar distinction: microeconomics and macroeconomics. *Microeconomics* refers to the study of how individual economic agents (such as households and firms) operate, whereas *macroeconomics* investigates the behavior of the overall economy. Real estate economics is divided in a similar way. In this book, the study of the use, development, or pricing of individual properties or parcels of land involves a microeconomic approach. In contrast, the study of the behavior of the overall market aggregating across individual properties involves using a more macroeconomic approach.

In real estate economics, location plays a crucial role in distinguishing between micro and macro approaches. Real estate microeconomics borrows heavily from the traditional urban economics literature, treating the operation of land and property markets with the explicit recognition of space or location. What is the demand for land at one site? What is that site's highest and best use? How do house prices vary across sites, and why? What factors determine office rents or the location of firms and their plants? Real estate microeconomics investigates these questions by studying the operation of urban land markets and developing theories and explanations for the spatial structure of cities.

Real estate macroeconomics abstracts from the spatial dimension and considers the overall market for housing, land, or office space. The simplification that results from such aggregation can be justified on two grounds. First, as with any type of inquiry, insight often is achieved, perhaps at the expense of some realism, by abstracting or making simplifying assumptions. Without aggregating across locations and dealing with a market as a whole, the detailed time series models in Chapters 10 and 12 of this book simply could not be developed. Second, many factors that affect real estate are largely independent of location. Consider changes in interest rates or variations in the growth rate of an area's economy. These are forces that move over time and impact real estate at all locations. In these cases, it makes sense to study a market as an aggregate entity.

The distinction between real estate micro- and macroeconomics clearly hinges on the notion of an aggregate market. Within this context, then, how should a market be defined? The answer is that a market should represent a group of properties that react similarly with respect to macro factors (such as interest rates and economic growth). If the behavior of properties within a market is similar, then the macro approach will work. If properties react very differently to macro effects, then such modeling will be largely unsuccessful.

DEFINING MARKETS: PROPERTY TYPES

In addition to the distinction between microeconomic and macroeconomic approaches to real estate, throughout this book we distinguish between residential and nonresidential property markets. This delineation has both advantages and disadvantages, but we believe there are net benefits to the distinction. At the macroeconomic level, housing markets clearly behave differently from those of nonresidential property. Movements in housing prices and residential construction do not relate closely to movements in rents or construction for office, industrial, or retail properties. The institutions that guide each of these markets also are quite different. Residential contractors rarely build commercial space. Industrial or office space brokerage firms have no connection to firms undertaking residential brokerage. The financing of residential properties also takes place through a distinct mortgage origination process, and the residential mortgage market has a very active secondary market (the market in which mortgages are purchased and sold). Commercial financing takes place largely through private placements, but there is only a small formal secondary market. Thus, at the macro level, there are good reasons to consider different property types as different markets.

At the micro level, the distinction between residential and nonresidential property is not as clear, largely due to the fact that both types of property use and compete for a common resource: land. The price of commercial property, for example, bears a direct relationship to the price of residential property, since both uses compete for the same fixed supply of land. The locations of commercial and residential property also are closely linked through the commuting of workers and travel of shoppers. At the same time, the behavior of participants in the residential and nonresidential property markets is based on different economic theories and motives. Finally, the extensive government regulation of land in the two uses (e.g., through zoning) has important impacts on both residential and nonresidential property markets.

DEFINING MARKETS: AREAS

The second issue in defining a property market involves the question of spatial aggregation: what is the appropriate geographic definition of a real estate market? Should markets be defined at the neighborhood, town, metropolitan, state, or national level? There is no definitive answer to this question, but there are both conceptual and pragmatic criteria for making the choice.

Conceptually, the geographic definition of a real estate market should encompass real estate parcels that are influenced by the same economic conditions. Clearly, national economic conditions, such as interest rate levels, influence real estate markets. But we also know that real estate markets are profoundly influenced by economic conditions such as employment and income, which vary widely across regions of the country. How should these regional or local economies be defined? Urban economists have long struggled with this question.

As a practical matter, the geographic definition of a local economy is generally settled by the way in which data on urban economies are collected. The U.S. Census Bureau defines metropolitan statistical areas (MSAs) on the basis of economic behavior rather than the legal, political, or historic precedent that delineates towns or states. An *MSA* is generally defined as a county with a central city with a population of 50,000 or more and adjacent counties that are metropolitan in nature. The decision to include a county in an MSA is based on population density, the percentage of the population that is urban, the nonagricultural employment level, and the commuting patterns among counties and with the central city. As a result, MSAs are drawn to reflect a single labor market and the mobility of workers; in addition, MSA boundaries often change over time.[1] Commuting within a metropolitan area should not be so burdensome that it prevents most households from living and working at any two locations. In other words, a worker at a particular location within a metropolitan area should not be severely constrained from taking any job within that area. Conversely, commuting between metropolitan areas should present enough potential obstacles to make it a rare occurrence.

This labor-mobility definition of a local economy has broad ramifications for how real estate markets operate. If a worker within a metropolitan area can be reasonably expected to live anywhere in that area, then all houses in that area are, in some sense,

---

[1]In recent years, the Census Bureau has regrouped some adjoining and economically linked MSAs into common Consolidated Metropolitan Statistical Areas (CMSAs).

competitive with each other. For example, by commuting more or less, any worker could, in principle, bid on any house. Locations for firms are similarly competitive, in the sense that a business could choose any site and, in principle, still find workers willing to commute there. Between metropolitan areas, this degree of competitiveness normally does not exist. Households in San Francisco cannot reasonably be expected to work in Los Angeles, which means that the real estate markets of the two areas are in some fundamental sense disconnected. The competitiveness of properties within a metropolitan area comes from the ability of workers to change houses without switching jobs, and change jobs without moving their place of residence. The absence of such mobility between metropolitan areas separates their real estate markets.

Conceptually, if we define our unit of analysis at the macro level as the metropolitan area, what is the appropriate unit of analysis for the micro level? Within a market definition, there are distinct factors that affect the behavior of individual properties that are different from those factors that affect the overall market. This effectively means that there is something to be gained from the whole micro-macro delineation; that micro analysis is different from macro analysis, and that the two complement each other. If there were little difference between the types of theories and arguments used at the micro and macro levels, then there would not be any clear advantage to the twofold approach. In real estate economics, the role of location helps to create the distinction between the two levels, particularly when markets are defined at the metropolitan level.

The mobility of households and firms across locations within metropolitan areas is fundamental to the microeconomic study of real estate. Since locations within a market differ (by commuting for example), mobile households will quickly generate higher prices for more desirable (lower commuting) sites. The theory of urban land markets provides a methodological approach based on this high degree of spatial mobility. The mobility of firms and workers within metropolitan areas also means that an economic shock occurring at one site (e.g., loss or gain of jobs) will have impacts on prices at all sites, as mobile workers adjust their demands. Thus, sites within metropolitan areas should react similarly to changes affecting the overall market.

Throughout this book, our macro analysis is generally focused at the metropolitan level, although occasionally we deal with a national housing or commercial real estate market—particularly when there appears to be systematic patterns of behavior across many metropolitan areas. For the micro level analysis, we generally look within a metropolitan area, often at cities and towns within an MSA.

REAL ESTATE MICROECONOMICS: URBAN LAND AND LOCATION

When defined at the metropolitan level, real estate property markets contain thousands, and even millions, of individual parcels (sites, houses, buildings). Each property occupies a location that is technically unique: adjacent sites may have similar, but not exactly identical, locations. A market in which each good is somewhat unique is referred to as a *product-differentiated market.* In addition to urban land, labor is another major market that is fully product-differentiated. This type of market may be contrasted with a *commodity market*, such as that for corn, in which goods are largely identical.

The observed behavior of individual parcels within the urban land market tends to follow several patterns that are quite characteristic of product-differentiated markets:

1. The prices of individual properties or land parcels vary widely and systematically with the physical or location characteristics of the property. The valuation that households or firms place on these characteristics determines the property's overall value.
2. The *relative* prices of different properties remain very stable over time and change little as the overall market undergoes either cyclic fluctuations or long-term growth. Overall market movements tend to raise and lower all prices by proportionate amounts.
3. The relative price of a parcel tends to change mainly when the characteristics of that parcel are altered. Such changes include physical alteration of the structure as well as changes in the characteristics associated with the parcel's location or neighborhood.

The theory of urban location and land markets has been developed essentially to explain these observed patterns. Since some readers may be troubled, or not completely convinced by the assertions above, let's consider their conceptual and empirical foundations.

The fact that house prices vary according to the size, quality, and character of a unit's structure probably comes as no surprise. It is also true, however, that units with similar physical characteristics will vary enormously in price by location. Location characteristics that have been shown to affect house prices include commuting time or access to jobs, public services and neighborhood quality (e.g., school performance, crime rates, etc.), and natural or environmental features (water frontage, terrain with views, air or noise quality). These characteristics of a location can account for more than half of the overall value of a house. As an example of how important public services are, Table 2.1 compares the average price of a single-family house in a range of towns in 1990 metropolitan Boston to the average score of high school seniors in the town's school system on the test administered by the Massachusetts Educational Assessment Program. Figure 2.1 is a scatter plot of the house values and test scores and shows the regression line between the two variables. The relationship is striking and the statistical correlation between the two is quite strong.[2]

---

[2]In Table 2.1, a simple bivariate regression between test score (*TEST*) and house price (*P*) yields the following relationship:

$$P = -280811 + 369.4\ TEST \qquad R^2 = 0.38$$
$$(-6.1) \qquad (4.3) \qquad\qquad N = 32$$

The t-statistics are in parentheses below the coefficients. Thus, across the sample in the table, towns with average test scores 100 points higher have houses that are worth almost $37,000 more. Of course, we must be careful in drawing strong conclusions from this simple regression. Certainly, some of this large effect is caused by the fact that towns with higher test scores may also have lower crime, a better park system, and so on.

TABLE 2.1 Boston-Area House Values and Student Test Scores, 1990

	House Values (1990 $)	12th-Grade Achievement Scores
Brookline	377,800	1430
Wellesley	349,500	1437.5
Belmont	307,800	1455
Newton	293,400	1435
Lexington	282,800	1525
Cambridge	263,800	1222.5
Marblehead	257,200	1395
Needham	256,500	1470
Rockport	227,500	1445
Milton	219,600	1315
Arlington	209,200	1375
Reading	204,100	1347.5
Watertown	196,700	1280
Stoneham	194,900	1292.5
Waltham	191,100	1267.5
Burlington	191,100	1350
Wakefield	190,600	1282.5
Framingham	184,700	1415
Medford	182,400	1207.5
Sharon	182,100	1427.5
Dedham	177,500	1327.5
Peabody	177,100	1270
Ipswich	174,000	1415
Woburn	172,600	1247.5
Braintree	168,700	1387.5
Somerville	165,800	1155
Hopkinton	163,200	1265
Malden	162,900	1207.5
Boston	161,400	1180
Quincy	161,100	1295
Revere	160,500	1212.5
Randolph	155,500	1297.5

Scores represent averages of reading, math, science, and social studies scores.
Source: House Values, 1990 Census of Population and Housing, *Summary Tape File 1A*; Scores, *State Results of Massachusetts Testing Program*, Massachusetts Education Assessment Program, 1990.

Strong statistical relationships, such as that in Figure 2.1, exist throughout the housing market between prices and many structural or location attributes. They also characterize other property markets as well. Retail space rents vary systematically with the expected pedestrian traffic on downtown streets, and office space rents are higher around mass transit lines. In each of these cases, well-established price premiums or discounts exist for locational or structural features of a property. Location theory holds that such

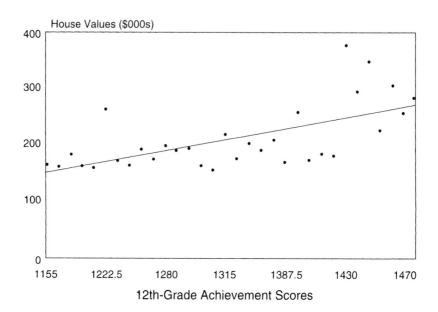

FIGURE 2.1 Relationship between house values and test scores of Boston-area towns, 1990.

Scores represent averages of reading, math, science, and social studies scores.

Source: House Values, 1990 Census of Population and Housing, *Summary Tape File 1A*; Scores, *State Results of Massachusetts Testing Program,* Massachusetts Educational Assessment Program, 1990.

price effects represent the long-term valuation of these attributes by households or firms. The theory also suggests that such valuations are relatively stable as the overall market undergoes growth or decline. In other words, rents or prices for all locations rise and fall with a market's fortune, but the relative price of more desirable versus less desirable locations changes very little.

The general stability of *relative* property prices or of property price premiums can be shown empirically. In Figure 2.2, the rents for office space during two very different periods are compared across several locations in the Boston metropolitan area. In 1980, the Boston office market was coming out of a long inactive period: construction was occurring everywhere and rents were rising rapidly. The economic growth of the defense, computer, and financial sectors in Boston created a real estate boom in the early 1980s. In contrast, by 1990, the economy had cooled and unemployment was rising. A changing computer technology market and the declining defense budget hit the area hard. In 1990, the real estate market had peaked and was declining rapidly; construction had almost ceased and rents were falling. Figure 2.2 shows that the relative rents for office space across locations changed very little between the beginning and end of this decade, despite considerable price inflation and very different overall market conditions.

The stability of relative property prices within metropolitan areas results from two features of the urban land market. The first is the high degree of household and firm

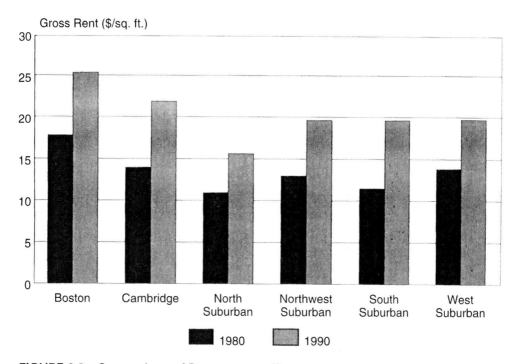

FIGURE 2.2 Comparison of Boston-area office rents, 1980 and 1990.
Source: 1980 Rents, Leggat and McCall and Spaulding and Slye, Inc.; 1990 Rents, CB Commercial.

mobility within metropolitan markets, as discussed in the previous section. Mobility acts to create a form of price "arbitrage." Locations within a market can rarely stay over- or underpriced with respect to other locations because of the mobility of potential property buyers or users. Another way of expressing this same condition is to say that the demand for any site or location is very *price elastic* with respect to its competitor sites. In this situation, small adjustments to prices (rents) should be sufficient to attract many buyers (tenants). Competition, demand elasticity, and arbitrage all imply that prices at one location cannot move independently of prices at other locations. Locations within a market are closely connected and rarely have independent price movements or cyclic behavior.

The stability of relative property prices also results from the manner in which such prices are determined within metropolitan land markets. The premium for property at one location should reflect the present discounted value of the consumer's *utility*, or cost savings, from that location relative to others. Thus, for example, the premium for sites with an easy commute should be the discounted value of the time and costs savings that results from such commutes. If the physical and locational attributes of properties change only slowly, and if consumer valuations of those attributes are reasonably fixed, then the relative prices of different parcels should also change very little.

In fact, urban location theory suggests that the relative prices of different properties should change only in either of two situations. The first situation in which relative prices within a metropolitan market might change is if consumer valuations of particular physical or locational attributes change. For example, a sudden increase in gasoline prices would lead consumers to value sites with shorter commutes more highly. The gradual demographic change of an area from having predominantly households with children to those without might be expected to alter the valuation of houses with many bedrooms versus smaller units. Similarly, long-term shifts in the spatial distribution of jobs might also change the relative valuation for certain kinds of office or industrial space. Generally, such price changes occur only very slowly, since they are based on fundamental shifts in the makeup of an area's population or economy.

The second source of shifts in relative property prices is change in the attributes of a property. Obvious examples include physical change in the property's structure such as rehabilitation, renovation, or expansion. Changes in locational or neighborhood characteristics may also dramatically impact property prices. A common example is the construction of a new highway or transit facility, which alters the pattern of commuting costs for many locations. In metropolitan areas with new transit systems or extensions of older systems, it is common to find new developments emerging around the transit system. It is often difficult to measure directly the impact of such changes in the transit system on land values and development because the impacts are too localized to demonstrate with publicly available data. Changes in neighborhood crime or town school quality can also be expected to affect relative property prices in one area versus another.

Real estate microeconomics involves more than just the study of how property rents or prices are determined across locations. It also focuses on how the land market uses these prices to determine both the density of development and the location of different land uses. One of the important lessons that microeconomics teaches us is that the price of land and its density, or use, are determined simultaneously: denser uses generate higher land prices, whereas more expensive land encourages denser use. Another precept of real estate microeconomics involves the separation of uses. The land market works much as an auction, with each site being developed or occupied by that use offering the most for it. In this process, it is a natural market outcome to have each use occupying separate areas or distinct locations. The development of land proceeds under a number of such microeconomic principles.

A thorough understanding of these principles of microeconomics allows us to understand the evolution of cities over time and the spatial patterns of land prices, land uses, and density. Why is residential density normally higher in downtown areas of a city, or along beaches and other natural amenities? How did Central Business Districts (CBDs) come into existence, and why has there been a recent explosive growth of suburban employment districts? What explains the distinct hierarchical pattern of retail establishments—a large number of smaller stores or centers and a small number of larger centers? Why do property prices and density eventually rise as a city grows? The study of metropolitan land markets provides answers to these questions by emphasizing the long-term equilibrium outcomes of spatial competition. This microeconomic approach, however, does not examine the economic determinants of long-term metropolitan growth or the short-run cyclic behavior of metropolitan economies. Real estate macroeconomics focuses on these topics.

REAL ESTATE MACROECONOMICS: MARKET GROWTH AND DYNAMICS

While microeconomics studies prices and land use across space within a particular market, macroeconomics examines the overall movement of prices and real estate development for the metropolitan market as a whole. By abstracting from the spatial dimension, macroeconomics is able to focus more specifically on the time dimension that emphasizes short-run movements and temporary disequilibrium. As a result, macroeconomics deals with aggregate variables that are averages or aggregations of data measured at each location within the market. Given the theory of real estate microeconomics, the presumption in macroeconomics is that such aggregate measures depict the behavior of variables at most locations within the market.

Some macroeconomic variables are most commonly measured as averages. These variables include market prices, rents, or vacancy. For example, samples of apartments are repeatedly surveyed by the U.S. Commerce Department to produce estimates of average rents in metropolitan areas. Brokerage companies periodically survey the inventory of office buildings to produce estimates of average market vacancy rates. The Federal Housing Finance Board maintains data on single-family house transactions through their survey of mortgage lenders and reports the average price of existing house sales. As an example of such data, Figure 2.3 traces house price series for the Dallas and Boston metropolitan areas in constant (1990) dollars.

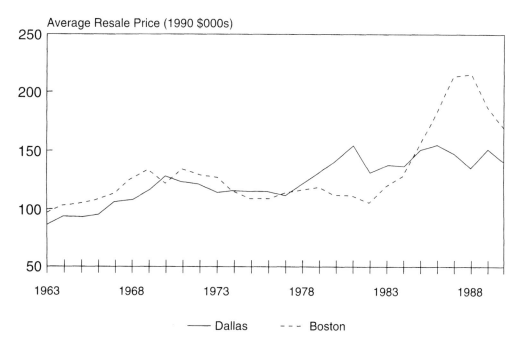

FIGURE 2.3 Boston and Dallas house prices, 1963–1990.

Source: 1963–72, average of monthly average purchase price for existing homes, Federal Home Loan Bank Board. 1973–90, annual average for existing and new homes, Federal Housing Finance Board.

One of the main objectives of real estate macroeconomics is to explain the long-run trends and short-run movements of price or rent data such as is shown in Figure 2.3. Sometimes house prices in many different areas are affected similarly by overall U.S. economic conditions. In both Boston and Dallas, for example, house prices dipped during the economic recessions of 1974 and 1982. At the same time, local market factors also are important. Dallas prices rose during the oil boom of the late 1970s, while Boston prices were flat. During the 1980s, Boston prices soared with the boom in technology industries, while the collapse in oil led to price declines in Dallas.

Often, the demand side of the market seems to account for much of the movement in prices. At other times, however, it is fluctuations in supply that explain price fluctuations. Consider the history of office-space vacancy rates in these same two markets in Figure 2.4.

In the market for office space, vacancy rates sometimes do move with a market's economic growth. For example, the vacancy rate soared in Dallas just after the recession of 1970 and during the Texas economic crash of the early 1980s. Similarly, Boston's vacancy rate peaked just after the recession of 1975. But why did Boston's vacancy rate rise in the mid-1980s, just when economic growth was strongest? Why did the vacancy rate in Dallas rise during the early 1970s, when its growth was strong? The answers lie with participants in the supply side of the market who built excessive amounts of new space, at least relative to market demand.

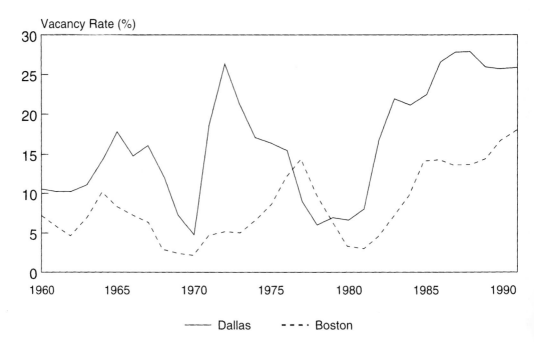

FIGURE 2.4 Boston and Dallas office vacancy rates, 1960–1991.
Source: CB Commercial.

Figure 2.5 portrays the growth in Dallas of office employment and office construction as a percentage of the stock of office space. Sometimes the two seem to move together, as during the period of Dallas's growing economy between 1972 and 1974, or during the decline in its economy in the mid-1980s. At other times, such as the periods between 1968 and 1970, 1974 and 1976, and 1988 and 1989, construction moved quite differently from employment growth. Clearly, the supply of real estate is not always in tune with demand, particularly over shorter intervals of time. Understanding the movements in supply and their determinants is as important as understanding the long- and short-term factors that affect property demand.

These examples illustrate some of the common patterns of behavior that real estate macroeconomics seeks to explain. These patterns give rise to three general principles that govern the aggregate behavior of metropolitan real estate markets:

1. The economic growth of each metropolitan area is determined in the short run by movements in the overall U.S. economy, together with the area's industrial mix and competitiveness. In the longer run, demographic changes and lifestyle preferences also play a role. Unlike different locations within a market, different metropolitan areas can simultaneously experience widely varying economic conditions. In the short run, there is no "arbitrage" between metropolitan areas.

2. The real estate market of each metropolitan area moves closely with the area's economic growth. In some situations, the supply or price of real estate can actually exert an influence on the area's overall economic development.

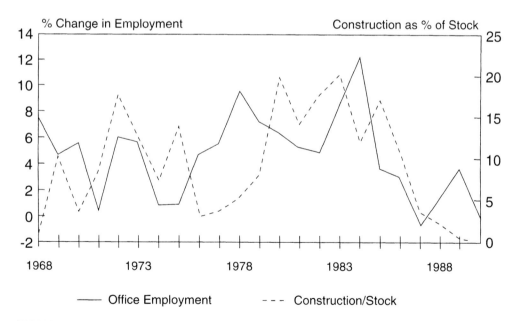

FIGURE 2.5 Dallas office employment growth and office construction, 1968–1990.
Source: Employment, adjusted U.S. government figures courtesy of Regional Financial Associates, Bala-Cynwyd, PA; construction/stock, CB Commercial.

3. Regions or metropolitan areas adjust slowly to economic change because resources are relatively immobile between markets. In response to changes in demand, the supply of factors into an area (labor, capital, structures) often occurs very gradually. Such slow adjustments give rise to temporary imbalances and help to generate cyclical patterns.

This macroeconomic behavior stands in noticeable contrast to the microeconomic principles discussed earlier. Within markets, individual parcels of real estate are intensely competitive with each other and have prices that adjust rapidly to maintain a degree of parity. While metropolitan areas also compete with one another over the very long run, the movement of economic resources between such areas is slow enough in the short run to largely uncouple the economies of different regions. Real estate microeconomics thus focuses on the equilibrium relationships between land or property parcels across locations within markets, while macroeconomics studies the disequilibrium that occurs as the markets grow and adjust to economic change.

SUMMARY

The micro and macro perspectives outlined in this chapter are the fundamental basis of analysis used throughout much of this book.

- The micro approach focuses on the importance of structural and locational characteristics on the prices and rents for a particular property or development. We often treat metropolitan areas as a single real estate market. While prices for real estate and land within a single market can vary enormously across locations, the relative price of real estate across locations is generally stable over time.
- The micro approach is examined in detail in the next four chapters. In Chapters 3 and 4 we explore the determinants of household location within a metropolitan area and examine the willingness to pay for structural characteristics, including the density of the development. In Chapters 5 and 6, we focus on the location decisions of firms within a metropolitan area.
- The macro approach examines how broad economic forces such as growth or decline in a metropolitan area's economy influence the area's real estate market. Metropolitan growth is determined by growth in the national economy as well as the area's industrial mix and competitiveness.
- The macro approach is examined in detail in Chapters 7 through 12. In Chapter 7 we examine the determinants of metropolitan growth. In Chapters 8 through 10 we provide a detailed examination of metropolitan housing markets, and in Chapters 11 and 12 we investigate metropolitan nonresidential real estate markets.

Section 2 Microeconomic Analysis of Property Markets

CHAPTER 3

THE URBAN LAND MARKET: RENTS AND PRICES

How is it that Manhattan has a dense urban skyline, while Los Angeles does not? How is it possible to find farmland within the city of Phoenix? Why is land in downtown Tokyo a thousand times more valuable than its suburban counterpart? This chapter begins a section of this book devoted to the study of residential development and the urban land market.

In economics, the markets for land and housing are often referred to as completely product-differentiated because each product sold in the market (every house or location) is unique. They stand in stark contrast to commodity markets, such as that for corn, oil, or minerals, in which a uniform good is traded in bulk quantities. The markets for most manufactured durable goods are considered partially differentiated, falling between these extremes. In the automobile market, for example, a large number of different models are regarded as being close, although not perfect, substitutes for each other. In the case of land or housing, no two parcels are exactly alike.

The fact that urban land is a completely differentiated product makes it difficult to speak about the supply or demand for sites at any particular location. By definition, the supply of land at each location is fixed; hence, it is quite price *inelastic.* The demand for a particular site, on the other hand, is likely to be quite sensitive, or *elastic,* with respect to its price. This results from the fact that numerous competitive sites, or substitutes, exist at adjoining locations. For almost two centuries, economists have recognized these distinctive features of the land market and have developed a simple approach for determining land or housing prices. The approach argues that land must be priced at each site so that its occupant is charged for the value of whatever locational advantages exist at that site. Understanding these advantages and how consumers evaluate them, therefore, becomes the key to understanding the spatial pattern of land or housing prices. This theory of *compensating differentials* assumes that only demand considerations determine the *relative* value of land or housing at different locations. The supply of land does play a role, but only in setting the overall level of prices.

We begin this chapter by examining a simple model in which the rent for housing and land is determined according to the compensation principle. This rent is referred to as *Ricardian rent,* since the approach was developed by Ricardo (1817). We then embellish this model to make it more realistic and examine what the model implies about how rents change over time and across cities. Ricardian theory also explains why land uses and different types of households tend to be separated spatially. Since sites go to those offering the highest rent, spatial separation occurs naturally in these markets. The chapter finishes by examining how Ricardian rent is converted into land or house prices. The capitalization of rent into prices is shown to vary by location within cities, particularly when urban areas are growing and such growth is anticipated to continue in the future. Finally, we examine data concerning house rents and prices, demonstrating that a century-old theory holds up fairly well against modern reality.

URBAN COMMUTING AND RICARDIAN RENT

The first fundamental characteristic of urban housing and land markets is that housing and land are more expensive at better locations and cheaper at less advantageous sites. This holds whether we consider natural locational amenities, such as lakes or an ocean, or man-made locational advantages, such as distance to employment or cultural centers. To illustrate how rent and locational advantage interact, we begin with a very simple city. In this city, commuting or access to a place of employment is the only locational advantage that is considered. Following a long literature, our city will be *monocentric,* meaning that it has only one employment center (Alonso 1964, Mills 1972, Muth 1969). Commuting to this center gives rise to what is called Ricardian rent. In the Ricardian definition, *rent* refers either to the payments that a tenant would offer for housing, or, alternatively, to the *annual* amount that an owner would be willing to pay for the right of occupancy or use. Later in this chapter we will examine how these rents get capitalized into prices. The model also assumes that the density of development is fixed, which means that structure capital cannot be substituted for land. This absence of any factor substitution may seem unrealistic, but we will deal with determining density in Chapter 4. Thus, our stylized city has the following features:

1. Employment is at a single center, to which households commute along a direct line from their place of residence. Commuting costs k dollars annually per mile. The location of a household thus refers to its linear distance (d) from the employment center.
2. Households are identical, and the number of workers (commuters) per household is fixed. Household income (y) can be spent on commuting, all other goods (represented in dollars by x), and on housing.

3. Housing has fixed and uniform characteristics at all locations. Housing rent is an annual amount $R(d)$, which varies by location (commuting distance d).
4. Housing is provided by combining a fixed amount of land per unit of housing (acres, q) together with a fixed amount of housing capital (materials and labor) that costs c (no factor substitution). Residential density, therefore, is $1/q$.
5. Housing is occupied by households who offer the highest rent, and land is allocated to that use yielding the greatest rent.

The last assumption is crucial, for it implies that when the housing market is in equilibrium in this stylized city, decreased rents as one moves out from the city center must exactly offset the increasing commuting costs. Since the quality and density of housing is fixed across locations, the only variation possible in household or consumer welfare is the amount of income left for expenditure on other goods (x). If housing rents do not exactly offset commuting costs, then consumers who live at closer locations will have more income left to spend on other goods. In this case, consumers at farther locations would seek to move to closer ones and would offer greater housing rent than current occupants. Since housing is rented to the highest bidder, rents at the closer locations would rise, while those at farther sites would fall. When rents exactly offset commuting costs, households would no longer have an incentive to move, and the market is then said to be in equilibrium.[1] In effect, mobility due to consumer welfare differentials is not possible when a private market is at equilibrium. As long as all households are identical, household expenditure on other goods (x) must be constant across locations at some level x^0. Using the definition of consumer income and expenditure, housing rents follow in Equation (3.1) below.

$$R(d) = y - kd - x^0 \qquad (3.1)$$

At the city center ($d = 0$), consumers will have no expenditure for commuting (at least in our stylized city), and so rent there, $R(0)$, will equal $y - x^0$. Moving outward, rent will decline dollar for dollar as commuting costs increase. At some distance, b, the city ends and housing rent will be at its cheapest. What determines this least expensive rent at the city's edge? The answer is the cost of constructing new units.

In many cities throughout the world, land beyond the edge of development is used for agriculture. In this use, it earns some rural rent *per acre* (labeled r^a).[2] In other situations, the land is simply held vacant with little or no meaningful rural rent. In the simple Ricardian model, assumption 5 implies that site or land owners seek the highest income from their land, just as housing is rented to those making the highest offer. Thus, as long as urban housing yields a rent for a site that exceeds that which the owner can receive from farming, land will be rented to urban households. We will see later that this simple criteria for the transition of land from rural to urban use still holds under a much more sophisticated analysis of the landowner's decision about when to develop land or convert it from farming to housing.

---

[1] This point is often referred to as a *spatial equilibrium*, since there is no incentive to change location.
[2] Throughout this book, capital letters will be used when referring to housing rent or price (R,P) while lower case letters will be used for land rent and price (r,p).

At the edge of the city (*b*), then, urban landlords can rent land for its agricultural or opportunity value of r^a per acre. With fixed density, a lot for each housing unit can be rented for $r^a q$. The rent for a housing unit at the edge of the city therefore has two components: the *land rent* $r^a q$ plus the *structure rent,* which is the *annualized* cost of constructing a unit (*c*). This structure rent could be measured by the annual mortgage payment necessary to cover the cost of constructing the unit. The sum of these two costs is the rent that is necessary to cover the creation of new housing at the city's edge. Combining this with Equation (3.1), we can determine that level of other expenditure x^0 that will prevail if a household that commutes from the city's edge must pay a rent for housing there equal to agricultural land rent plus the annual replacement cost of the housing structure:

$$x^0 = y - kb - (r^a q + c) \qquad (3.2)$$

Moving in from the edge of the city, Equation (3.1) defines how rents must rise as commuting costs decrease in order for households to maintain the level of welfare (or expenditure) defined in Equation (3.2). Combining the two, housing rents at any location will equal replacement costs plus the difference between commuting costs at the urban edge and those at the location in question. The rent gradient for housing is:

$$R(d) = (r^a q + c) + k(b - d) \qquad (3.3)$$

In effect, housing rent at any interior site absorbs the savings in commuting that result by moving in from the farthest location currently developed in the city. Only with these rents will (identical) households be willing to live at any location within the city.

Figure 3.1 traces the equilibrium rent gradient for housing (Equation (3.3)) as it varies along a radius (*d*) in our stylized circular city. There are three components to housing rent: (1) the rent necessary to convert a lot from farm land into urban land ($r^a q$), (2) the rent for the structure that sits on the lot, *c,* and (3) the location rent resulting from saved commuting costs, $k(b - d)$. It is important to note that both the agricultural rent and the structure rent are constant across locations. The slope of the housing rent gradient with respect to distance, $-k,$ is due to the location rent; rents fall away from the city center (per mile) by exactly the amount of additional commuting incurred by each household.

Those components of housing rent that involve location and agricultural land are often combined into a hypothetical rent for just urban land $r(d)$. Urban land rent can be thought of as a residual: the land rent that is left after subtracting the rent for the housing structure from the total housing rent. From Equation (3.3), Equation (3.4) describes urban land rent. It is important to remember that housing rent is measured per unit, or per household, while land rent will be measured as rent per acre. Thus, to convert housing rent $R(d)$ into land rent, $r(d)$, we must first subtract the structure rent and then divide by land per unit (*q*). This is the same as multiplying housing-minus-structure rent per unit by residential density ($1/q$).

$$r(d) = r^a + \frac{k(b - d)}{q} \qquad (3.4)$$

Urban land rent has two components. The first is the rent (per acre) for its alternative use (agricultural), while the second is the savings in commuting costs *per acre* that result when housing is placed on the land. At a density of $1/q,$ there are that many households per acre, each of which is saving $k(b - d)$ in commuting. The gradient for land rent

Chapter 3 The Urban Land Market: Rents and Prices

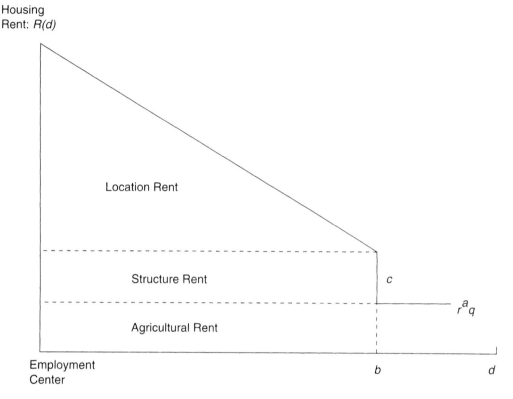

FIGURE 3.1 Components of housing rent.

with respect to distance has a slope of $-k/q$: the rent per acre of land falls by the increased total commuting of all who live in the $1/q$ units built on the land.

Numerical Example

Let's consider a typical example of rents in a simple city in which urban density averages around 4 units (households) per acre, or 2,560 households per square mile ($q = 0.0004$ square miles). A structure costing $100,000 to build would rent for $7,000 per year using a 7 percent interest rate. Annual agricultural rental income from farming tends to fluctuate around $1,000 per acre, or $640,000 annually, per square mile. Given our assumption of 4 units per acre, the agricultural rent per year for a house lot would be $250. Finally, the cost of commuting for an average household with income of about $40,000 could be about $200 per year per mile. With these values, annual house rent at the urban border will be $7,250 ($7,000 in structure rent plus $250 in agricultural rent). If the city's border is 20 miles away from the center, housing rent would be $11,250 at the center ($7,000 in structure rent plus $250 in agricultural rent plus $4,000 in commuting cost savings). Land rent per acre will range from $1,000 at the urban fringe (4 units per acre times $250 per unit) to $17,000 at the center (4 units per acre times the sum of $250 per unit in agricultural rent plus $4,000 in commuting cost savings).

How do housing rent and urban land rent vary across cities or within one city over time? Equations (3.3) and (3.4) permit us to draw some fairly powerful comparative static conclusions:

1. When the edge of the city (b) is farther from the center and involves a greater commute, housing and land rent at all interior locations is higher since at these locations there is a greater savings in commuting cost.
2. When commuting is more costly (per mile), interior housing and land rents will be higher relative to edge rents because, again, the commuting cost savings at interior locations are higher.
3. When urban land has a more productive alternative use or higher agricultural rent (r^a), urban housing and land rents will also be greater, because this land rent component of housing rent is higher.
4. When the density of urban housing is greater, the gradient for urban *land* rents will become steeper, with higher rents at the city center relative to those near the edge. (Remember, the slope of the land rent gradient is $-k/q$. If the amount of land used per housing unit, q, decreases, then the land rent gradient becomes steeper.)

POPULATION, LAND SUPPLY, AND RICARDIAN RENTS

Since urban rents depend crucially on the distance to the city edge, the next logical step is to examine how far a given city's edge will be. This involves three considerations: the population of the city, the density of housing, and the role played by the area's topography in determining the supply of land. Again, we will take the density of housing development as fixed here; in Chapter 4, we will relax this assumption and explore the implications of varying density.

One of the original assumptions of our stylized city was that of linear, radial commuting. If the city is located on a featureless plain, then this implies that the city will be circular in shape, with land rents equal for all points at a given distance (d) from the center. On the other hand, consider a city whose employment center is located at the coastline of a lake or an ocean. Many cities developed historically to serve as ports, and therefore have a semicircular structure. Commuting and prices will still be equal for a given radius, but the city's circumference may extend only 270 degrees (Boston), 180 degrees (Chicago), or even only 30 degrees (the peninsula of Bombay). In an even more realistic world, mountains, lakes, and manmade obstacles also can reduce the supply of land at any given radius from the employment center.

Since we are dealing with a very stylized city, let us characterize land supply with a variable (v) that ranges from 0 to 1. When $v = 1$, the city is fully circular. At the other extreme, if $v = 0.1$, the city is constrained on a peninsula with a circumference of only

Chapter 3   The Urban Land Market: Rents and Prices

36 degrees. If $v = 0.5$, the city center is located on the straight edge of a body of water. Alternatively, a fully circular city could have $v < 1$ if it contains lakes and hills that limit the land available for development at various distances. We must also consider the number of households in the city (n), and from the previous section, the amount of land used per housing unit (q). Given these variables, the area of the city divided by land usage per housing unit must equal the number of households in the city. Recalling the simple formula for the area of a complete or partial circle, we can define the border, b, as:[3]

$$b = \left(\frac{nq}{\pi v}\right)^{\frac{1}{2}} \qquad (3.5)$$

Numerical Example

We can again use the density of four households per acre (or land consumption of 0.0004 square miles per household) to calculate the border for a large city with 2 million households (n). In most American cities, almost 20 percent of urban land area is used for streets, 10 percent is used for commercial uses, and 10 percent is used for open space. This suggests that the value of v in a circular city would actually be closer to 0.6. Following Equation (3.5), a fully circular city has an urban border of slightly more than 20 miles (20.6), while a semicircular city with these parameters would extend to 29.1 miles.

The implications of Equation (3.5) are quite clear. All else being equal, cities that have greater population (n), lower density (larger lots, q), and are less circular (smaller v) will be spatially larger with a border (b) at a farther distance from the center. From comparative static result 1 in the previous section, this implies that such cities will also have higher housing and land rents. In fact, we can summarize the implications of Equation (3.5) into a fifth comparative static conclusion:

> **5.** A city with greater population, lower residential density, or that is less circular because of topography and land constraints will have a development edge that is at a greater distance from its center.

The combination of Equation (3.5) and Equation (3.3) or (3.4) provides a simple yet quite powerful model of urban land rents. Sometimes its implications are quite subtle. Consider two cities with equal populations and topography, but different residential densities. From Equation (3.5), the denser city will have a shorter distance to its edge, and from Equation (3.3) this will yield lower central housing rents. With respect to land, however, higher density increases the slope of the rent gradient at the same time it is shifted downward (from the nearer edge). Which of these two forces dominate? Will central land rents rise or fall with greater density? Combining Equations (3.4) and (3.5) with some

---

[3] The border, b, is the radius of a circular city. The land area of this circle is equal to πb^2. If the city is not fully circular, its area will equal $v\pi b^2$, where $0 < v < 1$. The land area of the city must be equal to the number of households, n, times the amount of land per household, q.

$$v\pi b^2 = nq \;;\; b = \left(\frac{nq}{\pi v}\right)^{\frac{1}{2}}$$

mathematics, we are able to deduce that on net, central land rents should be higher in cities with greater density, even as house rents fall.[4]

It is important to remember that the conclusions of the model only compare equilibrium solutions, just as in Chapter 1 with our four-quadrant diagram. The model is static in that it ignores expected future growth and does not pretend to portray how cities adjust gradually over shorter periods of time. It indicates only what the city eventually should look like. To incorporate expected growth, our model must deal with prices as well as rents, which we will do later in this chapter. The model is also extremely simple in its assumptions of fixed density and identical individuals. In Chapter 4, we will relax the assumption of fixed density. Now let's turn to the question of different households or land uses.

COMPETITION AND SPATIAL SEPARATION

The second fundamental characteristic of urban land and housing markets is that they tend to naturally separate different households or land uses spatially. To illustrate this, we extend our stylized city model to consider the situation in which there are two categories of households. Initially, let's assume that these household groups differ only according to their costs of commuting (perhaps from their valuations of time). There are n_1 members of the first group (Group 1) who dislike commuting intensely, whereas the n_2 members of the second (Group 2) mind it much less. As a result, we subscript the cost of commuting and have $k_1 > k_2$. Consider two questions. First, will the two groups choose separate or intermixed locations, and which group will locate where? Second, what will housing rents look like in this two-household city? In all other respects, our city is the same as in the sections above. Thus, there are $n_1 + n_2$ houses that are identical, with fixed lot sizes. There also is radial commuting, and the cost of constructing new housing at the city's edge again involves a rent both for structure capital and for agricultural land. Most importantly, rational owners will still rent housing to that household offering the most for it.

When there are multiple groups of households, there is no requirement that the members of one group must enjoy the same welfare (or level of expenditure) as members of another group. Markets treat equals equally and unequals unequally. To see this, let's examine the housing rents that will leave the members of *each* group with identical expenditure levels. We note such expenditure on other goods as x_1^0 and x_2^0 and pose the

---

[4]From Equation (3.4), we differentiate central land rents $r(0)$ with respect to the direct change in lot size, and the indirect effect of the altered border:

$$\frac{\partial r(0)}{\partial q} = -k\frac{(b-d)}{q^2} + \frac{k}{q}\left(\frac{\partial b}{\partial q}\right); \quad \frac{\partial b}{\partial q} - \frac{1}{2q}\left(\frac{nq}{\pi v}\right)^{\frac{1}{2}} = \left(\frac{b}{2q}\right)$$

Combining the two expressions and evaluating the result at the city center (d = 0), we have:

$$\frac{\partial r(0)}{\partial q} = -\frac{kb}{q^2} + \frac{kb}{2q^2} < 0$$

question of what rent exactly compensates the members of each household group for commuting. These housing rents are determined in Equation (3.6):

$$R_1(d) = y - k_1 d - x_1^0$$
$$R_2(d) = y - k_2 d - x_2^0$$
(3.6)

Suppose for the moment that $x_1^0 = x_2^0$; then at every location (d), the rent that Group 2 households would be willing to pay for housing would exceed that of Group 1 households. This follows simply from the fact that $k_1 > k_2$. In this situation, no landlord would rent housing to the members of Group 1. Clearly this is not an equilibrium. If, however, the incomes of Group 1 households were also greater than those of Group 2, it might by pure chance turn out that the two groups would have equal expenditure levels (x levels). This, however, is not a requirement of market equilibrium. The only equilibrium conditions are that rents must leave members within each group equally well off, and that all members of both groups must have housing. We can refer to the rent functions in Equation (3.6) as the *equilibrium rents* of each group.

The next question to examine is whether these two groups need not be spatially separated but could intermix over some range of locations. For this to be the case, it would have to be true that at such locations, the equilibrium rent levels for each group of consumers are the same so that landlords would be equally willing to rent to either group. Assume for the moment that one such location exists and call its distance from the center, m. To the right of m (at a farther distance), it must be true that the equilibrium rents of Group 2 will exceed those of Group 1. The slope of Group 2's rent gradient is less than that of Group 1, since Group 2 has milder distaste for commuting ($k_1 > k_2$). Moving in toward the city center, the equilibrium rents of Group 1 will exceed those of Group 2, because the members of Group 1 value more highly the commute savings from more central locations. Thus, in this model, there can be at most only one site where the equilibrium rents for the two groups intersect. Since landlords rent housing to the group with the maximum rent, there will be a spatially segregated occupancy pattern in either direction from such a common location, with Group 1 occupying houses closer to the center (Figure 3.2).

It is important to realize that one site of a common equilibrium rent must exist; for, without it, one group would have a higher equilibrium rent than the other group over *all* locations. Since there is enough housing for both groups, this would allow housing to be vacant while the members of the lower rent group go homeless. Because renting two houses brings no additional welfare, the higher-rent group would reduce its equilibrium rents, while the lower-rent group would raise its rents. Eventually an equilibrium necessitates an intersection point—the location (m). With this intersection point, spatial segregation necessarily results, with the more central houses being occupied by that group with the more steeply sloped housing rent gradient.

In Figure 3.2, houses from the center to a location (m) are occupied by Group 1. Houses further out are rented to Group 2. This makes economic sense, since Group 1 households find commuting more distasteful and, therefore, are willing to pay higher rents to be closer to the city center. As discussed above, any other pattern would violate one of the two central conditions of a market equilibrium: that housing must be rented for

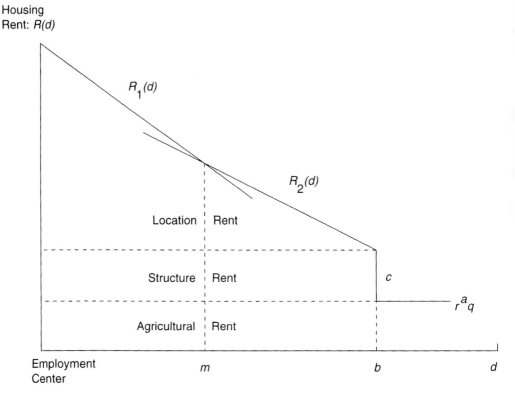

FIGURE 3.2 Housing rent gradient with two household types.

the maximum rent and that each household must occupy one house. To ensure the latter, the equilibrium rent at the edge of the city (the location b) must still equal the replacement cost of new units. As before, this covers a land rent per lot of $r^a q$ and a rent (c) for each housing unit's structure capital. This condition for the edge of the city, together with the definition of the intersection location (m), defines Equations (3.7) and (3.8):

$$R_1(m) = R_2(m), \quad \text{or,} \quad y - k_1 m - x_1^0 = y - k_2 m - x_2^0 \qquad (3.7)$$

$$R_2(b) = y - k_2 b - x_2^0 = r^a q + c \qquad (3.8)$$

The distance from the city center to the boundary between the two household groups (m) is determined from Equation (3.5) but is based on the number of Group 1 households (n_1). The urban border (b) is a distance such that $n_1 + n_2$ houses (with lot sizes q) can be built within that radius when the city circumference is v portion of a circle. These two conditions are used in Equations (3.9) and (3.10) to determine the intersection boundary and city edge distances (m,b):

$$m = \left(\frac{n_1 q}{\pi v} \right)^{\frac{1}{2}} \qquad (3.9)$$

$$b = \left(\frac{(n_1 + n_2)}{\pi v} q\right)^{\frac{1}{2}} \tag{3.10}$$

With m and b determined by Equations (3.9) and (3.10), Equation (3.8) gives the level of consumption or welfare of the second group (x_2^0), whereas Equation (3.7) determines the same quantity for the first group (x_1^0). With each of these known, Equations (3.6) determine the pattern of rents as shown in Figure 3.2.

An important extension of our two-household model can be formulated to describe the longer-term development of land and the separation of different uses or households. Suppose, for the moment, that the housing density that each household group desires is fundamentally different. In particular, let Group 1 continue to have a higher cost of travel ($k_1 > k_2$), but now let that group also demand houses that have larger lot sizes ($q_1 > q_2$). This set of preferences could easily characterize households of different income levels. Households with higher income will certainly demand more land, since land is a normal good. Higher wages, however, also mean that the commuting time of Group 1 is more valuable relative to that of lower-income households. In most U.S. cities, higher-income households tend to live further from the city center, whereas the poor are concentrated in cities. It has been suggested that this pattern might simply represent a long-run equilibrium configuration in the U.S. land market.

In the long run (when existing housing deteriorates and is replaced), the pattern of development will be determined based on a competition between the two groups over land rather than housing. That is, land at each site in the city will be developed by that household group for which land rent is highest. We continue to assume that the housing structures of both groups are identical and can be built for a common annual cost of c. The land rents that emerge from development by each group are contained in Equations (3.11):

$$r_1(d) = \frac{y - k_1 d - x_1^0 - c}{q_1}$$
$$r_2(d) = \frac{y - k_2 d - x_2^0 - c}{q_2} \tag{3.11}$$

The pattern of land development that will emerge in this longer-run model is similar to that depicted in Figure 3.2. The crucial issue of which household group develops land at more central land sites now depends on the relative slopes of the land rent gradients in Equations (3.11). The slopes of these gradients represent the additional commuting costs incurred from an acre's worth of development: $-k_1/q_1$ and $-k_2/q_2$. Even if Group 1 has a greater cost of commuting than Group 2, its land rent gradient might not be steeper if it demands houses with much larger lots than those of Group 2. When the two groups differ because of income, the outcome depends completely on the income elasticities of land consumption as opposed to commuting costs. With income elastic land demand and inelastic commuting costs, higher-income households will have much larger lots and only slightly greater commuting costs. In this case, they will outbid other households at peripheral locations—a result that is consistent with observed location patterns in the U.S. With income inelastic land demand and elastic commuting costs, higher-income households have steeper bids and should locate centrally.[5] With these elasticities, we would have to incorporate other factors, such as concern over the quality of public services (e.g., schools), in order to explain the suburbanization of wealthy households in the U.S. We consider a variety of such other factors in Chapter 13.

In a model with multiple household groups, the comparative static conclusions 1 through 4 in the previous section continue to be true. Less land supply, larger populations (of either type), or greater lot sizes all generate a farther city edge and, possibly, intersection distance (m). This, in turn, leads to higher housing and land rents throughout the city. The main lesson from our two-household city has to do with the separation of occupancy patterns. Locations are always rented to that use (in this case household group) that is willing to offer the most. It is only by chance that two uses will offer identical or similar rents and that intermixing will occur. As a general principle, land-use segregation is a common and natural outcome in private housing or land markets, rather than a result of government regulations.

GROWTH AND RENTS

The jump from housing (or land) rents to housing (or land) prices is a complicated one. In Chapter 1, we discussed how rents that are determined in the property market get converted into asset values by the capital market. Four factors are central to determining the *rate* at which income is converted into value: (1) long-term interest rates, (2) the expected future growth of current rent, (3) the risk, or variance, associated with that rent, and (4) the federal tax treatment of real estate. Together these four factors determine the capitalization rate. Throughout this text, we will focus mainly on the role of interest rates, taxes, and expected rental growth, leaving detailed discussions of risk and its role to texts on real estate finance. In this chapter, we ignore the federal tax treatment of real estate but will explore its impact later in Chapter 8.[6]

The historic growth of urban housing (or land) rent can depend on a number of factors, but the Ricardian model suggests that the most important of these is the growth of a city's population. Cities grow and expand gradually as the population of a region or nation increases, and this growth is largely responsible for increases in locational or land rents. Capital markets look forward, however, and consider the likely future growth of rental income when determining capitalization rates. A dollar of rental income that is expected to grow is worth considerably more today than one which the market expects to remain constant. In Chapter 10, we will discuss a number of theories about how future expectations of rental growth are formed. At this point, we will simply assume that the

---

[5]Wheaton (1977) empirically estimated these elasticities for households in San Francisco and found an income elasticity of demand for land that was quite close to the income elasticity of commuting.

[6]The approach to prices and growth taken here builds on Capozza and Helsley (1989, 1990), who consider the impact of risk and uncertainty as well as urban growth on urban land prices.

Chapter 3   The Urban Land Market: Rents and Prices

market expects current or historic growth to continue into the future. Thus, to understand how housing prices are determined at a particular location, we must examine what is happening to rents at that location as a city grows over time. Just as with our discussion of rents, we will begin by analyzing house prices and then derive land prices as a residual.

Equation (3.3) makes it clear that the rent for housing at any location depends on the rental cost of structures, c, the agricultural rent foregone on the house lot, $r^a q$, and the cost of commuting from that location as opposed to commuting from the city's border at distance b. This border, in turn, is related to the population of the city through Equation (3.5). If we examine Equation (3.5) in detail, we can see that as the population of a city increases, the city's border grows by one-half of the growth rate of its population. If the population of a city is increasing at a rate of 4 percent annually, then the amount of developed land (area) should be expanding at the same rate, but circularity necessitates that the radius increase by only 2 percent annually.[7]

If the city population is growing smoothly at some constant rate and its edge is expanding at one-half that rate, then the border distance is growing exponentially over time. We will denote time with the variable or subscript (t), which runs from the current period ($t = 0$) out to infinity ($t = \infty$). We denote the current border or city edge as b_0 and use (g) as the constant rate at which this edge is expected to grow in the future. This is equivalent to assuming that population will increase at a rate that is twice (g). Thus, at time $t > 0$, the city edge b_t will be $b_0 e^{gt}$.[8] This expression for where the border will be at each future time period also allows us to determine the future time that any site (beyond the current border) can be expected to become developed. This is tantamount to asking at what time the border will reach a given distance. Inverting the border function, the time until development (T) for a parcel of land located a distance $d > b_0$ is $\log(d/b_0)/g$. Thus, in a city whose population is growing at a constant rate $2g$, Equations (3.12) give the border as a function of time b_t and the time at which the border will reach a particular distance $T(d)$.

$$b_t = b_0 e^{gt}, \quad t > 0$$

$$T(d) = \frac{\log\left(\dfrac{d}{b_0}\right)}{g}, \quad d > b_0 \tag{3.12}$$

---

[7] If we take Equation (3.5) and differentiate it with respect to n, we get the following expression:

$$\frac{\partial b}{\partial n} = \frac{1}{2n}\left(\frac{nq}{\pi v}\right)^{\frac{1}{2}} = \frac{b}{2n}$$

Rearranging:

$$\frac{\partial b}{b} = \frac{1}{2}\frac{\partial n}{n}$$

[8] The Appendix at the end of this chapter provides a mathematical discussion of continuous compound growth and discounting.

Numerical Example

Returning to the example used throughout this chapter, consider a city with a current population of 2 million and a 20-mile border (b_0). If the population is increasing at 4 percent and the border is expanding by 2 percent each year, then Equation (3.12) indicates that after ten years, the border will stand at about 24.4 miles ($b_{10} = 24.4 = 20e^{0.2}$). At a 1 percent annual expansion rate, Equation (3.12) indicates that it will take almost twenty years for the border to increase from 20 to 24.4 miles: $T(24.4) = 19.9 = \log(24.4/20)/.01$.

As the city population grows at a constant rate, the increase in housing rents at any location will not be at a constant rate over time. Furthermore, the increase over any one time period will not be the same across different locations within the city. In fact, the largest percentage increases in housing rents will occur at the urban edge. To see this, we can examine Figure 3.3, where the housing rent gradient of the city is shown at two points in time, with the two city edges: b_0 and b_t. The percentage increase in rent at b_0, as the edge expands to b_t, is clearly greater than the percentage change near the center. Mathematically, we can take Equation (3.3) and examine how housing rents at any location (d) change in percentage terms as the city's edge expands at some constant percentage rate.[9]

Thus, in our highly stylized city, if the edge of development is expanding at some constant rate, the rate of increase of housing rents should be greatest at the city edge, and smallest at the city center. Furthermore, the percentage growth in rents at any given location declines over time as the border expands and that location becomes a more mature (interior) site. These features of rental growth only hold in a city where density is uniform and fixed.

Once the future border is known (or estimated) through Equation (3.12), we need only substitute this expression into Equation (3.3) to obtain the rent that should prevail at distance d at any future time period t: $R_t(d)$. Of course, housing will actually earn this rent only if it actually has been built; that is, if d is less than the (then) current border, b_t. For any site beyond the border, housing rent does not begin until construction takes place at the development date $T(d)$ specified in Equation (3.12). Thus, as the city grows over time and its boundary expands at the rate g, Equation (3.13) describes the rent for housing at any site that has already been developed, and at any time (t), when the urban border is b_t.

$$R_t(d) = r^a q + c + k(b_t - d), \qquad d \leq b_t, \text{ for all } t \qquad (3.13)$$

Numerical Example

As we calculated earlier, housing rents today (which we always denote as time $t = 0$) ranged from \$7,250 (at the current edge of 20 miles) to \$11,250 at the center. Using

---

[9]If we differentiate Equation (3.3) with respect to the urban boundary we get: $\partial R(d)/\partial b = k$. Dividing both sides by $R(d)$, and then multiplying both sides by ∂b, yields the following:

$$\frac{\partial R(d)}{R(d)} = \frac{k \partial b}{R(d)} = \frac{kb}{R(d)} \frac{\partial b}{b}$$

For a given percentage increase in b on the right-hand side above, the percentage change in rents on the left-hand side will be largest at that location d where $R(d)$ is least: the border.

Chapter 3 The Urban Land Market: Rents and Prices

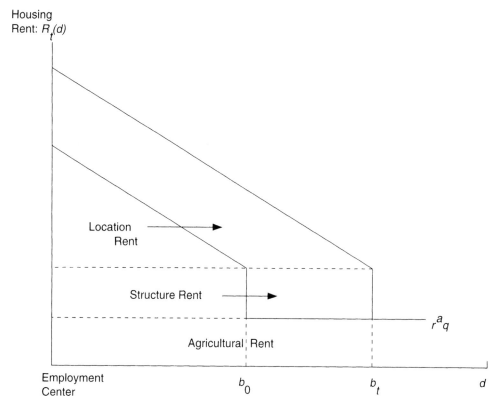

FIGURE 3.3 Housing rent gradient in a growing city.

Equation (3.13), we can calculate what the rent will be at these two locations in 10 years as growth expands the border outward. With the border expanding at 2 percent annually, Equation (3.12) says that in 10 years it will reach 24.4 miles ($24.4 = b_{10} = b_0 e^{0.02 \times 10}$). The rents at the old border will be $8,130 ($250 in agricultural rent plus $7,000 in structure rent plus $880 in location rent as a result of expansion of the border ($880 = 200(24.4 - 20)$)). At the same time, rents in the center will be $12,130 ($4,000 in initial locational rent plus $7,000 in structure rent plus the $880 in location rent as a result of expansion of the border). As the border expands, the location rent of interior sites rises due to the increase in commuting savings from a more distant border. Note that the percentage change in rents is higher at the old border, where rents increased 12.1 percent, than at the center, where rents increased by 7.8 percent.

GROWTH AND PRICES

At any time, and in any location that is already developed, the price of housing will simply equal the present discounted value (PDV) of the rental income stream that is defined in Equation (3.13). Using an interest or discount rate of i, and applying the continuous discounting mathematics in the appendix, we can obtain Equation (3.14) for the price of existing housing.

$$P_t(d) = \underset{t \to \infty}{PDV}[R_t(d)]$$

$$= \underbrace{\frac{r^a q}{i}}_{\substack{\text{Agric.}\\\text{value}}} + \underbrace{\frac{c}{i}}_{\substack{\text{Structure}\\\text{value}}} + \underbrace{\frac{k(b_t - d)}{i}}_{\substack{\text{Current}\\\text{location}\\\text{value}}} + \underbrace{\frac{kb_t g}{i(i-g)}}_{\substack{\text{Future}\\\text{growth in}\\\text{location}\\\text{value}}} \qquad d < b_t, \; i > g \qquad (3.14)$$

The four terms in Equation (3.14) are readily interpreted. The second term is the present discounted value of structure rent, or simply the cost of constructing the house. The first and last two terms together constitute the value of the house's lot. The first term is the present discounted value of the agricultural rent foregone on the lot when the house is developed. We call this the *agricultural value of land*. The third term is the present discounted value of the current location rent at the site (the commuting costs saved at the site (d) relative to the current urban border at time t (b_t). We call this the *current location value*. The final term is the discounted value of the increased commuting costs saved at the location in the future as the border grows (at the rate g).[10] This is the value of the expected increases in location rent, or the future growth in location value. The sum of these last two terms can also be thought of as the present discounted value of the location rent that will exist at the site from now on. We have separated the two so as to illustrate the following points. First, for a house located right at the border, the third term drops out. There is no current location rent at the border; the value of a house is composed only of structural rent, agricultural rent, and the expected future increases in location rent. Second, if the city is not expected to grow ($g = 0$), then the final term vanishes, and location value is composed only of today's location rent discounted forever.

It is useful to compare the house price in Equation (3.14) with the current rental income from housing as defined in Equation (3.13). As discussed in Chapter 1, the capitalization rate is defined as the ratio of rent to price or the rate at which rents are translated into asset value. Assets with growing income streams always have lower capitalization rates than assets with fixed or declining income streams. In the Ricardian model, the fact that house rents rise fastest nearer the border and slowest at the center suggests that for developed land, the capitalization rate varies across locations. If we

---

[10]In Equation (3.14), the last term can be derived mathematically as:

$$\frac{kb_t g}{i(i-g)} = \frac{kb_t}{(i-g)} - \frac{kb_t}{i}$$

The first term on the right-hand side above is the present discounted value of commuting costs to future borders—starting from the border at time t, b_t. We discount with the combined rate ($i - g$) as described in the Appendix, because the border is growing at the rate g, assuming that ($i > g$). The second term is the present discounted value of commuting costs to the (fixed) border that exists at time t. The difference is the present discounted value of the increase in commuting costs as the border grows (out from time t). These increased commuting costs will generate increases in locational rent.

compare the ratio of current ($t = 0$) rent-to-house price across locations, we get Equation (3.15).

$$\frac{R_0(d)}{P_0(d)} = \frac{i(i-g)R_0(d)}{(i-g)R_0(d) + kb_0g}, \quad d \leq b_0 \tag{3.15}$$

The expression for the capitalization rate in Equation (3.15) is complicated and somewhat difficult to interpret. To facilitate its interpretation, we can consider the inverse of a capitalization rate—a site's price-rent ratio, as expressed in Equation (3.16).

$$\frac{P_0(d)}{R_0(d)} = \frac{1}{i} + \frac{kb_0g}{i(i-g)R_0(d)}, \quad d \leq b_0 \tag{3.16}$$

The price-rent ratio in Equation (3.16) can be thought of as comparable to a price-earnings ratio for equity shares or common stocks (P/E). Since the P/E is the inverse of the capitalization rate, assets with growing income streams always have higher P/Es than assets with fixed or declining income streams.

How does the ratio of price to rent in Equation (3.16) change as the city grows? If the city is not growing ($g = 0$), then the entire last expression vanishes and the price-rent ratio is simply the inverse of the interest or discount rate, or $1/i$. Hence, with no growth, the capitalization rate for housing is the interest or discount rate and is the same throughout the city. When the city is expected to grow, the price-rent ratio exceeds $1/i$ (the capitalization rate is less than i). At sites closer to the urban border, $R_0(d)$ is lower, and, hence, the second term is larger. Within an urban area, the price-rent ratio will be somewhat greater (capitalization rate lower) at the edge of the city, where, in this model, rents increase the fastest. Moving toward the center, the expected increase in rents is slowest, and, hence, the price-rent ratio falls (capitalization rate increases).

Numerical Example

Let's continue by illustrating how house prices vary across locations in our stylized city. Assume that the long-term interest rate is 7 percent and the border is expanding at 2 percent per year. Remember that housing rents at today's fringe of 20 miles are $7,250. Plugging these figures into Equation (3.16) yields a price-rent ratio at the border of 17.4, or a capitalization rate of 5.7 percent. The price of housing at the border is simply the current rent at the border divided by this capitalization rate, or $127,193 ($7,250/.057). At the city center, current housing rent is $11,250. Following Equation (3.16), the price-to-rent ratio at the center will be 16.3, or a capitalization rate of 6.1 percent. Dividing current rents at the center by this rate yields a price for central housing of $184,426.

There are several important lessons from this simple model about house rents, prices, and capitalization rates.

1. When there is no expected growth in the city as a whole, the capitalization rate is simply the interest rate and is constant across all locations within the city.

2. As the city grows spatially (for example, from population increases), the capitalization rate becomes less than the interest rate and no longer is constant across locations. With faster rental growth at the urban edge, the capitalization rate is lower there than at the urban center. Over time, as the edge expands, the capitalization rate at interior sites rises.

3. House prices tend to grow over time at the same percentage rate as housing rents: faster at the urban fringe than at the urban center, and more slowly at interior locations.

Just as land rent was derived as a residual from housing rent, land prices are derived as a residual from housing prices. What this means is that land will absorb all of the anticipated increase in location rent as the city grows. If the structure cost is deducted from the price of housing, what is left is the value of the lot. Dividing by lot size (or multiplying by density) gives land price (per acre). This yields Equation (3.17) for the residual value of land that is already developed at location d and at time t (when the border is at b_t). The residual price of land at a developed site is composed of discounted agricultural rent (agricultural value), the discounted value of current location rent (current location value), and the discounted value of expected increases in location rent (future growth in location value).

$$p_t(d) = \left[P_t(d) - \frac{c}{i} \right] \frac{1}{q}$$

$$= \underbrace{\frac{r^a}{i}}_{\substack{\text{Agric.} \\ \text{value}}} + \underbrace{\frac{k(b_t - d)}{qi}}_{\substack{\text{Current} \\ \text{location} \\ \text{value}}} + \underbrace{\frac{kb_t g}{qi(i - g)}}_{\substack{\text{Future growth} \\ \text{in location} \\ \text{value}}}, \quad d \leq b_t \quad (3.17)$$

We now come to the question of how to value land that is today beyond the urban border ($d \geq b_0$) and, hence, vacant. At some future date T, this land will be developed. At that time, the land will collect its residual value according to Equation (3.17): $p_T(d)$. Until that time, vacant land will receive only agricultural rent. Thus, the price of vacant land today has two components. The first is the discounted value of agricultural rent collected between now and the time of development. The second is the residual value of the land at the time of development. Since the receipt of this residual value occurs in the future, it must be discounted back to today from the date of development. Combining these two components, Equation (3.18) gives the price of land today at a location that is currently vacant ($d \geq b_0$), and expected to be developed at the future date T. The value of vacant land is composed of its agricultural value and the expected increases in location value to be received in the future after development. For land that is today vacant, there is no current locational value.[11]

---

[11] The future value of land at the time it is developed $p_T(d)$ is simply Equation (3.17) evaluated at $t = T$, and at a distance equal to the future border: $d = b_T$.

Chapter 3 The Urban Land Market: Rents and Prices

$$p_0(d) = \underset{0 \to T}{PDV}[r^a] + e^{-iT} p_T(d)$$

$$= \frac{r^a}{i} + e^{-iT} \frac{kb_T g}{qi(i-g)}, \qquad d > b_0 \qquad (3.18)$$

          Agric.   Future growth in locational
          value   value, discounted

Throughout this chapter, we assumed that the city develops compactly from the center outward. At any point in time, development occurs out to a border that is defined as that location where urban and agricultural rents intersect. This is based on simple rent-maximizing behavior by landowners. Now, however, we are dealing with prices and expectations about future growth. Thus, we must at least raise the possibility of some noncompact form of development. Would a landowner decide to speculate and keep a site vacant that was closer than the current border even though the rent on the site would be greater from development? Would an owner prematurely develop a site that is farther than the current border even if its urban residual rent was less than agricultural rent? Rational owners of vacant land will select that development time in Equation (3.18) that maximizes the current value of that land. If we maximize Equation (3.18) with respect to the development date T, it can be shown that this date is such that $b_t = d$; or, alternatively, $T = T(d)$, as defined in Equation (3.12). The current value of a vacant site is in fact maximized when the site is developed precisely at that time when the border has moved out to the location of the vacant site. A strategy of either speculating (waiting for the border to pass by the site), or, alternatively, developing the site before the border reaches the site only reduces the value of vacant land.[12]

We can combine Equation (3.17) for the residual value of developed land with Equation (3.18) for vacant land to obtain a complete picture of land pricing throughout the city. The various components of land prices are shown in Figure 3.4.

In Figure 3.4, the first component of urban land price (agricultural value) holds at any location and is the present discounted value of perpetual agricultural rent. Farm land actually receives this income, whereas for urban land, the loss of this rent is an opportunity cost. The triangular component represents the site's current location value, or the current commuting costs saved, again discounted forever. The rectangular component

---

[12]To demonstrate this conclusion, we must remember that Equation (3.18) was derived from Equation (3.17), with the assumption that at the time of development, the border has just reached the location in question, $d = b_T = b_0 e^{gT}$. This allows the second term in Equation (3.17) to drop out. Without this assumption, the expression for the value of vacant land is:

$$p_0(d) = \frac{r^a}{i} + \frac{k}{qi}(b_0 e^{gT} - d)e^{-iT} + \frac{kb_0 e^{-(i-g)T} g}{qi(i-g)}$$

Maximizing this expression with respect to the development date, the derivative of p with respect to T must equal zero. This gives the following condition:

$$\frac{\partial p}{\partial T} = \frac{k}{qi}[-i(b_0 e^{gT} - d)e^{-iT} + gb_0 e^{-(i-g)T} - gb_0 e^{-(i-g)T}] = 0$$

The last two terms above cancel, and in order for the remaining expression to equal zero, it must be true that: $[b_0 e^{gT} - d] = 0$.

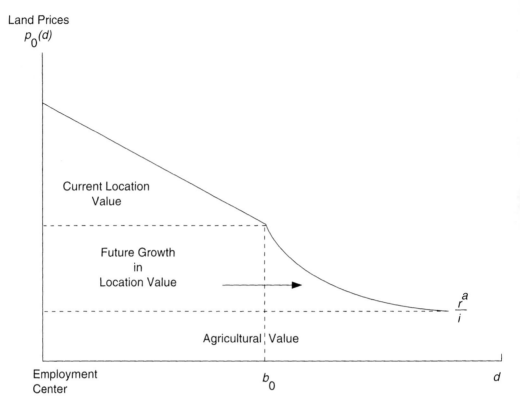

FIGURE 3.4 Components of land prices.

(future growth in location value) is the present discounted value of expected future increases in location rent at sites already developed. Beyond the current border, this value declines exponentially, since such increases in location rent will not begin until the date of future development, $T(d)$. As one considers ever more distant locations, the prospective date of development is so far into the future that, when discounted, these anticipated rental increases are worth close to zero. At this point, land has only its pure agricultural value.

Numerical Example

We can calculate the residual value of an acre of developed land today at the urban center. Remember that we assumed that there were four housing units per acre, which means that q is equal to 0.25. From Equation (3.17), we can calculate land prices by adding up the three terms. The first is the value of an acre of agricultural land: \$14,286 (\$1,000/.07). The current location value due to commuting cost savings is \$228,571 (at $t = d = 0$; (200 × 20)/(0.25 × 0.07)). The future growth in location value as a result of anticipated increases in commuting cost savings is \$91,429 (200 × 20 × 0.02/(0.25 × 0.07 × 0.05)). Summing the three terms yields a per-acre price for land at the center of \$334,286. In calculating the price of an acre of land at the current border, the middle term of Equation (3.17) drops out, so we get $105,715: the value of an acre of agricultural land ($14,286) plus the value of future commuting cost savings ($91,429). The price of land declines linearly from the city center to the current urban border (20 miles). From there out, vacant land prices decline exponentially, eventually reaching the value of pure agricultural land, $14,286. While these prices seem reasonable at the urban fringe, one might expect higher central prices, particularly for a large city with 2 million households that is growing at 4 percent annually. The explanation lies in our assumption throughout this chapter that density is uniform throughout the city at a level that is typical of U.S. suburban communities. We will see in the next chapter that densities tend to rise toward urban centers, which significantly increases central land prices.

It is important to point out how the various components in Figure 3.4 all change with market conditions. If the city is not growing, and is expected to continue not growing in the future, then $g = 0$ and both the rectangular area representing future value and its exponentially declining value (beyond b_0) collapse to zero. With no growth, there are no increases in location rent, and land beyond the current border will never be developed. In this case, land prices reflect only the discounted value of current location and agricultural rents. As the expected future growth rate of the market increases, the rectangular area rises and vacant land acquires considerable value because of its development prospects. This higher price for vacant land beyond the urban boundary gets reflected in higher housing prices and residual land values for sites already developed throughout the city.

This discussion of prices yields a final conclusion about the structure of land markets and how they may vary either between cities or within one city over time. Consider for the moment two cities whose current population, income, density, and transportation costs are identical. One city, however, has been at its current size for many years and is expected to remain so in the future. The other city has been growing rapidly and is expected to continue this growth in the future. The development edges of these two cities along with land and housing rents will be equal. The prices of land and housing, however, will be very different. The strong growth rate of the second city could yield prices that are significantly higher than those of its stagnant counterpart.

Within a city over time, economic or population growth often fluctuates with that of the surrounding region or the nation as a whole. As the current rate of growth fluctuates, the market may adjust its expectations about future growth. As these expectations adjust, there can be sharp changes in the value of urban land, even though current rents may not change at all. Returning to our simple numerical example, the value of an acre of land at the center and the border is considerably lower if our city of 2 million residents is not expected to grow at all (as opposed to 4 percent annually). In Equation (3.17), the third term drops out with no growth and central land is worth $242,857 rather than $334,286. Land at the border would plunge in value to $14,286 from $105,715. At the border, both the second and third terms of Equation (3.17) are equal to zero.

As we will see in Chapter 7, it not uncommon for urban growth rates to fluctuate in this range. Much of the variation of real estate prices over time is due to changes in the expected future growth of rental income, rather than to changes in the actual level of current rents. Faster expected growth of a city, all else equal, will yield lower capitalization rates. Thus, faster growing cities that are otherwise identical to slower growing cities (in population, income, and density) should have similar land and housing rents, but higher land and housing prices.

HOUSING PRICES: SOME EMPIRICAL EVIDENCE

How different are house prices across cities? Do the differences that exist correspond to those suggested by the simple Ricardian theories developed in this chapter? This is a question that a number of researchers have asked over the years but one that has proved elusive for two reasons: the lack of data and the confounding influence of other factors. In the stylized city developed in this chapter, housing structures were assumed identical and prices differed only because of the factors that affected land value: city size, geography, and residential density. In the real world, housing structures differ significantly because of history, climate, and varying regional preferences. In comparison to Minneapolis, many Los Angeles homes have swimming pools and air conditioning. Homes in the northeast have full basements—a feature rarely found in Texas. Thus, data on average sales prices by metropolitan area may not necessarily provide a good indicator of differences in house prices between markets when the typical unit can vary so much. In Chapters 4 and 8, we address the issue of quality-controlled house prices.

Keeping in mind these measurement problems, let's look at some data. Using 1990 Census data, Table 3.1 reports the median value of owner-occupied, single-family homes in each of 20 metropolitan areas.[13] We also include the three other variables that were used throughout this chapter to determine the price of urban land: the 1990 household population, the change in the number of households between 1980 and 1990, and a cost index for the construction of new homes.

Glancing at Table 3.1, it does seem the case that larger cities generally have higher house prices than smaller metropolitan areas (Los Angeles, San Francisco, Boston as opposed to New Orleans, Portland, Rochester, San Antonio). Within size categories, the relationship between values and growth is more difficult to discern. There also appears to be a relationship between house prices and the cost of residential construction. A more scientific approach to examining Table 3.1 involves a multivariate regression analysis. With the variables in Table 3.1, Equation (3.19) is estimated, with median house price (*PRICE*) as the dependent variable and metropolitan size (*HH*), growth (*HHGRO*), and construction cost (*COST*) as the independent variables.

$$PRICE = -298{,}138 + 0.019\ HH + 152{,}156\ HHGRO + 1{,}622\ COST$$
$$(10.0) \quad (2.4) \quad\quad (2.3) \quad\quad\quad (4.2) \quad\quad R^2 = .76 \quad\quad (3.19)$$

[13]In Table 3.1, we use Consolidated Metropolitan Statistical Areas (CMSAs) for a number of cities. These are larger areas that often include more than one city. For example, the Los Angeles CMSA includes Anaheim, Santa Ana, Long Beach, Oxnard, Ventura, San Bernardino, and Riverside. The idea behind a CMSA is that these areas in many respects reflect a single urban area rather than a collection of smaller distinct areas. For our purposes, CMSAs better reflect the size and growth of the area as a whole.

TABLE 3.1 Median House Values and Construction Costs

	1990 Value	1990 Construction Cost Index	1980 HHs*	1990 HHs	% Difference
Boston CMSA	$176,400	248.8	1,219,603	1,547,004	26.8
Cincinnati CMSA	71,400	203.9	586,818	652,920	11.3
Dallas/Ft. Worth CMSA	78,700	187.9	1,076,297	1,449,872	34.7
Denver CMSA	89,300	198.4	609,360	737,806	21.1
Detroit CMSA	69,400	227.4	1,601,967	1,723,478	7.6
Houston CMSA	63,800	192.8	1,096,353	1,331,845	21.5
Kansas City MSA	66,500	209.7	493,485	602,347	22.1
Los Angeles CMSA	211,700	239.8	4,141,097	4,900,720	18.3
Miami CMSA	88,700	191.1	1,027,347	1,220,797	18.8
Minneapolis MSA	88,700	213.7	762,376	935,516	22.7
New Orleans MSA	70,000	188.2	418,406	455,178	8.8
Philadephia CMSA	102,300	230.5	1,925,787	2,154,104	11.9
Phoenix MSA	85,300	195.4	544,759	807,560	48.2
Pittsburgh CMSA	55,200	213.9	828,504	891,923	7.7
Portland CMSA	72,600	216.3	477,513	575,531	20.5
Rochester NY MSA	86,600	218.4	342,195	374,475	9.4
San Antonio MSA	57,300	182.6	349,330	451,021	29.1
San Francisco CMSA	257,700	267.3	1,970,549	2,329,808	18.2
Tampa MSA	71,300	191.3	638,816	869,481	36.1
Washington DC MSA	166,100	205.6	1,112,770	1,459,358	31.1

*HH, household.
CMSA, Consolidated Metropolitan Statistical Area.
MSA, Metropolitan Statistical Area.
Source: 1990 Census of Population and Housing, *Summary Population and Housing Characteristics,* CPH–1–1, Table 5; 1980 Census of Housing, *Detailed Housing Characteristics, U.S. State Summary,* HC80–1–B1; *Historical Cost Indices from Means Square Foot Costs 1994.*

The t-statistics are in parentheses below the coefficients. These results are consistent with the theory developed in this chapter. The size of the metropolitan area has a positive and statistically significant impact on house prices as suggested by Ricardian theory. Our theory also suggests that the expected rate of metropolitan growth positively affects house prices, which is confirmed as well. Finally, Equation (3.14) indicates that the cost of constructing structures should influence house prices, and, clearly, this is true in our statistical equation. With only three variables, our model is able to explain 76 percent of the variation in house prices across our sample of metropolitan areas, suggesting that sometimes even a very simple or abstract theory can provide powerful explanations of real-world phenomena.

SUMMARY

In this chapter we have shown that even simple models can be quite powerful in explaining how urban land and housing markets operate. The Ricardian model of location based on a monocentric city with fixed residential density suggests the following:

- Rents for housing, and the derived residual rents for urban land, vary by location within cities so as to exactly offset the value that households place on the advantages of those locations.
- Households and other land users such as firms compete with each other for locations within a land market. Locations are occupied by that use that derives the greatest benefit from the site's locational characteristics, and, therefore, offers the highest rent.
- Cities with greater population tend to expand horizontally, to farther or less desirable locations. This makes existing developed sites more valuable, and increases housing and land rents at all locations.
- The rate of population growth of a city is a prime determinant of housing or land prices. With faster growth comes increasing land and housing rents. The capitalized value of these increases form the basis for prices. The rent-to-price ratio or capitalization rate for housing or land will vary both across locations at one point in time, as well as over time at one location.

APPENDIX: CONTINUOUS TIME DISCOUNTING[14]

A variable (such as rent r) that begins at r_0 and grows annually at a compound rate g, will after t years have the value: $r_0(1 + g)^t$. Now suppose that we compound the growth n periods annually, but use a growth rate of g/n. We get the expression below for the value after t years (tn periods), which in the limit (as $n = \infty$) yields the definition of a natural exponent:

$$\text{limit } (n \to \infty): \quad r_0\left(1 + \frac{g}{n}\right)^{tn} = r_0 e^{gt}$$

Following the same procedure, a variable (such as rent r) received t years in the future can be discounted at a compound annual rate i. Today, that rent is worth: r/e^{it}, or re^{-it}.

The value (p) of a fixed annual income r, received each year from time 0 until time T, is the sum of the discounted values of this income over the received years: its present discounted value. When time is continuous, and interest or compounding figured likewise, the sum of discounted values is replaced by the integral of the discounted value function. Integrating re^{-it} from 0 to T yields:

$$p = \text{limit}(n \to \infty) \sum_{t=0}^{Tn} \frac{r}{\left(1 + \frac{i}{n}\right)^t} = \int_0^T re^{-it} dt = (1 - e^{-iT})\frac{r}{i}$$

If the income is received forever ($T = \infty$), then $p = r/i$.

[14] See Chiang (1984) for a complete discussion of discrete and continuous time discounting.

If an income stream starts out at an initial value (r_0) and then increases (from $t = 0$) at a continuous compound rate g, the discounted value of the income received at time t is:

$$r_0 e^{gt} e^{-it} = r_0 e^{-(i-g)t}$$

Following the same procedure as above, the current present value of this growing income stream (p) will be the integral of the discounted values:

$$p = \int_0^T r_0 e^{-(i-g)t} dt = (1 - e^{-(i-g)T}) \frac{r_0}{(i-g)}$$

If the income is received forever ($T = \infty$), then $p = r_0/(i - g)$.

The formulas for the present value of a growing income stream are identical to those for a fixed income stream if the nominal discount rate (i) is replaced by a real discount rate ($i - g$). If the income stream is truly expected to grow at a rate that exceeds the discount rate ($i - g < 0$), then one has found the proverbial "free lunch," whose discounted value will be infinite.

The real discount rate ($i - g$) is the capitalization rate to be applied to a current dollar of riskless income expected to grow forever at the constant rate g.

REFERENCES AND ADDITIONAL READINGS

ALONSO, WILLIAM, *Location and Land Use.* Cambridge, Mass.: Harvard University Press, 1964.

CAPOZZA, DENNIS R., AND ROBERT W. HELSLEY, "The Fundamentals of Land Prices and Urban Growth." *Journal of Urban Economics* 26 (November 1989): 295–306.

CAPOZZA, DENNIS R. AND ROBERT W. HELSLEY, "The Stochastic City," *Journal of Urban Economics,* 28 (September 1990), 295–306.

CHIANG, ALPHA C., *Fundamental Methods of Mathematical Economics,* 3rd ed. New York: McGraw-Hill Book Company, 1984.

MILLS, EDWIN S., *Studies in the Structure of the Urban Economy.* Baltimore: The Johns Hopkins University Press, 1972.

MUTH, RICHARD F., *Cities and Housing.* Chicago: University of Chicago Press, 1969.

RICARDO, DAVID, *The Principles of Political Economy and Taxation* (1817; reprinted). London: J. M. Dent and Son, 1965.

STRASZHEIM, MAHLON, "The Theory of Urban Residential Location," in *Handbook of Regional and Urban Economics* (vol. 2), ed. Edwin S. Mills. Amsterdam: Elsevier Science Publishers B.V., 1987.

WHEATON, WILLIAM C., "Income and Urban Residence: An Analysis of Consumer Demand for Location," *American Economic Review,* 67 (September 1977), 620–631.

CHAPTER 4
The Urban Housing Market: Structural Attributes and Density

In Chapter 3, we began our examination of the urban housing market with a stylized and simple model of a city. In this city, all housing units were structurally the same and were built on identical plots of land. In reality, housing is a very heterogenous commodity. Lot sizes vary widely from single-family homes on several acres of land to apartment buildings where the land per unit is a small fraction of an acre. In most American cities, housing is more densely developed closer to the city center, where land values are high. Land parcels also vary widely in the amenities they provide. Lots may be level or sloped, wooded or cleared, with spectacular views, close to amenities such as a park or disamenities such as a polluting factory. The structural characteristics of housing also vary widely, from basic features such as the number of bedrooms and bathrooms, or the quality of kitchen facilities, to the more subtle features of architectural design and construction quality.

At any point in time, most houses available on the market are existing units, not newly constructed units. As a result, households rarely are able to assemble separately the individual attributes of a house into a custom package. Instead, they select that house that most closely meets their preferences and budget from a range of houses that offer different predetermined bundles of characteristics. While households must choose a complete unit, each individual characteristic of the house—from structural features to lot and location—is separately valued by the household. Hence, much can be learned about consumer preferences for individual housing characteristics by studying the patterns of choice and prices that emerge in a market of heterogeneous preexisting housing units.

Chapter 4 The Urban Housing Market: Structural Attributes and Density

The durability of housing units has a profound influence on the pattern of residential development in an urban area. In most U.S. urban housing markets, newly constructed housing units have tended to be larger over time, both in terms of interior space and lot sizes. This lower-density development pattern occurs at the fringe of the urban area, where land is more plentiful and less expensive, and stands in contrast with the older, higher-density development occupying central locations. As cities have spread out in this manner, average residential density has declined. Yet, at the same time, redevelopment has occurred at more central locations, frequently increasing residential density.

In this chapter, we build on the analysis presented in Chapter 3 by relaxing the assumptions of identical housing structures and lots to consider the heterogeneity of housing and how particular patterns of housing structures and density emerge over time. We set the stage for the chapter with a discussion of urban population density, focusing on how population density has changed over the last two decades within a particular metropolitan area. We then develop a way of statistically determining the value that households place on specific housing attributes. Finally, we present a simple model of how the density of development or redevelopment is determined over time and show how this model explains the patterns of density observed in most metropolitan areas.

URBAN DENSITY

Unlike the city in our simple model presented in Chapter 3, the density at which residential real estate is developed frequently varies widely within a metropolitan area. The underlying reason for variation in density is simple. As location rent increases the price of land, a substitution occurs between land and structure. Economists call this process *factor substitution.* At locations at which land is more valuable, development tends to use less land (the more expensive factor) per housing unit and relatively more structural capital (the less expensive factor). In other words, our models predict denser residential development at more central locations, where land is most expensive. As a result, we expect to find more multifamily buildings and fewer single-family homes as we move closer to the central city. As we will see, the relationship between density and land value moves in both directions: higher value not only encourages greater density, but greater density increases the value of land.

Casual observation in most cities suggests that residential density does indeed decline with distance from the central city. Empirically, this relationship is often measured by examining how gross population density (population divided by land area) varies with increasing distance from the center of the metropolitan area.[1] In Figure 4.1, we present the population density for 146 cities and towns in the Boston area based on the 1990 Census.[2] Together these 146 towns had a total population in 1990 of 3.86 million. The

---

[1]Alternatively, we could examine residential structure density—housing units per square mile. In these data, the pattern of residential structure density is very similar to that for population density.

[2]The 146 towns do not correspond to any Census definitions of the Boston metropolitan area. We defined the area to include towns within the region's outermost circumferential highway.

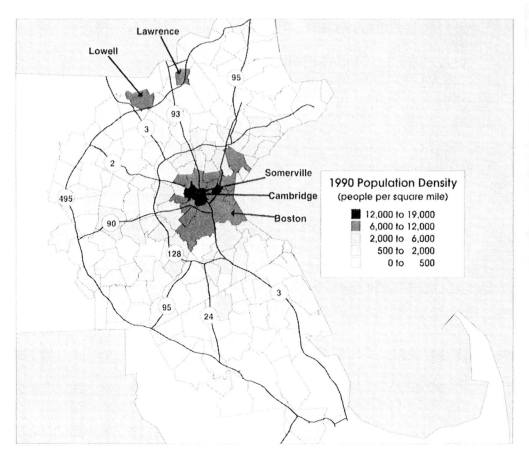

FIGURE 4.1 Population density for Boston-area cities and towns, 1990.
Source: 1990 Census.

average population density across these towns is 1,589 people per square mile, but density varies widely from 18,543 people per square mile in Somerville, which is just outside the city of Boston, to 157 in Bolton, to the far west of Boston. This wide variation and the general decline in population density with distance from the center are clear from the map.

There are some anomalies in our density data. For example, the city of Boston has a lower population density than several of its neighboring towns, such as Cambridge and Somerville. This is due to the fact that our measure of population density is based on the total land area of a city or town, not just land used for residential purposes. In the city of Boston, more land is used for commercial and institutional purposes (e.g., offices, hospitals, government, universities) than in some of its neighboring jurisdictions, a fact that drives down the population density as we measure it. Note also the two high-density towns to the northwest of Boston. These are Lowell and Lawrence, old manufacturing centers that developed historically as employment centers with dense residential development of their own.

Chapter 4 The Urban Housing Market: Structural Attributes and Density

The variation in population density with distance from the central city is often summarized through the estimation of a population density gradient. A *density gradient* is estimated by a simple two-variable regression model with population density as the dependent variable and distance as the independent variable. The standard specification is the negative exponential, which takes the form:

$$D(d) = D_0 e^{-\alpha d} \qquad (4.1)$$

Here, the population density at distance d miles from the center of the city, $D(d)$, has two components. D_0 is the model's estimate of the level of density at the center and α is the estimate of the coefficient on distance, which represents the percentage reduction in density with each unit increase in distance (i.e., each mile) from the center. In order to statistically estimate Equation (4.1), it must be transformed into a linear expression by taking the natural logs of both sides of the equation, which yields:

$$\log(D(d)) = \log(D_0) - \alpha d \qquad (4.2)$$

Equation (4.2) is estimated by an ordinary least squares regression, across observations consisting of towns, in which the dependent variable is the log of town density and the independent variable is the town's distance, d. In Table 4.1, we present estimates of Equation (4.2) for the Boston metropolitan area. For 1990, the coefficient on distance (α) is –0.09 and is statistically significant. This provides an estimate of the slope of the area's density gradient and means that with each mile increase in distance from the center, population density decreases by 9 percent. The constant in this model is the estimate of $\log(D_0)$, or the average density level at the center. In this sample, it is estimated at 6,634 people per square mile ($\log(D_0) = 8.8$, or $D_0 = e^{8.8} = 6{,}634$). The density 20 miles from the center is predicted to be 1,097 people per square mile. This simple model explains 53 percent of the variation in density in 1990.

In Figure 4.2, we present a scatter plot of actual town densities by distance from the center of the city of Boston with the line through the points representing our estimate of Equation (4.2). While the model fits the data well from about eight miles outward, it does considerably worse in fitting the data near the center. In fact, the actual population

TABLE 4.1 Population Density Gradients for Boston Metropolitan Area

			1990			1970		
	1990	1970	North	West	South	North	West	South
Constant	8.80	9.03	8.98	9.00	8.49	9.12	9.20	8.80
	(11.72)	(11.06)	(10.76)	(12.08)	(15.41)	(10.16)	(11.41)	(14.30)
Coefficient on	–0.09	–0.11	–0.09	–0.11	–0.08	–0.10	–0.13	–0.10
Distance	(–12.68)	(–14.14)	(–7.36)	(–8.42)	(–8.18)	(–7.80)	(–9.00)	(–9.79)
R^2	0.53	0.58	0.52	0.58	0.63	0.54	0.61	0.71
Observations*	146	146	53	54	41	53	54	41

Dependent variable: gross population density.
T-statistics are in parentheses.
*The city of Boston was used in each of the corridor density gradients.
Source: Authors' calculations, using the 1970 and 1990 Census, *Detailed Housing Characteristics*.

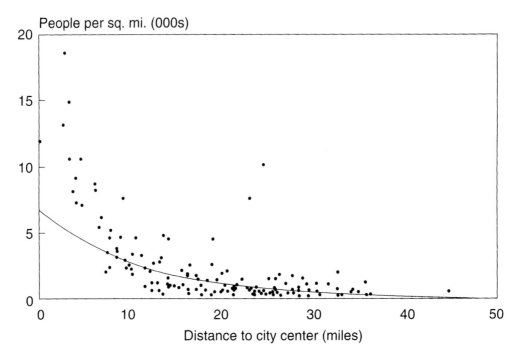

FIGURE 4.2 Boston-area population density, 1990.

Source: Authors' calculations, using the 1990 Census, *Detailed Housing Characteristics*.

density of the city of Boston in 1990 was 11,860, 79 percent higher than that predicted by the model. An inspection of the data suggests that the combination of the large number of cities and towns with relatively low density and the two major outliers between 20 and 30 miles from the city may be responsible for the flattening of the gradient at more central locations.

While it is clear that residential density tends on average to decline with distance, it is not necessarily true that density is the same at all points equidistant from the center. In Table 4.1, we also present density gradients estimated for three corridors in Boston, using only those towns to the north, west, and south. The coefficients on distance in 1990 vary from –0.11 in the west to –0.08 to the south. The flatter gradients to the north and south are largely due to older outlying employment centers (Lawrence and Lowell to the north; Brockton and Quincy to the south). The evidence presented in Table 4.1 suggests that densities vary considerably within a metropolitan area.

How does the pattern of residential density change over time? In Figure 4.3, we provide a graph comparing 1970 and 1990 estimated density gradients. The 1970 gradient is clearly steeper for the metro area. As shown in Table 4.1, the estimated gradients for the north, west, and south corridors for 1970 and 1990 all show a flattening effect over time. This illustrates a pattern of increased suburbanization of Boston's population over the past two decades.

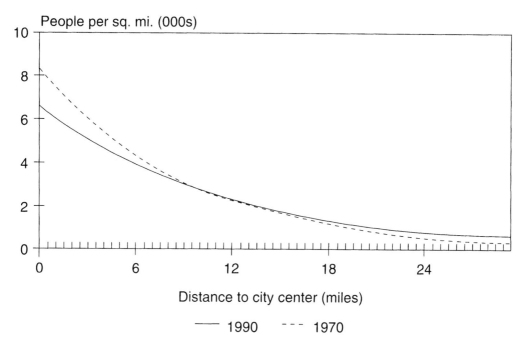

FIGURE 4.3 Boston-area population density gradients, 1970 and 1990.
Source: Authors' calculations, using the 1970 and 1990 Census, *Detailed Housing Characteristics.*

Between 1970 and 1990, the total population in these 146 cities and towns rose only 2.1 percent, or from 3.78 million to 3.86 million. However, Figure 4.4 illustrates that there have been dramatic shifts in the relative distribution of the population. The more central cities and towns lost population over the two decades, while towns at the fringe grew significantly.

While the density gradients of various cities can be quite different, in most cities researchers have observed the same trends over time that are occurring in the Boston area. During the last several decades, the population of most areas has become more decentralized in suburban communities, with a resulting flattening of the residential density gradient (Mills 1972).

HOUSING ATTRIBUTES AND HOUSEHOLD PREFERENCES

Consider two houses that are both purchased for $100,000. This purchase price reflects housing expenditures but does not imply that the quantity or quality of housing purchased is identical. In Houston, for example, $100,000 of expenditure might buy a three-bedroom ranch-style home with a large back yard in a middle-income suburban community. In New York City, the same $100,000 expenditure might purchase only a studio or one-bedroom condominium in a marginal neighborhood. Even within the same market,

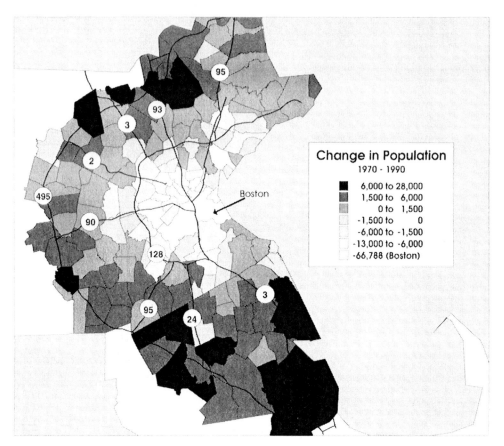

FIGURE 4.4 Change in population for Boston-area cities and towns, 1970–1990.
Source: 1970, 1990 Census.

$100,000 of expenditure might purchase a two-bedroom home with a large lot and swimming pool, or a four-bedroom house with zero lot line and no pool.

The point here is that housing is a heterogeneous commodity—houses differ in structure size and characteristics, as well as in the location and type of lot on which they sit. Because housing units are fixed in space, a household implicitly chooses many different goods and services when it selects a house, including neighborhood and school district, as well as the components of the structure itself. Identical houses on identical lots will often sell for very different prices depending on the quality of community schools or other public services. We will discuss the impact of local public services on property values in detail in Chapter 13.

In studying housing markets, it is important to distinguish between the expenditures that households make and a true measure of price. A true market price is defined for a fixed quantity of a good (e.g., price per pound of oranges or price per gallon of gasoline); expenditures are this unit price times the quantity purchased. In the housing market, we generally observe expenditures, not price per standard quantity (or quality) of housing. In this respect, housing is quite different from other markets that economists study where standardized unit prices are directly observed.

In Chapter 3, we introduced the notion that housing rents or prices compensate consumers for locational advantage. In a competitive market equilibrium in which all households are identical, households should be as equally well off paying less at less advantageous sites as they are paying more to occupy more desirable locations. This principle of compensation across locations continues to hold as we consider housing as a heterogeneous good with many different attributes. Households examine each house in the market and choose that unit which, considering price, makes them best off. Assuming (as we did in Chapter 3) that households have similar tastes and incomes, the price of each house will have to compensate exactly for its varied attributes. In Chapter 3, housing rents were hypothesized to exactly compensate for the commuting costs associated with different locations. In this chapter, housing rents or prices will have to compensate for all of the desirable or undesirable features of each unit, such as density, size, number of bathrooms, or construction quality, as well as the locational advantages associated with the site such as commuting. What amount of money would make a household indifferent between a three- and a four-bedroom house? What is an extra bathroom worth to a potential homebuyer?

When households evaluate a housing unit they apply a valuation process that is based on the unit's various individual attributes. It is important for both sellers of existing units and builders of new units to understand this implicit valuation process of buyers, because explicit prices for individual attributes are never directly observed in the housing market. As with any economic commodity, we expect that the implicit valuation of individual attributes, like bedrooms and bathrooms, will follow the law of diminishing marginal utility: the added value of additional consumption of a commodity drops as more is consumed. To illustrate this economic principle, we turn to Figure 4.5, which shows the amount a household is willing to pay for units of different size (measured in square feet of floor area, *SIZE*). The solid line depicts how the household's total valuation for a house varies with its floor area, while the dashed line depicts the implicit valuation of each additional square foot. Both demonstrate that a household is willing to pay less per square foot as more floor area is acquired.[3]

What are the specific slopes and shapes of the curves in Figure 4.5? How much does additional square footage actually add to the price of a house? How can we quantitatively estimate the implicit price of individual housing attributes, given that these prices are not directly observed? We can measure such consumer valuations using multiple regression analysis to estimate what is called an *hedonic price equation*.[4] An hedonic price equation considers the market price paid for a house, P, to be a function of the levels of all observable characteristics of that house, X_i, $i = 1, n$. The dependent variable (housing price or rent) can be developed by tracking actual sale or lease transactions or

[3]The dashed line (or marginal value of a square foot) is the derivative of the solid line (or total valuation of the unit).

[4]According to Berndt (1991, p. 111), Court (1939) coined the term *hedonic pricing* from hedonistic philosophies found in utilitarianism. Court estimated the enjoyment that consumers receive from the individual attributes of an automobile such as speed, internal comfort, safety, and so on.

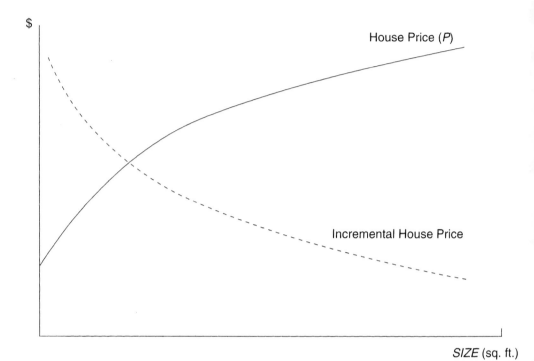

FIGURE 4.5 House prices and unit size.

by surveying current unit occupants and obtaining estimates of market price or rent. The characteristics used as independent variables include continuous variables such as square feet, integer variables such as number of baths, as well as discrete variables such as identifying whether the unit has a garage or a swimming pool. Often, qualitative judgments made by surveyors are included concerning the maintenance of the housing unit or the general quality of the neighborhood. Estimating such hedonic equations requires housing unit data that combines information on housing price or rent with a reasonably complete set of measures for the characteristics of the house and neighborhood. In its most simple form, linear hedonic equations look like the one shown in Equation (4.3).

$$P = \alpha + \beta_1 X_1 + \beta_2 X_2 + \ldots + \beta_n X_n \tag{4.3}$$

In Equation (4.3), the estimated coefficients on the housing characteristics, β_i, may be interpreted as estimates of an implicit price that households are willing to pay for more of each attribute. A linear hedonic equation assumes that this price is constant and does not depend on how much of each attribute the unit has. In other words, it assumes that all of a unit's square feet or space add the same value and that there is no diminishing marginal utility with additional space.

To illustrate the linear hedonic price technique, we have taken information from the U.S. Census Bureau's 1989 American Housing Survey (AHS) for the Boston metropolitan area. The survey provides a detailed set of unit and neighborhood attributes for a sample of

Chapter 4 The Urban Housing Market: Structural Attributes and Density

TABLE 4.2 Average Attributes of 1989 Boston-Area Houses

Attribute	Mean	Standard Deviation
House Value	199,720	75,445
Number of Bedrooms	3.201	0.890
Number of Bathrooms	1.624	0.680
Age of Structure	27.281	9.364
Single-Family Attached*	0.014	0.117
Garage*	0.632	0.482
Poor-Quality Unit*	0.024	0.154
Fair or Poor Neighborhood*	0.069	0.253
Central City*	0.036	0.187

* indicates a dummy variable: 0 for no, 1 for yes.
Source: U.S. Census Bureau, *American Housing Survey,* 1989.

1,648 owner-occupied, single-family housing units.[5] In Table 4.2, the characteristics of the houses used in this analysis are listed along with the sample means and standard deviations for each characteristic (the X_i above). In this sample, the average house has a price of almost $200,000, has 3.2 bedrooms and 1.6 bathrooms, and is an average of 27 years old.[6] One percent of the units are single-family attached, and 63 percent of the units have a garage.

The AHS survey also provides various measures of the quality of the structure. The U.S. Department of Housing and Urban Development aggregates these measures to determine whether the unit meets government adequacy standards. In this sample, 2 percent of the units are structurally inadequate by these government standards. The survey includes detailed characteristics of the neighborhood as well, covering the presence of abandoned buildings in the area and the occupant's view as to the quality of the neighborhood. These variables are combined to create a neighborhood quality variable that takes on the value 1 if the neighborhood is of fair or poor quality and 0, otherwise. In the Boston area, 6.9 percent of the units are defined to be in fair- or poor-quality neighborhoods. A final variable considers whether or not the unit is located in the central city; 3.6 percent of the units are in the central city. Using these AHS data, we estimate the linear hedonic regression equation described in Equation (4.4):

$$P = 61508 + 13935 \, BEDRMS + 50678 \, BATHRMS + 21681 \, GARAGE$$
$$(161.29) \, (146.40) \qquad (378.73) \qquad (134.75)$$
$$- 60 \, AGE - 3880 \, SFA - 3425 \, POOR\text{-}QUAL \, UNIT$$
$$(-7.45) \quad (-6.15) \quad (-7.18) \qquad \qquad (4.4)$$
$$- 6175 \, BAD \, AREA - 4997 \, CENTRAL \, CITY$$
$$(-21.18) \qquad \quad (-12.62)$$
$$N = 1168 \qquad R^2 = 0.38$$

[5] In this case, single-family units include both detached and attached units. An attached unit is a unit attached to another unit by a common wall (e.g., townhouses or row houses).

[6] The AHS is a survey of the housing stock, not a sample of housing transactions. As a result, the prices reported here are not transaction prices but rather the occupant's estimate of the value of the house. This raises questions about the accuracy of owners' estimates of value. In addition, the Census only reports value by ranges. Like other researchers, we assign each unit the midpoint value of that range. (See DiPasquale and Somerville 1995).

In Equation (4.4), t-statistics are in parentheses beneath the coefficients. More bedrooms, bathrooms, and the presence of a garage all increase the price of the home. Price declines if the unit is an attached rather than a detached unit (the variable *SFA*), or if the unit is of poor quality or located in a bad neighborhood. Price also declines if the unit is located in the central city. This result is the opposite of what is expected in the monocentric model presented in Chapter 3 in which the reduction in commuting costs closer to the CBD increases housing rents and prices. The negative impact of a central city location in Equation (4.4) may reflect other characteristics of the central city ignored in the monocentric model, such as high crime or poor-quality schools. The expected sign for the coefficient on the age of structure is unclear. Older structures could be expected to provide lower-quality services, but it is also true that older units often have unique features, such as charm or style, that home purchasers value. In this hedonic, age has a negative influence on house price. All of the coefficients are statistically significant.

Using Equation (4.4), we can explore the issue of how households value individual attributes of a housing unit, as well as how they value an entire house with a specific set of attributes. If, for example, we apply the estimated coefficients to the average characteristics provided in Table 4.2 and sum the terms, we can estimate the value of a house with those average attributes. That calculation produces an estimated average house price of $199,738, which is almost exactly the average value of houses in this sample.[7]

The coefficients in Equation (4.4) are estimates of the incremental value to be gained from more of each attribute. This hedonic equation indicates that a bathroom is the most valuable attribute, worth $50,678. A garage adds $21,681 to the value of a home. Holding all other characteristics constant, a single-family attached unit is worth $3,880 less than if the unit were free-standing.

While linear hedonic equations are frequently used in property valuations, they do have the unrealistic feature of assuming that each additional room or bathroom has the same value. As we discussed earlier in this chapter, it seems reasonable to expect that the law of diminishing marginal utility applies and that the value of additional bedrooms or bathrooms declines as more are added to a unit. By altering the specification of the hedonic model, we can permit the curvature between price and attributes implied by the law of diminishing marginal utility. A common model specification designed to address this issue takes the form:

$$P = \alpha X_1^{\beta_1} X_2^{\beta_2} \ldots X_n^{\beta_n} \tag{4.5}$$

To statistically estimate the parameters of Equation (4.5), we transform it into a linear equation by taking the natural logs of both sides. This yields:

$$\log P = \log \alpha + \beta_1 \log X_1 + \beta_2 \log X_2 + \ldots + \beta_n \log X_n \tag{4.6}$$

---

[7] A fundamental principle in regression analysis is that when an estimated regression equation is evaluated at the mean values of the independent variables (the estimated coefficients are multiplied by the mean values of the independent variables), the model predicts the mean value of the dependent variable (see Pindyck and Rubinfeld 1991). The small discrepancy between the calculated house value and the actual mean house value is caused by rounding.

Chapter 4   The Urban Housing Market: Structural Attributes and Density

The coefficients in this model are obtained by estimating a linear regression equation in which the dependent variable is the natural log of price, and the independent variables are the natural log of the original attribute measures. Rather than determining the (constant) value of an additional unit of each attribute, X_i, the coefficients of Equation (4.6) represent the elasticity of price with respect to increases in the attribute: the percentage change in the dependent variable that results from a percentage change in the independent variable.

Using the same AHS data, we can estimate the following hedonic equation using the log-log specification.[8]

$$\begin{aligned}
\text{LOG } P = {} & 11.71 + 0.165 \text{ LOG } BEDRMS + 0.473 \text{ LOG } BATHRMS \\
& (3563.6)\ (97.54) \qquad\qquad\qquad\quad (326.09) \\
& + 0.145 \text{ LOG } GARAGE - 0.004 \text{ LOG } AGE \\
& \quad (103.76) \qquad\qquad\quad\ (-5.06) \\
& - 0.001 \text{ LOG } SFA - 0.122 \text{ LOG } POOR\text{-}QUAL\ UNIT \\
& \quad (-0.27) \qquad\qquad\ (-29.70) \\
& - 0.103 \text{ LOG } BAD\ AREA - 0.015 \text{ LOG } CENTRAL\ CITY \\
& \quad (-40.77) \qquad\qquad\qquad\ (-4.34) \\
N = {} & 1168 \qquad\qquad\qquad\qquad R^2 = 0.286
\end{aligned} \qquad (4.7)$$

How do we interpret the coefficients in Equation (4.7)? These coefficients are estimates of the exponents in Equation (4.5). For a discrete variable, such as the presence of a garage, we do not think about percentage changes; rather, we think only about a house either having or not having a garage. If a house has a garage, the variable has been coded with the value 2; if it does not, the value is 1.[9] Using Equation (4.5), we find that the presence of a garage adds 10.6 percent to the value of the house ($2^{0.145} = 1.106$). If the house is located in an undesirable neighborhood (another discrete variable), its value is reduced by 6.9 percent ($2^{-0.103} = 0.931$).

We predict a house's price by simply inserting values for each attribute in Equation (4.5), using the coefficients estimated in Equation (4.7) as the exponents in Equation (4.5), and then multiplying all of the terms. The price for a single-family detached house that is 27 years old; has three bedrooms, two bathrooms, and a garage; is in good shape; and is located in a good neighborhood in the suburbs would be:

$$\begin{aligned}
P &= e^{11.71} 3^{0.165} 2^{0.473} 2^{0.145} 27^{-0.004} 1^{-0.001} 1^{-0.122} 1^{-0.103} 1^{-0.015} \\
&= 221{,}118
\end{aligned} \qquad (4.8)$$

Using our house with the attributes defined above but varying the number of bathrooms, we can illustrate the law of diminishing marginal utility. A house with those average characteristics that has one bathroom is valued at $159,308. With two bathrooms, an

---

[8] The R^2 value of this equation is not strictly comparable to that of the linear Equation (4.4) and so cannot be used to judge which model fits the data best statistically. There are more advanced statistical procedures for making this comparison (see Pindyck and Rubinfeld 1991).

[9] Since we cannot take the log of 0, those variables taking on the values of either 0 or 1 are entered as 1 or 2 in estimating Equation (4.6).

otherwise identical house is worth $221,118, an increase of $61,810, or 38.8 percent. With three bathrooms, its value is $267,865, an increase of $46,747 or 21.1 percent. These calculations clearly illustrate the law of diminishing marginal utility, and may be contrasted with the linear equation (4.4) where each bath added a constant $50,678 to house value.

HOUSING ATTRIBUTES AND NEW CONSTRUCTION

Understanding the value that consumers place on specific housing attributes can provide the key to successfully developing residential real estate. It also helps to explain the evolution of the housing stock in any particular city. In the long run, it is primarily the preferences of consumers and their willingness to pay for those preferences that dictate the type and configuration of housing that gets built. As with any economic good, however, consumer prices must be judged against the cost of providing that good. Consider as an example the question of how large to make a single-family home. We might assume as a starting point that the construction cost per square foot of space is roughly constant. If this square foot cost is (C), then to construct a house of $SIZE$ square feet costs $C \times SIZE$. As we have seen, however, the value of a house with $SIZE$ square feet should follow the law of diminishing marginal utility. Using the hedonic model of the previous section, the value of a home with $SIZE$ square feet, $P(SIZE)$, holding all other attributes fixed, will look something like the price function pictured in Figure 4.6. The cost of constructing housing will be represented by the linear ray out of the origin. At the size indicated as $SIZE^*$, the difference between house price or value and construction cost is maximized. At that level, the incremental value of an additional square foot will exactly balance the cost of construction.[10]

If over time, more modern homes tend to be larger, for example, this could be explained by one or both of two market changes. First, the cost of construction (per square foot) could have come down through technological improvements. This would flatten the cost ray in Figure 4.6 and lead to a higher value of $SIZE^*$, the most profitable home size. Second, consumers could have changed their preferences and become willing to pay more for additional space. This would lead to a willingness-to-pay function (P in Figure 4.6) that is less curved. This also generates a greater $SIZE^*$ solution.

Most attributes of a house can be evaluated against their cost of construction or installation in a similar manner. Thus, as market suppliers learn about their clientele, the homes that are constructed generally are those with the most profitable configuration of attributes. In this way, the units added to the stock each year tend to reflect both the market preferences and the construction technology prevailing at that time. Thus, in any given year, the overall stock of housing is an aggregation of units constructed at different

---

[10]At the profit-maximizing size ($SIZE^*$), the derivative of price (or willingness to pay) with respect to square feet, or the slope of the price function ($\partial P/\partial SIZE$), will equal the marginal cost of construction (C) or the slope of the cost function.

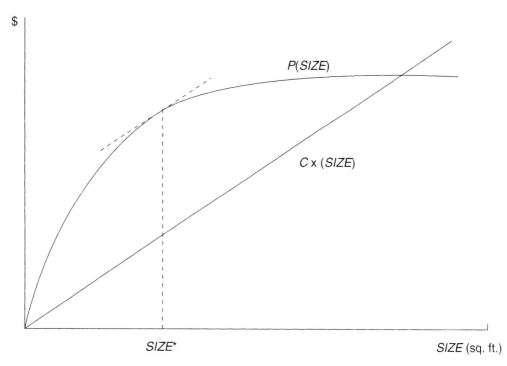

FIGURE 4.6 Willingness to pay and unit size.

periods with attributes based on the demand and costs in effect at the time each unit was built (Harrison and Kain, 1974). The one exception to the profit-maximizing principle just discussed involves unit density, or lot size. Determining the most profitable density for development is more complicated than the procedure for other attributes. Since density is the housing attribute that determines a city's overall pattern of residential development, we need to consider it in some detail.

RESIDENTIAL DENSITY, LAND VALUE, AND HIGHEST USE

When land is developed, its most central characteristic is the density of the development (i.e., the number of housing units per acre). As with any attribute, density is determined in a manner that maximizes the profit from development. As has been discussed both in this chapter and Chapter 3, a site's locational features and the structural characteristics of potential housing determine the amount of location rent that will accrue to any particular housing *unit*. In this respect, density is no different from any other attribute. As the first part of this chapter made clear, greater density should tend to reduce a unit's value through the loss of open space, green area, and privacy. However, density also determines the number of units to be developed per acre. In this respect, it is an important determinant of the location rent *per acre* that can be obtained from the site.

A landowner-developer contemplating the development of a site wants to maximize the residual profits to be obtained from the land, after construction costs. Thus, the density of development should be that which maximizes the potential residual value of the land. Let's assume here for simplicity that the only type of development is for residential use. In evaluating different densities of residential development, the developer must consider how the consumers' willingness to pay for units will vary with density, as well as how density increases the number of units to be placed on the site. Since consumers in general are willing to pay less per housing unit as density increases, there exists a tradeoff. Greater density reduces the value and, hence, profit from each unit, but increases the number of units that can be placed on the land. The former reduces site profits or value, while the latter increases it. A developer must balance these two forces in seeking the highest return to a site, rather than simply assuming that greater density yields higher profits and residual value. Let's work through this tradeoff more carefully.

Density can be measured in two ways: as the ratio of housing *units* to total land area of the property, or as the ratio of total housing *floor area* to total land area, commonly referred to as the FAR (*floor area ratio*). Throughout this chapter we will use the FAR measure, although our discussion can easily be recast using the units measure. We will refer to the FAR ratio with the variable F. As already discussed, we expect that, holding all other attributes of the unit and location constant, consumers will pay less for a housing unit that is in a taller building or a more dense development. In an hedonic model like those presented in the previous section, we would expect to get a negative coefficient on density. Using those hedonic models in the previous section, we can define an hedonic equation for the price per square foot of floor area (P) in a housing unit: $P = \alpha - \beta F$. The coefficient α represents the collective value of all other locational and housing attributes that can affect the price (per square foot of floor area) of a house, while β represents the marginal reduction in value that occurs as the house lot is reduced and its density or FAR ratio increased.[11]

We also expect that the cost (per square foot of floor area) of constructing housing units (C) will vary with the FAR of the residential development. In fact, the cost per square foot of construction tends to rise with greater FAR due to increased foundation work, greater structural support, or the necessity of elevators. For simplicity, we abbreviate the cost of construction as: $C = \mu + \tau F$. Here, μ represents a basic cost of construction (per square foot) and τ the incremental additional cost (assumed linear) as density is increased.

In the top panel of Figure 4.7, we present the price schedule and construction cost schedule per square foot of floor area as functions of FAR. The profit (per square foot of floor area) to be made from constructing a housing unit is simply $P - C$, or the vertical distance between the price and cost schedules. Clearly, profits per square foot of constructed floor area are reduced as the site's FAR of development is increased. Profits are

---

[11]As in Chapter 3, we will adopt the convention of using upper-case letters to refer to housing variables, lower-case letters for land variables, and Greek symbols for parameters or coefficients.

The assumption that the FAR reduction is linear is made only for ease of mathematical exposition. In fact, given that P is expressed per square foot, the negative relationship between P and FAR is actually somewhat curved.

Chapter 4 The Urban Housing Market: Structural Attributes and Density

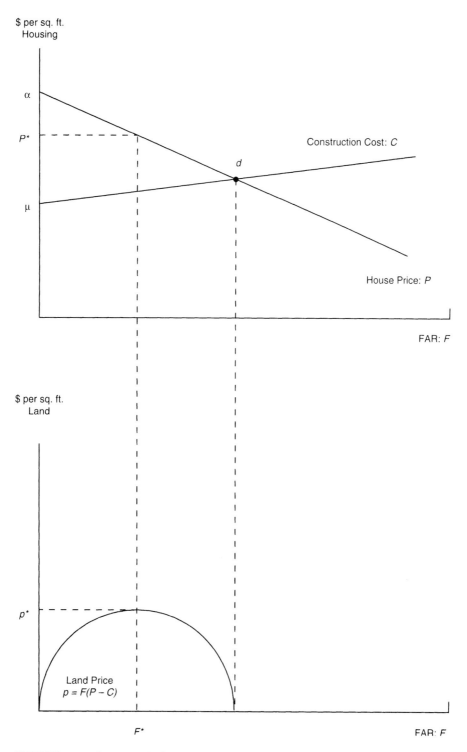

FIGURE 4.7 Optimal FAR.

zero at the point (*d*) where the two schedules intersect, positive to the left of (*d*) where price exceeds costs, and negative to the right where costs exceed price.

What is the profit that accrues to land? While both P and C depend on F, they each are measured in terms of square feet of *floor area*. The residual value of land will be measured as a profit per square foot of *land* area. To get the latter from the former is somewhat complicated, but is the key to determining a site's maximum profitability.

We begin by taking the housing profit (per square foot of floor area) illustrated in the top panel of Figure 4.7 as the difference between the price and construction costs schedules. We then multiply this profit per square foot of floor area by the value of F on the FAR axis (the ratio of floor area to land area). This yields a dollar value per square foot of land area—the residual profit $p = F[P - C]$. This residual profit per square foot of land is shown in the bottom panel of Figure 4.7. At the origin, the value of p must equal zero, since $F = 0$. At the point d where $P = C$ in the top panel of Figure 4.7, p must also equal zero, since with no profit per floor area, there can be no residual value to the land. In between, the value of p rises, reaches its maximum value at F^*, and then falls. Moving up from F^* and over to the vertical axis, p^* is the value (per square foot) of land evaluated at the FAR level F^*. Moving up from F^* to the house price function (P schedule) in the top panel of Figure 4.7, we can go over to the vertical axis and find the value of floor area at the optimal FAR, P^*. The mathematical expressions for F^* and p^* are:[12]

$$F^* = \frac{[\alpha - \mu]}{2[\beta + \tau]}$$

$$p^* = \frac{[\alpha - \mu]}{2} F = \frac{[\alpha - \mu]^2}{4[\beta + \tau]}$$

(4.9)

The development's maximum land profit per square foot is, in principle, an equilibrium value for what land is worth. Regardless of what was paid for the site, the density of development should follow Equation (4.9) even to minimize the losses from an overly high original purchase price. Of course, in the longer run, the maximum residual value from residential development at any site must exceed both the rural opportunity cost of

---

[12]The residual profit per square foot of land development (p) equals the floor area profit multiplied by the development FAR: $F[P - C]$. To find the value of F that maximizes land profit, we begin by substituting in the expressions for floor area price and construction costs:

$$P = \alpha - \beta F \quad , \quad C = \mu + \tau F$$
$$p = F[P - C] = F[\alpha - \mu] - F^2[\beta + \tau]$$

Setting the derivative $\partial p/\partial F$ equal to 0, we solve for the F value (F^*) where this condition holds:

$$\frac{\partial p}{\partial F} = [\alpha - \mu] - 2F[\beta + \tau] = 0$$

$$F^* = \frac{[\alpha - \mu]}{2[\beta + \tau]}$$

We can now obtain p^* by substituting our expression for F^* into that for p:

$$p^* = \frac{[\alpha - \mu]^2}{4[\beta + \tau]}$$

Chapter 4   The Urban Housing Market: Structural Attributes and Density

land and the value that other uses might yield in order for residential development to make sense. Or, put another way, for land to be developed residentially in equilibrium, the FAR chosen for each site must not only be that which maximizes residual land profit, but this land profit in turn must exceed that from other uses.

To illustrate the important role that density plays in determining a development's profitability, we can consider the market for condominiums in a fashionable and historic area of central Boston. To do this, we use data on 578 condominium sales transactions that occurred in the Beacon Hill and the Back Bay sections of downtown Boston in 1984.[13] The housing structures in this area are predominantly brownstones, or small brick walkup apartment buildings, but occasionally there is a larger elevator-serviced building. Our price data for these condominiums are all expressed as price per square foot. As can be seen in Table 4.3, the average price per square foot in 1984 was $150, with prices ranging from a high of $190 per square foot on prestigious Beacon Hill to $144 on Commonwealth Avenue. The average number of both bedrooms and bathrooms in the sample is 1.4 per unit. An important consideration in deciding to locate in a downtown area is the availability of parking; 25 percent of the units in this database had on-site parking. While we do not have detailed data on locational amenities, we defined the center of the downtown area as the Boston Common and calculated the distance of each unit to the Common. On average, these units are 5,167 feet from the Common, or just under 1 mile. Finally, the average number of stories in each of the buildings is 7.6.

Using these data, we can estimate an hedonic equation for sales price per square foot (rather than total sales price). Again, to keep the mathematics simple, we will estimate a linear equation, even though we argued earlier that a nonlinear function is more consistent with economic theory. Using 578 sales observations in 1984, the following equation was estimated:[14]

$$PSQFT = 181.0 + 6.2BED + 2.7BATH + 23.1PARK - 38.6BDUM$$
$$\quad\quad\quad (14.8)\ (2.6)\ \quad\ (0.8)\ \quad\quad (5.9)\ \quad\quad\ (-3.2)$$
$$\quad\ - 40.5MDUM - 49.1CDUM + 0.0007CDIST - 1.48STORY \quad\quad (4.10)$$
$$\quad\quad\ (-3.3)\quad\quad\ (-4.0)\quad\quad\quad (1.2)\quad\quad\quad\ (-3.8)$$
$$N = 578 \quad\quad\quad\quad\quad\quad\quad\quad\quad\quad R^2 = .16$$

Beneath each coefficient, the t-statistic is presented in parentheses. Given the linear specification, the coefficients in Equation (4.10) should be interpreted as dollars per square foot. If the unit comes with parking, it adds $23 per square foot to the value of the unit. As expected, bedrooms, bathrooms, and parking all have a positive impact on the price per

---

[13]The data for the Back Bay neighborhood encompassed only the three main streets in this area—Marlborough, Beacon, and Commonwealth.

[14]The variables in this equation are:

- *PSQFT*: Sales price per square foot
- *BED*: Number bedrooms
- *PARK*: Unit has parking
- *MDUM*: Unit on Marlborough St.
- *CDIST*: Distance from Common
- *BATH*: Number baths
- *BDUM*: Unit on Beacon St.
- *CDUM*: Unit on Commonwealth Ave.
- *STORY*: Number stories in building

Units not located on Beacon, Marlborough, or Commonwealth streets are on Beacon Hill.

TABLE 4.3 Characteristics of Boston Back Bay Condominiums, 1984

	Mean	Standard Deviation
Price per Square Foot	149.84	39.27
Beacon Hill	190.08	32.23
Marlborough St.	156.50	40.28
Beacon St.	150.90	41.22
Commonwealth Ave.	143.55	34.68
Parking	0.25	0.43
No. of Bedrooms	1.44	0.82
No. of Bathrooms	1.43	0.59
Distance to Boston Common (ft.)	5,167.41	3,112.47
No. of Stories	7.62	4.39

The following location distribution applied to the units used in this study: Beacon Hill, 1.73%; Marlborough St., 15.57%; Beacon St., 47.23%; and Commonwealth Ave., 35.47%.
Source: Greater Boston Board of Realtors.

square foot of the unit, although the coefficient on bathrooms is statistically insignificant. Locations on the three streets in the Back Bay has a negative impact on value relative to a location on Beacon Hill, which was the default location left out of the equation. Surprisingly, the coefficient on distance from the Boston Common is positive, but statistically insignificant. Finally, the taller the building that houses the unit, the lower the value of the unit.

The data in our sample suggest that the Boston Back Bay area has an average FAR of about 7.5, but this does not necessarily reflect the market demand for housing in this neighborhood. The older historic townhouses tend to be 4 to 5 stories tall, while many buildings constructed between 1920 and 1960 vary between 8 and 12 stories. Since 1960, the neighborhood has been an historic district in which a public board limits the FAR of new development to be compatible with the older townhouses. To determine the most profitable FAR (in 1984), we can take a prototypical two-bedroom, two-bath unit with parking and determine its base value for all terms in the hedonic equation above, except for number of stories. This becomes the value of the coefficient α in Equation (4.9). For Beacon Hill, the most prestigious location in the sample, these terms add up to a value of $222.04 per square foot $(181.0 + (6.2 \times 2) + (2.7 \times 2) + 23.1 + (0.0007 \times 200) = 222.04)$. The contribution of FAR to the price equation (the coefficient β in Equation (4.9)) is $–1.48 (for each additional story). Using these estimates, the price per square foot for the unit would be $222.04 − 1.48F$. If the unit was located on Commonwealth Avenue rather than Beacon Hill, the equation would be $176.89 − 1.48F$.[15]

For a construction cost equation, consultation with local architects suggests that in 1984, square-foot construction costs could be closely approximated with the function $C = 100 + 2F$. Following the steps in Equation (4.9), we find that the optimal FAR for new construction on Beacon Hill would be 17.5—more than twice the average height in our sample of buildings in this area ($F^* = (222.04 − 100)/2(1.48 + 2) = 17.5$). Using Equation

---

[15]In this example, the Beacon Hill value is calculated with the three locational dummy variables set to zero and distance to Boston Common set at 200 feet. The calculation for the Commonwealth Avenue location is based on $CDUM = 1$ and the average distance for units on that street to Boston Common of 5,855 feet.

Chapter 4   The Urban Housing Market: Structural Attributes and Density

(4.9), we can determine that at the suggested FAR of 17.5, land is worth $1,068 per square foot ($p^* = (222.04 − 100) \times 17.5/2$). With 43,560 square feet in an acre, the value per acre of land (at an FAR of 17.5) is $46.5 million. At a typical townhouse FAR level (four stories), land for new development would be worth only $10.6 million. In historic districts, or any other area in which height restrictions are in place, the reduction in land value because of lower FAR levels (relative to the optimal FAR) might be viewed as the cost of imposing such land-use regulations. In some situations, however, this cost may be justified by a broader increase in values, a topic that we will discuss in detail in Chapters 13 and 14.

LOCATION AND RESIDENTIAL DENSITY

At the beginning of this chapter, we argued that density increases at sites with greater location rent because as land rents rise, developers substitute away from land and use more structure capital. More valuable land is used more intensely. As we consider residential density at different sites within a city, density normally tends to be higher at more valuable locations where location rent is greater. This is a pattern seen in cities throughout the world, at least in those in which private land markets determine development. Along oceans, lakes or rivers, there are often walls of high-rise apartments. Real estate is developed at similarly high densities in downtown areas. Even in the suburbs, clusters of apartments and townhouses tend to be developed near shopping areas or business districts, or at town centers. Let's explore in more detail the argument that it is more profitable to develop more desirable sites at higher density.

Referring back to the expressions in Equation (4.9), as well as to the information in Figure 4.7, we pose the question of how the relationship between FAR and land price would change as the analysis is done at different locations. As we move to a more desirable location, the intercept of the house price function (α) increases. In the diagram, this shifts the price line upward. Of course, this will change the solution value for the optimal FAR (F^*), and the resulting residual value for land p^*. From the first part of Equation (4.9), it should be clear that a greater α will increase the solution value for F^*. In the second part of Equation (4.9), this in turn increases the potential value of land p^*.

To see this result graphically, we can imagine Figure 4.7 with a higher housing price (P) schedule—presented as the dashed line in the top panel of Figure 4.8. Let's assume that construction costs have not changed. With this higher price schedule, the maximum FAR that can still cover construction costs will shift outward. Thus, at any FAR, the profit per unit will be greater and the triangular area will expand. Increased location rent always generates greater potential housing profits (per square foot of floor area). When this greater profit per floor area is multiplied by FAR, the result is that the semicircular land profit value in the bottom panel of Figure 4.8 both rises and shifts to the right. This rise and shift means that the maximum value of the land profit function will occur at a higher value of F^*, which, in turn, generates a greater residual land value p^*.[16]

[16]Returning to the example of Boston's historic district, we can calculate the optimal FAR at the less prestigious location on Commonwealth Avenue, where the price equation is $176.89 − 1.48F$. The result is an optimal FAR of 11.0 (rather than 17.5) and a land value of $425 per square foot (rather than $1,068).

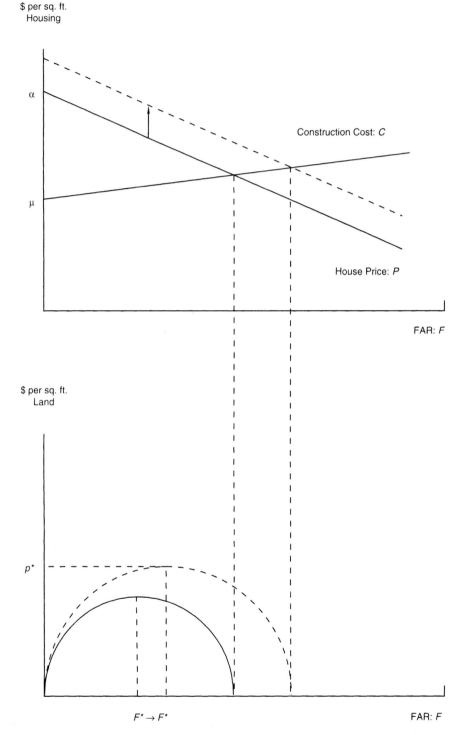

FIGURE 4.8 Optimal FAR: shift in housing price.

If this type of analysis were conducted at each location within the city, the result would be an ideal or potential market density gradient of residential development. Downtown sites would be more densely developed, as would sites at suburban transportation intersections. Sites near desirable natural or manmade amenities would also be developed at greater density, as well as would those locations with exceptional views or vistas. Wherever, the rule would apply: increased location rent encourages a substitution away from land usage, and this yields higher development density. Of course, in Chapter 3, we saw that greater density also increases the locational rent at desirable locations. When we compound these two effects, the result can be the extremely high densities and land prices often found in downtowns or along waterfronts.[17]

The question to ask is whether actual cities have patterns of residential density that look like this. In the beginning of this chapter, we presented some empirical density gradients for cities and towns that exhibited many of these traits (Figures 4.2, 4.3). In most cities, residential density is greatest both at the center and at strategic suburban nodes. It would be wrong to infer from this similarity, however, that cities generally have optimal or market development densities at most locations. Would the small single-family houses surrounding downtown Los Angeles be developed today if land were vacant, or does this pattern of housing belong to a period of 60 to 90 years ago when the structures in this area were built? Would Boston have the same extensive neighborhoods of row houses if that land were rebuilt today? In examining the determinants of actual residential density patterns, modern development at market density is always competing with the value of existing structures built years earlier. When little vacant land is available for development, the density observed at desirable sites may be more the product of market forces decades, or even centuries, ago. This is certainly the case in the Back Bay area of Boston that we examined in the previous section. Existing housing provides a large opportunity cost against which new development often cannot compete.

PATTERNS OF URBAN DEVELOPMENT AND REDEVELOPMENT

As cities grow over time, the location of new development tends to occur in distinct patterns. As a rule, new development mainly occurs on vacant land at the existing edge of the city. In this sense, the tendency is for population growth to increase urban development horizontally, much as in the simple model of Chapter 3. The density of development that occurs at the urban edge will be based on two considerations: the shape of the housing demand and construction cost schedules (in Figures 4.7 and 4.8) and the value of vacant fringe land (based on agricultural rent and the value of the development option).

---

[17]As an example of this compounding substitution effect, we can refer back to definition of p^* in Equation (4.9). As house prices increase at a better location (an upward shift in α), the residual land value rises not linearly but exponentially (to the power of 2) as α is increased.

In fact, the residual value per acre from new residential development at the fringe should, in equilibrium, exactly equal the price of vacant (agricultural) land.

For any city, the equality at the urban fringe between the residual value of developed land and vacant land prices serves to determine both the price of new housing and the density of new development. This condition for market equilibrium effectively links the results of Chapter 3 with those here. The price of new housing at the urban fringe will be such that when land is developed at its optimal FAR, its residual value [p^* in Equation (4.9)] will exactly equal the price for vacant agricultural land ($p_0(b)$) as defined by Equation (3.18).[18] This yields the important conclusion that the density of development at the edge of a city is *not* based on transportation costs, the size of the city, or other determinants of interior land prices. At the urban fringe, the price of land is fixed at its agricultural value plus the value of the development option; this dictates the density of fringe development.

It is important to reiterate that while the population of a city and its transportation system will surely determine how far the urban fringe extends, they do not have much impact on fringe land prices or density. Thus, the density of new fringe development in Los Angeles will be quite similar to that occurring in the tiny metropolitan area of Bakersfield, California, even though rents at interior locations in these two cities will be dramatically different. This important conclusion explains why there often exists low-density single-family housing at very central sites in many newer American cities. These interior sites often were the urban fringe just 50 years ago, and market conditions may not have changed over the intervening years. Thus, the housing built 50 years ago may use a similar density to that built at today's fringe, even though population growth has vastly expanded the city and pushed the fringe far past its original borders.

As cities grow horizontally, the price of interior housing, built years earlier, may rise or fall. If the housing is maintained, its price will normally increase because the growing city is creating more and more location rent for interior sites. If the housing is not maintained, its price could decline if the loss in value from the deteriorating structure exceeds the increase in locational site value. In some cases, older housing may completely deteriorate or be destroyed, creating pockets of vacant land. Such vacant land creates the opportunity for new development to occur within the city rather than just at the urban fringe.

When vacant land becomes available within the interior of a city, it is developed at a current market density, sometimes in stark contrast to the historic density of surrounding structures. This is easy to understand. The older structures were built at a time when the area was at the fringe of a much smaller city. Being at the (then) fringe, land had little location rent or value. Now in a much larger city, if the area has acquired location rent, the optimal FAR for modern development may have increased dramatically. These differences raise the question of whether the market must wait for housing to deteriorate or be

---

[18]In the housing demand equation, the price of housing is represented by $\alpha - \beta F$. In market equilibrium, and at the optimal density, this price must yield a residual land value ($p^* = F^*[\alpha - \beta F^* - \mu - \tau F^*]$), which, in turn, equals the price of vacant land. To meet this condition, α (the hedonic value of all housing attributes besides FAR) becomes endogenously determined, as was true of the models in Chapter 3.

Chapter 4 The Urban Housing Market: Structural Attributes and Density

destroyed before vacant land in the interior becomes available. Is it ever profitable to purchase and demolish perfectly sound housing simply because the value of a site as vacant land exceeds its value with the existing housing already on it?

When existing structures are purchased and demolished to create vacant land for new uses, we say that the site is being *redeveloped*. Historically, widespread redevelopment of urban sites has been an important force in shaping the land use patterns of many cities. Consider New York or Boston, for example. Around 1800, both of these cities had predominantly detached wood-frame housing. Over the next 50 years, most of this housing was replaced with three- to five-story row houses of masonry construction, at much higher FAR levels. Today, virtually none of the first-generation housing remains. While fires contributed some to this transition, historical documents clearly show that many owners simply demolished and rebuilt their sites as these cities grew very rapidly in the first half of the nineteenth century. After 100 or more years, these same cities experi-

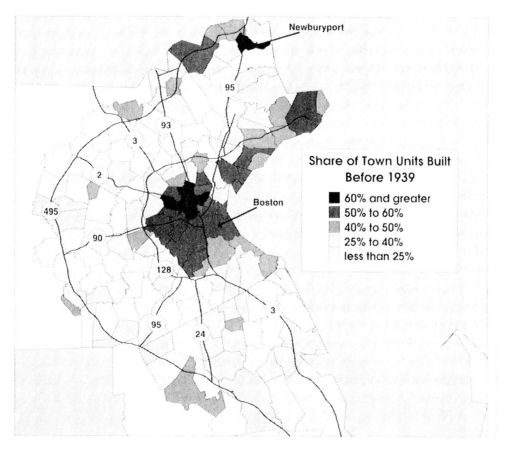

FIGURE 4.9 Town units built before 1939 in Boston-area cities and towns, 1990.
Source: 1990 Census.

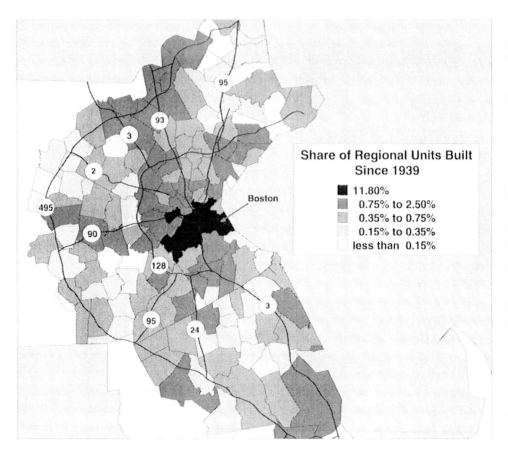

FIGURE 4.10 Regional units built since 1939 in Boston-area cities and towns, 1990.
Source: 1990 Census.

enced another wave of redevelopment to a third generation of housing. Particularly at very valuable sites such as those near parks and transportation terminals, row houses were replaced with elevator-serviced apartment buildings, involving a further increase in the site's FAR. Thus, in older cities, the higher-density structures that we often observe today are third-generation housing that resulted during more recent periods of vertical redevelopment.

To illustrate how such patterns of redevelopment can occur, we have displayed the fraction of housing units that were built prior to 1939 for each town in the Boston Metropolitan area (Figure 4.9). Clearly, there is a strong tendency for the average age of housing to decline as one moves from the center city outward.[19] To show the extent of redevelopment in the region, Figure 4.10 examines the locational distribution of housing

---

[19]Anomalies occur in some of the older outlying towns, which developed during the early colonial period.

Chapter 4 The Urban Housing Market: Structural Attributes and Density

built within the region since 1939. Almost 12 percent of all housing built during this period occurred on redeveloped sites within the fully developed city of Boston. Older center-city sites within the Boston metropolitan area have been the target of extensive redevelopment during recent decades.

Redevelopment represents an adjustment process by which housing capital is gradually replaced. In the process, historic density is upgraded to more modern market density. The speed and ease with which this adjustment occurs is very important. With rapid adjustment, cities will look quite modern, with vertical redevelopment occurring at the same time as horizontal development happens at the urban fringe. The result is that density throughout the city will be closer to those market levels dictated by today's economic conditions. With slow adjustment, the housing stock of cities will have an evolutionary character to it, with growth occurring primarily through horizontal expansion at the urban fringe. This suggests that we should closely examine the economic conditions that will generate redevelopment.

For redevelopment of a site to occur, the net residual value to land if developed optimally must exceed the gross value of *land and capital* that currently exists on the site plus the cost of demolishing the old capital. To illustrate the conditions under which this might happen, we can expand our previous discussion using the simple equations for housing and residual land prices. Let's suppose that the existing historic housing on a site has the value (per square foot of floor area): $P^0 = \alpha^0 - \beta F^0$. Here, the term α^0 represents the hedonic value of the existing housing capital on the site in contrast to the hedonic value of modern housing capital, the term α in Equation (4.9). Similarly, F^0 is the site's preexisting historic FAR in contrast to the optimal FAR, F^* in Equation (4.9). The total value (per square foot of land) of preexisting historic land use is: $p^0 = F^0 [\alpha^0 - \beta F^0]$. Redevelopment can occur only if the net land return (per square foot) from new development, p^* in Equation (4.9), exceeds p^0 by more than the cost of demolishing the existing structure. We can approximate the demolition costs associated with clearing a square foot of land through the term δF^0, where δ is the demolition cost per square foot of floor area. Substituting in, the condition that p^* exceed p^0 by these demolition costs reduces to:[20]

$$p^* - p^0 > \delta F^0 \text{ implies: } \frac{F^*}{F^0} > \frac{\alpha^0 - \beta F^0 + \delta}{(\alpha - \mu) - (\beta + \tau)F^*} \quad (4.11)$$

Examining Equation (4.11) more closely, it is possible to draw several conclusions. Suppose for the moment that the existing housing capital on the site has been completely maintained so that its value equals that of current new capital ($\alpha^0 = \alpha$). The right-hand side of Equation (4.11) then becomes the ratio of existing house value plus demolition

---

[20]In Equation (4.11) the right-hand side of the inequality is defined only for values of F^* where a positive profit from development exists; that is, $(\alpha - \mu) - (\beta + \tau)F^* > 0$. When density is so great that construction costs exceed floor prices, the return from development is negative and redevelopment obviously is unprofitable.

costs (per floor area) to newly constructed house profit (per floor area). The reader should be able to verify that for the inequality to hold when $\alpha^0 = \alpha$, F^* must be greater than F^0.[21] Thus, one way redevelopment can occur is when market conditions dictate an optimal FAR that is higher than that which already exists on the site.

How much greater does market FAR have to be for redevelopment to occur? Let's return to our example from Boston's Back Bay area. There, the average FAR among existing buildings was 7.6. In fact, the district is largely composed of brownstones and townhouse structures that are generally four stories tall and newer apartment buildings that are 8 to 12 stories tall. Consider two sites in the district: one with a four-story brownstone and the other with a 10-story apartment building. Using our previous estimates for α, β, μ, and τ and assuming that demolition costs (δ) are \$20 per square foot (of floor area) redevelopment becomes profitable for the site with a current FAR of 4 when the new proposed FAR for new development exceeds 12.[22] Since the optimal FAR from our earlier calculations (F^*), is 17.5, the redevelopment of existing townhouses would clearly be profitable. For a site with an existing 10-story apartment building, redevelopment is not profitable. The opportunity cost of existing structures at this higher density cannot be overcome with a current optimal FAR of 17.5. These results suggest that without the restrictions that are in place to maintain the low-rise historic buildings in the Back Bay, the district would seem to be ready for a major land-use transition, eliminating many of the older brownstones and replacing them with higher-rise apartment buildings.

Redevelopment may also be profitable at relatively low FARs if the housing capital that exists on a site has become seriously deteriorated or outmoded. Using Equation (4.11), we can see that for redevelopment to occur at a similar density to that which already exists ($F^* = F^0$), the criteria requires that α must exceed α^0. Again, using the Boston example, we determine that redevelopment at the current FAR of 4 would technically be profitable if the existing structure capital (per square foot) were to deteriorate to about 42 percent of what new structure capital is worth.

These examples illustrate that vertical redevelopment can be economically feasible under a range of market changes that might occur over relatively short intervals of time (decades). This is particularly likely in faster-growing economies in which location rents quickly build up and housing capital easily becomes outmoded. The fact that redevelopment is not always that common might be explained by two widespread institutional constraints. First, in order to acquire a substantial site, land often must be assembled from varied owners, a time-consuming and difficult process. Second, in the twentieth century, zoning and other land-use regulations have become widespread, and these often prohibit or slow down the process of land use change.

---

[21] If $F^* = F^0$, then the right-hand side of Equation (4.11) is greater than one, while the left-hand side equals one. Why would anyone tear down a house only to rebuild the identical structure?

[22] With $\alpha = 222.02$, $\beta = 1.48$, $\mu = 100$, $\tau = 2$, and $\delta = 20$, a new FAR of 12 just meets the criteria displayed in Equation (4.11).

Chapter 4 The Urban Housing Market: Structural Attributes and Density

REDEVELOPMENT, OCCUPANCY, AND LAND-USE SUCCESSION

As interior land is redeveloped to new density levels, the occupants of that land will often change. Such combined changes in occupancy and density of use frequently are referred to as *land-use succession.* These changes sometimes can involve the large-scale relocation of different groups of households. Understanding such patterns can be important in determining when and where redevelopment will occur and for whom the new uses should be built. To illustrate how the location of different households can change as land is redeveloped, we can return to a city with two types of households such as we used in Chapter 3.

In a city with two groups of households (labeled 1 and 2), the willingness-to-pay for housing (per square foot of floor area) is described in Equations (4.12). We integrate Chapters 3 and 4 now by making the demand for housing depend on both distance from the city center (d), as well as FAR (F). As in Chapter 3, the parameter k represents the marginal reduction in house prices (per square foot of floor area) with greater commuting, and we continue to use the parameter β to represent the marginal reduction in willingness-to-pay as a result of greater density.

$$P_1 = \alpha - k_1 d - \beta_1 F,$$
$$P_2 = \alpha - k_2 d - \beta_2 F, \qquad (4.12)$$
$$k_1 > k_2, \beta_1 > \beta_2$$

In Equations (4.12), we make the assumption that members of household Group 1 find commuting more burdensome than households of Group 2, and that they also value open space more, as evidenced by their greater distaste for higher FAR levels. This pattern of preferences is often thought to hold across households of different income levels: those earning more have both a higher value for time (hence, distaste for commuting) as well as a stronger demand for lower-density single-family housing (hence, distaste for FAR).

As the city develops initially in a horizontal manner, we could assume that the historic housing stock has evolved relatively homogeneously, with a relatively flat FAR gradient. As our earlier discussion suggested, this pattern is common in newer, faster-growing cities. With this historic stock of housing (and its constant FAR), the question of which household type locates where (closer or farther from the city center) will depend exclusively on the different preferences for commuting, as it did in Chapter 3. With the assumption in Equations (4.12), that Group 1 households have greater distaste for commuting, they will outbid Group 2 households for central housing, and vice versa for peripheral units. The pattern of house prices and occupancy will resemble the P_1, P_2 schedules shown in Figure 4.11.

Over time, selected units within the existing stock may deteriorate and vacant land will become available. The question is not just at what FAR will this land be developed, but for whom. Will the highest use for vacant land continue to involve development for households of Group 1 at central sites and households of Group 2 at farther sites? The answer will depend on which group is willing to offer the most per acre for land at central as opposed to peripheral sites.

To determine the willingness-to-pay for land by each type of household, we must determine which FAR represents the most profitable development at a given location. Using the construction cost function from the previous section, and following the procedures

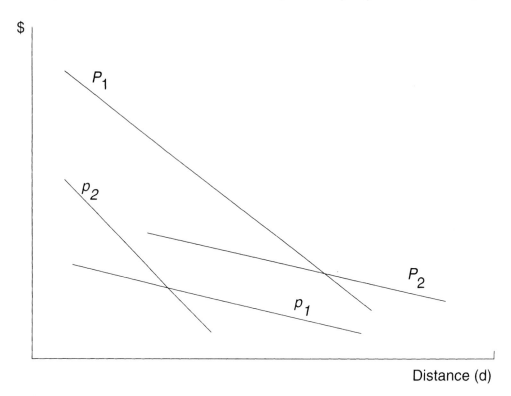

FIGURE 4.11 House and land price bids for two household types.

described with Equations (4.9), we solve for the optimal FAR levels for each household as a function of location (distance d). This, in turn, allows us to determine what is the maximum residual value for land, if developed for each type of household, and how this varies with distance from the urban center.

$$F_1^* = \frac{\alpha - k_1 d - \mu}{2[\beta_1 + \tau]} \quad , \quad F_2^* = \frac{\alpha - k_2 d - \mu}{2[\beta_2 + \tau]}$$

$$p_1^* = \frac{[\alpha - \mu - k_1 d]F_1^*}{2} \quad , \quad p_2^* = \frac{[\alpha - \mu - k_2 d]F_2^*}{2}$$

(4.13)

At a common site (or location d), the optimal FAR of development for Group 1 households will always be less than that for Group 2 households, since $k_1 > k_2$ and $\beta_1 > \beta_2$. As discussed in Chapter 3, the issue of which group will outbid the other for land at more central sites hinges on the relative *slopes* of the residual land price functions. In Equations (4.13), the slope of p_1^* with respect to distance (d) is $-k_1 F_1^*/2$, whereas that of p_2^* is $-k_2 F_2^*/2$. Given our assumptions about household preferences, it is easily possible for Group 2 households to have a more steeply sloped residual land price gradient than Group 1 households. This will be the case if the FAR of development for Group 2 households is significantly greater than for Group 1 households, whereas the distaste for commuting by Group 2 is only slightly less. This case is shown in Figure 4.11, with the p_1, p_2 schedules.

Chapter 4   The Urban Housing Market: Structural Attributes and Density

With the pattern of preferences shown in Figure 4.11, when vacant land becomes available at more central sites within the city, it not only will be developed at a higher FAR than surrounding historic housing, but it will be developed for and occupied by a different type of household than those occupying existing housing in the area currently. In principle, after a long enough period of time, the pattern of land use might eventually change from one in which Group 1 households occupy central sites to one in which Group 2 households live centrally. This is the process of land use succession—one use gives way to another, with a combined alteration of density or FAR as well as occupancy.

This example illustrates the complexity of determining the true highest and best use for urban land. In principle, the maximum value for any given site can be determined only by considering the optimal FAR that should be developed for each potential group of occupants or type of land use and then comparing these potential residual values across types or uses. If the land market is functioning well, it should be the case that at current housing density levels, the present occupants of an area do indeed represent the highest-paying users. At different potential densities, however, it may well be the case that other groups would generate greater residual value to the land.

SUMMARY

In this chapter we examined how housing development, particularly density, varies across locations within cities, and evolves over time as cities experience population growth.

- The price of a housing unit can be decomposed into implicit prices for each of the attributes that make up the unit, such as the presence of a garage, the amount of square feet, and the total density. There are distinct patterns to residential density in cities throughout the world.

- At higher density, otherwise identical housing units tend to have lower prices. The cost of constructing units, however, tends to increase with the density of development. Thus, the profit per housing unit tends to be lower at greater density, although more units can be placed on a given parcel of land. Determining the most profitable density of development requires trading off these two opposing considerations.

- At more desirable locations, this tradeoff leads to a highest and best use that involves greater density. In effect, higher prices for housing units lead to greater land values, and thus land is used more sparingly per housing unit. Most cities have density gradients, with denser residential uses located near transportation centers, highways, parks, waterfronts, or other amenities.

- As cities grow in population, new development initially tends to occur horizontally at the expanding border of the city. Thus, at any time, existing units reflect the history of development, with the oldest units at the center and the newest at the fringe.

- At critical times in the development of a city, it can become profitable to demolish existing housing units, built years earlier, particularly at more desirable locations. At such sites, the net return to just the land from new development can exceed the total price for existing housing. Normally, this occurs only when new development calls for much greater density than exists with the current housing.

REFERENCES AND ADDITIONAL READINGS

ANAS, ALEX, "The Dynamics of Residential Growth," *Journal of Urban Economics,* 5 (1978).

BERNDT, ERNST R., *The Practice of Econometrics: Classic and Contemporary.* Reading, Mass.: Addison-Wesley Publishing Company, 1991.

CAPOZZA, DENNIS, AND GORDON SICK, "Valuing Long Term Leases and the Option to Redevelop," *Journal of Real Estate Finance and Economics,* 4 (1991).

COURT, ANDREW T., "Hedonic Price Indexes with Automotive Examples," in *The Dynamics of Automobile Demand.* New York: The General Motors Corporation, 1939.

DIPASQUALE, DENISE, AND C. TSURIEL SOMERVILLE, "Do House Price Indexes Based on Transacting Units Represent the Entire Stock? Evidence from the American Housing Survey," *Journal of Housing Economics* 4, 3 (1995).

HALVORSEN, R., AND HENRY POLLAKOWSKI, "Choice of Functional Form for Hedonic Price Equations," *Journal of Urban Economics,* 10 (1981).

HARRISON, DAVID, AND JOHN KAIN, "Cumulative Urban Growth and Urban Density Functions," *Journal of Urban Economics,* 1 (1974).

MILLS, EDWIN S., *Studies in the Structure of the Urban Economy.* Baltimore, Md.: The Johns Hopkins University Press, 1972.

PINDYCK, ROBERT S., AND DANIEL L. RUBINFELD, *Econometric Models and Economic Forecast,* 3rd ed. New York: McGraw-Hill Book Company, 1991.

ROSEN, SHERWIN M., "Hedonic Prices and Implicit Markets: Product Differentiation in Pure Competition," *Journal of Political Economy,* 82, 1 (1974).

WHEATON, WILLIAM, "Urban Spatial Development with Durable but Replaceable Capital," *Journal of Urban Economics,* 3 (1978).

CHAPTER 5

FIRM SITE SELECTION, EMPLOYMENT DECENTRALIZATION, AND MULTICENTERED CITIES

In Chapters 3 and 4, we examined the location decisions of households and the operation of the residential land market within a metropolitan area. We now turn our attention to nonresidential land uses. How do firms choose their locations within a metropolitan area? Why do we tend to see spatial concentrations of commercial, industrial, or retail firms? How do we explain the decentralization of employment within metropolitan areas during the last half of the twentieth century? Our focus in this chapter is the operation of a land market in which space is used by commercial and industrial firms as well as by households.

Chapters 3 and 4 explained how residential land markets operate around a single employment center when workers must commute to that center. In Chapter 5, we extend that model to show why, historically, firms tended to concentrate in a single, central location. The traditional explanations for this phenomenon focus on the need of firms to transport both raw materials to their plants and goods to a central market through a transportation terminal such as a port. While this simple model does a fairly good job of describing firm location in nineteenth-century cities, employment today uses different production as well as transportation technologies.

Why has employment decentralized? Retail trade and personal service firms have simply followed their household clients as they have suburbanized over the last century. These patterns will be discussed in Chapter 6. Here, we focus on firms that produce and sell products on a broader national scale, and, therefore, are not tied to local residential clients as a market for their goods or services. In brief, production technologies changed in such a way that today manufacturing and wholesale firms must use more land per unit of output than they did in the previous era of employment centralization. This trend, in turn, has pushed these firms to fringe locations where land is cheaper. In addition, the rise in importance of truck transportation in getting goods to and from markets has made access to the interstate highway system important. For office-using commercial firms, the recent changes in telecommunication technology (e.g., e-mail and fax machines) have reduced the importance of physical proximity to both clients and other firms. Finally, for all types of firms, perhaps the most critical change has been the suburbanization of the major factor of production: labor.

While employment has been decentralizing, the spatial distribution of jobs in most cities is anything but uniform. Rather, metropolitan areas have become multicentered. Some of the forces that led to the original development of central cities are still at work and have led suburban firms to concentrate or cluster at peripheral locations. Such concentration results from the advantages of having similar and complementary firms in close proximity as well as from the importance of access to the highway system for getting products to market and employees to work. Thus, the modern multicentered city is the outcome of competing forces—the benefits of decentralization versus the benefits from concentration.

We begin this chapter with an examination of the spatial distribution of employment and how it has changed over time. Next, we discuss the traditional theories used to explain the existence of the central business district (CBD). Following that, we examine more modern explanations for why the forces that originally led to centralized employment have dissolved and have been replaced by forces encouraging employment dispersal. With this more current economic analysis, we find some close links between the urban land market and the labor market.

THE SPATIAL DISTRIBUTION OF EMPLOYMENT

As was the case with population density in Chapter 4, casual observation in most cities suggests that *employment density*—defined as employment divided by land area or jobs per square mile—declines with distance from the central city. Figure 5.1 displays employment density for 146 cities and towns in the Boston area in 1990. Together, these cities and towns had a total employment in 1990 of 2.07 million.[1] The average employment density across these towns is 1,025 jobs per square mile but varies widely from 16,062 in Cambridge and 11,104 in Boston to 29 jobs per square mile in Boxford at the far northern part of the region. This wide variation, as well as the general decline in employment density with distance, can be clearly seen in the map.

---

[1] In each state, a department is responsible for surveying businesses and tabulating data on jobs and wages as part of the U.S. unemployment insurance system. In Massachusetts, this information is collected by the state's Department of Employment and Training. The data are collected and organized by type of industry, as defined by the Standard Industrial Classification (SIC) system. For further explanation of SICs see footnote 6 in Chapter 7.

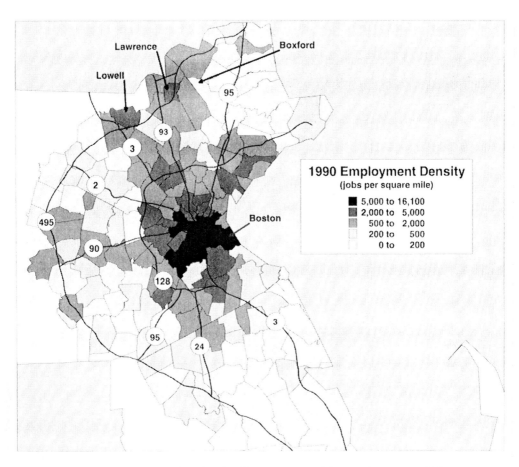

FIGURE 5.1 Employment density for Boston-area cities and towns, 1990.

Source: Massachusetts Department of Employment and Training, *Employment and Wages in Massachusetts Cities and Towns* (selected years), Boston, MA.

As expected, the anomalies in the employment densities closely match the anomalies in the population densities that were discussed in Chapter 4. The city of Cambridge has a higher employment density than Boston. Lowell and Lawrence to the far north also have relatively higher employment densities (2,911 and 3,360, respectively), given their more distant locations.

Empirically, we can measure the relationship between employment density and distance the same way we measured the relationship between population density and distance in Chapter 4. Using the negative exponential specification defined in Equations (4.1) and (4.2), we can statistically estimate a density gradient using the log of employment density as the dependent variable and distance as the independent variable:

$$\log [D(d)] = 8.05 - 0.10 \, d \qquad R^2 = 0.46 \\ (8.1) \quad (-11.15) \qquad N = 146 \tag{5.1}$$

In Equation (5.1), $D(d)$ is the density of employment at distance d. Our estimate of the coefficient on distance of –0.10 means that with each mile increase in distance from the center, employment density decreases 10 percent.[2] The constant in Equation (5.1) is the model's estimate of the log of the density at the center of the metropolitan area defined here as the city of Boston; the model predicts that Boston's density should be 3,134 jobs per square mile ($e^{8.05} = 3,134$). This estimate is far less than the city's actual density of 11,104. Figure 5.2 uses a scatter plot to compare actual town employment densities; the line represents Equation (5.1). Clearly, the model does far better in predicting employment density past mile 5 than within 5 miles of Boston. Even with these problems, this very simple model still explains 46 percent of the variation in employment densities.

For most of the towns in our sample, commercial or industrial uses take up only a small fraction of total land area. Thus, our measure of employment density may be

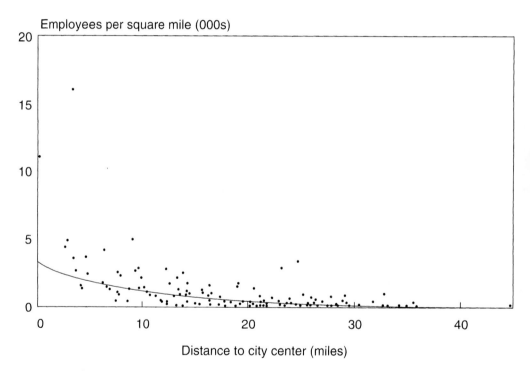

FIGURE 5.2 Boston employment density, 1990.

Source: Massachusetts Department of Employment and Training, *Employment and Wages in Massachusetts Cities and Towns* (selected years), Boston, MA.

[2]The employment density gradient in Boston has flattened over time. Estimating Equation (5.1) using 1967 employment densities yields the following equation, in which employment density decreases 12.6 percent for each additional mile from Boston:

$$\log [D(d)] = 7.75 - 0.126d \qquad R^2 = 0.47$$
$$(6.57) \quad (-11.35) \qquad N = 146$$

somewhat misleading. An alternative approach is to consider the town's share of total regional employment. For 1990, each town's share of the 2.07 million jobs in this region are displayed in Figure 5.3. While the general patterns are the same in Figures 5.1 and 5.3, there are some important differences. The city of Boston has far and away the largest share of the area's jobs, representing 25.9 percent of the total. Cambridge ranks second, with just 5.0 percent of total jobs, followed by Waltham and Newton, which have 3.0 percent and 2.2 percent, respectively. Lowell and Lawrence to the north have 1.9 percent and 1.1 percent of the area's jobs, respectively.

Over the past decades, employment has suburbanized in Boston. Figure 5.4 illustrates this by displaying the change in each town's share of the region's total employment between 1967 and 1990. The Boston share of total employment declined from 34 percent in 1967 to 25.9 percent in 1990, a decline of 8 percentage points. Declines in employment share were also realized by many of the cities and towns closest to the city of Boston as

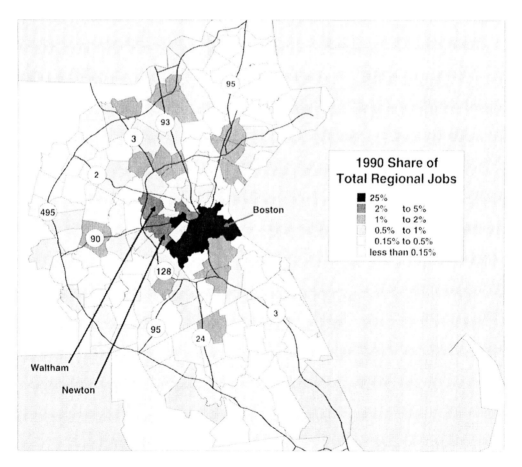

FIGURE 5.3 Share of regional jobs for Boston-area cities and towns, 1990.

Source: Massachusetts Department of Employment and Training, *Employment and Wages in Massachusetts Cities and Towns* (selected years), Boston, MA.

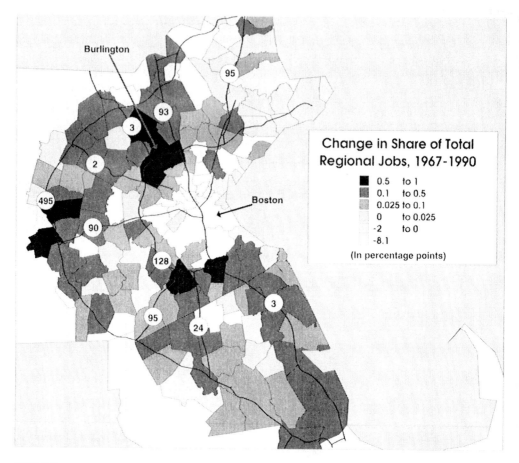

FIGURE 5.4 Change in share of total regional jobs for Boston-area cities and towns, 1967–1990.

Source: Massachusetts Department of Employment and Training, *Employment and Wages in Massachusetts Cities and Towns* (selected years), Boston, MA.

well as in older employment centers such as Lawrence, where the share fell from 2.1 percent to 1.1 percent. Growth in employment share over the period occurred mainly in suburban communities such as Burlington, a community in which the number of jobs more than tripled since 1967; its share of the area's employment went from 0.7 percent in 1967 to 1.6 percent in 1990. It should be noted that many of the towns that experienced growth in employment share are located at the intersections of major highways.

The patterns shown for the Boston region are quite typical of those in most older, mature, metropolitan areas. In newer metropolitan areas (e.g., Dallas, Los Angeles, Atlanta), the size and role of the core central city is much less than in Boston, and the extent of employment decentralization is far greater. We begin the task of explaining job decentralization by first considering the forces that originally created urban centers, focusing on the location decisions of firms that primarily export their products to clients or buyers outside of the region.

LAND MARKETS WITH A CENTRAL BUSINESS DISTRICT

In Chapter 3, we considered the location decisions of households in a city in which all workers commuted to a single employment zone located at the center of the city. The discussion in Chapter 3 suggests that for such a center to exist, firms must value central land more than households do. In a competitive, unregulated land market, a central commercial or manufacturing district can exist only if the land rent from these nonresidential land uses exceeds the land rent derived from housing for the surrounding workers. Let's begin our analysis of firm location by considering how the transportation system in eighteenth- and nineteenth-century cities and the shipping needs of firms might have been responsible for the creation of central business districts (CBDs). Our stylized city and the firms located within that city have the following characteristics:

1. The city has a single port or transportation terminal to which firms must bring their goods for export shipment and through which they receive their raw material or inputs from other cities. Similarly, imported consumer goods arrive through this facility. Within the city, the transport of goods (from the terminal) costs s dollars per unit per mile. Distance from this transportation center is denoted as d.
2. Firms produce an identical product using the same production process. The units of output produced per firm is fixed at Q.
3. There is no factor substitution. Both the lot size f and structure capital used by each firm are fixed. The rent for the structure used by firms is C, whereas the firm's residual land rent per acre varies with location, $r_c(d)$. With fixed land and structure, output per acre is fixed.
4. Output and input markets are perfectly competitive, with free entry into the industry. This means that each firm takes prices as given and economic profit is zero.
5. Land is allocated or rented to that use and to those plants or offices that yield the greatest rent.

The assumptions about our stylized city are, in many respects, analogous to the assumptions that we made at the beginning of Chapter 3. Using these assumptions, consider how firm profits (revenues minus all costs) would vary with location. If each firm sells Q units of its good and the unit price is ρ, then firm total revenues will be ρQ. Variable costs include wages and material production costs per unit, A, and transport or shipping costs to market per unit, sd. Firm fixed costs include the rent for the building, C, and land rent per acre, $r_c(d)$, times the number of acres used by the firm, f. Hence, profits, π, are:

$$\pi = Q(\rho - A - sd) - C - r_c(d)f \qquad (5.2)$$

With competition between firms ensuring zero profits, land rent per acre, $r_c(d)$, may be determined as a residual:

$$r_c(d) = \frac{Q(\rho - A - sd) - C}{f} \qquad (5.3)$$

In Equation (5.3), land rent is defined as that rent that gives firms the same zero level of profit regardless of location. Under the assumption that ρ, Q, A, and C, do not vary with location within a metropolitan area, land rents will exactly compensate firms for the increased transport costs that are associated with a farther distance to the transportation terminal. In this respect, the model is similar to that of Chapter 3, in which residential land rents exactly compensate households for the commuting costs associated with more distant locations. In this model, the transport costs at the city center ($d = 0$) are 0, and $r_c(0)$ equals $[Q(\rho - A) - C]/f$. Moving out from the center, land rents per acre decline by exactly the increase in transport costs per acre to firms: $-sQ/f$. If rents decline by more (less) than this, then firms could realize excess profits by moving out from (in towards) the urban center. In equilibrium, incentives to move must not exist; this equilibrium is analogous to the notion of *spatial equilibrium* that we defined for residential use in Chapter 3.

Returning to the main question of this section, we can see how a central business district comes into existence: the slope of the firm rent gradient must be steeper than the rent gradient of households. Recalling the results of Chapter 3, this means that as we move out from the transportation terminal, the shipping costs of firms (per acre of commercial use) must increase by more than the worker's commuting costs to the firm (per acre of residential use). This is likely to be the case if goods or materials are more expensive to move around than people (people frequently walked in nineteenth-century cities) and if commercial uses are more dense than residential. Under these conditions, firms constitute the dominant land use from the center to some intermediate boundary, m, and from m to the urban border, b, housing makes up the dominant use. At the intermediate boundary, the land rent from firms will equal residential land rent (labeled $r(m)$, as in Chapter 3). This pattern of rents is shown in Figure 5.5.

At the urban border, residential land rent must equal that from agriculture $[r(b) = r^a]$. Moving inward, land rent rises as commuting costs (per acre of residential development) fall until reaching $r(m)$ at the boundary between residential and business use (m). With the condition of equal rent at the boundary between business and residential land use, business land rent has two components: the opportunity rent from residential uses (who would occupy the land if firms did not) and the location rent or savings in transport costs associated with moving in from this boundary, $sQ(m - d)/f$. As a result, the land rent gradient for firms is:

$$r_c(d) = r(m) + \frac{sQ(m - d)}{f} \tag{5.4}$$

As with the discussion of residential land use in Chapter 3, we can relax the assumption that all firms have identical production processes and use identical amounts of land for their facilities. With different production processes and land requirements, there will be a systematic location pattern by type of firm. Suppose we identify types of industrial or commercial uses with the subscript i, and allow all firms within a type to have a specific output level Q_i, land usage f_i, and shipping or transport cost per mile to the terminal s_i. Firms that produce a great deal of output per acre—output which is also difficult or expensive to move around—will have a high ratio of $s_i Q_i / f_i$. Firms whose

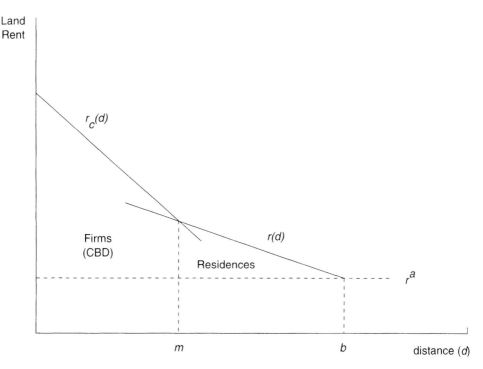

FIGURE 5.5 Spatial separation and land rents: firms and residences.

goods are easy to ship and who produce little output per acre will have a low $s_i Q_i/f_i$ ratio. Since the slope of a firm's zero-profit rent gradient is directly equal to this ratio, in a locational equilibrium within the central business district, firms will naturally tend to separate themselves spatially according to their ratio value.

Within the CBD, those types of firms that produce high output per acre and whose products are expensive to ship will have a steeper rent gradient. In a competitive land market, they will offer the highest rent for the most central sites. Firms with lower output per acre and/or firms whose goods are easier to ship will have a rent gradient that is somewhat flatter. They will tend to occupy sites farther from the transportation terminal and nearer to residential uses. The land market will allocate different commercial or industrial uses to sites within the CBD just as it allocated different types of households in Chapter 3. Land is always allocated to that use offering the highest rent and, in this case, central rents will be highest for those uses with the most output per acre.

The separation of different industrial or commercial uses within the CBD also leads to the emergence of a business density gradient. Since the level of output or production per acre is closely (and inversely) related to firm land consumption, f, those firms locating most centrally will tend to be those whose facilities are most dense. This pattern holds today in many cities in which the tallest office buildings tend to be developed on the choicest sites, adjacent to subways or other transportation terminals. At the edges of the business district, density is much lower.

TECHNOLOGY AND THE DECENTRALIZATION OF MANUFACTURERS

In the nineteenth-century city, offices, warehouses, manufacturing facilities and stores were all located in the central business district. Over time, the first firms to decentralize were industrial firms—those engaged in manufacturing or warehousing. The traditional explanation for this movement is that industrial technology changed to make the zero profit rent gradient of industrial uses much flatter across space. Before discussing this argument in detail, let's examine the extent of industrial decentralization within the Boston metropolitan region.

In the 146 cities and towns in our Boston-area sample, firms in the manufacturing and wholesale SIC categories provide 466,017, or 22.5 percent, of the area's jobs. While

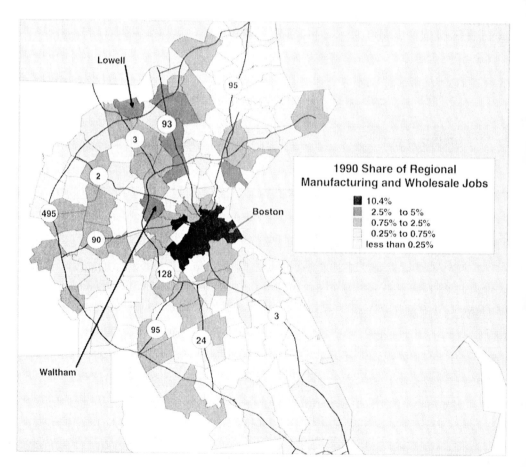

FIGURE 5.6 Share of regional manufacturing and wholesale jobs for Boston-area cities and towns, 1990.

Source: Massachusetts Department of Employment and Training, *Employment and Wages in Massachusetts Cities and Towns* (selected years), Boston, MA.

the city of Boston has the largest share of manufacturing and wholesale jobs (10.5 percent), these jobs are widely dispersed, with other cities or towns also having high shares (e.g., Waltham and Lowell have 4.7 percent and 3.5 percent, respectively). Figure 5.6 displays the share of metropolitan manufacturing and wholesale jobs by city and town. Outside of the city of Boston, those towns with a larger share of industrial jobs tend to be located near major highways.

The number of manufacturing and wholesale jobs in the Boston area has declined 8 percent since 1967. The spatial distribution of those jobs, however, changed more dramatically between 1967 and 1990. In Figure 5.7, we display the change in the share of regional manufacturing and wholesale jobs by city and town. The city of Boston's share dropped 12.3 percentage points over this period, from 22.8 percent in 1967 to 10.5 percent in 1990. It is clear from the map that Boston and nearby towns lost in their share of jobs, while more distant towns, particularly near major highways, gained considerably in their shares.

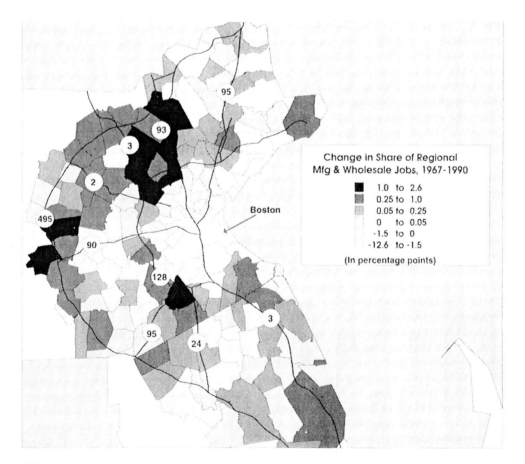

FIGURE 5.7 Change in share of regional manufacturing and wholesale jobs for Boston-area cities and towns, 1967–1990.

Source: Massachusetts Department of Employment and Training, *Employment and Wages in Massachusetts Cities and Towns* (selected years), Boston, MA.

Explanations for why manufacturing and wholesale jobs decentralized focus on two technological developments of the twentieth century. The first is the evolution of the transportation system. With the advent of railway lines, the central transportation terminal typical of the nineteenth century (e.g., a port) gradually gave way to a much more dispersed pattern of freight terminals. This pattern, in turn, evolved into an even more dispersed pattern of highways as manufacturers relied increasingly on truck transportation. The widespread adoption of rail and truck transportation meant that firms no longer needed to move their products to or receive their materials through the center of the city. The very rationale for a centrally oriented rent gradient by manufacturers virtually disappeared during the twentieth century.

In addition to changes in transportation technology, the methods of industrial production and storage technology were also evolving during this same period. Changes in both production and storage methods greatly increased the amount of land used per unit of output by industrial firms. During the later stages of the industrial revolution, manufacturers increasingly adopted production processes that were based on integrated horizontal assembly lines. It is argued that horizontal assembly increased the amount of land needed per unit of output. Modern inventory technology also has a high land requirement, because it requires manufacturers to store goods in large, single story horizontal structures.

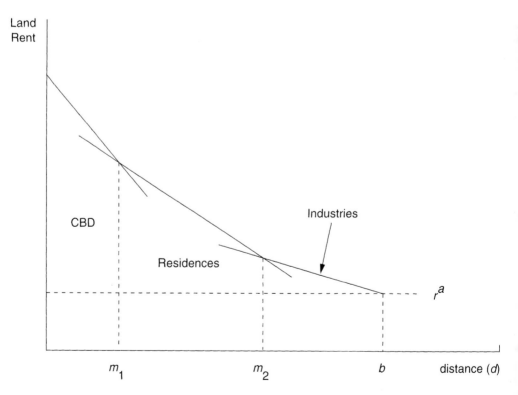

FIGURE 5.8 Spatial separation: land rents for commercial, residential, and industrial uses.

As a result of these changes, the zero-profit rent gradient of industrial firms became quite flat with respect to distance from the traditional urban center. Industrial firms thus were willing to pay less per unit of land for central locations than were most other uses. In the competitive land market, it became most profitable for them to choose more distant locations. Today, new industrial structures are almost always constructed at the very edge of cities in which land competition from other uses is minimal. This pattern of location and the land rents that result are shown in Figure 5.8. Commercial and office uses occupy a CBD (up to a distance m_1), followed by residences from distance m_1 to m_2. Beyond residences, land is used by low-density industries and warehouses.

The extensive land required for industrial uses has led some to argue that industrial land rent gradients are, in fact, virtually flat. As a result, industrial location may be determined more by where other land uses decide not to locate rather than by the explicit attractiveness of certain locations for industrial firms. For example, sites located right on major highways or near airports may be undesirable for many other uses because of noise or other aesthetic considerations. With little competition for these sites, industrial firms can find large tracts of cheap land.

WAGES, THE LABOR MARKET, AND OFFICE DECENTRALIZATION

While industrial land uses in the U.S. have been decentralizing from center cities for many decades, financial and service firms that use office space have remained much more centralized, at least until recently. Clearly, many American cities still contain large central business districts with numerous high-rise office buildings. However, since 1980, there has been an explosion of office construction outside of CBDs. Within the Boston metropolitan area, we can see this change in Figures 5.9 and 5.10.

In Figure 5.9, the 1990 share of regional jobs in the FIRE (financial, insurance, and real estate) and service SIC categories is still quite concentrated within the center city of Boston. In fact, Boston contains 35 percent of these jobs while having only 18 percent of the region's population. However, the map also shows that by 1990, several suburban communities adjacent to the inner circumferential highway (Route 128) had high concentrations of office employment (Newton 4 percent, Waltham 5 percent, Quincy 4 percent). If we look at Figure 5.10, in which the changes in regional service jobs shares between 1967 and 1990 are displayed, the decentralization of services becomes clearer. Boston's share dropped 12 percentage points (from 47 percent to 35 percent), while shares of numerous suburban communities rose. There was still absolute growth in office jobs within the CBD over this period, but it was far less than the growth of such jobs in the suburbs.

Within the framework that we have used to study the decentralization of manufacturing jobs, the movement to the suburbs of office jobs may seem somewhat puzzling. Don't offices tend to have high FAR (floor/area ratio) levels, which means that they should outbid other uses for desirable locations? While this is true, the key to understanding the decentralization of offices lies in defining what types of locations such firms find desirable. In fact, since office firms do not ship products or receive inputs, there was little

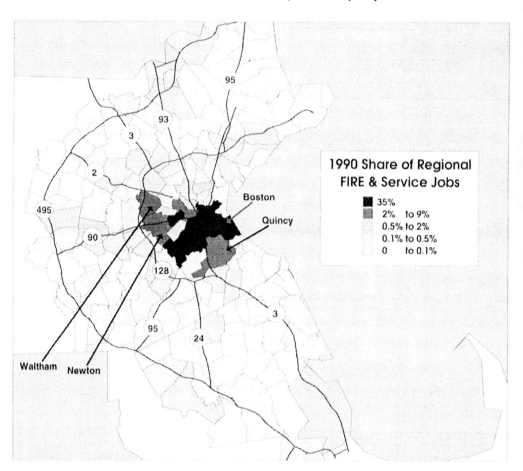

FIGURE 5.9 Share of regional FIRE and service jobs for Boston-area cities and towns, 1990.

Source: Massachusetts Department of Employment and Training, *Employment and Wages in Massachusetts Cities and Towns* (selected years), Boston, MA.

reason, historically, for them to use the central locations surrounding regional port or transportation facilities. Rather, for office firms, labor is by far the dominant and almost exclusive factor used in production. The locational incentives for office firms revolve around the costs associated with assembling their workforce.

When the location of firms is fixed at one urban center, we have seen how workers are compensated for commuting to that center through variation in land rents (or prices). But what happens if a firm currently located at that single center contemplates moving to some alternative location nearer to the residences of their employees? This question was first posed by L. N. Moses (1962), who argued that such a firm could hire those workers that lived next to it for a lower wage rate. Carrying the argument further, Moses hypothesized that there should be a location-specific wage rate at each distance from the center which a decentralizing firm could pay local workers. Since the only alternative

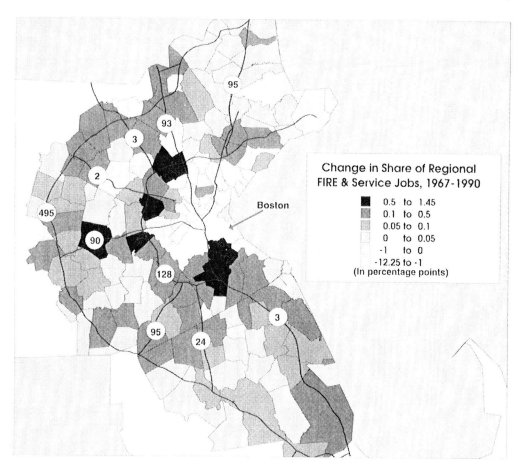

FIGURE 5.10 Change in share of regional FIRE and service jobs for Boston-area cities and towns, 1967–1990.

Source: Massachusetts Department of Employment and Training, *Employment and Wages in Massachusetts Cities and Towns* (selected years), Boston, MA.

source of employment is at the center, this decentralized firm could pay a wage that is lower than the wage paid at the center, reflecting the decrease in commuting costs to workers. In effect, there should be an urban wage gradient in addition to a land rent gradient. As a result, the urban labor market is closely intertwined with the market for land. Let's look at this argument in more detail by examining Figure 5.11.

In contrast to Figure 5.5, Figure 5.11 shows the CBD with a horizontal land rent from firm or business uses, r_c. We show this under the assumption that within the CBD, commuting costs are zero, so that workers must only pay to commute to the edges of the CBD (at distances d_1 or d_6). Within this city, a firm could decentralize its facility or office to some location d_2, using the land from d_2 to d_3. Remembering that in this model, all firms and workers are homogeneous, the decentralizing firm will be able to employ those

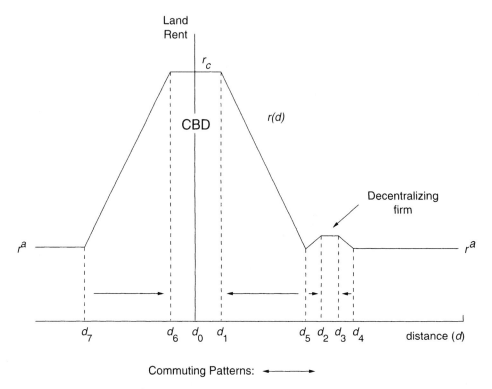

FIGURE 5.11 Decentralizing firms.

workers who live nearest its new location (to the right of d_3 and to the left of d_2). Since these workers are willing to pay more in rent as their commuting costs decrease (towards d_3 or d_2), workers employed at the decentralizing firm will bid up nearby residential land rents. Hence, we get the bump in the rent gradient between d_5 and d_4. At these locations, workers at the decentralized firm will outbid CBD workers for land. In order to actually occupy the land between d_2 and d_3, the land rent paid by the decentralizing firm must match the residential land rents paid by its workers. Let's first focus on the impact of firm decentralization on wages and commuting costs; we will examine the impact on firm land rents later in the chapter.

If workers at the decentralized firm are paid the same wages as CBD workers, then clearly they will have higher net wages since, on average, they have considerably shorter commutes. For example, at the distance d_5, workers commuting leftward to the CBD or rightward to the decentralized firm will both pay the same for land [$r(d_5)$]. Those working at the decentralized firm would have the shorter commute ($d_2 - d_5$), versus the longer CBD commute ($d_5 - d_1$). Since workers are identical and free to change jobs, a decentralizing firm will be able to pay less in wages. How much less? Just enough to leave workers indifferent between commuting to the decentralized firm and to the CBD. As in Chapter 3, we can assume that workers value their net income (gross income minus commuting expenses and rent for a standard house). Thus, the suburbanizing firm need pay

Chapter 5 Firm Site Selection

only a wage w_2 that yields the same net income to its workers as the wage w_1 at the CBD. If the cost (per mile) of commuting is k, this requires that for workers living at d_5:

$$w_2 - r(d_5) - k(d_2 - d_5) = w_1 - r(d_5) - k(d_5 - d_1); \text{ or, } w_2 = w_1 - k(d_5 - d_1) + k(d_2 - d_5) \quad (5.5)$$

Equation (5.5) is the spatial equilibrium condition for workers which permits us to identify some important implications. First, if the firm chooses to locate farther from the CBD, d_2 and d_5 increase, while the distance $d_2 - d_5$ remains fixed. This enables the firm to pay increasingly lower wages. Thus, there should be a wage gradient as one moves from interior to peripheral sites within a metropolitan area. Second, a firm contemplating decentralization with no costs other than wages should seek a location near the current edge of the city, where half of its workers can be accommodated on land between d_3 and the city's border, d_4. This is where its wages will be lowest.

While Equation (5.5) defines a spatial equilibrium with respect to workers, it does not address the question of whether firms are in a spatial equilibrium. Given our assumptions so far, the suburban firm with its lower wages has a clear cost advantage over firms in the CBD. Why won't all firms benefit from decentralizing and, in turn, move? Wages will be lowest when the commuting distances of workers are shortest and land rents are lowest. This argument leads to an ideal picture of the overall dispersal of firms, in which each firm is surrounded by its own workers. The metropolis becomes completely decentralized, with a sprawl of individual firm-worker subcenters, such as depicted in Figure 5.12.

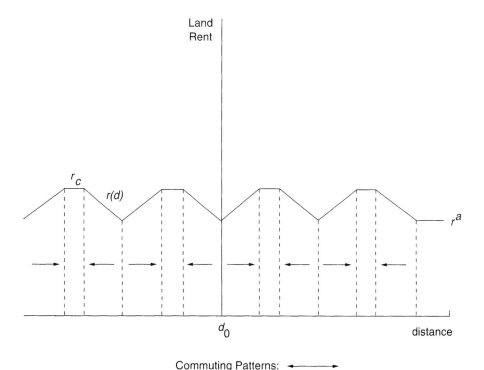

FIGURE 5.12 Subcenter sprawl.

As we have described it, the fully decentralized city in Figure 5.12 would have a number of advantages over the traditional monocentric city that we developed in Chapter 3 and that characterized nineteenth-century cities. To begin with, the average commuting time of residents would be very low, which, in turn, would generate lower average land (and housing) rents. Furthermore, as the population of the city grew over time, the commuting expenses of its workers (and, hence, land rents) would not necessarily increase, as was always the case with the monocentric city. In fact, larger metropolitan areas would simply have more subcenters rather than a larger single center. Do cities with more decentralized employment patterns have lower average commuting times relative to more centralized cities? (See (White 1988)). Gordon, Kumar, and Richardson (1989), for example, find strong statistical evidence that they do.

While this theory of employment dispersal is logically consistent and economically rational, in the real world, decentralization runs into several impediments that can severely limit its occurrence. First, our theory assumes that commuting in any direction is equally easy. Clearly, this need not be the case. Extensive transit infrastructure in many older cities has created a transportation system with far greater capacity to move people to the CBD than out or around to suburban subcenters. Even within the suburbs, the recent addition of circumferential highways concentrates highway capacity at a limited number of intersection points. Thus, it might be argued that older cities will never completely decentralize, whereas employment dispersal in newer cities will be determined by the extent and character of each region's transportation network.

Second, our theory was formulated with a homogeneous labor market in which all households/workers were identical. Clearly, this is not the case, and firms must employ workers of diverse skills at different wage rates. Such workers will also tend to live in different types of housing units at various density levels. Suppose for the moment that a firm contemplating decentralizing has a different mix of workers from other firms located at the CBD. Will the workers who currently live in the suburbs and work at the CBD be appropriate for the new firm? If not, the firm may have to hire workers from a much farther distance, which will limit its ability to pay a lower wage. Alternatively, could the firm's present workers, who currently live at other locations, move and buy the land or housing that is adjacent to the firm's new suburban site? Only if the housing on that land has the attributes desired by those workers. In short, assembling a workforce around a suburbanizing firm in theory is a simple task, but in reality can be quite difficult. Suburban workers will accept lower wages only if they can successfully switch jobs or housing in order to reduce their commute significantly.

During the last decade, researchers have begun to assemble enough empirical evidence to document that within many metropolitan areas, different wages are paid by location and that wage gradients do exist. Eberts (1981) found that comparable municipal workers are paid less in more distant suburbs. Ihlanfeldt (1992) found that suburban-based firms pay lower wages for a wide range of occupations in a sample of four metropolitan areas. Finally, Madden (1985) showed that when a worker changes jobs, a longer (shorter) commute is statistically associated with receiving an increase (decrease) in wages. All of this research seems to suggest that many workers are able to cluster close enough to their firms so that commute reductions are in fact being realized.

SUBCENTERS AND URBAN AGGLOMERATION

In the discussion so far, the only limiting factors that prevent firms from completely decentralizing are the impediments of the housing stock, local government institutions, and irregularities in the provision of infrastructure. There seem to be no economic limits to decentralization; or, alternatively, no economic forces that operate to encourage firm clustering in more centralized location patterns. But few, if any, metropolitan areas approach this pattern of complete decentralization. Instead, in most metropolitan areas, decentralizing firms tend to be clustered in any number of subcenters. To help explain this phenomenon, over the years, economists have developed several arguments suggesting that firms clustering in larger subcenters might receive some form of *agglomeration* benefit that could improve productivity, increase innovation, or reduce production costs. Let's examine these arguments in more detail.

One argument is based on the notion that, at least historically, there may have been productivity gains to an individual firm which are realized when all of its divisions or functions are located at the same point. Thus, if production, marketing, research, and administration are all carried out adjacent to each other, the ability to communicate face-to-face helps the firm operate more efficiently. This would clearly lead to the common clustering of facilities for one firm. In recent years, however, this argument has become less convincing as many firms seem to locate their various divisions in widely different locations. With the advent of vastly improved telecommunications, each division of a firm can be in constant contact with other units, operating with common information databases. Today, it may be quite economical for a firm to have its headquarters in downtown Manhattan, its production facilities in a New Jersey suburb, its clerical support in a Connecticut suburb, and its telemarketing unit in North Dakota!

A second explanation, also emphasizing the ability to easily communicate face-to-face, argues that *different* firms might desire to cluster together. Historically, urbanists have advanced this as a primary reason for the existence of a downtown CBD. It is unclear in the argument, however, whether the communication being undertaken is between similar firms (e.g., information sharing), between firms and their suppliers (e.g., informal vertical integration), or between firms and their clients (e.g., marketing). The distinction is important, for it suggests which kinds of firms may gain advantages from co-locating in the same cluster: firms in the same industry as opposed to firms in different industries vertically linked in business relationships.

These contact theories of urban agglomeration have been subject to little empirical research over the years. Surveys done in the 1960s and early 1970s did suggest that direct business contacts were then particularly important in the more skilled managerial occupations (Goddard 1973; Thorngren 1970). More recent interviews (Clapp 1980; Archer 1981) reveal that office firms located in the CBD explain their locational choice in terms of communicating with clients or other businesses. Those firms selecting suburban sites voice a greater concern for labor availability and accessibility. While these studies are suggestive, clearly more evidence is needed that *direct* business contacts play a significant role in determining firm locations, especially as new telecommunications media are more widely adopted.

If we assume for the moment that some form of agglomeration economy does exists within subcenters, we can develop a simple explanation of how the number of subcenters and their size is determined. In Figure 5.13, we illustrate how the cost of business for firms might vary with the size of the subcenter. The increasing schedule shows the rise in wages that must be paid at larger subcenters to compensate workers for increased commuting costs. This schedule must intersect the vertical axis, since a positive wage is required even at a single firm subcenter. Its rise should be linear if the density of residential development is fixed. The declining schedule shows a hypothetical agglomeration cost of production based on the informational or other benefits discussed above. It, too, must intersect the vertical axis (at A_0), but, from there, must eventually run parallel to the horizontal axis. This gives it a distinct nonlinear shape. The sum of the two schedules is the total cost of production. It will initially fall, reach a minimum, and then rise as the beneficial effects of better information wear off while increased commuting continues to drive up wages.

In Figure 5.13, it is interesting to estimate the impact of improvements in telecommunications on the shape of the schedules. The agglomeration cost schedule should not only be lower (shifting the intercept from A_0 to A_0'), but also flatter, as direct-contact costs are replaced by a medium that is almost insensitive to physical proximity. The end result is that with improved telecommunications, total production costs become lower, less U-shaped, and with a minimum point that is closer to the origin. The dashed schedules in Figure 5.13 show the impact of this technological change.

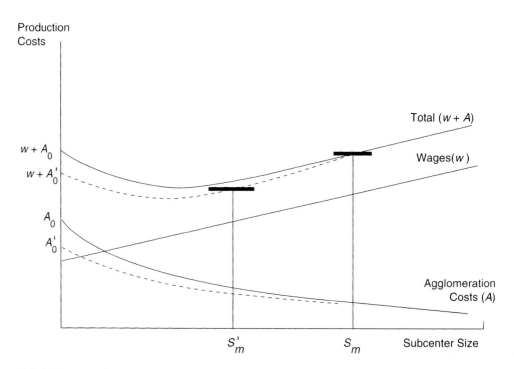

FIGURE 5.13 Subcenter size and firm costs.

Chapter 5 Firm Site Selection

Given firm production costs such as those in Figure 5.13, Helsley and Sullivan (1991) developed a simple model of how and why subcenters are formed. It begins with the assumption that as a region grows, new firms enter the region, select a location with the cheapest cost of production, and invest in a plant or facility. The plant or facility becomes a sunk cost which is assumed to make it prohibitive for the firm to move, even if its production costs (wages and agglomeration) would be lower at another site. Initially, there is one small center with low wages but high agglomeration costs (A_0). As the region grows, this center expands and total production costs move down at first. After the center reaches a certain size, total costs begin to rise, but a new center cannot yet form since total costs there ($w + A_0$) would still be higher. Eventually, as the center reaches some maximum level (S_m), its total costs of production rise to the same level as an isolated firm would experience ($w + A_0$). As the region grows, a second center is formed, and new firms are attracted to this center, where production costs are now falling, as opposed to the original center, where they remain at the higher level dictated by the size S_m.[3] As this second subcenter grows and reaches the size S_m, a third new subcenter forms, and so on. The end result is that after many years, there are a number of older centers, each of size S_m, together with one new center of some size less than S_m.

Within this framework, a technological improvement that reduces information costs (e.g., telecommunications) does have a decentralizing impact. The dashed schedules lead to lower agglomeration costs for the isolated firm (A'_0), but little cost change for firms at larger centers. For a city with the same number of total firms, the changing technology eventually dictates a larger number of smaller-sized subcenters (with size S'_m). As cities grow over time, a shift to the dashed schedule will also lead to the earlier formation of a second or third subcenter. As agglomeration or information costs become less important, cost-minimizing firms are better able to take advantage of the potential wage savings that come with more decentralized locations.

This discussion of urban agglomeration has omitted an important issue which will be raised in Chapter 14. If the location of a firm in a cluster contributes some distinct information benefit to the other firms located there, is the private market sending a sufficient signal to firms (through lower production costs) about the full benefit of clustering? A firm will certainly capitalize on the benefit of clustering, but will it consider the impact that it has on others? How can we take account of the benefits to other firms in a cluster as an additional firm enters? We discuss these external benefits, or externalities, in detail in Chapter 14.

SUBCENTERS, WAGES, AND THE URBAN LAND MARKET

Our theory of employment decentralization by firms has been depicted as a tradeoff between lower wages (caused by reduced worker commuting) and higher agglomeration or information costs (caused by the absence of many nearby firms). So far, we have not

---

[3] Firms at the older center do not move to the lower-cost, newer center because that would involve investing in a new plant.

fully integrated land rents into our discussion of firm decentralization. Residential land rents will vary with location as will wages, and to occupy land in a decentralized city, firms will have to match the land rents of residential users. In Figure 5.11, a decentralizing firm would not only pay lower wages, but would pay lower land rents as well. To understand more fully how businesses and households reach a spatial equilibrium when rents as well as wages vary across locations, we examine a city with two centers, a CBD and a suburban subcenter, and study the operation of the land market. We can generalize to many subcenters after completing our two-center example.

Our model has a CBD and a suburban subcenter located in a linear city, as illustrated in Figure 5.14. We choose a simpler, linear city rather than a circular one to keep our mathematics to a minimum.[4] The overall population of the city is fixed and is measured as the number of one-worker households N. N_1 of these workers are employed by firms in the CBD, while $N_2 = N - N_1$ work at firms in the second center. As in our previous discussion, we will assume for simplicity that all workers and all firms are identical. In this city, firms in the CBD occupy land between locations d_6 and d_1. To the left of d_6, land is occupied by residents who work in the CBD, out to the edge of the city at d_7. In the subcenter, firms use land between d_2 and d_3. To the right of the subcenter, land is used by subcenter workers, extending to the city's border farthest to the right, d_4. In between the CBD and the subcenter, there is residential land occupied by workers from both centers, and a boundary location d_5, to the left of which CBD workers live, and to the right of which subcenter workers reside.

Households-workers in our city have identical houses, as in Chapter 3, and a fixed amount of land per house: q. The firms that employ these workers at subcenters also build facilities (plants or offices) that occupy land at a fixed FAR. We combine the fixed firm FAR with a given amount of floor space per worker into a fixed overall usage of land per worker by firms: f. Thus, the density of workers at their place of work is $1/f$ while density at their place of residence is $1/q$. Workers commute to their firm along the line at an annual cost per mile of k dollars. Agricultural land to the right of d_4 and the left of d_7 is valued at r^a. Residential land rents will exactly compensate workers for the cost of commuting per acre.[5]

While land rents make the households who work at each subcenter equally well off at different residential locations, it is wages that will make mobile households equally well off *between* centers. Consider for the moment the workers who occupy land at the urban borders, d_4 and d_7. Both of these workers have land rent expenses equal to $r^a q$. They may, however, have quite different commuting expenses, depending on the commuting distances to the two centers. Denoting the wages paid at the CBD and subcenter

---

[4]In such a city, we must assume that there is actually a strip of land with some width, and that commuting occurs only linearly along this strip. To keep the mathematics simple, we assume that the width is 1 mile.

[5]Following the methodology presented in Chapter 3, residential rent, $r(d)$, can be defined as:

$$r(d) = r^a + k(d - d_7)/q, \quad d_6 > d > d_7$$
$$r(d) = r^a + k(d_4 - d)/q, \quad d_4 > d > d_3$$
$$r(d) = r(d_1) - k(d - d_1)/q, \quad d_5 > d > d_1$$
$$r(d) = r(d_2) - k(d_2 - d)/q, \quad d_2 > d > d_5$$

Chapter 5 Firm Site Selection

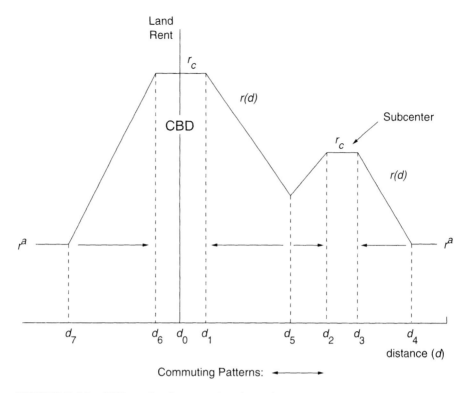

FIGURE 5.14 CBD and subcenter land markets.

as w_1 and w_2, the net income (after rent and commuting) of these two groups of workers must be the same:

$$w_1 - r^a q - k(d_6 - d_7) = w_2 - r^a q - k(d_4 - d_3) \text{, or,}$$
$$w_1 - w_2 = k[(d_6 - d_7) - (d_4 - d_3)] \tag{5.6}$$

Thus, as long as wages compensate workers for the commuting expenses made by the farthest worker at each subcenter, workers throughout the city will all be indifferent to location. Why? Because rents around each subcenter make workers at closer locations as well off as their colleague who commutes the farthest. Equation (5.6) is quite important, for it says that a system of different-sized subcenters can easily coexist within an urban land and labor market if higher wages at larger subcenters compensate workers employed there for the longer commute and higher land rents that inevitably result from greater size.

The population or employment of each subcenter is sufficient to determine all of the boundaries (d_1 through d_7), given the fixed location and distance between the center inner edges. Given the N_1 workers at the CBD (subcenter 1), its left boundary must extend far enough to accommodate that center's firms at the fixed worker density: $(d_1 - d_6)/f = N_1$. With a given overall workforce, the boundary to the right of the second center is determined from a similar condition: $(d_3 - d_2)/f = N - N_1$. The number of workers in each center also determines the various residential boundaries, given the fixed residential density. Remember that each household has only one worker in this model. In the interior between the centers, the boundary d_5 occurs where residential rents from each center are equal. The left extreme boundary, d_7, is determined such that enough land is developed for center 1 (CBD) workers: $(d_6 - d_7 + d_5 - d_1)/q = N_1$. Similarly, the right extreme boundary, d_4, is determined by $(d_4 - d_3 + d_2 - d_5)/q = N - N_1$. Thus, a center that has greater employment (i.e., the CBD) will have a larger land area to accommodate both its firms and households. These larger areas give rise to greater commuting distances and higher overall land rents, which necessitates paying higher wages.

Firms, like workers, are assumed to be all of the same type, exporting their products to world markets. Thus, as discussed earlier in this chapter, firms are price takers, and their profits depend only on the costs of producing their products. Some firm production costs will vary with location: wages, land rents, and any costs associated with center size or agglomeration. Other costs of business are exogenous, and do not vary appreciably across locations within the metropolis; for example, intermediate inputs and the capital costs of plant and equipment. We also assume that the cost of transporting products to world markets is exogenous, unlike in the monocentric model presented earlier in this chapter. In choosing a location, firms seek to minimize those costs that vary with location. Thus, any exogenous costs can be ignored in our model.

Let's now turn our attention to those costs that influence firm location. We define production costs due to agglomeration as $A(N)$ and we assume that these decline with center size, as was shown in Figure 5.13. Thus, firms operating at the CBD (center 1) have wage and agglomeration costs equal to $w_1 + A(N_1)$ dollars per worker, while those at the subcenter (center 2) have costs of $w_2 + A(N_2)$ dollars per worker.

With a competitive land market, commercial land within each center will have a rent equal to residential land rent at the edge of the subcenter. If we assume that there is effectively no cost of commuting within each subcenter, business land rents will be the same within the subcenter, and firms will have a uniform rental cost per worker equal to $1/f$ times this residential (and commercial) land rent.[6]

Just like households, firms in equilibrium must be equally well off, and this requires that the total costs of production be the same across centers. Aggregating the three components of business costs per worker (rents, wages, and agglomeration), we have the firm equilibrium condition:

$$A(N_1) + w_1 + r_1 f = A(N_2) + w_2 + r_2 f, \text{ or,}$$
$$A(N_1) - A(N_2) = w_2 - w_1 + f(r_2 - r_1) \tag{5.7}$$

Equation (5.7) can be used to identify the range of feasible sizes for each subcenter. We know that wage differences will simply equal the difference in commuting expenses to each subcenter's edge. We also know that firm rent differences will equal residential

---

[6]Business land rents at each center are r_1 and r_2. Under the assumption of a competitive land market, we have:

$$r_1 = r(d_1) = r(d_6) = r^a + k(d_6 - d_7)/q$$
$$r_2 = r(d_2) = r(d_3) = r^a + k(d_4 - d_3)/q$$

Chapter 5 Firm Site Selection   115

rent differences, which, in turn, also equal this same commuting expense difference to the two subcenter edges. As a result, when firms are in equilibrium, the difference in production costs from agglomeration between the two centers must exactly balance with the differences in firm rents and wages:

$$A(N_1) - A(N_2) = k[(d_4 - d_3) - (d_6 - d_7)] + (f/q)k[(d_4 - d_3) - (d_6 - d_7)] \quad (5.8)$$

$$\underset{\text{center 2 - center 1}}{\text{wage difference}} + \underset{\text{center 2 - center 1}}{\text{firm rent difference}}$$

It should be clear from Equation (5.8) that long-run differences in center size (employment and households) can exist only if production costs vary because of agglomeration in a manner that exactly offsets the increases in wages and rents that result from differences in center size. This is equivalent to saying that in Figure 5.13, the sum of agglomeration and wage-rent costs is relatively flat over some range of subcenter sizes. Let's consider more carefully how this balancing can occur.

If in Equation (5.8) we assume for the moment that there are no agglomeration impacts on production costs $[A(N_1) = A(N_2) = 0]$, then equilibrium requires that the centers must have equal commuting distances, land areas, and, hence, workers (households): $d_4 - d_3 = d_6 - d_7$. On the other hand, suppose that agglomeration does effect production costs and $N_1 > N_2$, so that $A(N_1) < A(N_2)$. In this case, center 1's land area and commuting distance $(d_6 - d_7)$ must exceed that of center 2 $(d_4 - d_3)$.[7] Center 1's larger size will generate lower agglomeration production costs, but the corresponding greater commuting costs will lead to higher land rents and wages than at center 2. For the larger center to be in long-run equilibrium with the smaller, the production advantage from agglomeration to firms must be exactly offset by the combination of higher land rents and worker wages. We can summarize this result:

1. Larger subcenters can coexist with smaller subcenters within a metropolitan area if they offer firms some production advantage through agglomeration. In equilibrium, the agglomeration advantage of greater size must be balanced by the larger subcenter's farther commuting distances, which increase land rents and necessitate paying higher wages to keep workers.

Numerical Example

Let's illustrate this conclusion with a specific example. A reasonable worker density for office firms would be $1/f = 500$ workers per acre (320,000 workers per square mile).[8] Our metropolitan area will begin with *two even-sized subcenters* of $N_1 = N_2 = 1$ million workers each and we assume that all development takes place on a strip of land that is

---

[7] Given the conditions in footnote 5 and Equation (5.6), it should be clear that the wage differences and rent differences between centers must be of the same sign to ensure that workers are paid. Thus, if the left-hand side of (5.8) is negative, both expressions on the right-hand side must be also.

[8] This worker density would exist with FAR levels of between 2 and 3, together with roughly 250 square feet of floor area per worker. These are very typical figures for suburban office space.

10 miles wide throughout.[9] Given our worker density, the total land area required for each center is 3.125 square miles. With a land strip 10 miles wide, each center must be 0.3125 miles long ($d_1 - d_6 = d_3 - d_2 = 0.3125$) to accommodate the workers at their firms. If the center inner edges are 20 miles apart ($20 = d_2 - d_1$), and the worker density of housing is $1/q = 4$ per acre (2,560 per square mile), then the 200 square miles of land area between the centers can accommodate a total of 512,000 workers (or 256,000 workers for each center). On the outer edges, each center will have to extend about 29 miles ($d_6 - d_7 = d_4 - d_3 = 29.06$) for there to be enough land to house each center's remaining 744,000 workers ($29.06 \times 10 \times 2560 = 744,000$).

Land rents in this city can be calculated using the same numerical examples as in Chapter 3. If agricultural land rents, r^a, are \$1,000 per acre at the edges of the subcenters (d_4 and d_7), and the cost of commuting, k, at each center is \$200 per mile annually, then at the core of each subcenter land will rent for \$24,248 per acre to both firms and households (\$1,000 in agricultural rent plus 4 households per acre times \$5,812 in commute savings to each household).

Suppose that we allow some form of agglomeration to affect the production costs of firms. For illustration, assume that a center that is twice the size of another has a 5 percent increase in labor productivity over the other city's, or a \$2,500 cost advantage per worker. The question is, how will this level of agglomeration alter the center sizes, land rents, and transportation expenses of our example? Will a \$2,500 cost advantage in a center that is twice the size of another be eroded by the additional commuting expenses and land rents that such a size increase would entail? The right-hand side of Equation (5.8) says that to balance a \$2,500 agglomeration cost advantage, the difference in edge commuting distances between the two centers must reach 12.4 miles [$2,500/(k + kf/q) = 2,500/201.6 = 12.4$]. Thus, if center 1 is the larger, it must expand so that its outer edge, d_7, is 35.26 miles from the center [$29.06 + 1/2(12.4)$]; while center 2's border, d_4, contracts to an edge of 22.86 miles from its center [$29.06 - 1/2(12.4)$]. Since commuting costs \$200 per mile annually, the travel expenses of the farthest worker at center 1 will increase by \$1,240 ($1,240 = 200 \times 6.2$), while maximum commuting expenses at center 2 decrease by this same amount. For workers to be indifferent between employment at each center, Equation (5.6) says that wages at center 1 will have to rise by \$2,480 relative to center 2.

With the new outer edges of residential development established, we can recalculate central land rents at each subcenter. With center 1's edge at 35.26 miles (d_7), central rents will be \$29,208 per acre, while center 2's 22.86-mile edge at d_4 creates central rents of \$19,288 per acre. In a competitive land market, as the central rents rise in center 1, it will expand to take more of the land between the two centers, and center 2 will shrink, taking less of this land. The boundary between the centers (d_5 in Figure 5.14) moves from halfway between the two when they were the same size to 16.2 miles from center 1 and 3.8 miles from center 2. Center 1 now has 6.2 miles of additional interior land and

---

[9]In footnote 4, we reminded the reader that our linear city must have a width. To simplify the mathematics we assumed that width was 1 mile. Here, to make our example more realistic, we assume a width of 10 miles.

another 6.2 miles from border expansion, while center 2 has lost this much through contracting its edge and share of interior land. The net result is that center 1 now has 93 percent more workers (households) than center 2. Center 1's total land area [now (16.2 + 35.26) × 10 = 514.6 square miles] multiplied by 2,560 households per square mile yields 1,317,376 workers at that center, with a residual 682,624 at center 2. This is almost exactly equal to the difference in center sizes that was assumed to generate the agglomeration advantage. In other words, with the *assumed* level of agglomeration, a center that is twice as large as another will require additional commuting expenses and rent that roughly match the agglomeration advantage.

In this example, households at the edge of the now-expanded center 1 will incur additional commuting expenses of $1,240 annually, while those living next to that center's employment zone will find that their annual rent for a lot has increased by $1,240. At center 2, both the commute from the edge and central rents fall by these amounts. Firms at center 1 must pay their workers $2,480 in additional wages relative to center 2 in order to successfully compete in the labor market. But what of the additional $20 that remains between the original $2,500 in agglomeration benefits and the $2,480 in higher wages? This is exactly made up (with rounding error) by the additional land rent that firms must pay (per worker) at center 1 versus center 2. With a worker density of 500 per acre, the $9,920 rent differential between center 1 and center 2 translates into a difference of $19.84 per worker (9,920/500 = 19.84).

Given Equation (5.8), it is not surprising that almost all of center 1's $2,500 agglomeration production advantage winds up getting absorbed by the difference between center wages. To make households equally well off, rents per acre at the core of center 1 rise from $24,248 to $29,208, while those at center 2's core are reduced to $19,288. The difference between core land rents per acre is $9,920, or $2,480 for each household's quarter-acre lot. This difference in lot rents is what must be compensated for in wages. The difference in core land rents also impacts firms, but, in this model, it does so only trivially. The $9,920 rent difference per acre at the core increases the firm's annual cost of land per worker by only $20, because firms use such little land per worker. A $9,920 difference in land rents per acre between centers translates into a difference of only $0.23 per square foot. If firm facilities have a FAR of 2.0, the floor space rent for those facilities should differ by less than $0.12 per square foot. This example illustrates an important conclusion that holds generally when there is a competitive land market in which firms and residents need only match each other's rents to occupy land.

> 2. At larger subcenters, with agglomeration advantages, workers will have to commute farther, increasing residential and commercial land rents per acre. Because households use much more land for their residence than workers use in their workplace, the impact of greater land rents is primarily to generate wage differences rather than differences in the rent for facility space to firms.

As we discussed earlier in this chapter, there is considerable empirical research which documents the existence of urban wage gradients; wage rates are higher at large urban CBDs and lower at suburban subcenters or more peripheral sites. These wage differences presumably exist because of differences in the commuting expenses associated with working downtown as opposed to working at various suburban locations. This is quite consistent with our model above, as long as agglomeration productivity factors compensate firms for the higher wages at CBDs. The model's conclusion that differences in the rent for facility space should be minimal across subcenters is more problematic. Let's examine some data on urban subcenters to see how they vary in size and rental rates.

SUBCENTERS AND RENTS IN GREATER BOSTON

At the beginning of this chapter, we focused on the changing employment patterns of the Boston metropolitan area, illustrating how manufacturing jobs and office and service jobs have been rapidly decentralizing. We now consider information from commercial real estate brokerage companies about the location of industrial or office buildings and the rents that they currently command in the marketplace. These kinds of data are widely available within many U.S. cities. In Table 5.1, we list those towns or subcenters within the Boston area that, in 1993, contained contiguous office buildings with a total of at least 1.5 million square feet (1.5 percent of the region's total office space). There are three such clusters within the city of Boston and 11 subcenters in the suburban towns that ring the center city. Included in the table are average market rent levels per square foot for that office space within each center that is in buildings over 50,000 square feet in size that were built during the last 15 years.

TABLE 5.1 Office Area, Buildings, and Asking Rents, Boston-Area Towns, 1993

Town (Cluster)	Square Feet (000s)	No. of Buildings	Rent
Boston (Back Bay)	10,675	66	25.19
(Financial District)	26,754	141	26.73
(South Station)	3,053	21	23.50
Andover	1,438	10	16.25
Burlington	3,498	43	18.90
Cambridge	11,103	116	18.64
Framingham	3,196	39	14.06
Lexington	2,320	38	19.41
Natick	1,518	19	15.50
Newton	1,973	38	18.32
Quincy	4,797	44	15.90
Waltham	5,843	60	19.60
Wellesley	1,774	36	19.45
Westborough	1,664	15	12.50
Residual	26,793	548	15.21
MSA	106,399	1,234	20.74

Source: Special tabulation from The Property Information Management System, CB Commercial, Inc., August 1993.

Chapter 5 Firm Site Selection

In the Boston office market, the three center-city clusters account for 35 percent of the region's office space, while the 11 suburban subcenters combined house another 40 percent of the market. The remaining 136 cities and towns contain only 25 percent of the office space, which clearly illustrates the tendency for office buildings to cluster. Across the 14 towns and clusters, average rental rates vary by almost 114 percent, from $26.73 in Boston's financial district to $12.50 per square foot at a distant subcenter. While the larger central-city areas clearly have higher rents than the suburban subcenters, within the suburbs, there remain large differences in rents that seem unrelated to the size of the center. For example, Wellesley has higher rent than Cambridge, despite the fact that Cambridge has over six times more space; there is a $3.70 rent difference between Waltham and Quincy, which have similar stocks of space.

In Table 5.2, we examine similar information for clusters or subcenters of industrial space within the Boston metropolitan area, using the same minimum-size criteria of 1.5 percent of the market. (For industrial space, this minimum would be 4.2 million square feet. The average rent levels are for warehouse space within each cluster that is less than 15 years old.) Comparing the data provided in Tables 5.1 and 5.2 yields two

TABLE 5.2 Industrial Area, Buildings, and Asking Rents, Boston-Area Towns, 1993

Town	Square Feet (000s)	No. of Buildings	Rent
Boston	8,969	116	NA
South Boston	5,170	92	5.00
Andover	5,192	49	5.56
Bedford	4,126	61	6.65
Billerica	8,430	161	4.26
Braintree	4,510	79	4.50
Burlington	4,353	106	7.12
Cambridge	7,351	128	NA
Canton	5,026	91	3.83
Chelmsford	4,565	58	1.87
Framingham	4,520	72	4.64
Lawrence	6,548	39	6.96
Lowell	11,350	111	2.54
Lynn	6,795	54	NA
Mansfield	5,432	53	5.53
Marlborough	5,567	86	5.73
Peabody	4,074	48	6.91
Quincy	4,197	18	NA
Waltham	5,877	149	5.50
Westborough	5,677	75	4.04
Wilmington	8,013	128	4.83
Woburn	12,233	249	5.51
Residual	139,658	2,490	3.94
MSA	277,633	4,513	4.40

NA, No available rental quotations.
Source: Special tabulation from The Property Information Management System, CB Commercial, Inc., August 1993.

important differences between office and industrial space in Boston. First, there is far less clustering of industrial space. The two industrial clusters within the city of Boston contain only 5 percent of the region's industrial space, and two suburban submarkets (Lowell and Woburn) have somewhat more than Boston's share of the market. Using the 1.5-percent-of-market minimum, there are more clusters (22, versus 14 for the office market), and, combined, they account for just under one-half of the region's industrial space (versus 75 percent for office). Thus, industrial space is far more dispersed and less likely to cluster than office space. Second, industrial rent for comparable space exhibits even more variation than was true for office buildings. Industrial rents range from $1.87 up to $7.12 per square foot, a 280 percent difference. Like the office market, there seems to be no association between subcenter size and rent level.

These Boston metropolitan area data suggest two important conclusions. First, the formation of subcenters is quite different across the two uses: office buildings tend to form fewer larger centers, while industrial buildings are more widely dispersed in a larger number of smaller clusters. If we rely on the arguments and models of the previous section, this systematic difference between the two uses suggests that whatever agglomeration economies exist must clearly be stronger for office firms than for manufacturers. Second, the tables also reveal significant differences for both types of property in rental rates across subcenters. This result seems to contradict a conclusion of our simple model, in which wages rather than rents varied most with different-sized subcenters. However, the variation in rents within Tables 5.1 and 5.2 does seem to be largely unrelated to the size of the subcenter. With the exception of Boston's higher office rents, larger subcenters do not systematically have higher rents than smaller ones. Perhaps wages, rather than rents, really do vary most across subcenters of different sizes, but other factors largely unrelated with subcenter size exert an influence over commercial and industrial rents.

SUBCENTERS, LOCAL GOVERNMENTS, AND LAND-USE RESTRICTIONS

Throughout this chapter, we have operated under the assumption of a competitive land market in which sites are eventually occupied by the use offering the highest return or rent. In reality, many cities and towns limit the area that certain uses may occupy. Thus, the size, growth, and existence of subcenters can be keenly influenced by the willingness of selected local governments to allow industrial or commercial uses within their boundaries. In Chapters 13 and 14, we will discuss the incentives and rationale for local governments to limit, regulate, or encourage the location of particular uses. At this point, we want to indicate only that the pattern of clustering within Boston or other metropolitan areas may be determined as much by land use regulation set by the local political process, as by underlying economic motives.

If local governments interfere with the land market through local zoning or other development regulations, then the rents for office or industrial space might vary far more across subcenters than is indicated by our simple model. If one use is not allowed to encroach or expand into the territory occupied by another, then there is no economic necessity for the land rents of these two uses to compete with one another. In the models above, we assumed that the rent for commercial land within each subcenter would equal or just exceed the rent for surrounding residential land. If the boundary between residential and commercial or industrial use is fixed institutionally rather than by market competition, this assumption no longer holds. Commercial rents within each subcenter can exceed or be less than residential land just across a border that is defined by regulation. Cities or towns that severely limit commercial or industrial development might have higher commercial land rents even if these developments are of smaller size. With land-use regulations, larger centers and suburban subcenters may coexist even if there are no agglomeration benefits.

Our simple model was also based on the notion that the cost of residential land varied only with subcenter size because of worker commuting. But suppose that residential density is not fixed, and, as in Chapter 4, larger subcenters tend to develop at higher residential density. With variable density, larger subcenters could have much higher residential land rents, and this, in turn, would generate a more pronounced variation of office or industrial rent with subcenter size. This might well explain the noticeably higher office rents within the city of Boston. The high historic urban densities in older cities can generate a powerful opportunity cost that commercial development must match if it is to acquire land.

There has been some limited empirical research on the role that local land-use regulations play in the commercial or industrial land market. A study within the Minneapolis metropolitan area demonstrated that the probability of industrial development occurring within a town was strongly influenced by the town's land-use policies (Wasylenko 1980). For land-use restrictions to have this effect, of course, they must not only be present but be binding.

More recent research has begun to examine directly the determinants of rent for comparable office space in the greater Los Angeles area. Sivitanidou (forthcoming) finds that office rents within the Los Angeles area vary by even more than the Boston data of Table 5.1. In order to explain statistical differences in subcenter office rental rates, she grouped explanatory variables into three categories: locational factors that firms would find desirable (e.g., proximity to the airport), factors that would influence the opportunity rent for residential land (e.g., school quality), and land-use regulations. Land-use regulations included measures of the FAR limits on commercial development, the scarcity of commercially zoned land, and the existence of various development moratoria. All of these factors had strong impacts on the rent for commercial space.

Throughout this chapter, we have seen that the location of industrial and commercial development has been influenced by long-run economic and technological change. Elevators for office buildings and horizontal assembly lines in factories have redefined the FAR levels of these two uses and given them distinct location patterns. The declining cost of transportation relative to labor has refocused business location decisions around their most important resource—labor. In this process of change, the public sector plays an increasingly important role. Would industries have decentralized in the early twentieth century without the initial construction of roads? Would office development have remained more centralized recently if urban centers had better transit systems rather than circumferential highway networks? Will local governments cooperate with business to provide the diverse housing needed to accommodate the business workforce locally? To what extent have some industries sought to flee the tax burdens of inner cities? In Chapters 13 and 14, we will further examine the role played by the public sector in development and track the evolution of public sector development policies.

SUMMARY

In this chapter, we have examined the location decision of firms within metropolitan areas, in particular those firms that export their products or services. These jobs have undergone extensive decentralization in most metropolitan areas since the early 1900s. As a consequence, the spatial structure of metropolitan areas is changing from one of monocentricity (single employment center) to polycentricity (many employment centers).

- Industrial firms have largely moved to suburban location because modern production and storage technologies make them extensive users of land. In part due to the spatially diffuse character of truck and rail transportation, industries decentralize because they are less willing to compete with denser (higher rent paying) land uses.

- More recently, many office-using firms are decentralizing to be closer to their workforce and, consequently, can pay lower wages. While land rent compensates workers for the commuting costs to a common employment center, variation in wages must exist to compensate workers for any differences in the average commuting costs that exist when there are multiple employment centers.

- Several factors can limit this trend toward decentralization. Local governments can hinder the ability of firms to match locations with their workforce by regulating the type of housing that is built. Also, firms may derive economic advantages from locating in larger, more central clusters, which facilitate communication and information sharing. With new telecommunications technology, this agglomeration effect may be diminishing, helping to encourage decentralization.

REFERENCES AND ADDITIONAL READINGS

ARCHER, WAYNE. "Determinants of Location for General Purpose Office Firms Within Medium Size Cities." *AREUEA Journal* 9 (1981): 283–297.

BRENNAN, T. P., R. E. CANNADAY, AND P. F. COLWELL. "Office Rent in the Chicago CBD." *AREUEA Journal* 12 (1984): 243–260.

CLAPP, JOHN. "The Intra-Metropolitan Location of Office Activities." *Journal of Regional Science* 20 (1980): 387–399.

EBERTS, R. W. "An Empirical Investigation of Intra-Urban Wage Gradients." *Journal of Urban Economics* 10 (1981): 50–60.

GODDARD, JOHN B. *Office Location in Urban and Regional Development.* Oxford: Oxford University Press, 1973.

GORDON, P., A. KUMAR, AND H. RICHARDSON. "The Influence of Metropolitan Spacial Structure on Commuting Time." *Journal of Urban Economics* 26 (1989):138.

HARTNETT, H. "A Location Analysis of Manufacturing in Chicago." *AREUEA Journal* (June 1973).

HELSLEY, R., AND A. SULLIVAN. "Urban Subcenter Formation." *Regional Science and Urban Economics* 21, 2 (July 1991).

IHLANFELDT, K. R. "Intra Urban Wage Gradients: Evidence by Race, Gender, Occupation and Class." *Journal of Urban Economics* 32 (1992): 70–91.

MADDEN, J. F. "Urban Wage Gradients: Empirical Evidence." *Journal of Urban Economics* 18 (1985): 291–301.

MCMILLEN, D., AND L. SINGELL. "Work Location, Residence Location and the Intraurban Wage Gradient." *Journal of Urban Economics* 32 (1992): 195–213.

MOSES, L. N. "Towards a Theory of Intra-Urban Wage Differentials and Their Influence on Travel Patterns." *Papers of the Regional Science Association* 9 (1962): 53–63.

SCHMENNER, R. "The Rent Gradient for Manufacturing." *Journal of Urban Economics* 9 (1981).

SIVITANIDOU, RENA. "Urban Spatial Variations in Office Commercial Rents: the Role of Commercial Zoning." Forthcoming in the *Journal of Urban Economics.*

SIVITANIDOU, RENA, AND WILLIAM C. WHEATON. "Wage and Rent Capitalization in the Commercial Real Estate Market." *Journal of Urban Economics* 31, 2 (1992), 206–229.

STRUYK, R., AND F. JAMES. *Intra-Metropolitan Industrial Location.* Lexington, MA: Lexington Books, 1975.

THORNGREN, B. "How Do Contact Systems Affect Regional Development?" *Environment and Planning* 2 (1970): 409–427.

WASYLENKO, M. "Evidence of Fiscal Differentials and Intra-Metropolitan Firm Relocation." *Land Economics* (August 1980).

WHITE, MICHELE. "Firm Suburbanization and Urban Subcenters." *Journal of Urban Economics* 3 (1976): 323–343.

WHITE, MICHELE. "Location Choice and Commuting Behavior in Cities with Decentralized Employment." *Journal of Urban Economics* 24 (1988): 129–152.

CHAPTER 6

RETAIL LOCATION AND MARKET COMPETITION

In the previous chapter, we examined the location decisions of firms when households represent workers. The choice of location by a firm determined the commuting pattern of its workers, which, in turn, affected wages, and, hence, a firm's cost of doing business. This model made sense when we were studying the location of industries or large scale office firms whose products and services are sold to regional or national clients. When firms sell their products strictly to local customers, however, the role played by location changes. The primary focus in firm location decisions shifts from the impacts of location on wages and input costs to the impacts of location on the firm's market size and its volume of business. In this chapter, we examine the theory of retail location, focusing on how stores compete with each other for business. As in previous chapters, distance and urban transportation costs still influence household behavior; but now, instead of influencing the cost of commuting, they determine the likelihood that customers will be drawn to a retail facility. This model can also be used to study those types of professional service firms that regularly deal with residential clients and for whom access to those clients is important.

We begin this chapter by examining the distribution of retail firms within a metropolitan area both by location and type of product. The data reveal a number of well-recognized patterns. Retail firms are widely dispersed and have been growing more so over time. There is also a hierarchy to the distribution of retail establishments by type of product. As a consequence, retail stores tend to cluster into centers with distinct characteristics. For example, a small strip shopping center may have a supermarket, drug store,

Chapter 6 Retail Location and Market Competition

liquor store, and video store; a regional mall may have a variety of discount or factory outlet stores. To understand these patterns, we develop a set of theoretical arguments that explain the pattern of shopping frequency, trip distance, and value of purchase.

We next consider the classical theory of retail competition. Stores are held to compete with each other in two different dimensions: price and location. Given the locations of competitors, most retailers are able to exercise some degree of monopoly power over local buyers. The closer the competitors, the more intense retailer price competition becomes. In the longer run, stores choose locations that maximize their local market power. This classic theory of location is able to explain the long recognized variations in store density and location that exist between different types of retailers.

The shortcoming of classical retail theory is that it ignores the fact that consumers can economize on transportation by purchasing many different types of products on a single shopping trip. These savings give rise to a fundamental reason for having stores cluster at centers or modern shopping malls. Retail centers compete not just on the basis of price, but also by offering consumers the most advantageous mix of stores.

In the final section of the chapter, we demonstrate how retailing theory can be applied to analyze empirically the drawing power and sales potential of competing retail shopping malls within a metropolitan area. Using household survey data on consumer shopping patterns, a demand model can be estimated statistically that predicts the probability that shoppers at each residential location will choose to patronize one of many possible alternative retail centers. Forecasting with this model permits developers and planners to evaluate the impact of and potential sales from new retail development, through either the expansion of existing centers or the construction of new ones.

RETAIL LOCATION PATTERNS

Since retail stores serve households, one might expect to find that the location of retail establishments is quite decentralized, given the decentralization of the population discussed in Chapter 3. At the same time, the propensity of stores to cluster will lead some areas to specialize in retail centers. Let's examine the spatial distribution of retail activity as measured by employment in firms whose SIC (Standard Industrial Classification) category is retail, for our sample of 146 cities and towns in the Boston MSA. Figure 6.1 provides the share of retail jobs by city and town for 1990. As expected, the city of Boston has the largest share, with 16.5 percent of the area's retail employment. The next largest share is Cambridge, with 3.6 percent of retail jobs. There are eight towns with between 2 percent and 4 percent of retail employment. Note that these towns tend to be located near major highways.

How has the spatial distribution of jobs changed over time? Total retail employment grew from 242,376 in 1967 to 345,702 in 1990, representing 42.6 percent growth. Retail employment has clearly decentralized over the period. As shown in Figure 6.2, the city of Boston's share of retail employment dropped 14.4 percentage points, from 30.9 percent in 1967 to 16.5 percent in 1990. Figure 6.2 clearly illustrates that the older

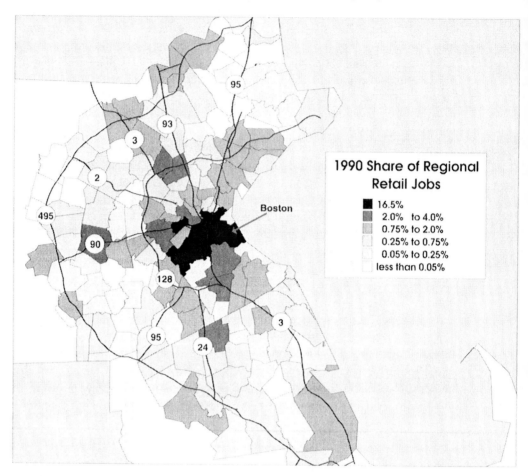

FIGURE 6.1 Share of regional retail jobs for Boston-area cities and towns, 1990.

Source: Massachusetts Department of Employment and Training, *Employment and Wages in Massachusetts Cities and Towns* (selected years), Boston, MA.

cities and towns near Boston and those that were once larger employment centers such as Lowell and Brockton have lost retail share. Three towns' shares of retail employment grew between 1 and 2 percentage points: Danvers to the north on Route 95, and Burlington and Woburn on Route 128 near Route 93. Again, growth in retail employment share has tended to occur in towns near major highways.

Since retail stores serve the population, an alternative way of looking at the spatial distribution of retail jobs is to consider the ratio of retail jobs to the population as shown in Figure 6.3. Two features of the retail landscape are immediately apparent in viewing Figure 6.3. First, retail employment is clearly clustered or concentrated in a select number of municipalities. Cities or towns that specialize as retail centers have five to six times as many retail workers relative to population as do towns that are not specialized. Second,

Chapter 6 Retail Location and Market Competition

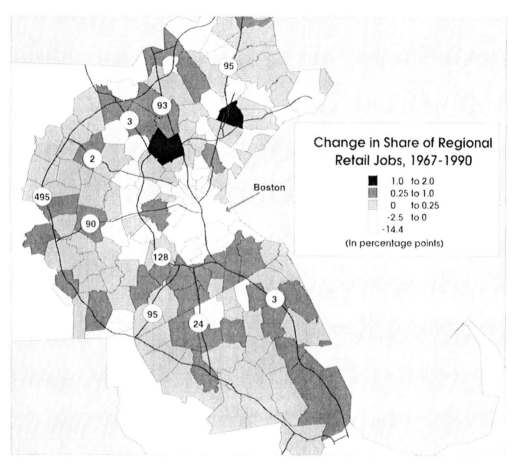

FIGURE 6.2 Change in share of regional retail jobs for Boston-area cities and towns, 1967–1990.

Source: Massachusetts Department of Employment and Training, *Employment and Wages in Massachusetts Cities and Towns* (selected years), Boston, MA.

over the region as a whole, there is no sense of centrality to the location of retail employment. While the city of Boston has many retail jobs, to a large degree, this seems to reflect the city's dominant size in relation to smaller surrounding suburban towns. When measured against its resident population, the city of Boston is actually not a retail center. Rather, the greatest concentrations of retail employment relative to population are located evenly throughout the suburbs at various transportation junctures.

To better understand these patterns requires that we examine two kinds of consumer behavior: First, how do consumers spend their money and in what kind of stores? Second, how often do they shop in stores, how far do they travel to shop, and what are their travel costs? The distribution of retail stores that emerges over the longer run will be a reaction to repeated patterns in consumer shopping behavior.

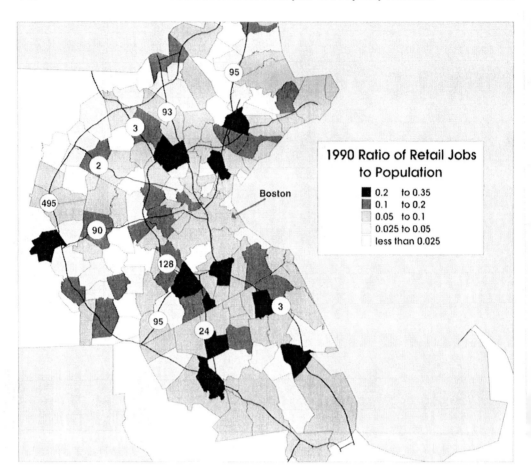

FIGURE 6.3 Ratio of retail jobs to population for Boston-area cities and towns, 1990.

Source: Massachusetts Department of Employment and Training, *Employment and Wages in Massachusetts Cities and Towns* (selected years), Boston, MA.

STORE FREQUENCY AND CONSUMER SHOPPING BEHAVIOR

Consumers spend approximately 37 percent of their total income on items purchased in retail stores. Taxes, housing, and medical services are major nonretail expenditure categories for households, although even within these categories, some purchases are made at retail establishments (e.g., prescription drugs). Most of what is known about consumer expenditure patterns comes from surveys of retail establishments.

The largest of these establishment surveys is the federal government's Census of Retail Trade, which is conducted every five years. In the Census, the government attempts to survey all retail establishments to determine both sales and employment. The sales data are reported by the detailed SIC category of the retailer, not by product lines. Thus, sales of shoes, for example, are counted in the total sales figures reported for a variety

Chapter 6 Retail Location and Market Competition

of establishments: shoe stores, discount outlets, and department stores. Likewise, not all sales reported for shoe stores are for shoes. This census also does not distinguish between those establishments that reside in retail centers and stand-alone stores. Individual establishment data is not revealed in order to preserve confidentiality. Table 6.1 illustrates the type of summary data available in the Retail Census for the Boston metropolitan area.

Establishment surveys are often used to infer conclusions about consumer expenditure patterns or expenditure shares of personal income. This can lead to problems, particularly in smaller geographic areas. The shopping expenditures made at establishments in New York City, for example, will include purchases made by suburban shoppers, international tourists, and many other consumers in addition to the residents of the city. Similarly, establishment data from rural areas will tend to underreport expenditure if mail-order business is significant or consumers travel outside of their immediate area to make major purchases. Over larger geographic areas, these problems are less present.

The Boston data in Table 6.1 suggest that about 8.2 percent of the region's total personal income is spent each year on automobiles, 10.8 percent on food and drink, 5.8 percent on merchandise in apparel or department stores, and 3.7 percent on home-related items. The data on the distribution of retail facilities is quite typical of most major metropolitan areas. The most numerous retail establishments are eating and drinking places, followed by food or grocery stores, and then apparel stores. There are almost as many automotive dealers as furniture and home-furnishings stores, and drug stores are no

TABLE 6.1 Boston CMSA Retail Census Data, 1987

SIC Code	Kind of Business	No. of Establishments	Sales ($000s)	Sales per Establishment ($000s)	Paid Employees	% of Personal Income ($000s)
	Total Retail Trade	25,419	$32,109,978	$1,263	375,662	37.2%
52	Building and Garden Materials	1,020	1,679,530	1,647	11,756	1.9
531	Department Stores	168	2,914,184	17,346	NA	3.4
54	Food Stores	3,075	5,756,751	1,872	66,223	6.7
541	Grocery Stores	1,794	5,178,412	2,887	51,992	6.0
546	Retail Bakeries	665	223,496	336	9,159	0.3
55[a]	Automotive Dealers	1,228	7,102,357	5,784	24,978	8.2
56	Apparel and Accessory Stores	2,585	2,051,969	794	26,684	2.4
562,3	Women's Clothing and Specialty Stores	1,076	809,699	753	11,754	0.9
566	Shoe Stores	712	321,123	451	4,304	0.4
57	Furniture and Home-furnishings Stores	1,887	1,555,169	824	13,442	1.8
58	Eating and Drinking Places	6,950	3,372,405	485	127,978	3.9
591	Drug and Proprietary Stores	900	1,148,159	1,276	12,978	1.3
59[b]	Miscellaneous	5,515	4,138,376	750	44,669	4.8
592	Liquor Stores	834	154,438	185	1,480	0.2
5944	Jewelry Stores	504	326,084	647	3,719	0.4
5961	Catalog and Mail-Order Houses	148	558,813	3,776	3,670	0.6

[a]Except 554, Gasoline Service Stations.
[b]Except 591, Drug and Proprietary Stores.
NA, not available.
Source: Census of Retail Trade, 1987; Boston MA–NH NECMA personal income, Survey of Current Business, April 1989.

more plentiful than building and garden material establishments. Finally, the region has only 168 department stores.

If stores all did equal volumes of business, then store frequency would be proportional to the volume of consumer purchases or aggregate sales. This is clearly not the case. In Table 6.1, average sales per retail establishment is $1.26 million. There is, however, wide variation in sales per store by SIC category. For example, eating and drinking establishments had average annual sales of $485,238, while automotive dealers had average annual sales of $5.78 million.

Many of the stores in metropolitan areas are clustered at retail centers. The National Research Bureau maintains a careful inventory of the nation's shopping centers. Let's consider their data for the Boston Metropolitan area in Table 6.2. The data in Table 6.2 reveal a clear hierarchy of retail centers. There are 144 smaller neighborhood centers and only 10 very large "super regional" centers. There are 112 community and 22 "specialized/regional" centers. It is interesting that there is no strong pattern of average store size within each category of center, although average gross leasable area per store is largest in community centers.

Unfortunately, we know very little about the clustering tendencies of different types of stores. Do apparel stores tend to locate in centers more than jewelry stores? Do food and liquor stores seek common locations? Is there any tendency for home-furnishings and department stores to cluster or to stay apart? To answer questions such as these we need location-specific data about retail establishments, data which the Census does not release.

More direct information about the patterns and ways in which households shop is sometimes gathered by small-scale interview surveys. These surveys tend to focus on two questions: the frequency and the length of shopping trips. Data about such behavior tends to be collected privately; there is no such information collected by the government. The bases of these market research surveys can be either the household at their place of residence or the shopper at the place of purchase. If we survey all households at their places of residence and all shoppers at their places of expenditure, we presumably would obtain identical information about average shopping frequency and trip length. This holds as well within retail categories. With more site-specific surveys, however, we must be careful about drawing general conclusions. A survey of shoe store patrons at a retail mall, for example, may find that reported trip lengths vastly exceed those of neighborhood-located stores and therefore cannot be used to draw region-wide generalizations.

TABLE 6.2 Boston Shopping Centers, 1992

	Neighborhood	Community	Specialized/Regional	Super Regional
Number of Centers	144	112	22	10
Average GLA (sq. ft.)	50,996	165,226	448,130	1,037,266
Average Number of Stores	11	20	69	139
Average GLA/Stores	4,540	8,196	6,504	7,494
Total Stores	1,584	2,354	1,518	1,390
Grand Total: 6,846				

GLA, gross leasable area.
Source: National Research Bureau, Shopping Center Directory, Chicago, Ill., 1992.

Chapter 6 Retail Location and Market Competition

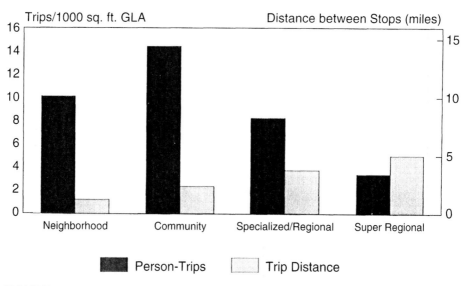

FIGURE 6.4 Travel behavior for retail shopping, 1991.

Averages for midday and P.M. trips; GLA, gross leasable area.
Source: Travel Characteristics at Large-Scale Suburban Activity Centers, Transportation Research Board, Washington, DC, 1992.

In Figure 6.4 we report the results of a broad patron survey undertaken in six metropolitan areas[1] across the four types of retail centers reported in Table 6.2. The survey provides a count of trips to each center as well as information about the origin, destination, mode of travel and trip length. The trip frequencies reported are hourly, averaged over the midday and afternoon peak periods, and the trip distances are averaged over trips coming to and going from the center.

The data in Figure 6.4 reveal the most fundamental property of shopping behavior: households make more frequent and shorter trips to neighborhood centers and less frequent, longer trips to the regional centers. However, do consumers shop this way because of the distribution of facilities, or does the distribution of facilities emerge to respond to the shopping needs of consumers? The frequency and distance that consumers travel to various stores involve questions both of economic demand as well as facility supply. The location patterns of retail stores will obviously determine the kinds of distances that consumers must travel to purchase various goods (Berry 1967). However, given the availability of retail outlets, consumers exercise considerable discretion over how often they choose to shop and how much they purchase on each trip. These decisions in turn will lead suppliers to locate differently. Let's begin by examining in more detail the decisions about shopping frequency and purchase amount.

---

[1]The shopping centers chosen were located in the following metropolitan areas: Seattle, Orange County, CA, Dallas, Atlanta, Washington, DC, and Minneapolis.

GOODS AND SHOPPING FREQUENCY

We consider the consumer's choice of shopping frequency as a simple inventory choice; should a monthly shopping trip be made to purchase and then store a whole month's supply of a good, or should a shopping trip be made daily with little or no storage involved? Obviously, the decision will depend on the type of commodity, the frequency of its use, and the cost of the trip to obtain it. In this inventory problem, we will assume that the consumer desires to obtain a given amount of a specific commodity each year at the lowest total annual cost. The following variables need to be defined.

- u: units of the good consumed annually.
- P: purchase price per unit.
- i: storage cost per year (including foregone interest).
- k: transport cost per purchase trip.
- v: frequency of trips per year.
- Q: quantity purchased per trip.

It must be remembered that the total annual consumption of the good will be simply the product of trip frequency and the quantity purchased on each trip ($u = vQ$). Perhaps less obvious is the average amount stored. Every time a trip is made, Q units are purchased. If the trip frequency is v, then $1/v$ represents the time between trips. During this interval, the consumer runs down his inventory from the Q units originally purchased to zero. Thus, the average inventory is always $Q/2$, or $u/2v$ units, and the purchase value of this average inventory is $Pu/2v$. The total cost of consuming this good annually has three components: initial purchase outlays (Pu), travel costs (kv), and storage expenses [$i(Pu/2v)$]. Storage expenses include the opportunity cost of the funds used to purchase the inventory. Thus, the total cost of consuming this good is CC:

$$CC = Pu + kv + i\left(\frac{Pu}{2v}\right) \tag{6.1}$$

The consumer selects the frequency of trips to minimize this total cost expression. This yields a value for v that will depend on the various parameters of this simple model (P, u, k, and i). The solution is:[2]

$$v = \left(\frac{iPu}{2k}\right)^{\frac{1}{2}} \tag{6.2}$$

---

[2] The minimum of Equation (6.1) can be obtained by taking its derivative with respect to v and then setting the resulting expression to zero. This yields:

$$\frac{\partial CC}{\partial v} = k - \frac{sPu}{2v^2} = 0$$

Solving for v yields:

$$v = \left(\frac{iPu}{2k}\right)^{\frac{1}{2}}$$

Examining Equation (6.2), we can see how the consumer's cost-minimizing trip frequency will vary with market and purchase parameters. If the good is consumed often (a nondurable as opposed to durable good), then more units per year (u value in Equation (6.2)) will be consumed, which will lead to more frequent trips. Likewise, if the good is more expensive (all else equal), or if storage costs are greater, then to reduce inventory costs, it will also be optimal to shop more frequently. Finally, if each trip to purchase the good is longer and more expensive (a higher k value), then the shopping frequency will be less.

This simple model could be consistent with the data on center travel behavior if we had better information about what goods shoppers purchased at each type of center; or, alternatively, what kinds of stores are located there. The hypothesis is that neighborhood centers contain stores that sell high-purchase-frequency goods: perishable goods that are hard to store (e.g., milk or fresh vegetables). Regional centers, on the other hand, should contain stores that sell low-purchase-frequency goods: small durables that are easy to inventory. The distribution of stores, however, will also be influenced by two other considerations. First, there are the fixed costs of establishing a retail outlet. If these costs are low, they could lead to a proliferation of small stores instead of a few larger ones. Second, retailers can adjust their prices to partially compensate the consumer for making a longer or shorter trip. Thus, a small number of larger centers could entice consumers to make the longer trip if they had lower prices. Clearly, retailers will adjust prices and select their locations in ways that try to increase market share and profits. To fully understand retailing, we must develop a more complicated and complete model of how retail competition and market areas emerge.

CLASSICAL RETAIL COMPETITION THEORY

In classical retailing theory, each type of commodity or good is considered to be purchased at a separate retail facility. The objective of the theory is to explain (1) the competitive pricing behavior of retailers offering the same good and (2) the density of their retail facilities and, hence, average length of purchase trip. While classical retail theory ignores the possibility of joint purchases of many goods (such as frequently occur on trips to shopping malls), the theory can explain many observed patterns in the distribution of more traditional retail facilities.

In our version of the classical theory, we will imagine that consumers are located evenly along a line at a uniform density of F households per mile, as shown in Figure 6.5. Stores also are located along this line at even intervals of distance D.[3] We will focus our attention on one representative retailer, who sets her price (for the standardized good) at P, when her competitors (on either side) charge the price P_0. All competing retailers face

---

[3]The model of space as a line suffers from the problem of how to handle the two "ends" of the line. A recent innovation in the model that avoids this problem bends the line into a circle (Tirole 1988; Stern 1972a, 1972b). Either topography is equally abstract. More realistic retail market models have been developed in two-dimensional space, but they are far more complex mathematically and have yielded little additional insight over that from the one-dimensional version.

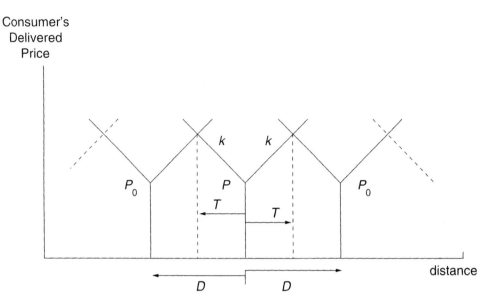

FIGURE 6.5 Retail market areas.

Note: Uniform buyer density (F) at each distance.

the same cost of retailing, composed of a marginal cost per each unit sold, *mc,* and a fixed cost of operating the store *C.*

Consumers are assumed to purchase the commodity with an annual frequency of v trips per year; on each trip, the consumer purchases one unit of the good. Consumers shop at the store whose *delivered price* is lowest, since the product is of uniform quality. The delivered price to the consumer combines the purchase price (P or P_0) with the travel cost necessary to reach the store. The cost of travel is k times the distance between the consumer and the store. Thus, emanating out of each store is a delivered price ray that represents the cost to consumers at that distance of shopping at the facility. When that ray intersects the ray (moving in the opposite direction) from a competing store, the store's *retail market area* is determined. All of this is shown in Figure 6.5, where the distance T represents the size (on one side) of our representative retailer's market area.

In this classical model of retailing, we take the frequency of purchase, the cost of travel, and the costs of retailing as parameters. The variables we determine as a function of these parameters are equilibrium prices, market areas, and the density of retail establishments:

PARAMETERS

v: frequency of purchase trips (good consumption).

k: trip cost per mile.

mc: marginal (wholesale cost) of good to retailers.

C: fixed cost for a retail facility.

F: buyer density along line.

Chapter 6 Retail Location and Market Competition

VARIABLES

P: unit price of good.
D: distance between retail stores.
T: market area boundary distance (one side).
S: individual store sales.

Market Area Boundary

The representative retailer with a price of P will find that sales S are proportional (by the purchase frequency v) to the size of its market area and density of buyers. The market area will extend to that distance T at which the delivered price of goods to a consumer is the same as that of a retailer's competitors. Since each store sells symmetrically on either side, the total market area is twice the distance of this boundary. When stores are spaced a distance of D apart, the market area boundary is determined by solving for that T at which delivered prices are equal:

$$P + kT = P_0 + k(D - T) \text{ implies } T = \frac{P_0 - P + kD}{2k} \tag{6.3}$$

Since consumers purchase one unit of the good per trip, annual sales per store, S, are:

$$S = 2TvF = vF\frac{(P_0 - P + kD)}{k} \tag{6.4}$$

Price Determination

In retail competition, each individual store faces an explicit demand curve for its product; sales depend on a store's price in comparison to that of its competitors. In effect, local stores are not price takers (as in a traditionally competitive industry), but rather set a price to maximize profits. A higher price expands unit profits, but reduces the market area and hence unit sales. The retailer's profits (π) are equal to the difference between price and wholesale costs ($P - mc$), multiplied by sales volume and minus the fixed cost of the facility (C):

$$\pi = (P - mc)vF\frac{(P_0 - P + kD)}{k} - C \tag{6.5}$$

The price that maximizes this profit function is determined with the following condition:[4]

$$P = \frac{P_0 + kD + mc}{2} \tag{6.6}$$

[4]Following the approach in footnote 2, to move from Equation (6.5) to Equation (6.6), we take the derivative of π with respect to P and set the derivative equal to zero to maximize profits:

$$\frac{\partial \pi}{\partial P} = \frac{P_0 vF - 2PvF + vFDk + (mc)vF}{k} = 0$$

Solving for P yields:

$$P = \frac{P_0 + kD + mc}{2}$$

Equation (6.6) implies that the price set by one store will react positively to a higher price set by its competitors. Every other store, however, will also follow this rule and base its prices on that of its competitors. How are these prices eventually to be determined? One theory of a competitive price game states that in equilibrium, everyone's price must be the same (Tirole 1988). If we require that $P = P_0$ and then combine this with Equation (6.6), we get the final equation for price in Equation (6.7). With this price, we also use Equation (6.3) to get market area distance T and Equation (4.4) to get the sales volume for each store, S:

$$P = kD + mc \; ; \; T = \frac{D}{2}, \; S = DvF \qquad (6.7)$$

The competitive price in Equation (6.7) involves a markup over wholesale costs. The markup increases when stores are farther apart (a higher value of D) and when trips are more costly (greater k). The reason for this behavior is that greater spacing between stores and more expensive travel confers a greater degree of monopoly power on each individual facility. When an individual store raises its price by a given amount, the percentage reduction in its market area is less when its competitors are farther away. In effect, a store's demand curve becomes more inelastic when its competition is more remote or more difficult to access.[5]

Entry and Store Density

Given the competitive equilibrium price, stores may or may not make profits. The question hinges on whether the markup in price (multiplied by sales volume) is sufficient to cover the fixed costs of running a store. If stores are sufficiently far apart, then excess profits will result, while an overly dense pattern of stores may yield losses. In the long run, stores will enter and exit the market until the profits earned (under the pricing rules in Equation (6.7)) equal zero. Given that prices follow Equation (6.7), this zero-profit condition yields Equation (6.8):

$$(P - mc)vFD - C = 0 \qquad (6.8)$$

The combination of Equations (6.7) and (6.8) represents a simple system that must be solved simultaneously in order to arrive at the final solution to the classical model. Equation (6.8) can be thought of as determining store density given prices, while Equation (6.7) determines prices given store density. Solving the two together yields:[6]

[5] Since sales equal $2vFT$ (Equation (6.4)), the percentage change in sales with respect to price is:

$$\frac{\partial S}{\partial P} \frac{P}{S} = \frac{-P}{(P_0 - P + kD)}$$

This demand elasticity is clearly smaller (inelastic) as kD increases.

[6] From Equation (6.7), $P - mc = kD$. Substituting this into Equation (6.8) yields:

$$(kD)vFD - C = 0$$

$$kD^2vF = C$$

$$D = \left(\frac{C}{kvF}\right)^{\frac{1}{2}}$$

Substituting this definition of D into $P = mc + kD$ yields the expression for P given in Equation (6.9).

$$D = \left(\frac{C}{kvF}\right)^{\frac{1}{2}} \; ; \; P = mc + \left(\frac{kC}{vF}\right)^{\frac{1}{2}} \tag{6.9}$$

The equations in (6.9) express the long-run equilibrium configuration of stores as a function only of the model's parameters. These equations have been widely used to predict how the distribution of retail stores will vary by the type of good or merchandise sold. In examining the solution equations, it is clear that:

1. Goods purchased more frequently will generate store networks that are denser, with increased competition and tighter profit margins.
2. When the fixed costs associated with retailing a particular good are higher, sparse store networks will emerge with higher profit margins.

Classical retailing theory, while simple, is able to explain some of the patterns in retail location that we observe in modern markets. Department stores have high fixed costs and tend to sell goods that are infrequently purchased. At the other extreme are food stores, establishments with low fixed costs that sell goods that have high purchase frequency. Despite having a similar aggregate business volume to that of apparel stores, building and garden stores have higher fixed costs, largely because of store size. Since they also deliver goods that are less frequently purchased than those in apparel stores, there are fewer building and garden stores in a defined area. Even within broad categories of goods, we find different retailing patterns that conform to the classical retailing model. The omnipresent convenience store has low fixed costs and sells primarily those food items purchased most frequently, relative to supermarkets.

NEOCLASSICAL RETAILING: JOINT PURCHASES AND CENTERS

While insightful, the classical theory of retailing does not explicitly consider the tendency of retail facilities to cluster at common sites in shopping centers or malls. This pattern is so pervasive it suggests that a significant expansion of the theory is needed to explain modern retailing behavior. Recent research has developed some convincing arguments to explain retail clustering that focus on the forces that link the business of different stores. Let's carefully consider first what these forces are, and, second, how they have led to clustering.

Joint Purchase Trips

In the classical theory, the consumption of each good necessitates its own set of shopping trips. Consumer shopping time and costs can be greatly reduced, however, if we assume that many purchases can be made with a single trip because those commodities are available at a common source. While the joint purchase of goods with a single trip may seem obvious, there is surprisingly little research about exactly what kinds of goods consumers like to shop for jointly (Stahl 1984). The tendency for hardware and liquor stores often to locate in the same strip centers as supermarkets suggests that these items may be frequently purchased together in a single trip. Similarly, the tendency for malls to house a wide range of goods suggests that shoes, clothing, jewelry, and housewares may also be items that consumers commonly seek on single trips. While these patterns are suggestive, it should not necessarily be presumed that modern retailing has uncovered all such linkages. The recent emergence of food vendors in shopping centers, for example, suggests that the ties between categories of consumption may change over time.

Interdependent Product Demand

With multiple purchase trips, the demand for one store's products depends not just on the store's own pricing policy, as suggested in the classical theory. In effect, the individual retail store within a center finds that its demand also varies with the general drawing power of the center as a whole. Several recent theories have elaborated this idea by defining a probabilistic measure of the demand for an individual store's products (Stahl 1984). With this approach, the likelihood of a given consumer purchasing an item from an individual store is divided into two components:

$$\text{Store Demand} = [\text{Probability: coming to center}] \times [\text{Probability: purchase at store}] \quad (6.10)$$

The first probability, that of a consumer coming to the center, is determined by the behavior of all stores at the center, as well as by that of the center's owner or manager. Consumers are more likely to shop at a center when that center has the "right" number and mix of stores in comparison to the composition of other competing centers. It is the center's management which is largely responsible for this. The probability of visits also will depend on the travel convenience of the center in relation to its competitors, or even to other stand-alone stores. Finally, the combined pricing policies of the other stores at the center also will influence the likelihood that shoppers select it as their shopping destination. The probability that a shopper will make a purchase at an individual store is influenced by the overall volume of shoppers at the center. Once shoppers are at the center, the individual store's sales largely will be determined by its own product offerings and its own price policy.

The fact that consumers shop for multiple goods on a single trip and choose the destination for this trip based on a center's overall mix and pricing policy has given rise to several kinds of retail behavior. The first of these is a leasing structure that provides the center's owner with a strong incentive to care about each tenant's business.

Retail Mix and Center Leases

Since the business of any individual store within a center depends on the center's overall mix of stores, it is important for the owner or manager of a center to consider the impact of his decisions on each of the stores in the center. For example, what assurance does an individual store have that the center's owners will not admit a strong competitor? Once initial leases are signed, what ensures that the owner will lease the center's remaining space to stores that tend to attract the kind of customers that patronize the existing stores?

If the owners of a center have a stake in the business of their tenants, then decisions about a center's mix of stores should, in principle, be based on what is in the collective best interest of the tenants. To provide this incentive, the leases for most retail space contain two types of rental payments: a normal fixed or prespecified *ground rent* and a variable *overage rent*. Overage rent is a payment which is based on the gross receipts of the tenant. Usually, overage rent is a fixed percentage of all gross receipts above an initial deductible amount. Over time, as a tenant's business grows, overage rent will increase. It is not uncommon for overage rent to comprise a significant source of income for owners of long-established and successful centers.

To understand the important role that overage rent plays in the operation of a center, consider the following dilemma faced by an owner-manager. When vacant space becomes available within a center, the type of tenant who will offer to pay the most rent for that space is that tenant for whom the existing shopper traffic in the center is most valuable. This is likely to be a tenant with little established retailing reputation, who can gain a "free ride" from the center's present clientele. If the center's owner received only ground rent, then, in principle, it would be tempting to lease the space to such a tenant. When the owner receives overage rent, on the other hand, there is a strong incentive to prefer a tenant who will also boost the sales of the existing occupants. With overage rent, the owner's income is maximized when the mix of stores reinforces each other, drawing clients who are likely to make joint purchases. This, of course, is also the mix that is most attractive to tenants.

In order to entice the "right" types of tenants into a center, owners will frequently offer identical space at widely varying ground rents to different types of stores. Such price discrimination is a feature of retailing which a number of researchers recently have studied (Brueckner 1993; Benjamin, Boyle, and Sirmans 1992). *Anchor stores* are those whose retailing reputation and name help identify the center's character, define its main clientele, and draw a core of customer traffic. As such, anchor tenants usually receive sharp discounts in ground rent. Conversely, much higher rents are normally charged to smaller stores whose business is largely dependent on attracting the eye of shoppers that come to the center because of the reputation of the anchors. Of course, owners also adjust a center's mix by simply denying tenancy to those applicants who might adversely impact a center's reputation or image.

Department Stores and Price Coordination

Since the volume of traffic at a center depends on the collective pricing policy of the stores as well as their number and mix, there is a second form of interdependence among the center's retailers. For example, when one store has a sale, the customers that are attracted to it provide an expanded client base for the other stores as well. Alternatively, if one store is failing to draw its normal clientele because its prices are not competitive, then all stores will tend to lose business.

A number of researchers have argued that this link between the prices for one commodity and the sales of others provides a strong rationale for the emergence of diverse-product department stores (Wolinsky 1983). In principle, offering many products at a single source can be accomplished with a large concentration of different individual specialty stores. The problem with this arrangement is that each individually owned store will not have an incentive to price their products aggressively in order to potentially benefit the other stores. The marginal revenue that accrues to the other stores in the center is not recouped by the individual store when deciding on its own prices.

If a concentration of specialty stores were owned by a single entity, then that owner would reap all of the gain when discounts for one commodity brought traffic—and, hence, sales—to goods that complement that commodity. Of course, these benefits will also exist when a single store offers a wide range of goods. Department stores often accept low margins on some product lines to draw customers and, hopefully, generate sales for commodities with higher markups. It is difficult to imagine an arrangement under which this form of cross-pricing could exist with a set of individually owned smaller specialty stores.

MODELING SHOPPING CENTER ATTRACTION

It should be clear now that shopping centers compete with each other in much the same manner as individual stores did in the classical theory explained previously. The difference is that a more diverse set of factors determines the customer draw of a center in contrast to the simple classical theory in which customers based their patronage on the cheapest delivered price of a single commodity. Rather than attempting to develop a mathematical theory of this more complex kind of competition, researchers have turned to simulating shopping center competition with computer models. These simulation models use data on actual shopping patterns to estimate, statistically, the factors that influence consumer patronage decisions. If done correctly, this approach not only yields some general insights about center competition, but provides a forecasting tool for evaluating the potential impact and likely patronage of new or redesigned retail facilities.

Our forecasting model will use an approach that has seen increasing application in urban research: *discrete choice analysis.* Discrete choice analysis is used to understand how economic actors select one option out of a field of mutually exclusive choices that are available to them. It has seen extensive application in market research (brand choice), in travel behavior studies (choice of travel mode), and, recently, in the locational choice made by households of where to live, or by firms of where to locate. In our application, consumers are assumed to select one and only one shopping center to patronize from among the region's competitive field. Before explaining how this choice is made, we need to first lay out the landscape of where potential consumers live and what retail choices are available to them for patronage.

The modeling begins by dividing up the market area (usually a metropolitan region) into zones. Often, these are census tracts or a combination of tracts. Let's assume that there are n of these zones and denote them with the subscript $i = 1,n$. Typically, there is considerable census information about consumers within these zones, but here we focus on the number of households and their income—the prime determinants of retail buying potential. Let's assume that there are h categories of household income and

Chapter 6   Retail Location and Market Competition

subscript them with $j = 1,h$. The median income of all households in category j is the census variable Y_j. Finally, the census data will give us the number of households in each income category, in each zone: N_{ij}.

Having dealt with the character and location of households or potential shoppers, we now turn to the region's system of shopping centers. With this model, we must identify some set of shopping centers that constitute a competitive market. We assume that m such centers have been identified and that each is located in one of the zones.[7] For convenience, we can assume that our zones have been numbered so that the first m zones ($m < n$) are those with shopping centers. We use the subscript $k = 1,m$ to refer to those zones with centers (or, alternatively, the centers themselves). Each center has a set of attributes that our households find desirable when shopping. These attributes can include the size and mix of stores, the availability of parking, the degree of enclosure of the center, and measures of the center's product pricing. As we will see later, information about the size and character of the center is widely available, while surveys of product pricing generally are not. Limited only by the availability of data, we assume that there are g such center attributes and call the level of attribute $l = 1,g$ at center $k = 1,m$: Z_{lk}.

Finally, we need some measure of travel cost (including time) between all of the zones in our system. Such travel matrices are frequently available from local planning agencies, who use them for long range development of a region's transportation system. In fact, we do not need the complete n-by-n set of travel costs, only those between the n zones in which households live and the subset of these (numbering m) that have centers. We label these costs T_{ik}, where the first subscript refers to one of the n residential zones, and the second refers to one of the m zones with centers.

Within this landscape, households will evaluate the desirability of each center as a shopping destination based both on the center's attributes as well as on the costs of traveling there. To keep our model as simple as possible, we assume that the desirability of a center to households in a particular income category can be expressed in terms of a simple linear utility measure. The parameters of this linear utility measure will be different for each category of income. Thus, the utility that a household of type j, living in zone i would derive from shopping at center k (U_{ijk}) can be written as a linear function of center attributes, travel costs, and a series of coefficients, or utility parameters, that depend on the category of the household.

$$U_{ijk} = \alpha_j T_{ik} + \sum_{l=1}^{g} \mu_{lj} Z_{lk} \qquad (6.11)$$

In Equation (6.11), the first term represents the (dis)utility that households of type j, living in zone i, derive from traveling to center k. This depends on the travel costs between i and k (T_{ik}) and the disutility of traveling. The coefficient, α_j, is the marginal disutility of traveling, and is allowed to vary by household income category. If wealthier households dislike traveling more than those that are less wealthy, then $\alpha_1 < \alpha_2 < \alpha_3$, and so on. Alternatively, if wealthier households can afford to travel farther, the magnitude of the αs will be the reverse.

[7] We have assumed here that each center is in a unique zone only to keep the notation simple. It is easy to incorporate more than one center into each zone, as long as we keep track of which zone each center is in.

The second part of Equation (6.11) is a summation of similar terms, numbering g. For each of the center attributes ($l = 1, g$), the coefficient μ_{lj} is the marginal valuation that a household in income category j places on a unit measure of shopping center attribute l. When multiplied by center k's level of that attribute, Z_{lk}, we get the contribution to utility from that center feature. Our linear model assumes that a household shopper's utility is the sum of all these terms.

The second part of a discrete choice model is to convert household shopper utilities into probabilities of actually patronizing a particular center. If consumer utilities were known and could be measured with certainty, then each shopper would simply select the center with the highest utility. More realistically, some attributes of a center are known by consumers only with uncertainty. It is also possible that consumer valuations of center attributes may contain random elements as well. If shopper utilities have a random term in addition to the variables in Equation (6.11), then, for each given shopper, there will be a probability that a particular center yields higher utility than all the others. If there is a probability that a particular center yields higher utility than all others, then there is also a patronage probability that each household from income category j, living in zone i, will shop in center k. This probability (P_{ijk}) often is written:[8]

$$P_{ijk} = \frac{e^{U_{ijk}}}{\sum_{k=1}^{m} e^{U_{ijk}}} \quad (6.12)$$

The summation in the denominator of Equation (6.12) covers all centers (including the particular center in the numerator). Thus, when the shopping probabilities are summed over centers, the result will always equal 1. In effect, a consumer must select one center (out of the m available), and Equation (6.12) determines how the utility that a household derives from each center leads, in turn, to shopping probabilities. It should be clear that no matter how large a particular center's utility is, the expression for P_{ijk} can never exceed 1. Similarly, no matter how low a center's utility is, P_{ijk} can only approach zero. The sensitivity of a center's probability to changes in one of its attributes (the Z_{lk}) depends on that attribute's coefficient in the utility expression: μ_{lj}. For example, if μ_{21} is large, then households in the first income category find the second attribute to be important in their shopping utility. In this case, the probabilities of patronage for these households will change sharply if the values of the Z_{2k} are different between the centers. Small values for an attribute's coefficients mean that both utilities and shopping probabilities are relatively insensitive to variation in this characteristic.

A center's *total patronage* depends on three considerations. The first is the center's attributes in comparison to those of other centers. The second is the center's location relative to its competitors. These two combine to determine the shopping probabilities for any given household. The third consideration is the spatial distribution, or location, of

---

[8]The derivation of the probability expression in Equation (6.12) depends completely on the nature of the random term that is added to the utility expression in Equation (6.11). If the random term obeys the Weibull probability distribution, then Equation (6.12) reflects the probability that a given center has the highest utility among all centers. A formal derivation and application of this approach to urban travel is found in Domencich and McFadden (1975).

households. A center can have the ideal mix of attributes, but if it is not located near a large number of households that value that mix, or if other centers are located closer to those households, it will not generate sufficient traffic. A center will be successful when those consumers for whom the center has a high shopping probability are both nearby and plentiful in number. Summing across the zones in which households live, i, the total patronage of center k by income group j (S_{kj}) is given in Equation (6.13). Overall patronage will be the sum of that patronage from each income group j.

$$S_{kj} = \sum_{i=1}^{n} P_{ijk} N_{ij} \qquad (6.13)$$

Thus, given the spatial pattern of households within a metropolitan area and an identifiable market of competitive centers, a discrete choice model can be developed to predict shopping center patronage. Two key ingredients remain to be discussed. The first is how to use information about current shopping patterns to estimate the parameters in the utility function (6.11). Without numerical estimates for α_j and μ_{ij}, the model cannot be used. The second is how to forecast with the model and evaluate the likely impacts of new centers or changes to existing centers. To implement the model, we consider a specific application in the Boston metropolitan region.

FORECASTING SHOPPING BEHAVIOR IN BOSTON

In the mid-1980s, the logistic choice model described above was implemented for the Boston metropolitan area to study the competition among the region's major shopping malls.[9] The metropolitan area was limited to include the central city of Boston and the approximately 104 towns covering the closer-in suburban communities. Towns were used as zones, with the exception of the city of Boston, which, because of its size, was split into 23 separate traffic zones. Using annual town data and the 1980 U.S. Census, the region's planners developed estimates of the number of households in each of these zones by five income categories. The field of large competitive malls was limited to 10 super regional and the three largest regional centers. Using only published information (mainly from the 1987 Census of Retail Trade), nine center attributes were identified, including size of the center (in square feet), number of parking spaces, total number of stores, number of stores in each of five categories, and parking costs. These attributes for each of the 13 Boston shopping centers are provided in Table 6.3.

In order to estimate shopper utility parameters, the Boston study used the results of a privately conducted (by telephone) home-interview survey undertaken during the mid-1980s about retail behavior. In this survey, households were asked whether they had visited each of the 13 centers within the last week. The interview covered a sample of residents in 40 of the towns used by the model, and respondents also reported the category of their household income. In total, slightly less than 4,000 households were

---

[9]An earlier version of the model is found in Weisbrod, Parcells, and Kern (1984). The model is now copyrighted by the MIT Center for Real Estate and Cambridge Systematics, Inc.

TABLE 6.3 Characteristics of Boston-Area Shopping Centers

	Size (000 sq. ft.)	Parking Spaces	Stores	Discount Stores	Department Stores	Variety Stores	Furniture Stores	Restaurants	Parking Costs[a]
Boston CBD	1,750	0	300	1	2	9	29	247	$3.50
Back Bay	886	0	402	0	3	0	15	250	3.50
Harvard Square	635	0	300	0	0	0	10	50	2.50
Chestnut Hill	440	2,400	67	0	2	2	11	17	0
New England	458	3,300	27	1	1	5	2	3	0
North Shore	1,550	6,700	102	1	3	5	7	8	0
Liberty Tree	1,020	5,500	118	2	0	2	10	22	0
Burlington	1,137	6,000	100	0	4	6	10	13	0
Dedham	575	2,500	50	2	1	3	4	4	0
South Shore	1,300	6,000	130	0	4	4	11	13	0
Natick	549	3,000	91	1	2	4	12	11	0
Lowell	400	3,000	161	1	2	2	15	40	0
Brockton	450	3,000	117	1	2	4	13	21	0

[a]Cost of parking is for two hours.
Source: Census of Retail Trade, 1987; and telephone surveys by the MIT Center for Real Estate.

surveyed. These survey responses were then used to estimate the aggregate shopping patterns for each town or zone. Based on the survey, the total number of shoppers from zone i with income j who went to shopping center k (S_{ijk}) was estimated.[10]

Given these data, the utility parameters in Equation (6.11) can be estimated using standard regression analysis.[11] Consider the ratio of the number of shoppers patronizing each center, relative to some other center. Arbitrarily selecting the first center, we calculate the ratio, S_{ij1}/S_{ijk}, and then take the natural log of this ratio as the dependent variable: $\ln(S_{ij1}/S_{ijk})$. If we do this calculation for the right hand side of Equation (6.12), we first get the ratio $e^{U_{ij1}}/e^{U_{ijk}}$; taking the log of this ratio yields: $U_{ij1} - U_{ijk}$. The final step in developing a regression equation is to substitute in the definition of shopper utility from Equation (6.11). The end result is a linear regression equation where the dependent variable is the log ratio of shopper frequencies and the independent variables are differences in center attributes and travel costs.

$$\ln\left(\frac{S_{ij1}}{S_{ijk}}\right) = \alpha_j (T_{i1} - T_{ik}) + \sum_{l=1}^{g} \mu_{lj} (Z_{l1} - Z_{lk}) \qquad (6.14)$$

Equation (6.14) was estimated with the dependent variable the log of patronage for center k ($k = 2,13$), versus center 1, for each of the 40 ($i = 1,40$) respondent residence

---

[10]Let R_{ijk} be the number of respondents in zone i, with income in category j, who shopped at center k; and let R_{ij} be the number interviewed. Then the estimated aggregate pattern of shopping (S_{ijk}) can be calculated from the responses using the known distribution of households (N_{ij}) as:

$$S_{ijk} = N_{ij}(R_{ijk}/R_{ij})$$

[11]An alternative approach is to take each respondent's answer as 13 discrete observations: a 1 if the respondent visited a particular center and a 0 if he or she did not. A technique called *maximum likelihood estimation* seeks to estimate utility parameters so that the predicted probabilities from Equations (6.11) and (6.12) are as similar as possible to this pattern of 0s and 1s.

Chapter 6 Retail Location and Market Competition

zones. A separate regression was estimated for each income category of households ($j = 1,5$), and each of these regressions had 480 observations (12×40 zone-center combinations). The independent variables for each observation are the differences in center attributes and travel costs. Table 6.4 gives the estimated values for the utility parameters from the Boston sample.

The first row in Table 6.4 gives the marginal disutility of travel distance (α_j) for households in each of the five income categories. It is clear that as income increases, households have less aversion to traveling and are therefore willing to shop at ever greater distances. The next nine lines give the estimated marginal utilities for each of the center attributes, again by the income category of household (μ_{lj}). The number of both discount and variety stores in a center, for example, create strong marginal utility for the lowest income categories, but this drops as income rises, and eventually turns strongly negative for the highest income group. With department and furniture stores, this pattern of utilities is just the reverse. The number of restaurants brings positive utility to all groups, but more so to households with greater income. Center size, as measured either by square feet or number of stores, is valued by lower-income households, but not by those with higher income.

The results in Table 6.4 illustrate the potential of this type of analysis in sorting out the importance of travel costs and center attributes in attracting different types of shoppers. From the parameters in Table 6.4, we predict the number of shoppers by income for each of the 13 centers in this example (Table 6.5). The center with the largest predicted total volume of trips is the South Shore center. While this center has one of the best attribute mixes (for a broad base of shoppers), its success is largely a result of location. It has only two small competitors (Dedham and Brockton) in the entire southern half of the Boston metropolitan area. By contrast, seven large centers split the equally sized western and northern parts of the region. By income class, Boston's prestigious Back Bay

TABLE 6.4 Estimated Values for Attributes of Major Boston-Area Shopping Centers

	Marginal Utility by Income Categories (j)				
	1	2	3	4	5
Travel, α_j:	−0.2962	−0.2224	−0.1486	−0.0748	−0.001
Center Characteristics, μ_{lj}:					
Square Feet	0.0021	0.0012	0.0003	−0.0006	−0.0015
No. Stores	0.0261	0.0162	0.0063	−0.0036	−0.0135
No. Discount Stores	1.154	0.488	−0.178	−0.844	−1.5
No. Department Stores	−1.35	−0.36	0.63	1.62	2.61
No. Variety Stores	1.595	0.83	0.065	−0.7	−1.465
No. Furniture Stores	−0.03	0.06	0.15	0.24	0.33
No. Restaurants	0.0118	0.0136	0.0154	0.0172	0.019
No. Parking Spaces	0.00028	0.00046	0.00064	0.00082	0.001
Parking Costs	−0.042	−0.024	−0.006	0.012	0.03

Source: MIT Center for Real Estate; Cambridge Systematics, Inc.

TABLE 6.5 Predicted Number of Shoppers for Major Boston-Area Shopping Centers, by Income

	Income Categories (j)					
	1	2	3	4	5	Total
Boston CBD	9,318	20,928	31,218	20,928	2,545	84,938
Back Bay	84	1,009	8,244	34,806	27,990	72,134
Harvard Square	25,517	23,196	9,021	1,496	46	59,276
Chestnut Hill	117	1,506	8,145	24,334	13,674	47,776
New England	19,959	11,047	1,639	42	0	32,687
North Shore	8,728	19,568	16,582	1,431	13	46,322
Liberty Tree	8,985	10,193	4,010	144	0	23,333
Burlington	7,020	20,864	31,160	15,868	932	75,843
Dedham	8,555	6,610	1,157	77	1	16,400
South Shore	8,799	23,400	45,283	56,054	12,529	146,066
Natick	7,669	15,974	15,530	3,052	137	42,363
Lowell	357	2,154	8,568	12,326	3,263	26,668
Brockton	9,806	18,175	12,119	2,751	149	42,999
Total	114,915	174,624	192,676	173,309	61,281	716,805

Source: MIT Center for Real Estate; Cambridge Systematics, Inc.

area and the Chestnut Hill Mall draw the largest predicted volume of wealthy patronage, both absolutely and as a percentage of their total traffic. The New England, Dedham, and Liberty Tree centers are predicted to attract mostly low- and moderate-income households. Remember that both attributes and location are important. Harvard Square, for example, attracts mostly low-income shoppers, which is largely due to its location in the midst of a very large student population.

As an exercise in market research, we can pose the question of where a new 300,000 square-foot department store would generate the most additional traffic. Since total shopper patronage is fixed in this model, expanding retail facilities at one center will merely draw business from competitors. To study this issue, we repeatedly solve the model with an additional department store and 300,000 square feet at each center. We then compare the increases in number of shoppers across the possible investments. Referring back to the coefficients in Table 6.4, we might suspect that the addition of a new department store would be most valuable to a center with a predominantly higher-income patronage. This is because the utility of a department store is slightly negative for the two lowest-income groups, and then switches signs and becomes highly positive for wealthy shoppers. Sure enough, simulations reveal that between 70,000 and 80,000 more shoppers are attracted to Back Bay, Chestnut Hill, and South Shore when a large department store is added to those centers. By contrast, only 8,000 to 19,000 new shoppers are attracted to the Liberty Tree or Dedham centers.

MARKETS AND RETAIL SALES

The retailing models developed in this chapter have all had as their premise the assumption that total retail sales or patronage (in a particular market) are fixed and that individual stores or centers simply compete for a share of the pie. To economists, who view sales or consumption as determined by income, this assumption seems obvious. Many experienced retailers, however, cling to the notion that new retailing facilities will actually expand aggregate sales or generate greater consumption within a market. In some situations it is possible to reconcile the two views, in particular when a market has been narrowly defined.

The creation of a large shopping facility on the north side of town, for example, could easily expand the aggregate sales of north-side retailers. All that would be needed is for south-side shoppers to begin patronizing the new facility and for northern residents to cease their occasional outings to retail facilities in the south. Total sales have increased because sales imports into the market have increased, while sales exports have decreased.

With almost any market definition, there will be some leakage of sales out of the area and some importing of sales into it. When the market area definition is appropriate, these flows of trade will be small and insignificant. When a market is too narrowly defined, however, external trade flows can be substantial and can be altered through the provision of more retail space.

Aggregate sales within a market can also change with retail facilities if the market is supply-constrained. Rural areas frequently export much retail expenditure through mail-order sales or through occasional long-distance shopping trips. The opening of a rural shopping center frequently attracts some of this business and creates the impression that aggregate retail activity has increased. Total consumer expenditure by local residents has not grown, it is only the *local* share of that consumption that has increased.

Throughout this chapter, we have assumed that retail expenditure requires the patronage of retail facilities, which, in turn, involves consumer travel. Clearly, technology is challenging this traditional notion. The rapid growth of mail-order catalog sales over the last 20 years is a testament to the desire by consumers to acquire the merchandise they demand with a minimum of effort. Television shopping offers the promise of somewhat better visual inspection of goods than can be accomplished through the printed medium. Whether these remote shopping technologies will ever be able to replace the desire of consumers to inspect goods personally is an important question. When the quality and character of goods is quite varied, nothing can replace direct inspection. When goods are more uniform or differ only in clearly obvious dimensions, remote shopping offers a viable alternative. Retail theory in the future may focus less on the competition among local retailers and more on the competition between local retailers and remote shopping sources.

SUMMARY

In this chapter, we explore the locational choice of retail firms that are linked to households as a market. As population has suburbanized, retail facilities have followed to the point where many center cities are no longer the major retail hub of a metropolitan area.

- There are distinct patterns to the location of retail facilities. A dense pattern of small, neighborhood shopping centers coexists with a sparse distribution of large, regional centers. Shopping trips to neighborhood centers are more frequent and of shorter length, while trips to regional centers are longer, but less frequent.

- Shoppers purchase different items with quite different frequencies that depend both on the inherent rate of use and also on the cost of inventorying or storing the item. The density of stores that provide certain items will depend positively on the frequency of purchase and negatively on the costs of establishing a retail facility. Thus, the mix of neighborhood and regional centers emerges naturally in reaction to shopper behavior.

- Retail stores often cluster together, historically in business districts, and more recently in shopping centers. Clustering occurs because consumers can visit many stores and purchase different items with a single trip, greatly economizing on retail travel. The mix of stores that cluster together can be quite different in a business district than in a shopping center. The single ownership of a shopping center allows the cluster or mix of stores to be specifically designed to complement each other.

- Competition among shopping centers largely is a zero sum game. One center's sales gains occur at the expense of other centers.

REFERENCES AND ADDITIONAL READINGS

BENJAMIN, J., G. BOYLE, AND C. F. SIRMANS. "Price Discrimination in Shopping Center Leases." *Journal of Urban Economics* 32 (1992): 299–317.

BERRY, B. *Geography of Market Centers and Retail Distribution*, chaps. 1–3. Englewood Cliffs, NJ: Prentice Hall, 1967.

BRUECKNER, JAN. "Inter Store Externalities and Space Allocation in Shopping Centers." *Journal of Real Estate Finance and Economics* 7,1 (1993): 5–17.

CAPOZZA, DENNIS, AND ROBERT VAN ORDER. "A Generalized Model of Spatial Competition." *American Economic Review* 68 (1978): 896–908.

DOMENCICH, T., AND DANIEL MCFADDEN. *Urban Travel Demand: a Behavioral Analysis*. Amsterdam: North Holland, 1975.

STAHL, K. "Location and Spatial Pricing Theory with Non-Convex Transportation Schedules." *Bell Journal of Economics* 13 (1982): 575–582.

STERN, N. "The Optimal Structure of Market Areas." *Journal of Economic Theory* (April 1972a).

STERN, N. "The Optimum Size of Market Areas." *Journal of Economic Theory* (April 1972b).

TIROLE, JEAN. *The Theory of Industrial Organization*. Cambridge: MIT Press, 1988.

WEISBROD, PARCELLS, AND KERN. "A Disaggregate Model for Predicting Shopping Area Market Attraction." *Journal of Retailing* 60, 1 (1984).

WOLINSKY, A. "Retail Trade Concentration Due to Consumers' Imperfect Information." *Bell Journal of Economics* 14 (Spring 1983).

Section 3 Macroeconomic Analysis of Property Markets

CHAPTER 7

ECONOMIC GROWTH AND METROPOLITAN REAL ESTATE MARKETS

The primary objective of this chapter is to provide an understanding of the underlying determinants of regional or metropolitan growth, and, hence, the demand for local real estate. In this analysis, we ignore how firms and households locate *within* regions (the *intraregional* location decision), and consider the economic activity of a metropolitan area as a monolithic market. As a result, we focus on the longer-run issues of how and why economic activity chooses to locate *among* different regions (the *interregional* location decision). It is these decisions that ultimately determine how fast a region grows or declines. As discussed in Chapters 3 through 6, the size and rate of economic growth in a metropolitan region are the crucial determinants of how its real estate market evolves and changes over time. Thus, the first task in real estate macroeconomic analysis is to understand regional or metropolitan economies, the factors that determine their economic growth, and the impact that this growth has on a region's various markets. We build this understanding of regional growth using a simple comparative static analysis similar to that used in Chapter 1.

We begin with the definition of a regional economy and the particular economic features that distinguish regions from nations. Regions are more open economies than nations, meaning that there is a greater flow of products and services among a nation's regions than between nations. The openness of local economies gives rise to a range of conceptual as well as measurement issues. Two main forces tend to propel regional economic growth: demand for regional products (which generates jobs), and the supply of regional factors (mainly the work force to fill those jobs).

To understand how these supply and demand factors determine regional growth, we build a simple three-sector model of a metropolitan economy. The three markets in the model are the output market for goods and services produced in the region and two factor markets—the labor market and the real estate market (composed of both structures and land). These three markets are closely interrelated. Labor and real estate are inputs required to produce regional output and are paid for with the income generated from the sale of that output. The payments necessary to attract labor and develop real estate determine the cost of local production, which then affects an area's competitiveness and, ultimately, the sales of its products. The relationship among these three metropolitan markets and the national economy shapes the sources of economic growth or decline.

One source of economic growth is the sale of products produced within one region to customers outside of that region. Such exports bring economic resources into the area. The national business cycle, an area's industrial mix, and the competitiveness of local industries all help to determine the demand for a particular area's output.

To produce regional output, however, the primary factors of production (labor, structure, and land) must be readily available within the region. The demographic makeup of an area and the mix of skills embodied in the current workforce provide an important indigenous source of labor. Without local labor, a region must attract workers from other areas, which is generally more difficult than retaining local workers. An area's climate, amenities, and public services all contribute to determining how easy it is to attract (and keep) a supply of labor.

A metropolitan area's stock of real estate structures (residential, commercial, and industrial), together with its ability to develop land, represents the other important resource. Without affordable housing for the area's workers and buildings for its firms, output cannot be produced. The capacity of a region to readily expand its supply of real estate is a crucial ingredient for ensuring continued economic growth. Without this capacity, real estate rents will rise, eventually increasing both the wages that must be paid to labor and the prices that must be charged for output. Such increases in the cost of local production can eventually choke off economic expansion and stifle long-term growth.

REGIONAL ECONOMIES

Regions are like nations with two important exceptions. First, regions do not have a separate currency and, as a result, do not control their own supply of money. The absence of local currency means that regions cannot expand or contract their money supply in order to stimulate or slow down their economic growth. Thus, regions largely are at the mercy of their broader national economies. The lack of local currencies also means that fluctuations in exchange rates cannot act as a buffer to broader economic shocks. A region experiencing a decline in demand for its products cannot devalue its currency so as to reduce imports and stimulate exports. Rather, local employment and wages must absorb the full negative impact of the change.

Second, regional economies, unlike national economies, are fully open. This implies that there are no legal impediments (tariffs, quotas, or other barriers) to the flow

Chapter 7 Economic Growth and Metropolitan Real Estate Markets

of goods, labor, or investment across their borders. Together with a common language and culture, openness permits a high degree of trade in goods and services among regions. Open economies can specialize, trade with one another extensively, and provide each other with needed factors. A slow-growing region normally will save more than it invests, passing the excess funds to a rapidly growing region. A region with a high birthrate may send its workers (through out-migration) to fast-growing regions with lower birthrates.

To illustrate the openness of regional economies, we examine the regional accounts for two states, Florida and Pennsylvania. We use state data because information on regional accounts is not available by metropolitan area. We divide each state economy into income accounts (the value of all payments received) and output or product accounts (the value of all goods and services produced). States often tax the income of individuals and firms and usually require companies to report their output, payroll, workforce, and investment expenses. In theory, these data permit construction of a system of accounts for state output and income not unlike that created by nations. In practice, such efforts present significant problems, and there is no single source of data on state output and income accounts. The task of constructing account data for a state is complicated by two implications of the openness of regional economies. First, with free state borders, state governments do not directly record imports and exports. These figures must be estimated from surveys of firm shipments. Second, large firms frequently do business in a number of states, and often do not record the value of the goods or services produced at each branch plant. Therefore, states must estimate the value of the output produced within their boundaries. Despite these limitations, state output accounts sometimes are produced by government agencies or private consulting firms. Income accounts are somewhat easier to construct and are often produced by states and consulting firms.

Table 7.1 provides income and product accounts for Florida and Pennsylvania for 1991, courtesy of Regional Economic Modeling, Inc. As shown in Table 7.1, Florida and Pennsylvania are somewhat similar in terms of value of income received and output produced. This is not surprising, given that the two states have similar populations; in 1990, the resident populations of Florida and Pennsylvania were 12.9 million and 11.9 million, respectively.

The first series of accounts in Table 7.1 examines total regional income or factor payments (Y). Regional income has two components: wages and salaries, and other income. Other income is composed of all unearned income (y) (e.g., dividends and interest) and government transfers (G) (e.g., social security and welfare payments). In these data, we have reliable figures for total income and wages but no explicit measure of the various components of other income. As a result, we estimate other income as a residual, $Y - w$. The value of wage income (w) is quite similar in the two states, but other income in Florida is noticeably higher than in Pennsylvania. Some of this other income represents a distribution of profits or interest income (y) to local residents from the national capital market. The magnitude of this income depends on the wealth of local residents through their ownership of stock, bonds, and savings accounts. It should be pointed out that unearned income received by residents of a region (y) may have little relationship to the profits of local companies (π). Locally-generated profits may go to investors in other

TABLE 7.1 Summary of Output and Income Accounts for Florida and Pennsylvania, 1991

	Florida ($ billions)	Pennsylvania ($ billions)
Income Accounts *		
Income (Y)	262	242
Wages (w)	126	127
Other Income ($y + G$)	136	115
Consumption (C)	260	193
Private	214	161
Government	46	32
Federal Taxes (T)	38	41
Savings (S)	−36	8
Output Accounts†		
Output (Q)	219	211
Wages (w)	126	127
Profits and Rents (π)	93	84
Consumption (C)	260	193
Investment (I)	44	27
Imports (M)	175	153
Exports (X)	92	144
INCOME (Y) − OUTPUT (Q)	43	31

*Other Income is calculated as ($Y - w$); savings are calculated as ($Y - C - T$).
†Profits and rents are calculated as ($Q - w$); in Florida, $C - M + I + X$ does not quite equal Q due to rounding.
Source: Regional Economics Modeling, Inc.

states and much unearned income is derived from companies located outside the state. Regional unearned income depends heavily on the national economy, particularly on interest rates and corporate profits. It is not surprising that other income in Florida is 18.3 percent higher than in Pennsylvania, given its larger proportion of elderly residents.

The next set of entries under the income account for Table 7.1 examines how regional income is spent. Regional consumption (C) is divided into two components: private and public. Private consumption is simply the value of all privately produced goods and services used by state residents. Public consumption represents the estimated value of government services produced within the state (e.g., education, law enforcement) and consumed by local residents through the payment of state and local taxes. Thus, this entry in Table 7.1 implicitly accounts for the payment of most nonfederal taxes.

The role of the federal government in a region's economy is more complicated. Unlike state and local governments, federal taxes paid (T) by a region need not balance with federal services or transfers received (G). Regional residents pay taxes to the federal government and receive various forms of federally assisted cash payments. Taxes are separately recorded in Table 7.1 (T), while federal receipts (G) show up largely within the other income category. With progressive federal income taxation, poorer regions tend to receive more of these payments (e.g., social security or unemployment insurance) than they pay in taxes. For wealthier regions, the reverse is true.[1]

Income that is not spent on taxes or consumption must be saved (S). The savings rate for individuals in the U.S. is typically very small, in the neighborhood of 4 percent of income. Local savings get reinvested around the country through the operation of an efficient national capital market. Accumulated local savings brings unearned income back to the region. Savings within a state are not explicitly measured and must be estimated as a residual from income: $S = Y - C - T$. The savings estimate for Pennsylvania (3 percent of disposable income) is consistent with national savings behavior. In Florida, however, there is a large dissavings. This dissavings might be expected in a state with a large retired population, and helps to explain how Florida's consumption can be so much greater than Pennsylvania's, despite having similar income. The income accounts of a region can be summarized with the following equation:

$$Y = w + y + G = C + S + T \tag{7.1}$$

The second set of accounts in Table 7.1 measures regional output (Q), the value of all goods and services produced within the two regions. Total output equals wage payments (w) plus locally earned rents and profits (π). In the data, we have estimates of total state output and wages but no explicit measures of local profits and rent. We estimated local profits and rents as a residual, $Q - w$. Comparing the investment (I) and savings (S) figures in the table illustrates how little local profits or savings have to do with regional investment. Pennsylvania shows less investment than Florida but a savings rate of 3 percent while Florida is dissaving at a rate of 14 percent of income.

Goods produced within each region are exported (X) or are used either for local consumption or for building new local capital (investment, I). The consumption of locally produced goods can be estimated from total consumption (C) by simply subtracting imports (M). Investment (I) will generally depend on the region's rate of growth. Exports (X) traditionally were thought to consist mainly of manufactured goods. In today's economy, however, there is a growing recognition that many services can be export goods as well. Examples of exported services include an educational institution with many out-of-state students, an investment bank with worldwide clients, or an advertising firm with national clients. As shown in Table 7.1, Florida's more service-based economy exports 42 percent of its output—considerably less than the manufacturing-oriented economy of Pennsylvania, which exports 68 percent of its output. Despite having fewer exports, Florida imports more than Pennsylvania. These import-export figures show that states are far more open than the U.S. national economy, where foreign trade typically constitutes only about 10 percent of output. The output account data can be summarized in Equation (7.2).

$$Q = w + \pi = C - M + I + X \tag{7.2}$$

If we examine the difference between income received and output produced within a region, Equations (7.1) and (7.2) yield two definitions:

---

[1] Purchases of regional goods and services by the federal government (e.g., through defense or public works contracts) are not a transfer, but rather represent an export.

$$Y - Q = y + G - \pi = S - I + T - X + M; \text{ or:}$$
$$X - M = [S - I] + [T - G] + [\pi - y] \tag{7.3}$$

Equation (7.3) clearly shows, as Table 7.1 also illustrated, that a region's income need not equal its output. Given the openness of state economies, there is no reason to expect that output and income will be the same. Equation (7.3) shows that a region's trade balance in terms of goods and services must be counterbalanced by the sum of three financial flows: a net capital flow, a net federal government transfer flow, and a net profits flow. A state with a trade surplus must contribute money to the national economy, while that with a deficit needs financial infusions. Florida has a strongly negative trade flow ($X - M = -83$), whereas Pennsylvania has a closely balanced one ($X - M = -9$). In terms of capital, Florida's negative savings rate and high investment level represent a strong inflow of funds ($S - I = -80$), whereas in Pennsylvania, positive savings and smaller investment generate a much smaller capital inflow ($S - I = -19$). The type of accounting data in Table 7.1 does not allow us to separately distinguish transfers from the federal government nor profits generated by local businesses within each state. However, the sum of the two can be estimated as a residual. In Florida, there is a slight positive net combined transfer of federal government and profit income ($G - T + y - \pi = 5$). This same net combined transfer in Pennsylvania is negative ($G - T + y - \pi = -10$). Through the positive inflow of capital and transfer income, Florida is able to consume all of its income and import almost twice what it exports. Pennsylvania's more normal pattern of trade and consumption matches much smaller net capital flows.

Using data such as that in Table 7.1, it is possible to illustrate how the demand for a region's products or the infusion of new investment and transfers gets translated into regional income or output. A dollar that enters the region through any of these channels gets recycled many times. It first goes to pay for local factors of production in the form of wages or structure rents. When received, the dollar becomes income for factor owners. This income is then spent, partially on imported goods (the exports of other regions), but also on goods and services produced for local consumption only (e.g., dry cleaning, restaurants, utilities, etc.). Expenditures on imported goods leak out of the region, while expenditures on locally-produced goods and services form the income of other local factor owners. When they, in turn, spend it, some portion again escapes out of the region, while some is retained. In the end, a dollar of export sales or transfers generates some amount of local production (or income) that significantly exceeds the original dollar.

The relationship between exports (or transfers and investment) and the resulting local income or production generated is often referred to as a regional economic *multiplier*. A simple model can illustrate how such a multiplier is determined if we add the following two behavioral equations to the accounting identities in Equations (7.1) through (7.3):

$$C = bY$$
$$M = mC \tag{7.4}$$

Multiplier models generally have at least two such behavioral equations. These involve parameters which are based on assumptions about economic actions (as opposed to identities which are true by definition). The first of these assumes that some constant fraction (*b*) of income is consumed (the remaining fraction of income (1 − *b*) is saved); the second assumes that some fraction (*m*) of consumption is imported.² Using the identities in Equations (7.1) through (7.3) and Equations (7.4), we can solve for regional income as:

$$Y = \frac{X + I + G + y - \pi}{1 - b(1 - m)} \qquad (7.5)$$

In Equation (7.5), $1/[1 - b(1 - m)]$ is the multiplier. For every dollar of exports sold, investment made, or transfers received (*X,I,G,y*), $1/[1 - b(1 - m)]$ dollars of income are eventually generated. Much research has been undertaken on the magnitude of such multipliers. The data in Table 7.1 suggest that the import share (*m*) is about 0.7, and the consensus is that the marginal propensity to consume (*b*) is about 0.8 or 0.9. This gives a multiplier of 1.3—$1 of exports generates about $1.30 of local income or production.

While regional accounts and multiplier analysis are used quite often with state data, the only comparable information available at the metropolitan level is data about employment. Using such information, economists have developed metropolitan employment multipliers. This analysis assumes that export sales are proportional to employment in export industries and that each job created in an export industry translates into some multiple number of total local jobs. Movements over time in export-sector jobs and total regional employment confirm this relationship and yield similar estimates to those based on output and income accounts for long-run multipliers.

The regional multiplier model presents an extremely simple view of a region's economy, one that is mostly of illustrative value. Multiplier models assume that local production is never supply-constrained; hence, demand is the sole determinant of regional growth. But labor, capital, and real estate are all essential to the local production of output. What if these factors are not easily available and production cannot be readily expanded? Equally important, is it ever the case that regional growth results from changes in a region's supply situation, rather than from expanded demand? To investigate these possibilities, we need to develop a more complete model of a region's economy.

A THREE-SECTOR MODEL OF METROPOLITAN ECONOMIC GROWTH

To better understand the simple relationships between economic growth and a region's real estate market, we need a complete picture of the local economy. We begin this model by dividing a regional economy into three markets: that for regional output, labor, and real estate (covering both structure and land). The model will be a simple static one much like the four-quadrant diagram developed in Chapter 1. We will deal first with the output market for regional goods and services.

---

²This regional multiplier model is one of the simplest possible. For example, it assumes that exports and investment are exogenous, or at least do not depend on local economic conditions. Classic references on multipliers are Isard (1960) or Richardson (1979).

Following the multiplier theory discussed previously, the demand for total regional output will depend primarily on the demand for exports. In the short run, the sales of export goods will vary with the price of those commodities relative to the price of similar goods produced for export in other regions (or nations). Thus, we can imagine that exports are some negative function of the price of local production: $X(p)$. Equation (7.2) therefore implies that the demand for overall regional output, Q_d, covering both locally consumed and exported products, will also be a negative function of local output prices. In the first diagram of Figure 7.1, we depict the demand schedule for a region's output of all goods and services. This schedule can be thought of as that price of local goods that is necessary to sustain the level of output demand on the horizontal axis. A nearly vertical schedule suggests that demand for the region's exports is very inelastic with respect to price; while with a nearly horizontal schedule, the region's exports are sold in very competitive national markets.

To deal with the supply side of a region's economy, we consider the various components that go into the cost of producing goods. First, there are intermediate inputs or raw materials. Since most of these inputs are generally shipped into the region, their prices tend to be similar across regions. Thus, intermediate goods' prices normally have a minor influence on the relative cost of production between regions. The primary factors of production—labor and real estate—are more local, however, and their prices do vary among regions. These differences can generate significant variation in local production costs. The real estate market is the factor market where land is combined with structures to produce the real estate used by both firms and households. The other factor market is for labor. We assume that there is no substitution possible between real estate and labor. Thus, there will be fixed amounts of real estate and labor required to produce each unit of output (α_K and α_L). The production cost per unit of output (C) is therefore $\alpha_K r + \alpha_L w$, where r and w are the annual costs of using real estate and labor (a rental and wage rate).[3]

The second and third diagrams in Figure 7.1 depict the two regional factor markets: the labor market and real estate market. In each diagram, the vertical line depicts the demand for that factor that originates from the level of production in the output market. In the labor market, worker demand (L_d) equals $\alpha_L Q$, while in the real estate market, demand (K_d) is $\alpha_K Q$. With the assumption that there is no factor substitution, the demand for each factor depends only on output, not the price of the factor. This is why the factor demand schedules are vertical, or perfectly inelastic, and shift proportionately with the level of output. The upward-sloping schedules in each of the diagrams represent the supply of that factor into the region.

In the labor market, the horizontal axis measures the size of the region's labor force. On the vertical axis is the region's wage rate divided by the price level of its goods and services (the price level from the vertical axis in the first diagram). The ratio (w/p)

---

[3] If $\alpha_K = K/Q$, and $\alpha_L = L/Q$, then: $r\alpha_K + w\alpha_L = (rK + wL)/Q$, or the average cost of producing Q. In the national economy, the share of the value of output which goes to wages is around 75 percent, with the remaining 25 percent being used to pay for structure, land, and equipment. Average factor shares vary widely by industry, and, hence, across regions as well.

Output Market
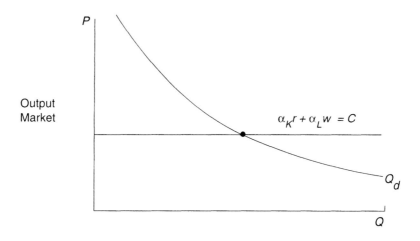

Labor Market
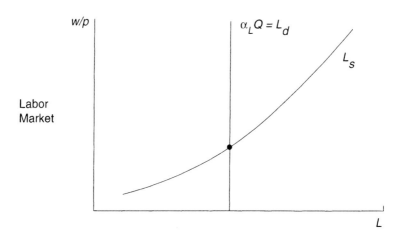

Real Estate Market
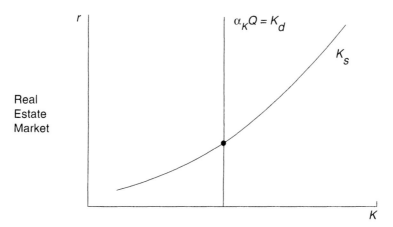

FIGURE 7.1 Three-sector model of regional economy.

might be called the region's *effective wage*—the wage rate deflated by the price index or cost of living in the area. In the long run, it is this effective wage (and not simply nominal wages) that determines the regional supply of labor. The upward-sloping supply schedule indicates the effective wage that is necessary to sustain the labor force on the horizontal axis. Labor force migration into a region that occurs because of an increase in wages represents a movement along this labor supply curve. A more horizontal (elastic) schedule indicates that labor easily moves into the region in response to a higher effective wage. A more vertical or upwardly sloped curve suggests a region that has difficulty in attracting labor.

The diagram for the real estate market is identical to that for labor. On the vertical axis is the rent for real estate (r). Following our discussion in Chapter 3, this rent covers both structure and land. On the horizontal axis, we can measure the stock of real estate. The vertical line gives the demand for real estate (K_d), which is simply proportional to the region's output: $\alpha_k Q$. The supply schedule depicts that rent (for both land and structure) that is necessary to bring into existence the stock of real estate on the horizontal axis.[4] We know from Chapter 3 that in order to expand, a metropolitan area must develop more land, which, in turn, necessitates higher real estate rents. With topographical constraints, building restrictions, and other impediments to development, this supply schedule can be quite vertical or inelastic. Limitless land with few development restrictions should lead to a more horizontal or elastic schedule. Since our model here is static, we are ignoring the question of how long it takes to develop real estate.

The three diagrams in Figure 7.1 are closely linked. Given the output demand schedule in the first diagram, wages and rents determine production costs and, hence, the level of output. In the second and third diagrams, this output level determines factor demand, which, with the given supply schedules, determines the price of factors. A region is in equilibrium when the solutions in each graph are internally consistent: the values of Q and p in the first diagram must lead to the values of w and r (in the other two diagrams), which, back in the first diagram, generate the original Q, p intersection. In such an equilibrium, a region is stable and not growing.

Growth in this regional model can be thought of as a comparative static shift. We consider two sources of economic growth. Demand-induced growth occurs when the demand schedule for a region's output increases. Supply-induced growth responds when the supply schedule for the factors of production (labor or real estate) increases. As we will show, the market reacts quite differently when growth occurs as a result of output demand shifts than when it occurs because of labor supply changes.

---

[4]Following the lessons of Chapter 3, we could decompose real estate rents into a land component (which rises with the amount of real estate built in the region) and a structure component, which, in the long run, should be constant or independent of the structure stock. The structure component of rent, however, would depend on the regional price level since labor and materials required to build a structure are tradeable among regions. Land, however, is fixed and not tradeable among regions. Because we are including land in our definition of real estate, we do not divide rent by p in the real estate market as we do with wages in the labor market.

Chapter 7 Economic Growth and Metropolitan Real Estate Markets

Demand-Induced Regional Growth

Shifts in the demand for a region's exports can come about from one of several changes. The region's existing products can become more fashionable, or the prices of competitive products made in other regions can rise. In both cases, the region's firms face rising orders for their current exports. It can also be the case that firms within the region modify their products or design new ones that become more widely accepted and popular. We will discuss these types of changes in more detail later in this chapter. For the moment, we want to focus on how such shifts in product demand lead to a pattern of response in the region's markets that has several characteristics. These reactions can be summarized in two conclusions:

1. With demand-induced regional growth, output prices, wages, and real estate rents all rise, as do the quantities of output produced, employment, and stock of real estate. The percentage rise in wages must exceed that of prices, which, in turn, must be greater than the increase in real estate rents.
2. With an elastic supply of regional factors, demand-induced growth will generate large increases in quantities (output, employment, and real estate) and small increases in prices, wages, or rents. With inelastic factor supplies, demand-induced growth creates large increases in prices, with less resulting growth in quantities.

To demonstrate these conclusions, we analyze the impact of a demand shift within our three-sector model. In Figure 7.2, the region initially is at an equilibrium defined in all three markets by the values: Q^0, p^0, L^0, w^0, K^0, and r^0. The expansion of export demand first takes the form of an upward shift in the export demand schedule of the first diagram, from Q_d to Q'_d. At the current cost of production in the region (C^0 or p^0), this shift leads to a large increase in production orders (to Q''), well above the output level denoted as Q'. Can these orders be filled, and what is the impact of this output expansion on production costs? As depicted in the first diagram, wages will rise from w^0 to w', real estate rents from r^0 to r', and, hence, production costs will rise from C^0 to C'. The rise in production costs that accompanies the growth in production tends to choke off some of the initial increase in export demand. Thus, the actual level of output that results from the demand shift will only be from Q^0 to Q'. To see how factor prices rise and how this in turn raises production costs, we look to the second and third diagrams in Figure 7.2.

The increase in desired output from the first diagram in Figure 7.2 is represented by the outward shifts in the factor demand schedules of the second and third diagrams. Labor demand increases from $\alpha_L Q^0$ to $\alpha_L Q'$, and real estate demand from $\alpha_K Q^0$ to $\alpha_K Q'$. To provide this increased labor, nominal wages must rise to w', and this rise must be great enough so that in combination with higher prices, effective wages will increase (to w'/p'). In the real estate market, the increased demand generates the higher level of real estate rents, r'. This new solution, like the initial equilibrium, must be internally consistent. The new factor prices (w', r') generate a cost of production (C'), that, together with the new output demand schedule, results in factor demands that match factor supplies at

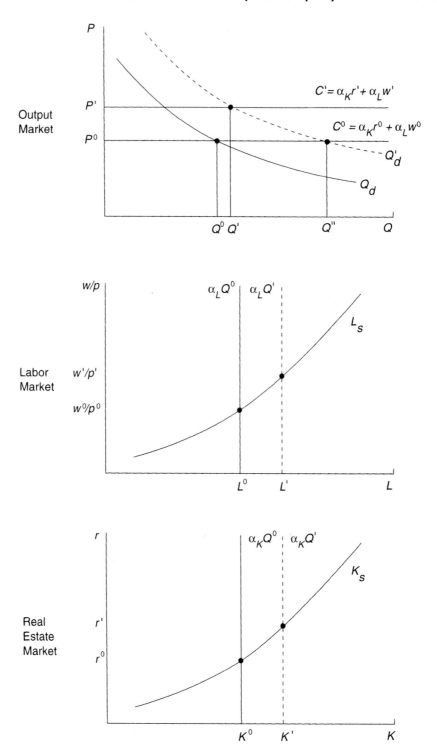

FIGURE 7.2 Three-sector model: output demand shift.

the new factor prices. This new equilibrium is: Q', p', L', w', K', r'. Remember from Chapter 1 that with a static model, it is possible to describe only the new equilibrium solution and not the actual time path of adjustments that the market experiences in moving to this new equilibrium.

It should be clear from Figure 7.2 that the new solution must involve values for *all* variables that are *greater* than the original solution. A decrease in any value would be internally inconsistent. For example, were factor prices to rise so much that the higher production costs reduced output, then the demand for these factors would actually be less. With rising factor supply schedules, this reduced demand could not sustain the higher factor prices. In reaction to an increase in export demand, regional output, employment, and stock of real estate all must increase. More importantly, output prices, wages, and real estate rents all will rise as well. There is a tradeoff, however, between the two sets of variables. The more prices, wages, and rents increase, the less output, labor, and structures will grow. Conversely, if the former increase only slightly, then the quantity variables can grow significantly. The solution to the tradeoff depends on the various elasticities of factor supply.

Returning to Figure 7.2, imagine a case in which both the labor and structure supply schedules are nearly vertical, or very inelastic with respect to their factor prices. Against these schedules, increased factor demand results in a large rise in rents and wages, which, in turn, shifts the cost line (in the first diagram) markedly upward. The end result is only a small increase in regional output, and, likewise, small increases in the actual growth of employment and real estate. Inelastic factor supplies mean that in reaction to an increase in demand, large increases in wages and rents are necessary to bring forth any new factor supplies. This change increases the cost of production and chokes off much of the initial increase in regional output demand.

In the case of very elastic factor supplies, the supply schedules in the second and third diagrams of Figure 7.2 are nearly horizontal. The increase in factor demand in this case has almost no impact on wages and rents, and, hence, the cost line in the first diagram barely moves upward. Almost all of the initial increase in regional product demand is able to be fulfilled.

The two polar cases of factor supply also generate quite different impacts on the qualitative demand for real estate. With inelastic factor supplies, the region does not grow much physically in response to increases in output demand. The number of new houses or buildings needed is limited. On the other hand, the rapid increase in prices means that most residents (workers and landlords) become wealthier. Thus, the character of the real estate demanded may change significantly, and existing buildings may have to be renovated, expanded, or adapted. With elastic factor supplies, workers and resource owners may not become much wealthier, but the physical expansion of the region will be much more rapid given an otherwise similar demand shift.

There may also be mixed cases in which one factor has a very elastic supply, while the other is inelastic. In the short run, the supply of labor is often thought of as more elastic, since the durability of real estate limits the ability of the stock to grow or decline rapidly. In this case, wages will rise very little, while real estate rents will increase more rapidly. Regional production costs will rise somewhere between these two and output growth will likewise be intermediate in magnitude.

It is important to remember that for any pattern of factor supply elasticities, an increase in regional product demand will raise wages more than goods prices, and goods prices more than real estate rents. Wages must rise faster than goods prices so that the effective wage can increase and bring forth the additional labor for output expansion. Since the growth in output prices is a weighted average of the increase in factor costs, rents cannot increase more than prices.[5]

The demand for regional products can decline as well as grow. The same logic applies to a decline in demand, only the signs of the impacts are reversed. Declines in product demand reduce all quantities (output, employment, real estate) as well as all prices (rents and wages). With inelastic factor supplies, the declines in prices, wages, and rents are large, whereas the declines in output, employment, and real estate are more modest. With elastic factor supplies, the price drops are modest, whereas the reductions in output, employment, and real estate almost match the initial decrease (shift) in demand.

Supply-Induced Regional Growth

Economic growth can also occur as a result of shifts in the supply of resources into a region, most commonly from changes in the supply of labor. The labor supply curves in Figures 7.1 through 7.3 trace the quantity of labor supplied at different wage rates. *Labor force migration into a region that occurs because of an increase in wage rates represents a movement along this regional labor supply curve. Labor force migration into a region that occurs because of events in other regions (or nations) represents a shift in the labor supply curve.* As we will illustrate later, such shifts in labor often result from foreign immigration, regional demographic forces, or from changes in lifestyle preferences. These shifts in regional labor supply have impacts that can be quite different from those experienced under the demand-induced growth scenario. Whenever regions grow in response to shifts in labor supply, the reaction of prices and quantities can be summarized as follows:

1. With supply-induced regional growth, output prices and wages fall, while the quantity of output produced and employment both rise. The percentage fall in

---

[5] Noting the change in variables with the differential (d), this assertion can be written as:

$$\frac{dw}{w} > \frac{dp}{p} > \frac{dr}{r}$$

The first inequality follows because the *effective wage* (the ratio w/p) must increase to attract more labor. The second inequality is shown by recalling the definition of price ($p = \alpha_K r + \alpha_L w$). We differentiate this price to yield:

$$\frac{dp}{p} = \frac{(\alpha_L w)}{p}\frac{dw}{w} + \left(1 - \frac{\alpha_L w}{p}\right)\frac{dr}{r}$$

Since wages must rise (in percentage terms) faster than prices, then rents cannot also rise faster than prices, since the rise in prices is simply a weighted average of the two factor price increases.

Chapter 7 Economic Growth and Metropolitan Real Estate Markets

wages must exceed that of prices. The stock of real estate must increase, necessitating a rise in rents.

2. With an elastic demand for a region's products, a positive shift in labor supply generates large increases in output and employment, and only slight declines in wages and prices, as the expanded labor force is easily absorbed. Substantial expansion of the real estate stock requires that real estate rents increase. With inelastic regional demand, labor absorption will be more difficult, wages and prices will fall more significantly, while output and employment will rise only modestly. Rises in the stock of real estate and rents also will be more modest.

To demonstrate these results, we turn to Figure 7.3, where the initial equilibrium in the region's three markets is shown as: Q^0, p^0, L^0, w^0, K^0, and r^0. The shift in labor supply takes place in the second diagram with the outward movement of the schedule from L_s to L'_s. The magnitude of the horizontal movement in the schedule represents the number of new workers entering the region's labor force.

If the demand for labor were to remain unchanged (at $\alpha_L Q^0$), because output continued as before, then effective wages would have to fall well below the level indicated by w'/p'. This would encourage as many workers to leave the region as initially entered (from the schedule's original shift). As wages fall, however, the cost of production in the first diagram shifts down. Higher output results, and this expands labor demand from $\alpha_L Q^0$ to $\alpha_L Q'$. Eventually, wages fall only to w'/p', which is enough so that employment increases from L^0 to L'. In effect, some but not all of the new migrants have been absorbed by a growth in output, caused by falling production costs. Costs have fallen because wages have dropped, in an attempt to absorb the new workers.

While prices and wages fall in the markets for the region's output and labor, in the real estate market, rents must rise. In order to house the increase in employment and the new production, more development must occur. This expansion of the region's stock of real estate requires that more land be brought into development, and this, in turn, necessitates higher rents (as described in Chapter 3). The reader, at this point, might legitimately question whether the rise in real estate rents might not outweigh the fall in wages and lead to an increase in the cost of production. This cannot occur. If rents were to rise by this much, then the resulting rise in output prices would reduce production and thereby the demand for real estate. With lower real estate demand, rents would have to fall. Supply-induced growth always results in a fall in wages that exceeds the fall in prices, so that real wages drop. The rent for real estate, however, must rise, as of course will output, employment, and the stock of real estate.

Since quantity variables (output, employment, and real estate) are moving in the opposite direction from wages, prices, and rents, it is important to analyze the magnitudes of these relative changes. Here the elasticity of regional product demand plays a critical role. If the region's products are sold in highly competitive national or international markets, then the demand schedule that the region faces for its products will be nearly perfectly elastic. In the first diagram of Figure 7.3, this will imply an almost horizontal Q_d schedule. The impact of a labor supply shift in this case will be to reduce prices and wages only slightly, expand output considerably, and employ almost all of the migrants

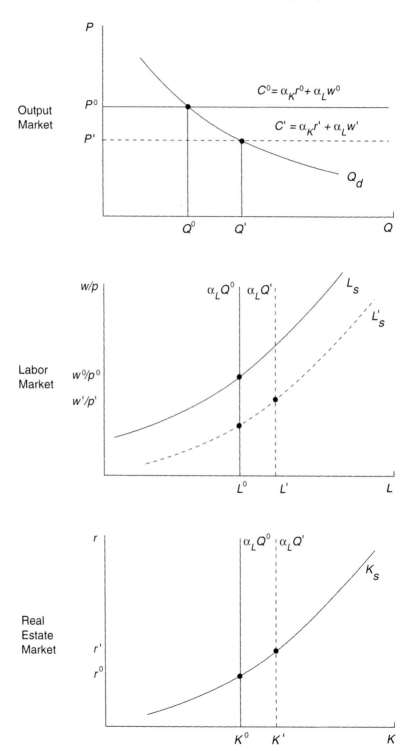

FIGURE 7.3 Three-sector model: labor supply shift.

that caused the original supply shift. An elastic product demand makes the absorption of an expanding labor supply relatively easy. In the real estate market, the large growth in output and employment necessitates a significant increase in the stock and, hence, rents.

The polar case occurs when the region is a dominant producer of goods within a very limited national market, and so aggregate product demand is quite inelastic. This implies that the Q_d schedule in Figure 7.3 is nearly vertical. In this situation, the absorption of labor will be far more difficult. Product prices will have to fall significantly to generate any growth in output, which, in turn, will require an even larger decline in wages. This combination causes many workers to leave the region, almost as many as entered with the initial supply shift. The meager growth in output and employment means that only a slight increase in real estate is necessary so that rents will rise likewise.

In between these two extreme cases, more mixed configurations of output and price changes are possible. It may also be possible that a region's labor supply occasionally shifts downward. This has the same pattern of reactions, only with opposite signs. The labor market tightens, and wages and prices rise as output and employment fall. On the other hand, rents and the supply of real estate decrease.

REGIONAL EXPORTS AND PRODUCT DEMAND SHIFTS

The central role that a region's exports play in demand-induced growth has generated considerable interest and research over the years. There are many causes of growth or decline in a region's exports, and local decision makers continually search for policies that will help to stimulate such demand. When export demand increases, jobs are created as existing firms expand or new firms move into the region. In this section, we briefly review some of the more common theories and factors that play a role in shaping the growth and composition of a region's export base.

The National Business Cycle

As the national economy experiences cyclic fluctuations, regional exports tend to be influenced particularly severely. This is due to the high concentration of manufactured durable goods in the composition of most regions' exports. While national gross domestic product (GDP) typically fluctuates only 5 to 8 percent during the trough-to-peak of a business cycle, consumer or producer expenditures on durables can vary by far more. Thus, few regions escape the impacts of national business fluctuations. Consider the growth of total nonagricultural employment in two quite different metropolitan areas, Los Angeles and Chicago. As Figure 7.4 illustrates, national employment dropped during national recessions, which occurred in 1969–70, 1975, 1980–82 and 1990–91. The years just following these recessions are periods of strong economic expansion.

The similarity in the timing between the economic growth in Chicago and Los Angeles and the national trend is no accident. Among a much larger sample of metropolitan areas, few have escaped recessions, and most have undergone significant growth

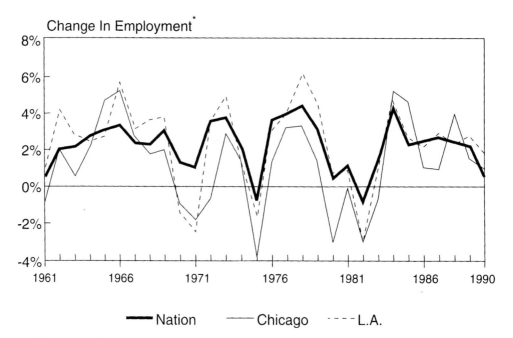

FIGURE 7.4 Employment growth for the nation, Chicago, and Los Angeles.

*Civilian nonagricultural employment.

Source: National employment, *Economic Report of the President 1991*, Washington, DC, February, 1991; metropolitan employment, adjusted U.S. government figures courtesy of Regional Financial Associates, Bala-Cynwyd, PA.

during periods of national expansion. In the short run, movements in the national economy play a strong role in local export demand.

Industrial Mix

Over longer periods of time, the growth rates of certain industries exceed that of the economy as a whole, while other sectors of the economy lag behind. During the two decades from 1945 to 1965, for example, heavy consumer durables grew rapidly, only to fall prey to foreign competition in the 1970s and 1980s. The aerospace industry grew steadily throughout the last 40 years because of the rapid expansion of both civilian and government demand. With fewer defense needs in the coming decades, however, aerospace growth is expected to slow. Health care services and the pharmaceutical industry experienced strong growth during the 1980s as the nation's demographic profile continued to age. In addition to demographic trends, rapid developments in biotechnology point to continued growth in these sectors in the future.

As long as regions specialize in the production of certain goods or services, one region's industrial mix may generate much greater export growth than another's, even for

Chapter 7   Economic Growth and Metropolitan Real Estate Markets

quite prolonged periods of time. For the moment, we will leave aside the question of why regions specialize or industries concentrate. Regional economists have developed a simple technique—*shift-share analysis*—which decomposes a region's growth into different components, including the effect of a region's industrial mix. Shift-share analysis is usually based on employment growth, since employment data, unlike output or income data, is available by detailed industry categories. The following data form the basis of most shift-share analyses:

N, n: total employment growth rate nationally, and in a particular region.
N_i, n_i: employment growth rate in industry (i) nationally, and in a particular region.
E_i, e_i: industry (i)'s level of employment, nationally and regionally.

The growth of a region is first decomposed into a share component, which estimates how much growth would have occurred if each industry category in the region grew at the common rate of all industries nationally (N). This component captures the region's share of the nation's overall employment growth. The shift component includes two effects: the *industry mix effect* and the *competitive effect*. The industry mix effect calculates what additional growth occurred because of the region's particular industry mix. Here, we take the additional employment growth (positive or negative) that each industry experienced nationally ($N_i - N$) and weight these changes by the region's industry mix. This effect measures how much more (or less) the region should have grown because it contained a mix of industries that was growing relatively fast or slow nationally. The competitive effect takes the growth rate of each industry within the region (n_i) and subtracts the national growth rate for industries of the same type (N_i). Weighting these differences by the region's industry mix produces an estimate of how regional firms within industry categories grew relative to identical firms nationally. In effect, this term measures the competitiveness of regional firms in each industry with firms in that industry nationally. Using the variables defined above, the three components of a region's growth are:

$$\sum_i e_i n_i = \sum_i e_i N + \sum_i e_i (N_i - N) + \sum_i e_i (n_i - N_i) \qquad (7.6)$$

$$\text{Share} \quad \underbrace{\text{Mix} \qquad \text{Competitive}}_{\text{Shift}}$$

Tables 7.2 and 7.3 provide a simple example of an actual shift-share analysis. Using 1980 and 1990 SIC (Standard Industrial Classification) level employment data, we calculate the share, mix, and competitive components for the Phoenix and Pittsburgh metropolitan areas. The data illustrate some interesting differences between the economic structure and performance of the two metropolitan areas. From Table 7.2, we can calculate that, in 1980, Pittsburgh had 23 percent of its workforce employed in manufacturing (213,600 of 908,500), whereas Phoenix had only 18 percent (114,000 of 636,200). Over the next decade, manufacturing grew in Phoenix by 21 percent, but the region as a whole saw a huge 55 percent increase in jobs, with service jobs soaring to total a 108 percent increase for the decade. Thus, by 1990, manufacturing represented only 14 percent of

TABLE 7.2 Nonfarm Employment for Phoenix, Pittsburgh, and the U.S. (Annual Average)

	Phoenix			Pittsburgh			U.S.		
	1980	1990	%	1980	1990	%	1980	1990	%
Sector	(000s)	(000s)	Change	(000s)	(000s)	Change	(000s)	(000s)	Change
Mining	0.4	0.8	100.0	11.8	4.5	−61.9	1,027	711	−30.8
Manufacturing	114.0	138.2	21.2	213.6	119.4	−44.1	20,285	19,111	−5.8
Construction	50.6	55.5	9.7	44.0	43.6	−0.9	4,346	5,136	18.2
Transport + Public Utilities	30.7	58.4	90.2	54.4	54.1	−0.6	5,146	5,826	13.2
Wholesale	39.2	60.4	54.1	52.9	54.2	2.5	5,292	6,205	17.3
Retail	122.8	187.8	52.9	153.9	171.4	11.4	15,018	19,683	31.1
FIRE	44.9	75.4	67.9	45.7	55.4	21.2	5,160	6,739	30.6
Services	132.8	275.9	107.8	211.1	310.9	47.3	17,890	28,240	57.9
Government	100.8	133.3	32.2	121.1	106.4	−12.1	16,241	18,322	12.8
TOTAL	636.2	985.7	54.9	908.5	919.9	1.3	90,405	109,973	21.6

Source: Employment and Earnings, Bureau of Labor Statistics, Washington, DC, 1980 and 1990.

TABLE 7.3 Shift-Share Analysis for Phoenix and Pittsburgh

	Phoenix				Pittsburgh			
		SHIFT		Total		SHIFT		Total
Sector	SHARE	Mix	Competitive	Change	SHARE	Mix	Competitive	Change
Mining	0.1	−0.2	0.5	0.4	2.6	−6.2	−3.7	−7.3
Manufacturing	24.7	−31.3	30.8	24.2	46.2	−58.6	−81.8	−94.2
Construction	11.0	−1.8	−4.3	4.9	9.5	−1.5	−8.4	−0.4
Transport + Public Utilities	6.6	−2.6	23.6	27.6	11.8	−4.6	−7.5	−0.3
Wholesale	8.5	−1.7	14.4	21.2	11.5	−2.3	−7.8	1.4
Retail	26.6	11.6	26.9	65.1	33.3	14.5	−30.3	17.5
FIRE	9.7	4.0	16.8	30.5	9.9	4.1	−4.3	9.7
Services	28.7	48.1	66.3	143.1	45.7	76.4	−22.3	99.8
Government	21.8	−8.9	19.6	32.5	26.2	−10.7	−30.2	−14.7
TOTAL	137.7	17.2	194.6	349.5	196.6	11.1	−196.3	11.4

Source: Employment and Earnings, Bureau of Labor Statistics, Washington, DC, 1980 and 1990.

Phoenix's workforce. Pittsburgh, on the other hand, saw its manufacturing workforce drop almost in half. It was only because of strong growth in the service sectors that total employment managed to remain stable over the decade. With this very different employment history, manufacturing accounted for 13 percent of Pittsburgh's workforce in 1990.

Table 7.3 assigns each area's total employment change for the decade into the three shift-share components. (Thus, the total employment change for Phoenix, 349,500, is equal to the total change in Table 7.2, 985,700 minus 636,200.) The share components show what the increase in employment would have been in each region had it grown at the overall national rate of 21.6 percent. The industry mix components give the adjustment to this share component that is due to the region's unique industrial composition. At least when done with data at the two-digit level of detail, the industry-mix effects in the two areas are both small and quite similar. The mix in Phoenix was favorable and accounted for an additional 17,000 workers, while that in Pittsburgh was slightly less so and contributed 11,000 workers. In other words, both cities benefited slightly from having an industrial mix made up of more industries that were growing relative to the industrial mix in the country as a whole. The third column gives the competitive portion of the shift component for each region, and it is here that the difference between the two areas stands out. In Phoenix, employment in eight of the nine industries provided grew faster than employment in those industries nationally. The one exception was construction. In stark contrast, employment in all nine industry categories in Pittsburgh grew at a slower rate than employment in those industries nationally. Pittsburgh firms in these industries seem to be less competitive nationally than Phoenix firms.

If shift-share analysis is done with more detailed data (two-, three-, or four-digit SIC categories[6]), the industrial mix portion of the shift component tends to stand out more. The use of one-digit data masks important differences in the growth of various manufacturers. Recent research has suggested that over the last several decades, about 50 percent of the overall variance in total growth across regions can be explained by the industry mix effects when done with quite detailed data. The remaining half is explained by the fact that within specific industry groups, new firms are created or existing firms grow faster in some regions than in other areas (Terkla and Doeringer 1991). The answers to the question of why some firms in the same industry outperform others and what systematic role regions play in such success stories, lie at the heart of some intriguing questions in regional economic theory.

The Product Cycle and Regional Growth

One theory of export demand and industrial job growth focuses on the cycle that products seem to go through as they are invented, produced, and eventually standardized (Norton and Rees 1979). According to this theory, a firm experiences its most rapid growth in jobs or income right after a new product is invented, during the period of initial production as the product gains buyer acceptance. During these early stages of the cycle, product development, refinement, and marketing are the dominant concerns of the producer. The theory asserts that firms at this stage in the product cycle typically tend to cluster near concentrations of existing firms in the industry.

The advantages to firms in the same industry of clustering together can be many (Henderson 1988). Through close proximity to each other, firms can exchange ideas, share input resources, and exploit labor market economies. These external benefits

---

[6]In the SIC classification system, the number of digits in the code corresponds to a level of industrial detail. For example, manufacturing is a major industrial division; textile mill products (22) is one of the two-digit levels within that division. At the three-digit level, 228 represents yarn and thread mills, with thread mills alone being 2284. The SIC is periodically updated and reorganized.

among firms generate a form of agglomeration referred to as a *localization economy*.[7] An additional aspect of this phenomenon suggests that not only are static business costs lower in such agglomerations, but new business creations and inventions also occur more easily in regions with a concentration of particular industries. Thus, when new business activity is generated, there are strong reasons for that activity to be generated as an offshoot of existing industry activity.

For industrial concentrations to be maintained over time, however, firms that initially cluster must choose to continually expand and concentrate their production activity at one site. If greater size increases production efficiency for individual firms, then there will be a natural tendency for firms to locate all their activity at a single common site. If firms within an industry compete with each other in a monopolistic competitive manner, then competition and equilibrium pricing will result, despite the increasing returns to scale at the firm level (Krugman 1991).[8]

The argument suggesting that industrial growth comes from concentration and innovation has received only mixed support in recent empirical investigations. In Table 7.4, we examine new business growth in the five major industry groups, as defined by first-level SIC division codes. For purposes of illustration, we present two indicators that might explain this new business growth. The data are presented for 11 quite diverse states. The first indicator is *concentration,* which is defined as the percentage of jobs in that state accounted for by the SIC industry. At the bottom of each industry block of columns is the average for the 11 states, as well as the total for the U.S. as a whole. From the second block of columns, for example, we see that Georgia, Illinois, Massachusetts, Michigan, Missouri, and Pennsylvania have economies with higher than average concentrations of manufacturing firms. The middle column of each block provides the second indicator, *share,* which is the percentage of national jobs in that industry in each state. The third column within each block provides the measure of new business growth by industry, which is each state's percentage of national new business creations in that industry.[9]

When a state's share of new business starts in an SIC category exceeds its share of that SIC employment, then, in some sense, the state has become a center of entrepreneurial activity in that industry. Within manufacturing, California, Florida, Texas, and Arizona have high new business activity shares relative to employment shares. All of

---

[7] In the parlance of regional economics, *agglomeration* refers to any production-enhancing effect across firms that occurs with some form of locational concentration. If the effect comes from identical firms sharing information, it is referred to as a *localization economy*. If the effect comes from diverse firms helping each other with inputs and services, it is called an *urbanization economy*. *Economies of scale* refers to increases in production that are greater than proportional to the increase in inputs used as a firm grows. In other words, with input prices held constant, the long-run average total cost curve of the firm is declining.

[8] When there are increasing returns at the firm level, then eventually larger firms will underprice smaller ones and a single large monopoly will emerge. Under *monopolistic competition,* firms offer uniquely different, but competing products. Krugman argues that this model not only characterizes most modern manufacturing, but it explains how price competition, increasing returns to scale, and firm clustering can all be reconciled.

[9] The Dun & Bradstreet Corporation maintains a database on approximately 9 million business establishments in the U.S. New business creations is a gross measure defined by Dun & Bradstreet. It covers the number of jobs created in establishments that existed in 1987, but not 1986, and that are not a subsidiary of any existing company in the D&B data file.

TABLE 7.4 Business Starts and Employment Concentration and Share by Industry Sector by State (1987)

	Construction		Manufacturing			Wholesale and Retail Trade			FIRE			Services			Total All Sectors			
	Employment Concentration* (%)	Business Starts Share† (%)	Employment Concentration (%)	Share (%)	Business Starts Share (%)	Employment Concentration (%)	Share (%)	Business Starts Share (%)	Employment Concentration (%)	Share (%)	Business Starts Share (%)	Employment Concentration (%)	Share (%)	Business Starts Share (%)	Employment (000s)	Share (%)	Business Starts	Share (%)
Alaska	4.8	0.2	6.1	0.1	0.1	19.6	0.2	0.2	5.4	0.2	0.2	20.2	0.2	0.3	210.1	0.2	547	0.2
Arizona	7.4	2.1	13.5	1.0	1.8	24.6	1.4	1.7	6.8	1.4	2.3	24.9	1.4	2.0	1,385.8	1.4	4,385	1.9
California	4.9	11.5	18.0	11.1	16.5	23.6	11.3	13.2	6.9	12.2	12.5	25.1	12.1	14.2	11,678.5	11.4	30,809	13.2
Florida	7.0	6.8	11.0	2.8	5.8	27.2	5.4	7.1	7.4	5.5	7.0	26.9	5.4	5.9	4,848.1	4.7	15,088	6.5
Georgia	5.5	3.0	20.5	3.0	2.9	25.3	2.9	3.1	5.6	2.4	2.7	19.4	2.2	2.9	2,782.0	2.7	6,972	3.0
Illinois	4.0	3.9	19.1	4.9	3.8	24.8	5.0	3.8	7.3	5.5	3.3	23.7	4.8	4.6	4,928.3	4.8	10,032	4.3
Massachusetts	4.5	2.8	19.6	3.1	2.5	23.6	3.0	2.2	7.1	3.3	3.1	27.9	3.5	2.3	3,061.8	3.0	5,426	2.3
Michigan	3.3	2.5	26.0	5.1	4.1	23.0	3.5	3.0	4.8	2.7	3.4	22.1	3.4	3.6	3,735.8	3.7	7,716	3.3
Missouri	4.5	2.0	19.3	2.2	1.7	24.6	2.2	1.7	6.2	2.1	1.5	23.1	2.1	1.7	2,197.8	2.1	3,893	1.7
Pennsylvania	4.4	4.4	21.2	5.5	4.1	22.8	4.6	4.2	5.9	4.5	4.4	25.9	5.3	4.6	4,915.1	4.8	10,257	4.4
Texas	5.3	6.9	14.3	4.9	7.0	25.2	6.7	7.4	6.8	6.8	8.8	22.2	6.0	7.9	6,516.9	6.4	17,029	7.3
Total 11 States	5.0	46.0	18.0	43.7	50.4	24.4	46.2	47.5	6.6	46.6	49.2	24.3	46.4	49.9	46,260.2	45.2	112,154	48.0
Total U.S.	4.9	100.0	18.6	100.0	100.0	23.8	100.0	100.0	6.4	100.0	100.0	23.6	100.0	100.0	102,310.0	100.0	233,710	100.0

*Concentration measures the portion each industry has of the state's total (industry sector for state as percent of total for state).
†Share measures the share each state has of the U.S. total for each industry (industry sector for state as percent of industry sector total for U.S.).

Source: *Business Starts: Business Starts Record 1986/1987*, The Dun & Bradstreet Corporation, New York; *Employment and Earnings*, Bureau of Labor Statistics, Washington, DC, May 1989.

these states have average or below-average concentrations of manufacturing employment. Georgia, Illinois, Michigan, Missouri, and Pennsylvania have relatively low new business activity shares, despite having the highest job concentrations in manufacturing. Clearly, when done with first-level manufacturing data, the concentration theory does not seem to hold.[10]

The questionable connection between industrial concentration and new business creations does not mean that concentration is undesirable. Regions with high industrial concentrations might generate new ideas and products, but the jobs created to produce these products could occur in other areas. For example, a recent study of patent filings clearly found that inventions were more likely in states with a relatively high volume of both corporate expenditure on R&D and university-funded research. Academic research also induced greater corporate expenditures on R&D (Jaffe 1989). Thus, areas of concentrated activity might promote research and idea innovation, but it is not always clear that such innovation leads to more job growth in that same region. Some parts of the country might be responsible for the lion's share of innovative activity, while the eventual manufacturing of new products (and hence job creation) may occur elsewhere.

A second portion of the product cycle theory expands on this view and argues that innovation and product development may take place in certain locations, but once products mature and are mass-produced, firms frequently move and seek those locations where overall production costs are lowest. Sometimes this may involve moving production to an offshore manufacturing facility; but, more frequently, it may lead firms to seek a different region within the U.S. Thus, product cycle theory holds that regions or metropolitan areas may undergo sustained growth if they are low-cost producers and can continually attract mature firms that are producing more standardized products.

The notion that firms that produce standardized products choose plant locations that minimize costs has been the subject of considerable study over the years. In order to understand the location decisions of these firms and the relative abilities of regions to attract them, the questions most often posed are what costs seem to matter most to firms and how do they vary across alternative regional locations. Clearly, the answer to these questions will vary by the type of firm or industry. Industries that are labor intensive or energy intensive, for example, would give the greatest weight to the relative cost of these inputs in making their location decisions.

State and local governments have long been concerned with understanding firm location decisions as they consider economic development strategies to attract firms to their jurisdictions, hoping to expand jobs and increase income. Such strategies require an understanding of the comparative advantages and disadvantages of the jurisdiction with respect to those costs that matter most to firms considering locating there. Such information helps states and localities target their efforts toward industries that may find their jurisdictions attractive. Since taxes are one of the few levers that they control, an important question for state and local policy makers is how important are state and local tax incentives in firm location decisions.

---

[10]When the analysis in Table 7.4 is done with more detailed four-digit SIC categories, researchers tend to find a positive connection between concentration of existing activity and new business creations. See Carlton (1979).

Chapter 7 Economic Growth and Metropolitan Real Estate Markets

In many manufacturing industries, intermediate inputs (goods that are in the production of a good that will be purchased by consumers; e.g., glass used in assembling a car) can account for a significant portion of final production costs. Since such inputs are freely traded, the primary variation in their cost is transportation. For heavy or bulky inputs, it is not uncommon to find both producers and suppliers locating together in a common region. This form of vertical industry organization is particularly strong in the heavier metals and chemical industries. Aside from the cost of intermediate inputs, the other costs of a manufacturing plant (value-added costs) can also vary across locations, primarily due to differences in labor wages, local taxes, and final good shipment expenses.

As an example of how labor costs, shipping costs, and taxes can vary across regions, we examine the location of General Motors' Saturn plant in Tennessee during the 1980s. Tennessee won out over nine alternative sites that were actively campaigning for the plant. Table 7.5 examines some estimates of what Saturn costs would be at each of these 9 sites out of the 130 analyzed.

The Saturn case can provide several broad-based lessons, despite having some unique characteristics. Because of the size and weight of an automobile, one would expect that shipping costs would play an important role in locating the Saturn plant. Using assumptions about the distribution of the potential market for Saturn cars, Bartik et al. (1987) were able to calculate the likely transport costs from each alternative site. The variation in estimated final shipping costs across sites was only 27 percent, or $122 per car. Proceeding in a similar manner, data about state and local tax rates, rebate programs,

TABLE 7.5 Estimated Saturn Costs* per Car

		Labor Costs			Total Measured Costs	
Location	Average Cost of Transport to Market	5,000 Local Supplier Labor Costs Only[†]	11,000 Jobs at Local Wages[‡]	State and Local Taxes	With Local Supplier Labor Only	With All Jobs at Local Wages
Nashville, TN	426	159	350	118	703	894
Lexington, KY	423	186	409	106	715	938
St. Louis, MO	419	172	378	134	725	931
Bloomington, IL	417	202	444	162	781	1023
Terre Haute, IN	413	209	460	168	790	1041
Kalamazoo, MI	430	244	537	116	790	1083
Marysville, OH	427	219	482	169	815	1078
Minneapolis, MN	494	195	429	—	689[§]	923[§]
New York, NY	535	184	405	—	719[§]	940[§]

*1987 dollars.
[†]This calculation represents cost per car for the 5,000 local labor jobs only. In addition, 6,000 union jobs were contracted at the same wage rate regardless of location.
[‡]This calculation estimates cost per car if all 11,000 jobs were at prevailing wages, derived by multiplying the Local Supplier Labor Costs in column 2 by the ratio of 11,000/5,000.
[§]Labor and transport costs only. Tax costs were not available for these states.
Source: Timothy J. Bartik et al., "Saturn and State Economic Development," *Forum for Applied Research and Public Policy* (Spring 1987).

and incentives were used to estimate the total taxes that would be paid (per car) by the plant (tax estimates for New York and Minneapolis were unavailable). Listed in the fourth column, these were estimated to differ by 59 percent across the nine locations, or $63 per car.

The Saturn plant involved some unique labor negotiations. A special contract between General Motors and the United Auto Workers (UAW) union required that union plant workers would receive the same wage regardless of the plant's location. Saturn was to employ 6,000 plant workers, with an additional 5,000 jobs being created by local suppliers that would locate near the plant. These 5,000 jobs would pay prevailing local wages. The column labeled Local Supplier Labor Costs in Table 7.5 reports the variation in these labor costs across the nine locations. The labor costs for local suppliers range from $159 per car in Nashville to $244 per car in Kalamazoo, a 53 percent difference in costs.

Since the UAW contract is a special case, we also estimate the labor costs per car if all 11,000 jobs were at prevailing local wages (without the UAW contract). In this case, total labor costs would have varied $187 per car across the nine sites (from a low of $350 to a high of $537). These recalculated labor costs, assuming that all jobs are at local wage rates, provide a better general indication of how important regional variation in wages might be to the automobile industry.

Summing transport costs, labor costs and taxes across the nine sites examined in the table, Nashville, Tennessee was the lowest-cost location regardless of how labor costs are defined. Across the seven sites for which all costs are available, total production costs vary 16 percent to 21 percent, or $112 per car when only local supplier labor is considered, and $189 per car if plant jobs paid local wages. While seemingly small, variation in costs of this magnitude are important to many domestic and foreign automobile producers. During the 1980s, a number of new auto assembly plants were opened in this same region, including a Nissan plant in Smyrna, Tennessee.

Clearly, a region will grow if it is a low-cost producer and can attract firms who are seeking the cheapest manufacturing cost. The question remains, however, whether low-cost regions can continue both to attract new economic development and keep their costs low. Won't wages eventually rise as demand grows, and taxes increase to provide more services? To the extent that these factor costs are endogenous, wages and taxes will rise with economic development. In fact, a frequent stated goal of economic development is to increase wages and incomes for local residents.

A region can continue to attract firms and keep its costs low only if at least some production cost differentials are truly exogenous. For example, if certain regions have lower energy needs or lower energy costs because of climate or natural resource endowments, then such areas will always appeal to energy intensive firms.

It is also important to understand that growth through being a low-cost producer can go only so far. Other regions must invent the products which eventually become standardized and then seek sites of low-cost production. In this sense, the cost-based economic growth of one region may be highly dependent on the innovation growth occurring in other areas.

The Government and Regional Demand

There are several other sources of demand for regional products, and one of the more important of these is the federal government. We have already discussed how the federal government affects income through its system of taxes and transfer payments. More important, the government also acts as a direct purchaser of regional products, chiefly through the defense department and federal public works projects. Many of the U.S. aerospace and electronics industries owe their existence to government purchases. When the government builds highways, housing, mass transit facilities, or water projects, the construction jobs created constitute a form of regional export. It's no accident that members of Congress lobby vigorously to have such projects undertaken in their state or district. The spatial distribution of government contracts can have a significant impact on the pattern of regional growth.

REGIONAL LABOR SUPPLY: MIGRATION AND DEMOGRAPHY

A region's labor market can be an important consideration when it comes to stimulating and sustaining economic growth. Much of the empirical research on firm locational choice points to the importance of labor availability and wage costs (Carlton 1979 and Schmenner 1982). Producing exports requires that enough workers with the necessary skills can be found at competitive wages. The ease with which labor can be acquired to accommodate new economic growth depends on the elasticity of regional labor supply: for a given increase in wages, how large will the increase in the area's workforce be and how quickly will this increase occur?

The slope of the labor supply schedule, or the elasticity of labor supply, depends on how easily interregional migration occurs. If labor (both within the region and in other regions) is mobile and reacts strongly to small changes in relative effective wages, then a region's labor supply will be responsive to new demand. An inelastic labor supply results if workers are immobile because they have become attached to their current locations for family or other personal reasons. Immobility of factors of production give rise to factor price differentials across regions. It is important to remember that it is a region's *relative effective wage* that determines labor supply, and not *nominal wages*.

There has been considerable research on the various determinants of interregional migration (Greenwood 1975), much of it based on using census data to examine the decade-long movements in population between regions. In this research, the net flow of workers between regions has historically been related to the interregional differences in wages. Such studies also find that effective wage measures (deflated with either regional cost indices or data on area house prices) provide better explanations of migration flows than do nominal differences in wages. In addition to wages, younger and better-educated workers are more likely to move, and the propensity to move is negatively related to the distance between regions. Thus, on average, U.S. labor seems to be reasonably mobile between areas, although there is little consensus about the wage supply elasticity of labor between regions. There is some evidence that various regions may have quite different labor supply elasticities, and this is an important subject of ongoing research in regional economics today.

While a region's labor supply elasticity is crucial for sustaining economic growth, movements along a region's labor supply schedule do not initiate growth. Exogenous shifts in labor supply occur for other reasons. The most common historic pattern of shifting labor supply is immigration into selected regions. To make such movements truly exogenous, the immigration has to result because of changes occurring outside of the region into which the population eventually flows. For example, a downturn in the Mexican economy helped to send many Hispanics into Texas and California during the 1980s. Within the country, the movement of population between regions frequently meets this criteria of being exogenous. A recent hypothesis of shifting labor supply holds that since the late 1960s, workers seemed to have shifted their preferences with respect to either climate or geography. Warm areas may have become more attractive, and so labor supply has shifted to the "sunbelt" regions. This explains, the theory contends, why many areas with warmer climates grew rapidly over the last several decades—in many cases, with little or no increase in real wages. Florida, Arizona, and southern California are held up as examples of this climate-shift notion. While strong job growth in conjunction with stagnant wages provides some evidence of shifting labor supply, it does not explain why such labor supply changes occur.[11]

Labor supply shifts also can come about internally from changes in a region's effective birthrate. If there are changes in a region's age distribution or age-specific fertility, the impact on the area's labor supply can be pronounced, but will lag almost two decades behind. Since offspring have some preference to work in the region in which they were raised, a region experiencing a high birthrate will eventually find itself with a plentiful supply of young workers. By contrast, a region with a low effective birthrate will eventually face the task of having to attract workers from other regions. To illustrate that regions do grow due to such labor supply shifts, as well as export demand, we turn to Table 7.6.

In Table 7.6, we examine growth in eight major metropolitan areas over the 1960 to 1990 period.[12] Atlanta and Dallas show extraordinary growth in both wages and population (or employment). Thus, they exemplify the scenario of a positive shift in regional product demand. Chicago and Pittsburgh likewise exhibit a pattern induced by a negative shift in demand, leading to little population or job growth and well-below-average wage growth. With Miami and San Diego, however, rapid increases in population over the long term have been accompanied by negative wage growth. This would seem to illustrate a strong positive shift in labor supply. Our final two cities, St. Louis and Detroit, show virtually no population increase over 30 years, but high wage growth. These areas might

---

[11]Although there is little empirical evidence to support the notion, a common explanation for the "sunbelt" shift is the rapid technological improvement in air-conditioning systems that occurred during the late 1950s and early 1960s.

[12]In Table 7.6, we use the growth in real wages adjusted for changes in the cost of living over time, but not across areas. The data necessary to compute individual city changes in effective wages over time (a comparative price index over time and across regions) does not currently exist.

TABLE 7.6 Regional Differences in Labor and Wage Growth, 1960–1990

Metropolitan Area[*]	Population (% Change)	Employment		Wages[†] (% Change)
		Total (% Change)	Manufacturing (% Change)	
Atlanta	179	312	109	19
Chicago	18	54	−21[‡]	3
Dallas	136	NA	140	19
Detroit	16	71	−9	18
Miami	107	191	109	−8
Pittsburgh	−7	31	−52[§]	−8
San Diego	142	275	103	−3
St. Louis	19	64	−12	18

[*]1960 figures based on 1960 Census Bureau MSA definitions; 1990 figures based on 1990 Census Bureau definitions.
[†]Real average hourly earnings of production workers in manufacturing, 1990 dollars.
[‡]1990 wage figure based on weighted average of Aurora–Elgin, Chicago, Joliet, and Lake County PMSAs.
[§]1990 wage figure based on weighted average of Pittsburgh and Beaver County MSAs.
Source: Population from *State and Metropolitan Area Data Books,* Bureau of the Census, Washington, DC, 1979 and 1991; employment and wages from *Employment and Earnings,* Bureau of Labor Statistics, Washington, DC, February 1961 and March 1991.

have experienced negative labor supply shifts; while population remained roughly constant, the labor force may actually have been declining.

What Table 7.6 illustrates is how complicated and difficult it is to disentangle the various causes of historic economic growth in any particular area. The complexity exists because many potential factors can cause shifts in the labor supply schedule of a region. Furthermore, the demand for a region's products may be shifting independently, but at the same time as the labor supply schedule is changing.

REGIONAL COMPETITION, WAGES, AND REAL ESTATE MARKETS

The discussion so far has emphasized how individual regions grow or decline and what factors contribute to these trends. We conclude this chapter by considering the system of regions within the U.S. and how that system evolves over time. There has been considerable recent evidence that documents the persistence of long-term growth differences between the various states and areas within the U.S. (Barro and Sala-i-Martin 1991). It is also clear that the causes of these long-term growth differences are quite complex. Climate, firm innovation, cost competitiveness, and immigration can all be contributing factors to regional growth. Regardless of the cause, regions cannot continue to grow unless they can attract labor with a competitive effective wage. Without a competitive effective wage, a region's labor supply will slowly erode. Thus, the hypothesis is sometimes advanced that across regions within a country, effective wages tend to converge even though nominal wages may differ. To examine this hypothesis, Table 7.7 presents data on wages and local living costs.

TABLE 7.7 Metropolitan Competitiveness*

Metropolitan Area	Actual Wage[†]	Skill-Adjusted Wage[†]	Median House Value[‡]	Cost of Living Index[§]
Anaheim	11.22	11.09	237,184	132.3
Birmingham	9.27	9.08	79,662	98.5
Boston	11.88	11.31	200,000	164.1
Buffalo	9.34	9.50	78,614	107.2
Cincinnati	10.19	10.00	78,745	102.4
Cleveland	10.36	10.16	83,855	109.5
Dallas	10.62	10.44	85,000	103.8
Denver	10.89	10.35	86,335	101.5
Ft. Worth	10.33	9.96	80,000	103.2
Indianapolis	9.62	9.61	78,614	99.3
Kansas City	10.69	10.22	71,155	95.1
Los Angeles	10.90	10.83	225,000	126.5
Miami	9.43	9.75	94,874	110.1
Milwaukee	10.11	9.91	92,240	102.0
Minneapolis	11.22	11.10	95,000	99.8
New Orleans	9.42	9.45	68,309	97.8
Philadelphia	10.98	10.72	139,000	127.2
Pittsburgh	9.84	9.56	71,155	102.5
Portland, OR	10.34	10.19	80,643	103.0
San Francisco	12.62	11.94	250,000	144.5
San Jose	13.06	11.83	251,564	129.9
Tampa	9.07	8.97	85,000	100.7
Washington, DC	11.97	11.22	170,000	128.4
Average	10.58	10.31	120,954	112.6

*1989 dollars.
[†]Actual and skill-adjusted wages calculated by multiplying wage differential indices by the December 1989 seasonally adjusted average hourly earnings of production or nonsupervisory workers on private, nonagricultural payrolls.
[‡]Median house value from American Housing Survey median house values for 1988, 1989, or 1990, converted to real 1989 dollars.
[§]Cost of living index is from 3Q 1989, except Boston (3Q88), Cincinnati and San Jose (4Q89), and Tampa (1Q90).
Source: Actual wages, *Employment and Earnings,* Bureau of Labor Statistics, Washington, DC, 1990; skill-adjusted wages, Randall W. Eberts and Joe Allan Stone, *Wage and Employment Adjustment in Local Labor Markets,* W. E. Upjohn Institute for Employment Research, Kalamazoo, MI, 1992; median house values, American Housing Survey, Washington, DC, 1988, 1989, 1990; cost of living index, American Chamber of Commerce Research Association, Louisville, KY, 1992.

The first column in Table 7.7 gives the average wage earned in 1989 by manufacturing workers in a sample of metropolitan areas. Since metropolitan areas differ in their industrial mix, the second column examines wages, controlling for differences in each area's industrial mix as well as average levels of education and job training.[13] The third column reports the average price of a three-bedroom home in the area, as determined

---

[13]The adjustment to the average manufacturing wage takes the same form as the hedonic equations in Chapter 4 that were used to adjust house prices. In effect, the adjusted numbers in Table 7.7 are calculated based on metropolitan area regression coefficients from an equation that explains individual earnings using variables related to education, industry, and job experience.

from the American Housing Survey. The last column gives a more comprehensive cost of living index, compiled by the American Chamber of Commerce Research Association, that includes regional variation in food and energy costs as well as housing.

The data in Table 7.7 show that there is a strong correlation between wages and the cost of living. Birmingham, Buffalo, Indianapolis, New Orleans, Pittsburgh, and Tampa all have low skill-adjusted wages. The average cost of living index for these areas is 101, compared with the 112.6 average for the 23 cities in the table. At the other extreme, Anaheim, Boston, Los Angeles, Minneapolis, Philadelphia, San Francisco, San Jose, and Washington, DC have the highest wages. The average cost of living for these cities is 131.6. The simple correlation between wages and living costs is 0.75. However, there are exceptions to this strong positive relationship. In Minneapolis and Kansas City, wages are high but living costs are low, whereas Miami has low wages and higher living costs. In general, the data in Table 7.7 is consistent with the notion that differences in nominal wages reflect differences in the cost of living, leading to a convergence of effective wages across cities.

The data in Table 7.7 also reinforce a primary assumption embedded within the regional model of this chapter: that an area's cost of living is largely determined by the cost of developing real estate. All of the areas that have high cost of living indices have high median house prices. The converse holds as well, and the correlation is exceptionally strong. In fact, across the 23 areas, the simple correlation between house values and the more general cost of living index is 0.86. Thus, an area may experience strong demand-induced economic growth pressures, but unless it can easily produce housing, such growth will drive up real estate rents and reduce effective wages, perhaps to the point of curtailing growth. In the longer run, the ability of an area to produce a reasonably priced and plentiful supply of housing and industrial structures may be one of its strongest assets in the competition with other regions for scarce economic resources.

SUMMARY

In this chapter, we examined how regions grow, focusing on the interregional location decisions of firms and households. We examined two sources of regional growth:

- Increased demand for a region's exports which brings more resources into the area. Demand for an area's exports are determined by conditions in the national economy, a region's industrial mix, and the competitiveness of a region's firms.
- Readily available factors of production that permit rapid expansion of a region's output. Labor and real estate structures are crucial factors of production. Effective wages and a region's attributes such as climate, amenities, and public services determine the supply of labor. The availability of affordable housing and commercial and industrial real estate are essential to expanding a region's output.

In the simple three-sector model presented in this chapter, we illustrated the important differences between demand-induced growth and supply-induced growth.

- An increase in the demand for a region's products increases regional output, employment, and stock of real estate, as well as output prices, wages, and real estate rents. Output, employment, and stock rise more than output prices, wages, and rents when factors are readily available and elastically supplied.

- An increase in the supply of labor (an outward shift in the supply curve) increases output, employment, the stock of real estate, and real estate rents, but wages and output prices fall. The increase in quantities and rents is large relative to the decreases in wages and output prices when output demand is price elastic.

REFERENCES AND ADDITIONAL READINGS

General

HENDERSON, J. VERNON. *Urban Development: Theory, Fact, and Illusion.* New York: Oxford University Press, 1988.

RICHARDSON, HARRY W. *Regional Economics.* Urbana: University of Illinois Press, 1979.

WHEATON, WILLIAM C., ed. *Interregional Movements and Regional Growth.* Washington, DC: The Urban Institute, 1979.

Regional Economies

ISARD, WALTER. *Methods of Regional Analysis: An Introduction to Regional Science.* Published jointly by the Technology Press of the Massachusetts Institute of Technology and Wiley (New York), 1960.

MATTILA, JOHN M. "A Metropolitan Income Determination Model and the Estimation of Metropolitan Income Multipliers." *Journal of Regional Science* 13, 1 (1973):1–16.

A Three-Sector Model of Metropolitan Economic Growth

BARTIK, TIMOTHY J. *Who Benefits from State and Local Economic Development Policies?* Kalamazoo, MI: W. E. Upjohn Institute for Employment Research, 1991.

ENGLE, ROBERT F. "The Regional Response to Factor Supplies: Estimates for the Boston SMSA," in *Interregional Movements and Regional Growth*, ed. William C. Wheaton, pp. 157–196. Washington, DC: The Urban Institute, 1979.

WHEATON, WILLIAM C. "Metropolitan Growth, Unemployment and Interregional Factor Mobility," in *Interregional Movements and Regional Growth*, ed. William C. Wheaton, pp. 237–253. Washington, DC: The Urban Institute, 1979.

Regional Exports and Product Demand Shifts

BARTIK, TIMOTHY J., CHARLES BECKER, STEVE LAKE, AND JOHN BUSH. "Saturn and State Economic Development." *Forum for Applied Research and Public Policy* (Spring, 1987):29–40.

CARLTON, DENNIS W. "Why Do New Firms Locate Where They Do: An Econometric Model," in *Interregional Movements and Regional Growth*, ed. William C. Wheaton, pp. 13–50. Washington, DC: The Urban Institute, 1979.

DIPASQUALE, DENISE, AND KAREN R. POLENSKE. "Output, Income, and Employment Input-Output Multipliers," in *Economic Impact Analysis: Methodology and Applications*, ed. Saul Pleeter, pp. 85–113. Boston: Martinus Nijhoff, 1980.

ENGLE, ROBERT F. "A Disequilibrium Model of Regional Investment." *Journal of Regional Science* 14, 3 (1974):367–376.

HEKMAN, JOHN S. "Branch Plant Location and the Product Cycle in Computer Manufacturing." *Journal of Economics and Business* 37, 2 (1985):89–102.

JAFFE, ADAM B. "Real Effects of Academic Research." *American Economic Review* 79, 5 (1989):957–970.

KRUGMAN, PAUL. "Increasing Returns and Economic Geography." *Journal of Political Economy* 99, 3 (1991):483–499.

NORTON, R. D., AND J. REES. "The Product Cycle and the Spatial Decentralization of American Manufacturing." *Regional Studies* 13, 2 (1979):141–152.

PAPKE, JAMES A., AND LESLIE E. PAPKE. "Measuring Differential State-Local Tax Liabilities and Their Implication of Business Investment Location." *National Tax Journal* 39, 3 (1986):357–366.

PAPKE, LESLIE E. "Subnational Taxation and Capital Mobility: Estimates of Tax-Price Elasticities." *National Tax Journal* 40, 2 (1987):191–203.

SCHMENNER, ROGER W. *Making Business Location Decisions*. Englewood Cliffs, NJ: Prentice Hall, 1982.

TERKLA, DAVID G., AND PETER B. DOERINGER. "Explaining Variations in Employment Growth: Structural and Cyclical Change among States and Local Areas." *Journal of Urban Economics* 29, 3 (1991):329–348.

Regional Labor Supply: Migration and Demography

GRAVES, PHILIP E. "Migration and Climate." *Journal of Regional Science* 20, 2 (1980):227–238.

GREENWOOD, MICHAEL J. "Research on Internal Migration in the United States: A Survey." *Journal of Economic Literature* 13, 2 (1975):397–433.

Regional Competition, Wages, and Real Estate Markets

BARRO, ROBERT J., AND XAVIER SALA-I-MARTIN. "Convergence across States and Regions." *Brookings Papers on Economic Activity* 1 (1991):107–158.

EBERTS, RANDALL W., AND JOE ALLAN STONE. *Wage and Employment Adjustment in Local Labor Markets*. Kalamazoo, MI: W. E. Upjohn Institute for Employment Research, 1992.

GYOURKO, JOSEPH, AND J. TRACY. "The Importance of Local Fiscal Conditions in Analyzing Local Labor Markets." *Journal of Political Economy* 97, 5 (1989):1208–1231.

ROBACK, JENNIFER. "Wages, Rents and the Quality of Life." *Journal of Political Economy* 90, 6 (1982):1257–1278.

CHAPTER 8

THE MARKET FOR HOUSING UNITS: HOUSEHOLDS, PRICES, AND FINANCING

There is no question that each metropolitan area has its own local housing market. The national housing market represents the average behavior across these different local markets. Rather than examining prices and density gradients within a single market as we did in Chapters 3 and 4, in the next few chapters we aggregate across space and examine housing markets at the metropolitan and national levels. Tracking trends in the national market over time provides a useful basis for comparing movements in individual markets. How does the housing market in Boston or Pittsburgh compare with what is happening in the national housing market? Trends in the national market provide useful information for developing federal housing policy, which must address needs across many diverse markets.

In studying housing markets, we use two different measures of housing: housing units and housing services. The market for housing units is simply the demand for and supply of dwelling units. The dwelling unit is any residence, including single family detached homes, row houses, townhouses, apartments, condominiums, and so on. This definition makes no distinction between unit quality, range of unit amenities (e.g., garages, jacuzzis, ocean views, etc.), or the unit's neighborhood location. In other words, when examining the market for housing units, we count all units equally regardless of their characteristics.

In studying the market for housing services, we attempt to sort out the differences in housing units. *Housing services* are defined as the total quantity *and* quality of housing consumed. Housing services include the size of the structure and lot, the characteristics of the unit, and any locational amenities (e.g., quality of public schools, parks, and local

Chapter 8   The Market for Housing Units   183

taxes). Clearly, housing units are easier to measure (they can simply be counted) than housing services. In this chapter, we focus on the market for housing units; in Chapter 9, we will consider the market for housing services.

In the next section, we examine the various determinants of the demand for housing units and the decision of whether to own or rent housing. Then we take up the issue of measuring the true price of housing, focusing on the difference between this price and what consumers spend. This is followed by discussions on the importance of mortgage markets and federal tax policy in determining the annual costs of owning a home. Finally, we end with a discussion of the impact of federal tax policy on the supply of or investment in rental housing.

HOUSEHOLD FORMATION AND THE DEMAND FOR HOUSING UNITS

The demographic makeup of the population plays an important part in the operation of the housing market. By definition, a household is a single individual or a group of individuals (related or unrelated) living in the same dwelling unit. In 1989, the resident population of the U.S. was 248 million people. These 248 million people grouped themselves into 93.7 million households, which implies an average household size of 2.65 people (Statistical Abstract 1991).

The demand for housing in the U.S. can be measured by the number of households. Annual growth in this number, or net household formations, indicates the change in overall housing demand. Net household formations have ranged from 500,000 to 2 million over the last three decades. Household formations rose as the post–World War II baby boom began to form households in the late 1960s through the 1970s. Since the early 1970s, baby-boom households have delayed marriage and childbearing, resulting in a "baby bust." During the 1980s, the number of households grew by 1.25 million per year on average; for the 1990s, net household formations are projected to be about 1.1 million annually.

Figure 8.1, derived from figures from the U.S. Census, provides the number of households by age for 1960 through 1990. The Census also provides a projection of the distribution of households by age through 2000. The figure clearly shows the aging of the baby boom. In 1980, there were more household heads aged 25 to 34 than any other age category. By 2000, the largest age category for head of household will be between the ages of 35 and 44, with the 45 to 54 year olds close behind. The figure also clearly shows the effects of the baby bust. Since 1980, the number of household heads under age 35 has decreased, as opposed to increases in all other age brackets. This pattern will continue into the 1990s. The number of elderly household heads (over age 65) has been rising steadily over the past three decades relative to the number in other age categories, and this increase will accelerate into the next century as the baby-boom generation ages.

How important a factor is age in the decision to form a household? We can answer this question by estimating the number of household formations, based only on the changing age distribution of the population. Consider the following calculation. Take the

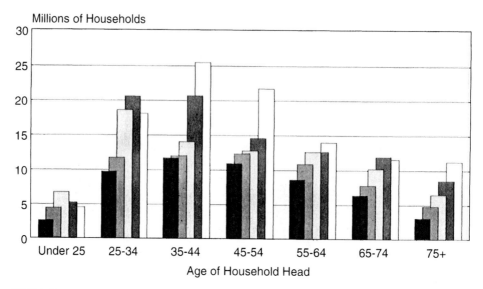

FIGURE 8.1 Distribution of households by age of household head, 1960–2000.

Source: Household and Family Characteristics, Series P-20, U.S. Bureau of Census.

rate at which persons in each age group of the population form households (the "headship rate") in a given year. (Any year could be used; in this case we chose 1973.) Apply these headship rates to the age distribution of households in prior and subsequent years to estimate an "age-expected" number of households. This measure of household formations isolates how changes in the age distribution of the population can be expected to alter the number of households formed from year to year. In Figure 8.2, actual and age-expected household formations are presented for the period between 1960 and 1990. A comparison of the two formation rates shows that during much of the early 1960s, they moved in a similar pattern. From 1966 to 1980, however, actual household formation ran way ahead of that predicted by the age distribution. By contrast, in the 1980s, actual household formation lagged slightly behind the age-expected formation.

Figure 8.2 makes clear that, while age is important, there must be other factors influencing changes in household formation. Are household formations independent of the housing market? It has been argued that high housing costs can delay the move of young adults from their family homes to their own households or result in the doubling up of families into a single unit (e.g., children moving their families into their parents' home or adults living with roommates).

Changes in lifestyles, such as delays of marriage and childbearing or increases in the divorce rate, are other factors that can influence both the number of new households and the types of household formations. In Figure 8.3, we trace the increase in population and households for 1989. This year is typical of recent periods, in that the number of households is growing faster than the population. Lower birthrates, continued high rates of divorce, and fewer remarriages have all contributed to smaller household sizes

Chapter 8   The Market for Housing Units

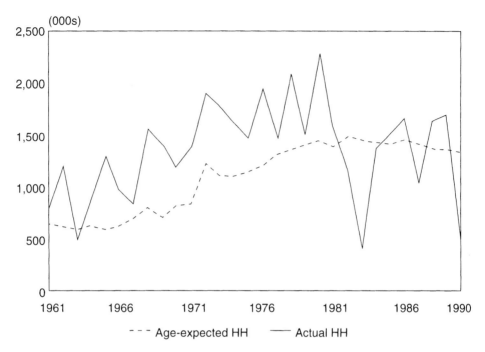

FIGURE 8.2 Household formation, 1961–1990.

Source: Denise DiPasquale and William C. Wheaton, "Housing Market Dynamics and the Future of Housing Prices," *Journal of Urban Economics,* 1994.

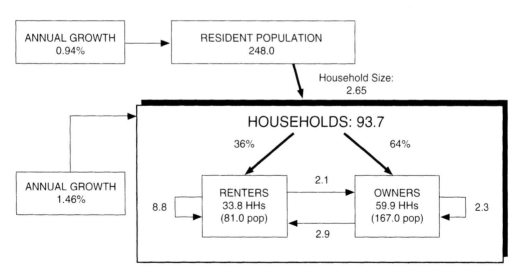

FIGURE 8.3 Household movement, 1989.

Figures in millions.

Source: Data from American Housing Survey, 1989.

over the last decade. Changes such as these can significantly impact the type of housing unit demanded.

TENURE CHOICE

At the time households are formed, they must also make the decision of whether to own or rent. In this chapter, we study this decision as part of the demand for housing units. As shown in Figure 8.3, 64 percent of all households owned their homes in 1989, while 36 percent lived in rental units. In the previous 12 months before the 1989 American Housing Survey, 17.3 percent of all households moved. As one might expect, the majority of these moves (54.1 percent) were made by renters to another rental unit. Moves by renters to owner-occupied units accounted for 13.4 percent of total moves. Moves by owners to other owner-occupied units accounted for 14.4 percent of moves. Perhaps most surprising, moves by owners to rental units accounted for the remaining 18.2 percent of moves.

Tenure choice—the decision to rent or to own a home—is an important one for most households. As will be discussed later in this chapter, the initial cash required to purchase a home (down payment and closing costs), as well as the income required to qualify for a mortgage, may limit the ability of some households to own their homes. Setting aside the ability to clear these hurdles, it is not obvious that all households want to own their own home. Households that move frequently for work or recreational opportunities (e.g., skiing in winter and sailing in the summer) may find renting less costly. The data provided in Figure 8.3 show that mobility rates are higher among renters than homeowners.

An important reason that more mobile households might choose to rent is that the transaction costs associated with renting are far lower than those connected with homeownership. For homeowners, the fees for lawyers, insurers, and the mortgage lender can range from 1 percent to 3 percent of the purchase price. Many homeowners must also sell their current home in order to move. Selling a home requires time to search for a buyer and, in many cases, the payment of realtor fees to complete the sale. Realtor fees range between 3 and 6 percent of the purchase price. Finally, searching for a new home can be a time-consuming and, therefore, a costly process. For renters, the typical transaction costs are a security deposit of one or two months' rent and the search costs to find a new unit. Tenants leaving a rental unit at the end of a lease typically do not incur any costs. Given these differences in costs, households whose employment situation or age require frequent moving may prefer renting to owning their homes. A homeowner who must move annually could lose as much as 10 percent of her house value every year simply in transactions costs.

How does the attractiveness of homeownership change over one's lifetime? Mobility tends to decline with age as workers settle into their careers or begin having children. It is also true that older workers have had time in the labor market to accumulate the savings required to make the down payment on a house. Finally, wages tend to rise with work experience. All of these factors should increase homeownership with age. Table 8.1 examines the variation in homeownership rates both by income and age. The table shows that homeownership rates rise dramatically with income overall, as well as within every

Chapter 8 The Market for Housing Units

age bracket. The overall homeownership rate also rises with age, at least up through 64 years of age. After that it declines slightly. Within each income group, however, the rate always rises with age. Thus, the decrease in overall homeownership among the elderly is probably tied to the general decline in their incomes.

As with household formations, age does not tell the whole story of homeownership rates. If we use the homeownership rates by age for a given year (again, we use 1973) and then apply these rates to the age distribution of households for different years, we can generate an "age-expected homeownership rate." As shown in Figure 8.4, the

TABLE 8.1 Homeownership Rates by Age and Income

Age of Household Head	Incomes ($000s)					All Incomes
	<20	20–29	30–39	40–49	50+	
25–34	21.7%	37.3%	53.4%	58.9%	68.5%	44.3%
35–44	36.6	55.2	68.3	77.6	85.4	66.5
45–64	59.4	73.1	81.5	85.6	90.5	78.1
65+	67.5	84.9	87.6	89.6	91.7	75.5
All Ages	48.3	58.3	68.0	74.9	84.3	64.1

Source: Authors' tabulations of 1990 Current Population Survey.

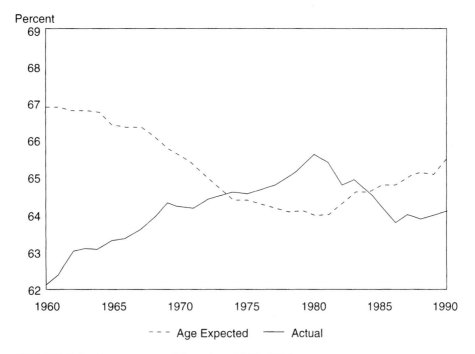

FIGURE 8.4 Homeownership rates, 1960–1990.

Source: Denise DiPasquale and William C. Wheaton, "Housing Market Dynamics and the Future of Housing Prices," *Journal of Urban Economics,* 1994.

age-expected homeownership rate fell from 1960 through 1980. During this period, baby boomers were just beginning to form households, and young households tend to have lower rates of homeownership. From 1980 forward, the age-expected rates increase because as the baby-boom generation ages it shifts into age groups with higher rates of homeownership. Age-expected rates continue to rise through the 1990s. Surprisingly, as shown in Figure 8.4, actual homeownership rates *rose* during the 1960s and 1970s and *fell* throughout the 1980s.

Why is there an inverse relationship between age-expected and actual homeownership rates? From Table 8.1, it is clear that income as well as age matters. For example, the more rapid income growth of the 1960s may have contributed to the increase in homeownership during that decade. In addition, the relative costs of owning vs. renting have fluctuated over the last three decades (Rosen and Rosen 1980). As Figure 8.5 illustrates, the cost of owning a home rose slowly from 1967 to 1977, increased rapidly through the early 1980s as real interest rates rose, and then declined somewhat as real interest rates fell. Over the same three decades, real rents have remained relatively stable. In order to determine more fully the influence of these relative costs on tenure choice, it is important to measure carefully the full costs of owning as opposed to renting a home. The first step in this process is to measure accurately the price of housing, how it changes over time, and the investment return that this gives homeowners.

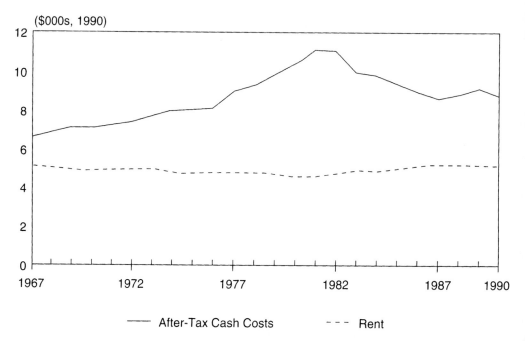

FIGURE 8.5 Costs of homeownership and renting, 1967–1990.

Source: State of the Nation's Housing 1991, Joint Center for Housing Studies, Cambridge, MA, Table A-1.

Chapter 8 The Market for Housing Units

THE PRICE OF HOUSING

As discussed in Chapter 4, in studying housing markets, it is important to distinguish between the expenditures that households make and a true measure of price and consumption. *Price* is the market price for a *defined* quantity of a good (e.g., price per pound of oranges or price per gallon of gasoline); *consumption* is the quantity or quality of the good purchased; *expenditures* are the unit price times the consumption. In the housing market, we generally observe expenditures, not consumption nor the price per standard unit of housing. In this respect, housing is quite different from other markets that economists study in which prices per standard unit and the units consumed are directly observed.

The house price data reported in the popular press generally refer to the average resale price of existing homes. This is the average price paid or expenditure made by homebuyers for a unit with a previous occupant. The problem with tracking expenditures (or price paid) over time is that movements in expenditures may reflect changes in both unit price as well as average unit quality. From year to year, the mix of houses that are bought and sold may change. If the houses that sell in one year are of higher quality than those in another year, then expenditures will rise but true prices may not. In order to separate changes in house prices from changes in house quality, economists have used a variety of statistical techniques that estimate prices for a uniform, or *quality-controlled,* house. The difference between a quality-controlled house price and actual housing expenditures is a measure of housing consumption (both quantity and quality). We discuss measures of housing consumption in more detail in Chapter 9. As for measuring housing prices, there are two approaches: the hedonic approach and the repeat sales approach.

Hedonic Price Indices

In Chapters 3 and 4, we described a microeconomic theory of how consumers value housing attributes and use this valuation to develop corresponding rent or price offer functions. While we never observe the value placed on the individual attributes, the offer price reflects these valuations. In equilibrium, each house is purchased by that household whose offer price exceeds that of all other households. Thus, actual market transaction prices represent the outer-envelope of individual offer functions. This theory has led many researchers to hypothesize that market prices are likely to have the same kind of functional relationship with housing attributes that individual offer price functions do. For example, since individual households obey the law of diminishing marginal utility, market prices as a whole should as well.

As we discussed in Chapter 4, a *hedonic price equation* is simply a relationship between housing unit attributes and market prices (rather than individual household offer prices). Following the offer price functions of Chapter 4, then, we might expect to observe the multiplicative relationship (Equation 8.1) between a house's market price, P, and its n measured structural and locational attributes ($X_i, i = 1, n$). As long as each of the αs in (8.1) are positive but less than 1, then prices increase with more of each attribute, but at a decreasing rate.

$$P = X_1^{\alpha 1} X_2^{\alpha 2} X_3^{\alpha 3} \ldots\ldots X_n^{\alpha n} \quad (8.1)$$

Over time, the valuation of housing attributes by households is likely to shift because of income growth, overall inflation, and specific conditions in the housing market. If we assume that the *relative* market valuation of housing attributes does not change, then these shifts over time can be incorporated by adding an additional term to Equation (8.1). Let time periods (years) be denoted with the letter t, and let D_t represent a dummy variable which has the value 1 for period t and zero for all other periods ($t = 1,T$). We let the parameter β_t represent how much house prices in period t have shifted since the base period ($t = 0$). The sum of the $\beta_t D_t$ ($t = 1,T$) terms are then added exponentially to Equation (8.1), yielding the following expression for the price of a house:

$$P = [X_1^{\alpha 1} X_2^{\alpha 2} X_3^{\alpha 3} \ldots\ldots X_n^{\alpha n}] e^{\beta_1 D_1 + \beta_2 D_2 + \ldots \beta_T D_T} \quad (8.2)$$

In the base period ($T = 0$), all of the D_t terms are zero, and house prices are determined by the expression in brackets. In period 1, only D_1 takes the value of 1, and the expression within brackets is multiplied or scaled by e^{β_1}. Thus, the ratio of current prices ($t = T$) to those one period back ($t = T-1$) is simply $e^{\beta_T - \beta_{T-1}}$ (the terms within brackets cancel out).

The value of the attribute parameters ($\alpha_1 \ldots \alpha_n$) and the time shift parameters ($\beta_1 \ldots \beta_T$) can be estimated statistically using a sample of house sales within a market over time—provided that the characteristics of the sold houses (the X values) are known—in addition to sales price and the date of sale. The data required are similar to those we used in estimating hedonic equations for single-family homes in the Boston metropolitan area and for condominiums in the Back Bay area of Boston in Chapter 4. The only difference is that, in Chapter 4, all the data were for the same year, whereas in this case data are combined across many years. Dividing the sales dates into T intervals and creating the dummy variables for each year, the statistical estimation can be made quite easily by taking the natural logarithm of Equation (8.2). This yields a linear regression equation between the log of house attributes, the dummy variables, and the log sales price:

$$\log(P) = \alpha_1 \log(X_1) + \alpha_2 \log(X_2) + \ldots \alpha_n \log(X_n) + \beta_1 D_1 + \beta_2 D_2 + \ldots \beta_T D_T \quad (8.3)$$

Again, as we showed in chapter 4, a regression equation of the form in Equation (8.3) provides estimates of the parameters in the price function. Using these parameters, we return to Equation (8.2) and calculate the price of a standard housing unit (one with "typical" attribute values). This is done for each time period (through the dummy variables) and the result is an estimate of what price the same unit would sell for over time, which is a true housing price index.

While conceptually sound, the hedonic approach suffers from rather extensive and stringent data requirements. Publicly available sales data often do not contain detailed information about unit attributes. Collecting such data can be difficult and expensive. If information about important unit characteristics is omitted from the data, and these housing characteristics have changed over time, then there will be systematic bias in the estimated hedonic price index (Epple 1987; Palmquist 1980; Haurin and Hendershott 1991). The repeat sales methodology, which does not require detailed information about unit attributes, avoids this problem.

Repeat Sales Price Indices

This technique also uses market sales or transactions data to track changes in prices over time. The repeat sales method, however, examines only transactions in which the same house has sold more than once during the time period under examination. Since the repeat sales approach is based on multiple transactions of the same house, the repeat sales estimates are automatically quality-controlled if there have been no alterations or renovations to the housing unit between the two (or more) transactions. If improvements or renovations have occurred between transactions, the repeat sales methodology will overstate the increase in house prices.

The regression equation used to estimate the repeat sales index can be derived from Equation (8.3). We denote P_2 as the most recent sales price of a unit, and P_1 as the earlier sales price. We also denote D_t^1 ($t = 1,T$) as a set of dummy variables for the *first* sales date and D_t^2 as the corresponding set of dummy variables for the *second* sales date. Thus, a house that most recently sold in period 6 will have only D_6^1 equal to 1, while all the other D^1 values are set equal to zero. Equation (8.3) characterizes house prices in any period. If a house transacted twice, we can subtract the *second* transaction price from the *first* and the X terms will cancel (assuming no alterations or renovations). This will leave Equation (8.4) as the difference in prices for the same house in two periods.

$$\log(P_1) - \log(P_2) = \sum_{t=1}^{T} \beta_t D_t^1 - \sum_{t=1}^{T} \beta_t D_t^2 \qquad (8.4)$$

In Equation (8.4), the estimated values for the β_t terms are the log of house prices in each period. The repeat sales method provides a price index but not price levels; in contrast, the hedonic approach provides price levels that can be translated into price changes. The advantage of the repeat sales methodology over the hedonic approach is that far less data are required about each sales transaction; only the selling price and year of sale are needed. However, since only houses that were sold more than once are included, the method ignores information on the vast majority of transactions. Certain types of homes sell more frequently than others (e.g., moderate to middle-priced homes in neighborhoods in which households are more mobile, such as college towns or towns near large corporate headquarters). The repeat sales methodology will tend to reflect changes in the prices of those types of homes.

Figure 8.6 illustrates changes in national house prices over the past two decades. The price index is a quality-controlled price index estimated using the repeat sales methodology; the existing sales price is the average price of existing houses sold annually and does not control for quality. Clearly, the basic patterns of change are the same with both price series. However, the decline in house prices in the late 1970s and early 1980s is sharper for the quality-controlled index, as is the upswing in the mid-1980s. This suggests that houses that sold in the early 1980s were better than average, while houses that sold in the late 1980s were worse than average.

This discussion of house prices has focused on prices for single-family owner-occupied homes. Identical methodological issues arise when considering apartment rents. Simply tracking average rents paid will indicate changes in the quantity and quality of

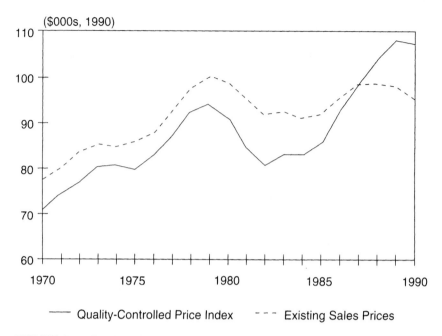

FIGURE 8.6 Real national house prices, 1968–1990.

Price index scaled using 1987 existing sales price.

Source: Price index, Freddie Mac Weighted Repeat Sales Index; existing sales price, sales price of existing single-family homes, *Homes Sales Yearbooks,* National Association of Realtors, Washington, DC.

rental units over time as well as the changes in rent. The Bureau of Labor Statistics (BLS) surveys rents for a sample of housing units as part of constructing the housing component of the consumer price index (CPI). To create a quality-controlled rent index, the BLS repeatedly surveys the same units. Hence, the BLS rent indices may be viewed as quality-controlled in much the same way that the repeat-sale index is quality-controlled. However, given that the units in the sample depreciate over time, the BLS index understates rent inflation. The BLS recently acknowledged the problem of ignoring depreciation and introduced a depreciation adjustment to the rent index.[1]

Figure 8.7 presents percent changes in quality-controlled rents and house prices for Houston and Los Angeles. The two cities exhibit dramatically different patterns. The crash in the Houston housing market during the early to mid-1980s is evident in the sharp declines of house prices and rents. In Los Angeles, the boom in house prices in the mid- to-late 1980s and the decline in 1989 and 1990 are clear. Rents are far less volatile than

---

[1]The BLS adjustment for depreciation in the rental series is made for 1988 forward. For a description of the BLS adjustment see Lane, Randolph, and Berenson (1988). Unfortunately, the BLS made no adjustments to the historical series. Lowry (1982) suggests that the average depreciation in rental housing units nationally is between 0.5 and 0.9 percent annually. The rent indices presented in this book assume a 0.75 percent annual depreciation rate.

Chapter 8   The Market for Housing Units

FIGURE 8.7 Changes in metropolitan rents and house prices,* 1980–1990.

*1990 dollars.

Source: House prices, *Metropolitan House Prices and the Costs of Homeownership,* by Denise DiPasquale, C. Tsuriel Somerville, and John H. Cawley, Jr., Joint Center for Housing Studies Working Paper W92-6, 1992; rent, Bureau of Labor Statistics, Residential Rent Index Component of the CPI-U.

house prices in Los Angeles, but, in Houston, rents seem nearly, but not quite, as volatile as house prices.

Given that home prices and rents are influenced by the same economic conditions and depend on the same underlying housing production costs, their divergence in a given metropolitan area may seem surprising. While the cost of construction and land will limit price declines over the long haul, there can still be short-term fluctuations in home prices or rents because of changes in regional economies or imbalances between the supply of and demand for units. Even within the owner-occupied market, prices for homes of differing quality or type may move temporarily in opposite directions. Housing is a durable good, and changing the stock of units with particular characteristics takes time.

While comparing percentage changes in rents and house prices provides useful insights into the operation of housing markets, in the tenure-choice decision, households ultimately compare rent levels to the annual cost of homeownership. Since, in the U.S., the vast majority of home purchases are financed with mortgages, mortgage interest rates and the structure of mortgage instruments play crucial roles in determining the annual cost of owning a home.

FINANCING HOMEOWNERSHIP

When purchasing a home, a household typically is required to pay between 10 percent and 20 percent of the purchase price in the form of a cash down payment, financing the remainder with a mortgage. A *mortgage* is a secured loan in which the borrower pledges the home being financed as security for payment of the loan. A mortgage has three important features: the interest rate, payment schedule, and amortization period (the term of the loan). These three features determine how much the borrower must pay each period and how quickly the homebuyer builds equity through repayment of principal. The standard mortgage instrument in the U.S. is the 30-year, *fixed-payment mortgage* (FPM), which has a fixed interest rate, a fixed payment, and is *self-amortizing*.[2]

With an FPM, the borrower pays the lender the same amount each month and at the end of the term the loan is paid off. Let's consider the mechanics of an FPM. How much would a mortgage lender loan today in return for payments of $1,000 per month for 30 years? Since a $1 payment in year 30 is worth less than a $1 payment today, the lender would calculate the present discounted value of the payment stream. The constant payments per period is an annuity. The present discounted value of an annuity (PDV) is:

$$\text{PDV} = R \frac{1 - [1/(1+i)^n]}{i} \tag{8.5}$$

where R is the payment, i is the interest rate, and n is the term. For a 30-year FPM with monthly payments, $n = 360$ (in months). Assuming an annual interest rate of 10 percent, i would equal 0.1/12, or 0.0085. Using Equation (8.5), payments of $1,000 per month for 30 years would yield a present discounted value of $113,950. Hence, a lender would loan $113,950 today in return for $1,000 per month for 30 years. If a homebuyer purchased a $125,000 home, and made a down payment of $25,000 (20 percent of the purchase price), she would need a $100,000 mortgage. Assuming a 30-year FPM with a 10 percent mortgage rate, what monthly payment would be required? Rearranging Equation (8.5) yields:

$$R = \text{PDV} \frac{i}{1 - [1/(1+i)^n]} \tag{8.6}$$

where the PDV is now the mortgage amount, $100,000. The monthly payments would be $878.[3] The monthly payments cover interest due and part of the principal. Early in the mortgage, the majority of each payment goes to interest. As the principal is paid off, the interest due declines and more of the payment goes to paying off principal. At the end of the term, both interest due and the total principal are fully paid.

In the U.S. mortgage market, the size of a mortgage that a borrower can obtain is limited by the borrower's income in relation to the required monthly payment. Current industry guidelines suggest that monthly housing expenses (mortgage payment, taxes, and insurance) cannot exceed 28 percent of gross monthly household income. As will be

---

[2] A *self-amortizing mortgage* is one in which, by making all scheduled periodic payments, the amount borrowed is fully repaid at the end of the term.

[3] Alternatively, we can calculate mortgage payments using continuous discounting, which was discussed in detail in the Appendix to Chapter 3. The PDV:

$$\text{PDV} = \int_0^n R e^{-it} dt$$

$$= \frac{R}{i}(1 - e^{-in})$$

Rearranging, the monthly payments are:

$$R = \frac{i\text{PDV}}{(1 - e^{-in})}$$

discussed in the next section, these guidelines are set by the federal credit agencies (Fannie Mae and Freddie Mac), which provide liquidity to the mortgage market by purchasing and selling mortgage loans. If a local lender wants to sell a mortgage loan through one of these agencies, it must conform to these standards.

It is important to point out that the FPM has fixed payments over the term of the loan. However, if there is inflation in the economy over the term of the loan, these payments will decrease in real (CPI-adjusted) terms. This decrease in real payments is often referred to as the *mortgage tilt*—real payments are higher in the initial period and decrease over time. Within limits, this tilt in payments may be viewed as a benefit. The lender as well as some borrowers may prefer a mortgage with declining real payments. For example, assuming that incomes keep pace with inflation, the mortgage payments become less of a burden over time, decreasing the risk of mortgage default. On the other hand, why should consumers sacrifice to pay high initial payments when years later they will have excess funds? Does it make any sense to limit mortgage lending by the ratio of the initial payment to initial income, when that income will normally rise rapidly relative to the payment? Do these mortgage provisions constrain the demand for housing?

An alternative mortgage to the FPM is the *price-level-adjusted mortgage* (PLAM) which, by design, eliminates mortgage tilt, keeping payments fixed in real terms. While not used in the U.S., PLAMs are widespread in many other countries, particularly those with higher inflation. With a PLAM, the borrower makes a payment that rises exactly with inflation or the country's price index (that is, payments in real terms are constant). The initial payment is determined by Equation (8.6). However, the PLAM payment is calculated on the basis of a real mortgage interest rate, $i - g$, where g is the inflation rate and i is the nominal mortgage interest rate. If there is no inflation, then the PLAM is equivalent to the FPM. If there is inflation, the initial payment on the PLAM is always less than the initial payment on the FPM. In subsequent years, payments rise with the rate of inflation, g. For example, if inflation was running at 5 percent and the nominal mortgage rate was 10 percent, the real rate would be 5 percent.[4] The initial monthly payment on a $100,000 mortgage would be $537, 39 percent less than the payment on the FPM ($878). As a result, the homebuyer can qualify for a larger mortgage loan. With the PLAM, however, both future payments and the outstanding balance on the loan (the principal) are indexed to inflation. If inflation continues to run at 5 percent per year, PLAM payments will rise at 5 percent a year.

In Figure 8.8, real and nominal annual payments for the FPM and PLAM are provided, using a $100,000 mortgage, a nominal mortgage interest rate of 10 percent, and an inflation rate of 5 percent (a real interest rate of 5 percent). Figure 8.8 shows that the nominal FPM payments are constant, but real payments decline over the term of the mortgage. The nominal PLAM payments rise with inflation over the term of the mortgage, but remain constant in real terms. The PLAM offers considerably lower initial

---

[4]Subtracting the current inflation rate from the current interest rate gives the *ex post* real rate. One practical problem with originating PLAMs is that the real mortgage interest rate is not known *ex ante,* since the rate of inflation is not known. Surveys of businessmen are sometimes used to provide estimates of expected future inflation.

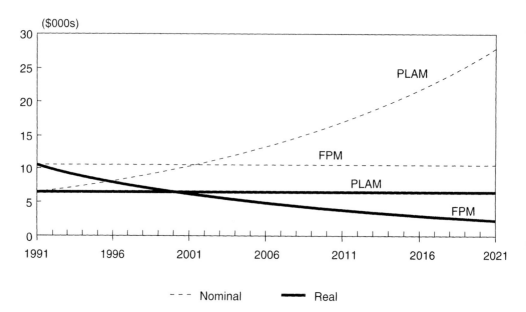

FIGURE 8.8 FPM and PLAM mortgages, real and nominal payments, 1991–2021.
$100,000 30-year mortgage; FPM at 10 percent, PLAM at 5 percent; real 1991 dollars.

payments, but the borrower takes on a liability that rises at the rate of inflation. By year 10, payments on the PLAM will equal the payment on the FPM; after year 10, PLAM payments exceed FPM payments.

Under both the PLAM and the FPM, the principal is paid off by the end of the term of the mortgage. However, with the FPM, the nominal as well as the real principal always declines over the term of the mortgage; with inflation, the balance due on the PLAM decreases in real terms but not in nominal terms. Hence, under a PLAM, it is possible for the borrower to owe more than the price paid for the house for some period during the term. The fact that the balance due does not rise in real terms allows the full amortization of the loan at the end of the term. A repayment schedule in which the outstanding principal increases in nominal terms is referred to as negative amortization. As long as house values rise with inflation, however, the borrower will not owe more than the house is worth. Figure 8.9 illustrates the schedule of repayment of principal under both mortgages in real and nominal terms.

The *homeowner's equity* in the house is defined as the market value of the house minus the outstanding balance on the mortgage. The day the house is purchased, the homeowner's equity is the down payment that was made. The homeowner accumulates equity in the home over time through both house price appreciation as well as the repayment of principal on the original mortgage.

With the FPM, the homeowner decreases the outstanding balance on the mortgage with every mortgage payment. Over time, more of the monthly payment goes to repayment of principal. In addition, all house price appreciation belongs to the homeowner in the form of increased equity. With the PLAM, the borrower builds equity at a much slower pace. This is because the outstanding principal grows at a rate only slightly less

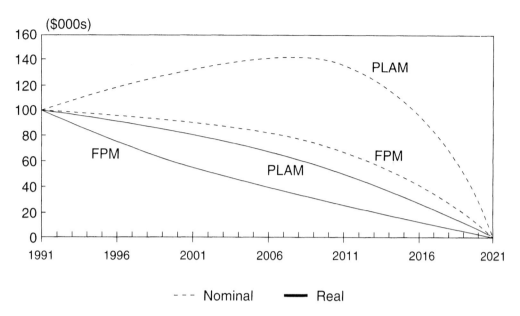

FIGURE 8.9 FPM and PLAM mortgages, real and nominal outstanding principal, 1990–2020.

$100,000 30-year mortgage; FPM at 10 percent, PLAM at 5 percent; real 1991 dollars.

than inflation (to allow for eventual amortization). If house prices appreciate at the same rate as overall inflation, the homebuyer's equity accumulation will be very slow. Much of the inflationary gains on the house go to the lender in the form of the increase in the outstanding principal. In effect, with an FPM, the borrower is foregoing current income and paying high initial payments in exchange for faster wealth accumulation through building home equity. This will allow the household to have greater disposable income in the future. With a PLAM, the borrower has a more gradual buildup of equity, foregoing some future wealth in exchange for lower payments and greater current disposable income.

In setting a fixed long-term nominal mortgage interest rate for an FPM, the capital market will incorporate its best guess about anticipated inflation. Who bears the risk of unanticipated inflation? Since the standard FPM does not give the lender a call option (the option to force the borrower to refinance the mortgage before the end of the term), the lender bears the risk. The lender must hold the mortgage even if it no longer provides a market rate of return. Does the FPM borrower bear the risk of unanticipated deflation? In practice, the answer is no. Borrowers have the option to refinance if interest rates fall. There are costs to refinancing, so the savings from getting a new mortgage at a lower interest rate must be greater than the costs of applying for a new mortgage. Current rules of thumb suggest that refinancing is cost-effective when interest rates fall between 1 and 2 percentage points. In the mid-1980s, when mortgage rates came down from the historic highs of the early 1980s, there was an explosion in mortgage refinancing.

With a PLAM, who bears the risk of unanticipated inflation? Since payments and the outstanding principal are both indexed to inflation, the PLAM, in effect, continuously refinances the original debt. Both the lender and the borrower are unaffected by inflation.

This conclusion, however, assumes that the borrower's income at least keeps up with inflation. While payments are fixed in real terms, income may fall in real terms, making it difficult for the borrower to keep up with the payments. The lender is protected from the risks of unanticipated inflation but retains the risk associated with rises in the real interest rate. The borrower retains the risk associated with real interest rate declines unless the borrower has the option to refinance.

When PLAMs have been considered in the U.S., three major objections have blocked their use. First, the negative amortization in nominal terms is considered a major problem. Two decades of research on the determinants of *mortgage default* (failure of the borrower to meet the mortgage payments) indicate that the most important factor is equity in the home. If the homeowner has little equity invested in the home, the likelihood of default increases. As a result, mortgage lenders and investors are reluctant to consider a mortgage instrument with negative amortization, particularly with low down payments. Second, homeownership in the U.S. is largely viewed as a major savings vehicle. The home is the largest single asset of most American households, who may prefer an FPM, which promotes savings, rather than a PLAM, which enhances current consumption. Finally, based on recent economic trends, there is concern that incomes may not always keep pace with inflation, making it difficult to meet the rising mortgage payments under the PLAM.[5] In other countries with higher inflation, PLAMs are viewed as a necessity. With the triple digit inflation in many Latin American countries in the 1980s, initial payment under an FPM would be prohibitive.

With borrowers resistant to PLAMs in the U.S., mortgage lenders have developed another form of mortgage instrument: the *adjustable rate mortgages* (ARM). Like the PLAM, the ARM enhances affordability, but shifts some of the risk of inflation from the lender to the borrower. Under an ARM, the borrower is charged the floating short-term nominal interest rate that adjusts periodically (e.g., every one, three, or five years). Since short-term rates are usually less than long-term rates, initial payments under an ARM are generally lower than with an FPM. When the short-term rate changes, monthly payments are calculated so as to ensure amortization of the unpaid balance over the remaining life of the loan. In today's market, most ARMs carry limits, or "caps," on the allowed increases in the interest rate each time the rate is adjusted. Caps also apply to the cumulative interest rate increase over the life of the loan. Typical caps limit the periodic increase in interest rate to two percentage points; over the life of the loan, the interest rate charged typically cannot exceed 6 percentage points above the initial rate.

Since the ARM is based on nominal interest rates, the tilt problem remains. Borrowers may pay a substantial price for the decrease in initial payments further down the road, since, even with the caps, there exists substantial risk of "payment shock" resulting from rising interest rates. For lenders, the ARM offers the opportunity to share the risk of unanticipated inflation with the borrowers. However, lenders may fail to receive the full short-term market return if the ARM caps bind at some point over the course of the loan.

---

[5]In order to address this concern, mortgage instruments in which payments are indexed to wage inflation rather than economy-wide inflation are receiving more attention. This type of instrument has been used in Mexico.

The mortgage instruments offered to borrowers are determined by the various institutional actors in the mortgage market. In the U.S., there is an extensive housing finance system that has grown over time, increasing the flow of capital to the home mortgage market. We now turn to the operation of this housing finance system.

THE U.S. MORTGAGE MARKET

Today, the housing finance system in the U.S. is composed of a primary mortgage market and a secondary market. The *primary mortgage market* is the market through which funds are actually provided to the borrower. That provision of a mortgage to a borrower may be carried out by a depository institution such as a commercial bank or thrift or by nondepository institutions such as mortgage banks. The *secondary mortgage market* is the market in which existing mortgage loans are bought and sold by investors.

Historically, local banks, particularly thrifts (savings and loan institutions), provided the funding for the majority of mortgage loans. These institutions took in short-term deposits, which represented household savings, and used those funds to make long-term mortgage loans. The availability of mortgage credit within a particular local area depended on local savings. When interest rates were relatively stable, funding long-term mortgages with short-term deposits proved to be a profitable business. However, in an environment characterized by rising interest rates, institutions had to pay higher rates on short-term deposits than were earned on their existing portfolio of long-term fixed-rate mortgages. Without call options, long-term mortgages could not adjust to higher rates, while rates on short-term liabilities increased. An additional problem was that mortgage loans were long-term assets with little liquidity; once a mortgage was in the portfolio, there was little prospect of selling it if the need arose to restructure the portfolio.

The fundamental idea underlying the creation of the secondary market is that while housing markets are inherently local in nature, the system of finance for home buying need not be. Rather than local banks being the ultimate funder of mortgage loans, the national capital markets now can provide the funds. Local lenders originate mortgage loans and can then sell those loans to a secondary market participant, who in turn sells the loans to an investor. The investor may be a pension fund or insurance company with a long investment time-horizon, willing to hold the mortgages in its portfolio. Such investors can take capital from areas with excess funds and move it into areas that have a shortage of funds. Meanwhile, the local lender can originate more mortgages by recycling the proceeds from the sale of previous mortgages. Since the 1930s a major goal of federal housing policy was to create a national mortgage market to replace the large number of independent local markets.

In order for a national secondary mortgage market to operate efficiently, mortgage loans must be standardized regardless of the local market in which they are originated. To be easily priced, mortgages must be commodities with similar structures and terms (e.g., 30-year, fixed-rate self-amortizing) and with similar borrower qualification requirements. As discussed in the previous section, for example, borrowers cannot qualify for a mortgage if annual housing expenses for that mortgage, plus taxes and insurance, exceed

28 percent of annual household income. With such standards, investors providing funds for mortgages are assured that all mortgages meet certain minimum requirements and, hence, need not inspect each individual mortgage before making a purchase. At the same time, it is important to remember that housing market conditions vary considerably across markets. Local originators offer the secondary market crucial expertise on local market conditions.

The federal government made a commitment to the development of a secondary market in the 1930s by creating the Federal National Mortgage Association (Fannie Mae) with the mandate to create a secondary market for mortgage loans and take a leadership role in creating standards for mortgage loans. In 1968, Fannie Mae was divided into two institutions, resulting in the creation of the Government National Mortgage Association (Ginnie Mae), an agency of the federal government housed in the Department of Housing and Urban Development (HUD). Its mandate is to make a secondary market in government-insured mortgages (often insured by Federal Housing Administration, or FHA). Fannie Mae became a federally chartered but privately held corporation. Fannie Mae's stock is traded on the New York Stock Exchange. Its charter mandates that Fannie Mae be exclusively in the business of making a secondary market for mortgages, primarily conventional (non-FHA insured) loans.

Finally, the Federal Home Loan Mortgage Corporation (Freddie Mac) was created in 1970. Like Fannie Mae, it also is a government-sponsored enterprise (GSE) with a federal charter that is privately owned and whose stock trades on the New York Stock Exchange. Originally, Freddie Mac was created to make a secondary market for mortgages originated by thrifts. Today, Freddie Mac and Fannie Mae compete to serve the broad spectrum of mortgage originators. In the last decade, investment banking firms have increased their role in buying and selling mortgage loans, but the market is clearly dominated by the federal credit agencies (Fannie Mae, Freddie Mac, and Ginnie Mae).

Mortgage investors include traditional institutions such as pension funds and life insurance companies. Commercial banks and thrifts continue to hold mortgages in portfolio as well. Of the secondary market conduits, Fannie Mae is the only one that plays a major role as a portfolio investor. In 1991, Fannie Mae had $129 billion in mortgage loans in its portfolio.[6]

As shown in Figure 8.10, in the current mortgage market, when a depository institution originates a mortgage loan, it can either hold the loan in portfolio or sell it. Non-depository institutions only sell loans. Originators can sell loans either directly to an investor or to the secondary market conduit. The secondary market conduit then makes the sale to an investor.

The secondary market conduits may simply sell whole loans to investors, or they may pool a group of mortgages and package them into mortgage-backed securities (MBS). They can also issue bonds backed by a pool of mortgages and sell the bonds or securities to investors. An MBS may be backed by thousands of mortgages or just a few. An investor in an MBS purchases shares of the pool of mortgages. Investors often prefer

---

[6]Fannie Mae funds its purchases of mortgage loans for its portfolio by selling short to intermediate term debentures.

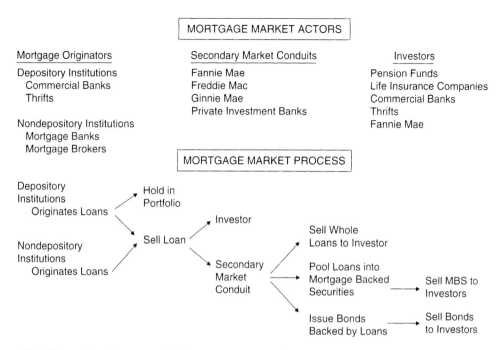

FIGURE 8.10 Diagram of U.S. mortgage market.

purchasing an MBS to an individual mortgage loan for much the same reason that investors prefer a diversified portfolio. Rather than take the risk that an individual borrower will make timely payments of principal and interest, the investor takes on the risk that a large group of borrowers will make timely payments (Fabozzi and Modigliani 1992).

With any mortgage investment there are two types of risk: *default risk* and *prepayment risk*. In the event of a default, the investor in an MBS takes the loss associated with his number of shares in the pool, whereas an investor in a single mortgage loan realizes the entire loss. Because the borrower has the option to prepay a mortgage at any time, the eventual term of an individual mortgage can be very uncertain. When a mortgage in the pool is prepaid, the prepayment of principal is passed through to the investors in proportion to their shares in the pool.

MBS issued by the federal credit agencies provide some security to investors. Fannie Mae and Freddie Mac guarantee the timely payment of principal and interest to the investor. Ginnie Mae's MBS are guaranteed by the full faith and credit of the U.S. government.

During the 1980s, there was enormous growth in the secondary mortgage market in general and in the market for MBS specifically. Rising interest rates in the late 1970s and early 1980s made funding mortgages from short-term deposits very unprofitable for thrifts and banks. Many thrifts moved away from the role of portfolio investors, limiting their activities to originating mortgage loans. In many cases, thrifts swapped their portfolios of individual mortgages for Fannie Mae or Freddie Mac MBS, backed by the very same mortgages. In this manner they limited their exposure to risk.

The growth in the role of the secondary mortgage market in providing funds for home mortgage loans has increased the importance of the standards set by secondary market institutions. These agencies greatly influence the types of mortgage instruments that are offered to borrowers. As we showed in the previous section, the mortgage instrument translates the purchase price of a home into an annual cost of homeownership. However, the annual cost of owning a home also is influenced by the treatment of the mortgage payment under federal income tax law.

FEDERAL TAX POLICY AND THE COSTS OF HOMEOWNERSHIP

In the U.S., there is a long tradition of encouraging homeownership through explicit and implicit federal government intervention. Over the past four decades, policy makers have argued that homeownership should be given a priority status because it provides households with a stake in their communities, ensures better quality housing, and provides an important vehicle for promoting saving over a household's life cycle.

By far, the largest federal subsidy to housing comes through the federal tax code. For federal income tax purposes, interest payments on both home mortgage loans and local property taxes are deductible from taxable income. In addition, the capital gains when the home is sold are exempt from taxation if the homeowner uses the gain to purchase another home within two years of the sale.[7] For homeowners over age 55, there is a one-time exclusion from capital gains tax, making it easier for the elderly to sell their homes and use the proceeds for other retirement needs.

What is the impact of this favorable tax treatment on the cost of homeownership? To answer this question, Table 8.2 examines in detail the costs of homeownership to the "typical" first-time homebuyer and how these costs changed over the 12 years between 1978 and 1990. This discussion is focused on the first-time homebuyer because the rationale for federal tax subsidy is largely based on the goal of promoting the transition from renter to homeowner.

In Table 8.2, the house-price series is quality-controlled; it is the hedonic price of the median bundle of characteristics purchased by first-time homebuyers in 1983. The mortgage rate is the annual average Federal Home Loan Bank Board contract rate, a standard measure of mortgage interest rates. Mortgage rates skyrocketed in the early 1980s, reaching a high of 14.78 percent in 1982. By 1990, they had declined to 9.74 percent. The calculations are based on a 30-year, fixed-rate mortgage with a 20 percent down payment. The initial cash required includes both the down payment and the closing costs (assumed to be 2.13 percent of the mortgage amount). These required initial payments range from a high of $17,359 in 1980 to a low of $15,997 in 1990. The up-front cash required to purchase a home is daunting to many potential first-time home buyers. In fact,

---

[7]In the case of other assets, when an asset is sold, a tax is due on the gain (sales price minus original purchase price) in the year of the sale.

TABLE 8.2 Homeownership Cost Components

	1978	1980	1982	1984	1986	1988	1990
House Price (1990 dollars)	$79,666	$79,983	$75,602	$75,076	$76,069	$77,357	$73,706
Mortgage Rate	9.40%	12.53%	14.78%	12.00%	9.80%	9.01%	9.74%
Marginal Tax Rate	22%	21%	19%	18%	18%	15%	15%
Mortgage Amount	$63,733	$63,986	$60,481	$60,061	$60,855	$61,885	$58,965
Upfront Cash Required:							
Downpayment (20%)	$15,933	$15,997	$15,120	$15,015	$15,214	$15,471	$14,741
Closing Costs	+ $1,358	$1,363	$1,288	$1,279	$1,296	$1,318	$1,256
Total:	$17,291	$17,359	$16,409	$16,295	$16,510	$16,790	$15,997
Annual Cash Costs:							
Mortgage Payment*	$6,375	$8,213	$9,049	$7,414	$6,301	$5,981	$6,076
Plus Other Costs[†]	+ $3,214	$3,223	$3,268	$3,298	$3,212	$3,107	$2,988
Before-Tax Cash Costs	$9,589	$11,435	$12,318	$10,711	$9,513	$9,088	$9,064
Less Tax Savings	− $435	$979	$1,201	$899	$665	$266	$308
After-Tax Cash Costs	$9,155	$10,456	$11,117	$9,813	$8,848	$8,822	$8,756
Less Nominal Equity Buildup	− $8,393	$8,206	$3,810	$2,430	$2,705	$3,274	$1,815
Subtotal:	$761	$2,250	$7,307	$7,383	$6,143	$5,548	$6,940
Plus Opportunity Cost	+ $1,233	$1,742	$1,674	$1,490	$923	$1,103	$1,083
Total Annual Costs:	$1,995	$3,992	$8,981	$8,873	$7,067	$6,651	$8,024

*Assume 30-year, fixed-rate mortgage. May not add due to rounding.
†"Other Costs" include hazard insurance, maintenance, property taxes, fuel, and utilities.
House price, *State of the Nation's Housing 1991*, Joint Center for Housing Studies, Cambridge, MA, 1991.

a number of studies have shown that the initial funds required to purchase a home is the most significant barrier for renters who are trying to make the transition to homeownership (Linneman and Wachter 1989; the U.S. Census Bureau 1991).

The bottom panel of Table 8.2 presents the annual costs of owning this typical first home. The before-tax cash costs include the mortgage payment as well as other normal operating costs. These include hazard (or fire) insurance required by most mortgage lenders, property taxes, maintenance expenses, fuel, and utilities. The before-tax annual costs peaked in 1982, largely because of the high mortgage interest rate at that time.

To measure the tax savings associated with owning a home, we must know the *marginal tax rate* of the typical homebuyer. The marginal tax rate depends on taxable, rather than gross income, which must be estimated by subtracting allowable deductions from income. In addition to the housing deductions (mortgage interest and property taxes), households can take deductions for other expenditures such as state and local taxes, charitable contributions, medical expenses above a set minimum, and so on.[8] Using

---

[8]Prior to the Tax Reform Act of 1986, interest payments for consumer debt (credit cards, car loans, student loans, etc.) were also deductible from income. For our calculations, we assume total nonhousing deductions of 5 percent of income prior to 1986 and then phase in the reduction in nonhousing deductions under Tax Reform, decreasing the deduction to 4.25 percent for 1987 and 3.5 percent for 1988 and beyond.

these total deductions, we can estimate the marginal tax rate for first-time homebuyers.[9] As shown in Table 8.2, the marginal tax rate was highest prior to 1981. The Economic Recovery Tax Act of 1981 cut marginal tax rates, as did the Tax Reform Act of 1986. By 1990, the marginal tax rate for first-time homebuyers is estimated at 15 percent.

All taxpayers are granted a standard deduction from income, regardless of expenditures on deductible items. In order to calculate the tax savings from homeownership, we must consider only deductions above the standard deduction. In 1991, the standard deduction for a married couple jointly filing a federal tax return was $5,000. Therefore, we subtract the standard deduction from total nonhousing and housing deductions and multiply this amount by the marginal tax rate to get the effective tax savings from homeownership. Again, the tax savings peaked in 1982 when mortgage interest rates peaked. In recent years, the tax savings for first-time buyers have been relatively small. This is due to a combination of declining mortgage interest rates, the decline in marginal tax rates, and the increase in the standard deduction. Lower marginal tax rates decrease the value of the homeowner deductions. The total deductions of first-time homebuyers, who typically purchase less-expensive homes, do not exceed the standard deduction by much. In Table 8.2, the tax savings for this group represented almost 10 percent of before-tax cash costs in 1982, but fell to just over 3 percent in 1990. For higher-income households with higher-priced homes, higher mortgage interest and property tax payments, and higher marginal tax rates, the value of housing deductions is considerably larger.

Taking before-tax cash costs and subtracting tax savings provides the after-tax cash costs. However, because housing is a capital good, this is not the end of the story on the costs of homeownership. As a capital asset, the value of a home may be expected to appreciate over time. As such, households view homeownership as an investment and are concerned with the expected return on that investment. When a household makes the decision to purchase a home, part of the decision is based on the expected appreciation in the value of the home. The total cost of homeownership takes into account the expected appreciation in the price of the home and subtracts this from the annual after-tax costs. This approach counts capital gains as they accrue, rather than when they are realized at the time of sale. While accrued gains are not directly comparable to the cash costs of housing, they do represent real wealth, which, potentially, can be converted to income.[10]

When homeowners contemplate the cost of owning housing they must estimate the expected future appreciation that will determine the investment return of their house. Economists suggest that consumers may use one of two approaches for this estimation: backward-looking expectations or forward-looking (rational) expectations. For the

---

[9]Marginal tax rates were calculated for the income decile that characterized first-time homebuyers in the 1985 American Housing Survey (AHS) (see DiPasquale 1989). That decile was then used in all other years, together with each year's tax schedule and estimated housing and nonhousing deductions, to arrive at the appropriate marginal tax rate.

[10]Remember that we are using an FPM for this analysis. With an FPM, all house-price appreciation accrues to the homeowner as it occurs. If we used a PLAM in this analysis, virtually none of the appreciation goes to the homeowner during the initial years of the mortgage—most goes to the lender in the form of a rising loan principle (to compensate for lower initial payments). Eventually, at the end of the PLAM mortgage term, the homeowner recoups all of the appreciation that has occurred during the intervening years. The timing of this appreciation, however, is quite different from that of the FPM.

example in Table 8.2, we used backward-looking expectations. In Chapter 10, we will develop the rational expectations approach. With backward-looking expectations, the household is assumed to use the price appreciation from the previous few years as a basis for forecasting future house price movements. In our example, we used a weighted average of nominal house price appreciation for the previous three years, with the most recent year given the highest weight. We need not consider federal taxes in this calculation since capital gains are only realized when the property is sold and are excluded from taxation if they are used to purchase a new home. The expected appreciation, or expected equity buildup, in Table 8.2 changes significantly over time. House prices rose dramatically in the mid- and late 1970s, generating high estimates of expected capital gains between 1978 and 1980. Actual house-price appreciation slowed considerably in the 1980s, resulting in much smaller expectations about future price growth. When expectations about house-price appreciation are taken into account, the costs of homeownership in the late 1970s through 1980 are much lower than throughout the rest of the 1980s and early 1990s.

Finally, to complete the calculation of the total cost of homeownership, we must consider the fact that the down payment and closing costs are financed with household savings. The opportunity cost of those savings is measured as the yield those savings would bring in alternative investments such as certificates of deposits, stocks or bonds. In Table 8.2, the opportunity cost is measured as the income that would have been earned if the funds were invested in one-year U.S. Treasury bills. The total annual cost of homeownership includes this opportunity cost.

An alternative approach to illustrating the costs of homeownership is to develop a summary measure called the *cost of capital* to homeowners, U (Dougherty and Van Order 1982). Let's define U as the total annual cost of purchasing \$1 of housing. This is equivalent to an after-tax interest rate less the rate of house-price appreciation plus the opportunity cost of the down payment. For simplicity, we assume that the opportunity cost of the down payment is equal to the mortgage interest rate. The standard measure of the cost of capital to homeowners (often referred to as the user cost of capital) is:

$$U = (i + t_p)(1 - t_y) - E\left(\frac{\Delta P}{P}\right) \tag{8.7}$$

In Equation (8.7), i is the nominal mortgage interest rate and t_p and t_y are the property tax rate and the marginal income tax rate. The expected rate of future nominal house-price appreciation is $E(\Delta P/P)$. Figure 8.11 presents a calculation of this cost of capital to homeowners over the last three decades. Note that the rapid house-price appreciation of the mid- to late 1970s was sufficient to make this cost negative for a few years.[11] At that point, homeownership was an extraordinarily profitable investment. In the 1980s, with slow house-price appreciation and lower marginal tax rates, the cost of capital rose.

It is clear that the preferential treatment of homeownership for federal income tax purposes has important impacts on the cost of homeownership. Current estimates suggest that the mortgage interest and property tax deductions alone cost the U.S. Treasury in the

---

[11]The negative user cost in the 1970s is the result of the fact that our measure of expected house-price inflation is based on actual recent price appreciation, which was larger than current after-tax interest rates.

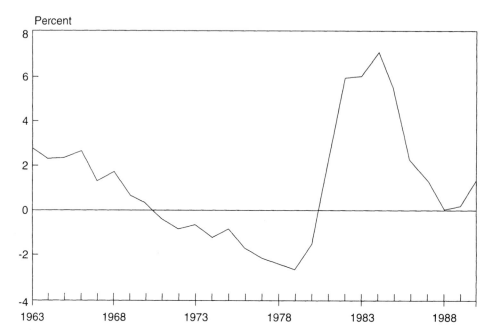

FIGURE 8.11 Homeowners' cost of capital, 1963–1990.
Source: Authors' calculations.

neighborhood of $70 billion annually. The capital gains exclusion adds further to this subsidy. The calculations presented in this section show that the impacts on first-time buyers are relatively small; instead, the policies tend to benefit those with greater income or value in a home. In this sense, homeowner deductions are an entitlement program with the perverse feature that the benefits rise with income and the wealth of homeowners. However, in recent years, some modest limits have been placed on the mortgage interest and real estate tax deductions for high-income households.

FEDERAL TAX POLICY AND THE RETURN TO INVESTORS IN RENTAL HOUSING

Federal tax policy also assists rental housing, but it does so by providing tax advantages to the owner-investor of units, rather than to the occupant. These advantages help to boost the asset price or value of rental housing, given a particular rental income stream. The supply of rental housing ultimately depends on the difference between the asset price of that housing and the cost of constructing or replacing it. The framework developed in Chapter 1 suggests that in long-run equilibrium, builders supply new rental units until the cost of constructing those units equals their asset price. In the short run, however, asset prices may bear little resemblance to longer run replacement costs. Since housing units take time to construct, sudden increases in demand can drive asset prices far in excess of construction costs. The difference between asset price and construction cost accrues to the landowner in the form of increased land rents. Thus, when federal tax policy assists investors and raises asset prices, this ultimately winds up increasing the supply of rental housing and reducing rents. In this way, assistance to the supply side of the rental housing market can eventually benefit the occupants.

An apartment building generates income from the rents paid by tenants and incurs expenses in the form of maintenance and repair expenditures. The *net operating income* (rents less expenses) is the flow of net income to the investor or owner of the building. As shown in Chapter 1, the ratio of current net income to market asset price is the capitalization rate—the rate at which current income is capitalized into asset value. If there were no special federal tax provisions for rental housing and the current rental income stream continued forever, the capitalization rate would simply equal the long-term interest rate.

More realistically, housing rents will grow over time, and a variety of federal tax provisions will further generate uneven income over the life or holding period of the investment. Capitalizing this more complicated income stream is the objective of this section. Our goal is to derive an expression for the cost of capital to investors in rental housing (a *cap rate*) that is analogous to the expression for the cost of capital to homeowners provided in Equation (8.7). The following discussion will outline, in some detail, the relevant aspects of the tax code and how each influences this capitalization rate.

For federal income tax purposes, owners of rental housing consider rent as taxable income and expenditures for maintenance and repair are deductions from income. Any interest payments on debt to finance the building are deductible from income. Finally, the tax code recognizes that buildings depreciate over time and permits an annual deduction from income for that depreciation. While the rationale for depreciation for tax purposes is the economic depreciation of the building, the implementation of the tax code may bear little resemblance to the actual economic depreciation of buildings.

The tax code sets a *tax life* for buildings, which over the past two decades has ranged from a high of 40 years to a low of 15 years; tax life currently stands at 27.5 years. The full purchase price less the value of land is depreciated over this tax life. The tax code provides a depreciation schedule, which determines the amount of depreciation that may be taken as a deduction in each year. The simplest depreciation schedule and the one currently used is the *straight-line method,* in which the annual depreciation deduction is simply the purchase price less the value of the land divided by the tax life.[12] Hence, if the building is purchased for $500,000 and the tax life is 15 years, the owner can take a depreciation deduction of $33,333 for each of the 15 years; if the tax life is 40 years, then the annual depreciation is $12,500. While the building depreciates each year, the cumulative depreciation for tax purposes that a specific owner can take is limited to the purchase price. Thus, an owner who holds the building until the property is fully depreciated finds it advantageous to sell the building to a new owner, who can then begin to take the annual depreciation deductions again based on the new purchase price.

---

[12]During other tax regimes, such as the Economic Tax Recovery Act of 1981, an alternative method of depreciation was used (a version of what is referred to as the double-declining balances, or DDB, method), which takes a higher fraction of the depreciation in the earlier years.

Finally, unlike owner-occupied housing, any capital gains realized with the sale of an apartment building are subject to federal capital gains tax. At the time of sale, the capital gain is defined as the sales price minus the original purchase price *plus* the sum of all depreciation taken while the property was owned. Thus, the depreciation is recaptured at the time of sale. Assuming that the building is held for a long period of time, the depreciation deductions taken earlier in the holding period have a much greater present discounted value to the investor than the cost of the recapture of depreciation at the time of sale.

The tax treatment of rental housing has changed significantly over the past two decades, undergoing three major tax regimes: pre-Economic Recovery Tax Act (ERTA) of 1981, ERTA, and the Tax Reform Act (Tax Reform) of 1986. As shown in Table 8.3, the tax life and the depreciation method for rental housing varied widely during these three periods. The tax life varied from 40 years pre-ERTA, to 15 years under ERTA (1982), to 27.5 years where it currently stands under Tax Reform (Follain, Hendershott, and Ling 1987).

The last line of Table 8.3 shows the percentage of historic costs (purchase price) that would be depreciated by the thirteenth year of ownership under the different tax regimes, given the assumptions made in the table. In the pre-ERTA years (before 1981), with a long tax life and the DDB method of depreciation, 61 percent of historic costs were depreciated by year 13. The short tax life under ERTA meant that 88 percent of historic costs were depreciated by year 13, while the longer tax life and straight-line method of depreciation under tax reform resulted in only 47 percent of historic costs being taken in depreciation by year 13. In terms of present discounted value, depreciation deductions in the early years are worth more than deductions in later years.

The magnitude of tax-depreciation benefits to an apartment building investor depends critically on the owner's marginal tax rates. Maximum marginal tax rates have ranged from 70 percent in the late 1970s, to 50 percent under ERTA, to 28 percent under Tax Reform. The table provides assumptions about the marginal tax rate of the "typical" investor in an apartment building under the three tax regimes. The lowering of marginal tax rates under Tax Reform significantly decreased the benefits of investing in rental housing. The tax rate on capital gains is also relevant to the investor in rental housing, since a gain may be realized when the building is sold. As shown in the table, the current

TABLE 8.3 Changes in Tax Variables: 1960–1990

	Pre-ERTA	ERTA 1981–1986	Tax Reform 1987–1990
Method*	DDB	DDB	SL
Tax Life (years)	30–40	15–19	27.5
Tax Rate on Income For Investors	0.50	0.45	0.28
Tax Rate on Capital Gains	0.25	0.18	0.28
Percent Depreciated (13 years)†	61	88	47

*Method refers to depreciation based either on double-declining balances (DDB) or straight-line (SL).
†Percent Depreciation (13 years) is the percentage of historic costs depreciated by the thirteenth year the property is held. The percentage of historic costs depreciated is based on the tax-rate assumptions on income and capital gains for rental housing investors provided in the table.
Source: Denise DiPasquale and William C. Wheaton, "The Cost of Capital, Tax Reform, and the Future of the Rental Housing Market," *Journal of Urban Economics,* 1992.

tax rate on capital gains is higher than under ERTA or pre-ERTA, again decreasing the tax benefits to investing in rental housing.

The federal tax provisions just discussed and shown in Table 8.3 can significantly alter the magnitude and pattern of a building's net after-tax income. To determine a capitalization rate for rental housing, we need to lay out these various income streams, discount them by a market after-tax interest rate, and determine what a willing buyer would offer for them. The ratio of this price to the current rent of the building is the *rental property capitalization rate*. With some simplification, rental housing generates three basic income streams for its owner.

The first income stream is *net rental income*. The building's initial net rent, R, includes gross income minus operating expenses and local property taxes. We assume that this income increases at a market inflation rate, g, and decreases with the economic obsolescence of the individual building (assumed to occur at a constant rate, δ). We also denote the capital market's risk-free interest rate as i, and the marginal income tax rate of the investor as t_y. Thus, we must discount an income stream that grows at the rate $(g - \delta)$ by an effective interest rate which equals $(1 - t_y)i$. Our assumption is that the owner of the building will hold it for n years at which time it will be sold. Using the continuous discounting procedure discussed previously, the present discounted value of this rental income stream is shown in Equation (8.8).[13]

$$\text{PDV(rental income)} = \frac{R(1 - t_y)(1 - e^{-un})}{u} \tag{8.8}$$

where: $u = g - \delta + (1 - t_y)i$

The second income stream of the building is the *discounted value of the depreciation deduction for tax purposes* (as opposed to economic depreciation, δ). For the purpose of illustration, we can assume straight-line depreciation over the same number of years that the building is held, n. In effect, we are assuming that it is optimal to hold the building for its tax life. It is never optimal to hold a building beyond this, since the depreciation deduction vanishes, and the building is more valuable to a new owner (who can start the depreciation cycle all over again). Under some situations, it can be profitable to hold a building for less than its tax life (Hendershott and Ling 1984). In our case, we take t_y times $1/n$th of the building's original purchase price, P, as the depreciation deduction each year. Discounting this benefit with the after-tax interest rate yields Equation (8.9):[14]

$$\text{PDV(depreciation)} = \frac{Pt_y(1 - e^{-i(1-t_y)n})}{ni(1 - t_y)} \tag{8.9}$$

---

[13]We obtain Equation (8.8) by using continuous discounting as shown in the appendix to Chapter 3:

$$\text{PDV(rental income)} = \int_0^n R(1 - t_y)e^{-ut}dt = \frac{R(1 - t_y)(1 - e^{-un})}{u}$$

[14]Again using continuous discounting, we obtain Equation (8.9) by:

$$\text{PDV(depreciation)} = \int_0^n \frac{Pt_y}{n} e^{-i(1-t_y)t}dt = \frac{Pt_y(1 - e^{-i(1-t_y)n})}{ni(1 - t_y)}$$

The final income stream is the *net proceeds from the sale of the building* in year n. If the building has been held for its tax life, then it will be fully depreciated, and capital gains tax will be due on the full sale price, and not just the difference between sales price and original purchase price. The capital gains tax rate is noted as t_c. The building's residual sales price will depend on how fast economic depreciation has been relative to market inflation. Since the 1960s, the inflation in market rents has generally exceeded the rate of economic obsolescence, which typically averages only about 1 percent annually. Again, for purposes of illustration, we make the simplifying assumption that these two rates offset each other and that the residual sales price equals the initial purchase price, P. Since the sale occurs n years into the future, this must be discounted by the after-tax interest rate:

$$PV(\text{sales proceeds}) = (1 - t_c)Pe^{-i(1-ty)n} \qquad (8.10)$$

In a competitive capital market, the original price paid for the building will equal the discounted value of all its income streams. As a result, we must combine Equations (8.8) through (8.10) and solve for that value of P where:

$$P = PDV(\text{rental income}) + PDV(\text{depreciation}) + PV(\text{sales proceeds}) \qquad (8.11)$$

The solution to Equation (8.11) is complicated because terms on the right-hand side as well as the left-hand side involve P. The rental property capitalization rate is the ratio

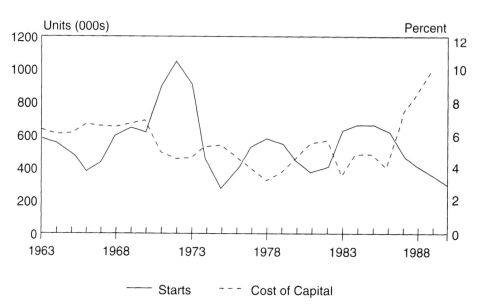

FIGURE 8.12 Multifamily construction and investor cost of capital, 1963–1990.

Source: Multifamily starts, *Economic Report of the President,* Table B-53, Washington, DC, February 1991; investor cost of capital, authors' calculations.

of current rent, R, to this solution price (R/P). In Figure 8.12, numerical estimates of this rental capitalization rate over the last three decades are presented along with annual levels of multifamily construction (units in structures with two or more units). While other supply and demand factors influence multifamily construction, there is a clear pattern of increases (decreases) in construction when the cost of capital decreases (increases). The historic movements in the cost of capital over time are caused by a complicated interaction between interest rates, tax treatment, and rental inflation. The rise in the cost of capital in the late 1970s, for example, is largely because of the increase in interest rates, while the rise after 1986 is mainly because of the changes in tax policy that followed Tax Reform. The combination of less-favorable depreciation allowances, together with the decline in marginal tax rates, was responsible for a rise of almost 4 percentage points in the rental cost of capital since the Tax Reform Act of 1986.

In the market for housing units, then, federal tax policy operates in two different directions. For owner-occupied housing, interest deductions and a capital gains exclusion lower the annual costs of ownership. By making housing more affordable, these policies stimulate demand. Using the four-quadrant analysis of Chapter 1, this raises home prices and eventually expands the supply of housing. With rental housing, tax policies stimulate the demand by investors, which then raises asset prices. Rising asset prices eventually expand the stock of rental units, and this then benefits tenants through lower rents. The pattern of such changes over time is the subject of Chapter 10.

SUMMARY

In this chapter, we illustrated the importance of demographic factors in determining the demand for housing units.

- Housing unit demand is based on household formations, which are not independent of the housing market. When housing is expensive, young people may decide to live with their parents longer or older households may double up with relatives or friends.
- Households tend to move more when they are younger. Renters are considerably more mobile than homeowners, partly because there are higher transaction costs for movers that own rather than rent.

Tenure choice—the decision to own or to rent—is influenced not only by demographic factors, but also by income, wealth, and the relative costs of owning versus renting.

- Homeownership rates rise with age, income, and wealth.
- The appropriate approach for comparing the costs of renting versus owning is to compare annual rent to the annual costs of owning a similar home. Examining rents and the annual cost of owning a home requires quality-controlled rents and house prices.

- The annual cost of owning a home is the purchase price times the user cost of capital. The user cost of capital includes the after-tax cost of mortgage financing and the after-tax opportunity cost of equity or the down payment. The user cost of capital must also include any expected house price appreciation. Capital gains from the sale of a home are generally free from federal tax.

- Federal tax policy has an important impact on the supply of rental housing. Net rental income is taxable, as are any capital gains at the sale of the property. However, the federal tax code permits a deduction from income for depreciation. The price of the rental housing asset is the sum of the present discounted value of the rental income stream and the depreciation benefits plus the present value of the after-tax gain at the sale of the property.

REFERENCES AND ADDITIONAL READINGS

General

DiPasquale, Denise, and Langley C. Keyes, eds. *Building Foundations: Housing and Federal Policy*. Philadelphia: University of Pennsylvania Press, 1990.

Fair, Ray C. "Disequilibrium in Housing Models." *Journal of Finance* 27, 2 (1972): 207–221.

Mills, Edwin S. *Studies in the Structure of the Urban Economy*. Baltimore: Johns Hopkins University Press, 1972.

Muth, Richard F. *Cities and Housing*. Chicago: University of Chicago Press, 1969.

Quigley, John M. "What Have We Learned About Urban Housing Markets?" in *Current Issues in Urban Economics*, eds. Peter Mieszkowski and Mahlon Straszheim, pp. 391–429. Baltimore: Johns Hopkins University Press, 1979.

Rothenberg, Jerome, George C. Galster, Richard V. Butler, and John R. Pitkin. *The Maze of Urban Housing Markets: Theory, Evidence, and Policy*. Chicago: University of Chicago Press, 1991.

Household Formation and the Demand for Housing Units

Borsch-Supan, Axel. "Household Formation, Housing Prices, and Public Policy Impacts." *Journal of Public Economics* 30, 2 (1986): 145–164.

DiPasquale, Denise, and William C. Wheaton. "Housing Market Dynamics and the Future of Housing Prices." *Journal of Urban Economics* 35 (1994): 1–27.

Haurin, Donald R., Patric H. Hendershott, and Dongwook Kim. "The Impact of Real Rents and Wages on Household Formation." *The Review of Economics and Statistics* 75, 2 (1993): 284–93.

Jackson, Gregory, George Masnick, Roger Bolton, Susan Bartlett, and John Pitkin. *Regional Diversity: Growth in the United States, 1960–1990*. Boston: Auburn House, 1981.

Mankiw, N. Gregory, and David N. Weil. "The Baby Boom, the Baby Bust, and the Housing Market." *Regional Science and Urban Economics* 19, 2 (1989): 235–258.

Muth, Richard F. "The Demand for Non-Farm Housing," in *The Demand for Durable Goods*, ed. Arnold Harberger, pp. 29–96. Chicago: University of Chicago Press, 1960.

Tenure Choice

HENDERSHOTT, PATRIC H., AND JAMES D. SHILLING. "The Economics of Tenure Choice, 1955–1979," in *Research in Real Estate* (vol. 1), ed. C. F. Sirmans, 105–133. Greenwich, CT. JAI Press, 1982.

JAFFEE, DWIGHT M., AND KENNETH T. ROSEN. "Mortgage Credit Availability and Residential Construction." *Brookings Papers on Economic Activity* 2 (1979).

ROSEN, HARVEY S., AND KENNETH T. ROSEN. "Federal Taxes and Homeownership: Evidence From Time Series." *Journal of Political Economy* 88, 1 (1980): 59–75.

The Price of Housing

CASE, BRADFORD, HENRY O. POLLAKOWSKI, AND SUSAN M. WACHTER. "On Choosing Among House Price Index Methodologies." *AREUEA Journal* 19, 3 (1991): 286–307.

CASE, BRADFORD, AND JOHN QUIGLEY. "The Dynamics of Real Estate Prices." *Review of Economics and Statistics* 73, 1 (1991): 50–58.

CASE, KARL E., AND ROBERT J. SHILLER. "Prices of Single-Family Homes Since 1970: New Indexes for Four Cities." *New England Economic Review* (Sept/Oct 1987): 45–56.

CASE, KARL E., AND ROBERT J. SHILLER. "The Efficiency of the Market for Single Family Homes." *American Economic Review* 79, 1 (1989): 125–137.

DIPASQUALE, DENISE, AND C. TSURIEL SOMERVILLE. "Do House Price Indexes Based on Transacting Units Represent the Entire Stock? Evidence from the American Housing Survey." *Journal of Housing Economics* 4, 3(1995).

DIPASQUALE, DENISE, AND WILLIAM C. WHEATON. "Housing Market Dynamics and the Future of Housing Prices." *Journal of Urban Economics* 35 (1994): 1–27.

EPPLE, DENNIS. "Hedonic Prices and Implicit Markets: Estimating Demand and Supply Functions for Differentiated Products." *Journal of Political Economy* 95, 1 (1987): 59–80.

HAURIN, DONALD R., AND PATRIC H. HENDERSHOTT. "House Price Indexes: Issues and Results." *AREUEA Journal* 19, 3 (1991): 259–269.

LANE, WALTER F., WILLIAM C. RANDOLPH, AND STEPHEN A. BERENSON. "Adjusting the CPI Shelter Index to Compensate for Effect of Depreciation." *Monthly Labor Review* (October 1988): 34–38.

LOWRY, IRA S. "Inflation Indexes for Rental Housing." Rand Corporation WD-1081-HUD, 1981.

PALMQUIST, RAYMOND B. "Alternative Techniques for Developing Real Estate Price Indexes." *Review of Economics and Statistics* 66, 3 (1980): 442–228.

Financing Homeownership

BRUECKNER, JAN. "Why Do We Have ARMs?" *AREUEA Journal* 21, 3 (1993): 333–345.

DIPASQUALE, DENISE, AND FRANCO MODIGLIANI. "Mortgage Design and Affordable Homeownership." Cambridge, MA: Joint Center for Housing Studies Working Paper W92-1, 1992.

DIPASQUALE, DENISE, C. TSURIEL SOMERVILLE, AND JOHN H. CAWLEY, JR. "Metropolitan House Prices and the Costs of Homeownership." Cambridge, MA: Joint Center for Housing Studies Working Paper W92-6, 1992.

FABOZZI, FRANK J., AND FRANCO MODIGLIANI. *Mortgage and Mortgage-Backed Securities Markets.* Cambridge, MA: Harvard Business School Press, 1992.

HUANG, DAVID S. "The Short-Run Flows of Nonfarm Residential Mortgage Credit." *Econometrica* 34, 2 (1966): 433–459.

JAFFEE, DWIGHT M. "An Econometric Model of the Mortgage Market," in *Savings Deposits, Mortgages, and Housing; Studies for the Federal Reserve-MIT-Penn Economic Model*, eds. Edward M. Gramlich and Dwight M. Jaffee. Lexington, MA: Lexington Books, 1972.

JAFFEE, DWIGHT M., AND KENNETH T. ROSEN. "Mortgage Credit Availability and Residential Construction." *Brookings Papers on Economic Activity* 2 (1979).

KEARL, JAMES R. "Inflation, Mortgages and Housing." *Journal of Political Economy* 87, 5 (1979): 1115–1138.

SMITH, LAWRENCE B. "A Model of the Canadian Housing and Mortgage Markets." *Journal of Political Economy* 77, 5 (1969): 795–816.

The U.S. Mortgage Market

FABOZZI, FRANK J., AND FRANCO MODIGLIANI. *Mortgage and Mortgage-Backed Securities Markets*. Cambridge, MA: Harvard Business School Press, 1992.

LEA, MICHAEL J. "Housing and the Capital Market," in *Building Foundations: Housing and Federal Policy*, eds. Denise DiPasquale and Langley C. Keyes, pp. 187–208. Philadelphia: University of Pennsylvania Press, 1990.

Federal Tax Policy and the Costs of Homeownership

DIPASQUALE, DENISE. "Homeowner Deductions and First-Time Homebuyers." Cambridge, MA: Joint Center for Housing Studies of Harvard University Working Paper W89-2, 1989.

DOUGHERTY, ANN, AND ROBERT VAN ORDER. "Inflation, Housing Costs and the Consumer Price Index." *American Economic Review* 72, 1 (1982): 154–164.

HAMILTON, BRUCE W., AND ROBERT M. SCHWAB. "Expected Appreciation in Urban Housing Markets." *Journal of Urban Economics* 18, 1 (1985): 103–118.

HENDERSHOTT, PATRIC H. "Real User Costs and the Demand for Single Family Housing." Washington, DC: *Brookings Papers on Economic Activity* 2 (1980).

HENDERSHOTT, PATRIC H. "The Tax Reform Act of 1986 and Real Estate," in *Building Foundations: Housing and Federal Policy*, eds. Denise DiPasquale and Langley C. Keyes, 241–262. Philadelphia: University of Pennsylvania Press, 1990.

HENDERSHOTT, PATRIC H., AND DAVID C. LING. "Trading and the Tax Shelter Value of Depreciable Real Estate." *National Tax Journal* 37, 2 (June 1984): 213–224.

LINNEMAN, PETER, AND SUSAN M. WACHTER. "The Impacts of Borrowing Constraints on Homeownership." *AREUEA Journal* 17, 4 (1989): 389–402.

POTERBA, JAMES M. "Tax Subsidies to Owner-Occupied Housing: An Asset-Market Approach." *The Quarterly Journal of Economics* 99, 4 (1984): 729–752.

ROSEN, HARVEY S. "Housing Decisions and the U.S. Income Tax: An Econometric Analysis." *Journal of Public Economics* 11, 1 (1979): 1–23.

SCHWAB, ROBERT M. "Inflation Expectations and the Demand for Housing." *American Economic Review* 72, 1 (1982): 143–153.

U.S. BUREAU OF THE CENSUS. "Who Can Afford to Buy a House?" Survey of Income and Program Participation, Current Housing Reports H121/91-1. Washington, DC: U.S. Bureau of the Census, May 1991.

Federal Tax Policy and the Return to Investors in Rental Housing

DIPASQUALE, DENISE, AND JEAN L. CUMMINGS. "Financing Multifamily Rental Housing: The Changing Role of Lenders and Investors." *Housing Policy Debate* 3, 1 (1992): 77–116.

DIPASQUALE, DENISE, AND WILLIAM C. WHEATON. "The Cost of Capital, Tax Reform, and the Future of the Rental Housing Market." *Journal of Urban Economics* 31, 3 (1992): 337–359.

FOLLAIN, JAMES R., PATRIC H. HENDERSHOTT, AND DAVID C. LING. "Understanding the Real Estate Provisions of Tax Reform: Motivation and Impact." *National Tax Journal* 40, 3 (September, 1987): 363–372.

HENDERSHOTT, PATRIC H. "The Tax Reform Act of 1986 and Real Estate," in *Building Foundations: Housing and Federal Policy,* eds. Denise DiPasquale and Langley C. Keyes, pp. 241–262. Philadelphia: University of Pennsylvania Press, 1990.

HENDERSHOTT, PATRIC H., AND DAVID C. LING. "Trading and the Tax Shelter Value of Depreciable Real Estate." *National Tax Journal* 37, 2 (June 1984): 213–224.

HENDERSHOTT, PATRIC H., AND JAMES D. SHILLING. "The Economics of Tenure Choice, 1955–1979," in *Research in Real Estate* (vol. 1), ed. C. F. Sirmans, pp. 105–133. Greenwich, CT: JAI Press, 1982.

CHAPTER 9

THE MARKET FOR HOUSING SERVICES: MOVING, SALES, AND VACANCY

The aggregate supply and demand for housing units characterizes only part of the operation of the nation's housing market. What's missing from this discussion of housing units are important questions such as what kinds of units households desire, how households acquire such units, and how the configuration of the nation's housing stock changes gradually over time. This part of the housing sector is known as *the market for housing services*. A capital good such as housing is valued because of the flow of utility or services that it provides to its users over time. A factory machine provides work (perhaps in place of labor); and, so, a housing unit provides shelter, prestige, or other services that consumers desire.

Chapter 4 showed that the types of services provided by a particular house depend very much on its configuration. A home with many bedrooms and a large lot, for example, provides space in which children can live and play. On the other hand, a house with fewer bedrooms and a smaller lot but with large living areas and a pool may offer better prestige or entertaining services for its occupants. The utility that a household derives from certain types of houses and their associated services certainly depends on the type of household and its particular needs. Household age, income, and size are just a few of the many individual characteristics that influence the demand for houses with specific features. Chapter 4 also demonstrated how a competitive housing market will efficiently match each type of house with those households willing to pay the most for that unit's particular features.

This chapter proceeds further and examines how this matching process operates dynamically over time. It is clear, for example, that the demand for housing services changes significantly over the life cycle of any individual household. The arrival of children, increasing economic success, and retirement can each generate major shifts in the demand for housing services. Such shifts in housing demand lead households to move—to seek a new and more appropriate unit and then vacate the unit previously occupied. This dynamic process of household mobility generates a large volume of housing transactions each year (sales or leases), and it is through such transactions that households achieve the type of housing services that they demand.

The housing vacancy rate (the excess of units over households) plays an important role in facilitating this transactions market. Vacant units (for sale or rent) provide the inventory through which households search when seeking a new unit. When this inventory is large, potential buyers have a wide choice, can easily find the unit they want, and can offer lower purchase prices. For sellers, on the other hand, a large inventory spells difficulty in finding buyers and leads to considerable flexibility in accepting purchase offers. Thus, house prices are strongly influenced by the combination of the vacancy rate and the fraction of households who are seeking to move. If household mobility is high and the vacant inventory low, prices will rise rapidly, eventually dissuading households from seeking a new house. Conversely, a large inventory and low mobility will lower prices, encouraging households to move and make the needed adjustment to their consumption of housing services.

HOUSEHOLDS AND THEIR HOUSING CONSUMPTION PATTERNS

The observation that household characteristics will influence the type of housing consumed may seem on the surface to be obvious. Yet the exact link between households and units often reveals some surprising patterns. The most extensive survey of households, which contains information both about the respondents' housing as well as their socioeconomic characteristics, is the decennial U.S. Census. A more frequent source, but one based on a much smaller survey of housing units, is the American Housing Survey (formerly called the Annual Housing Survey) by the Census Bureau and the Department of Housing and Urban Development. Many of the tables in this section come from analyzing the data in the 1989 American Housing Survey.

INCOME AND HOUSING CONSUMPTION: THE ELASTICITY OF DEMAND

The overall consumption of housing services is often difficult to measure. In past chapters, we have dealt with this problem in two ways. In Chapter 8, we measured aggregate housing consumption over time by calculating it as a residual from the changes in prices for certain housing units. A true price index for identical units was determined either by surveying repeated house sales, or by statistically estimating a quantity-quality controlled price equation (the hedonic approach). The difference between the movement of this index and the movement in overall average house prices measures changes in the provision of housing services.

In Chapters 3 and 4, it was also argued that *within* a given housing market, differences in house prices reflected only variation in housing consumption or services. Thus, the difference in price between a two-bedroom home and a four-bedroom home within the New York area reflects mostly the value of the additional space. However, a two-bedroom house in New York may cost much more than a four-bedroom unit in Columbus, Ohio, because the two markets have different price indices. Comparing the housing expenditure of wealthy and poor households that live in the same market, or markets, provides a valid estimate of the link between income and housing consumption. Comparing the expenditure of wealthy households in one market with poor ones in another does not.

Table 9.1 presents the average value of owner-occupied housing units by income and by age categories, using the 1989 national American Housing Survey. Because housing units in this survey are chosen at random from a set of local markets across the country, the survey ensures that the units belong to the same collective or national market. Thus, expenditure or value should reflect overall housing services. The table examines married households with children for household heads aged 25–34, 35–44, and 45–54, but married couples with no children in the age categories 55–64 and 65 and over. This allows us to isolate the impact of income on families at the same stage of life and to trace how changes in the stage of life alter housing consumption for households of similar means. There is a clear positive relationship between income and housing consumption but it is not quite proportional. Households with incomes in the $30,000–39,999 range, for example, have homes that are worth more than half as much as households in the $50,000–74,999 income bracket. The average income in the latter bracket is roughly twice of that in the former, while housing consumption is only between 35 and 77 percent greater, depending on age category.

The data in Table 9.1 permit the simple estimation of an income elasticity of housing demand. This *elasticity* is defined as the percentage change in housing consumption

TABLE 9.1 Average Value of Home Owned by Married Couples As a Function of Income, 1989

| Household Income | Age of Head of Household | | | | |
| | (With Children) | | | (Without Children) | |
	25–34	35–44	45–54	55–64	65+
Less than $20,000	43,822	70,817	65,407	72,928	81,514
$20,000–$29,999	51,145	73,206	77,353	76,427	100,750
$30,000–$39,999	61,964	75,588	77,720	87,030*	101,464*
$40,000–$49,999	93,814	98,544	111,975	102,495*	113,643*
$50,000–$74,999	109,679	122,282	114,804	117,287	152,532*
$75,000+	182,377	190,244	196,848	171,571	160,292*

Value of home as reported by homeowners; *indicates small sample size.
Source: Authors' tabulations of American Housing Survey, 1989.

that results from a percentage change in household income. For the data in Table 9.1, the income elasticity is estimated to be around 0.8—that is, a doubling of income leads to nearly an 80 percent increase in the amount of housing consumed.[1] This income elasticity is quite typical of numerous housing demand studies (Quigley 1979).

In tracking household expenditures by income, the exact definition of that income becomes an important issue. In Table 9.1, the survey data reports actual or current household income. There is good reason to expect that this definition of income is not the best measure and may be less strongly correlated with housing consumption than other possible definitions. For example, an unemployed household will report very low current income, but may not immediately adjust its housing consumption downward. Likewise, a student nearing completion of medical or law school will have very low current income, but much higher long-term potential earnings. The student's housing purchase may be based mostly on this anticipated growth in income, so reported current income would not be a good indicator of housing consumption.

For the purchase of long-lived durable goods, a more reasonable measure of household buying power is permanent rather than current income. *Permanent income* might best be thought of as the average income likely to be available over the anticipated occupancy of the house. For the medical student or the temporarily unemployed household, permanent income exceeds current income. A household nearing retirement has less permanent income than a 30-year-old with identical current income. The younger household might reasonably anticipate future income growth through job promotions, while the older household anticipates declining income during retirement.

There are several different approaches to measuring permanent income. One is to examine average income over the past few years. Another uses a statistical forecast of income based on not only current income, but other information about the respondent's age, education, and training—variables which clearly affect the household's expected future earnings. Whatever the approach, research consistently indicates that permanent income is a better predictor of housing consumption than current income. In fact, studies using some measure of permanent income generally report higher estimated income elasticities than those based on reported current income.

---

[1] The income elasticity of housing consumption (expenditure, E) is defined as:

$$\frac{\partial E}{\partial Y} \frac{Y}{E} \quad \text{or} \quad \frac{\partial \log E}{\partial \log Y}$$

Given the data in Table 9.1, the income elasticity of demand can be estimated from a statistical equation in which the natural log of household income (Y) is regressed on the natural log of housing expenditure (E). Using the mean expenditure and midpoint of the income category for the six categories in the first column of the table, the estimated equation in the case of 25–34-year-olds is:

$$\log(E) = 1.31 + .78 \log(Y) \qquad R^2 = 0.94$$
$$N = 6$$

Similar equations estimated for the other age groups yield income elasticities that generally decline with age.

HOUSING CONSUMPTION AND LIFE CYCLE

Household income is just one important determinant of the consumption of housing services. Life cycle and demographic factors also influence the preferences of households not only for overall housing consumption but for specific housing characteristics as well. In Table 9.1, for example, we can trace housing expenditure by income and age of household head. Table 9.2 shows how total housing consumption varies by income and household size, with the age of household head fixed. Table 9.3 looks at the same types of households and measures their consumption of a specific housing attribute—bedrooms—instead of overall housing consumption.

In Table 9.2, household size generally has little impact on total housing expenditure or the consumption of housing services. Intuitively, one might expect a positive effect, arguing that larger households need more shelter. The problem, of course, is that larger households also need more food, clothing, and other necessities as well. If satisfying these other items is more important, the consumption of housing might actually decrease with household size, at least when income is fixed. In fact, for households earning $25,000–59,999, Table 9.2 does show slightly decreasing expenditures as size increases. Another way of explaining the absence of a positive household-size effect is to note that when total household income is fixed, household income *per capita* actually decreases with greater size. Thus, while larger households may indeed want more housing, their diminished per capita resources may impede these desires.

TABLE 9.2 Average House Value for Homeowners by Income and Household Size for Households with Head Aged 35–44, 1989

| | Household Size | | | | |
Income	1 Person	2 People	3–4 People	5+ People	All
Less than $25,000	52,506	51,438	69,840	57,516	60,648
$25,000–$39,999	79,327	80,365	75,599	81,564	77,868
$40,000–$59,999	113,421	106,365	104,897	107,873	106,247
$60,000+	150,791	161,205	162,889	165,728	163,023
All	83,840	104,787	109,993	111,307	107,519

Value of home as reported by homeowners.
Source: Authors' tabulations of the American Housing Survey, 1989.

TABLE 9.3 Average Number of Bedrooms for Homeowners by Income and Household Size for Households with Head Aged 35–44, 1989

| | Household Size | | | | |
Income	1 Person	2 People	3–4 People	5+ People	All
Less than $25,000	2.37	2.54	2.92	3.23	2.83
$25,000–$39,999	2.45	2.80	3.01	3.35	3.00
$40,000–$59,999	2.33	2.72	3.17	3.59	3.15
$60,000+	2.72	2.93	3.39	3.76	3.40
All	2.43	2.76	3.16	3.53	3.13

Source: Authors' tabulations of the American Housing Survey, 1989.

The impact of household size on the consumption of bedrooms, on the other hand, is uniformly positive (Table 9.3). Thus, the presence of children creates an important change in housing consumption. Since the consumption of all housing services does not increase with household size, the increase in bedrooms must come at the expense of other housing services as reflected in the consumption of fewer amenities or lower quality of structure (e.g., fewer baths, smaller kitchens, less land, worse location, etc.).

The effect of household age on housing consumption, again holding income fixed, can be at least partially analyzed by returning to Table 9.1. Within every income category, as the household head ages from the twenties to the mid-forties, housing consumption noticeably increases. While along each row of Table 9.1, marital status and the presence of children are held constant, the number of children per household typically increases between the ages 25 and 45, which might explain the increase in housing consumption. However, in Table 9.2, increases in household size (holding income constant) have little impact on total housing consumption. An alternative explanation for this phenomenon is that household wealth tends to increase with age, and households tend to accumulate and keep this wealth in housing rather than in more liquid assets.

As households age, particularly from the mid-thirties to the mid-fifties, they tend to accumulate significant wealth. Some of this may be inherited from parents. The accumulation of wealth also occurs during this period in preparation for retirement. Finally, because a household's initial house may have appreciated in value, additional equity has often been created, which can be used to trade up to more or better housing. Chapter 8 showed that there is a strong tendency for households to reinvest their appreciated housing equity in more housing rather than refinance and then use the money either for current consumption or for investment in other assets. Some of this behavior can be explained by the fact that, historically, housing has been a good investment, particularly with the provisions in the U.S. tax code for mortgage interest and real estate tax deductions and the deferred taxation of housing capital gains.

Beyond the age of 55, the impact of age on housing consumption becomes somewhat mixed. It has been argued that there is some tendency for housing consumption to decrease after age 60, again holding income fixed. This could be a pure taste effect—older households might prefer other forms of consumption, particularly households that have seen their children leave the nest. This effect, however, is difficult to ascertain from Table 9.1. In all but the highest income category, housing expenditure is greater for households with a head aged 65+ than it is for households aged 45–54. Again, this may be due to the fact that Table 9.1 uses current rather than permanent income. A retired household with current income in the $40,000-49,999 category is likely to have made much more than that at age 45–54. Thus, in comparison to younger households *with the same income,* retired households are likely to have considerably more assets, presumably including a house.

The combination of Tables 9.1, 9.2, and 9.3 provides an interesting and useful picture of individual housing consumption over one's life. As one might expect, housing consumption tends to rise quite rapidly from a combination of several changes that normally occur between the ages of 25 and 54. The first and most important of these is that household income, as measured here, tends to rise over time until peaking for most heads of households when they reach their fifties. From then on, it declines. Thus, much of the increase in housing consumption can be explained by the normal pattern of household earnings. Surprisingly, household size during one's life plays a more mixed role in housing demand. While the presence and then departure of children has an effect on the *composition* of housing services, this factor seems not to influence overall housing *expenditure*. Finally, after age 55, there are mixed age effects, which, in Table 9.1, make it difficult to draw conclusions about the changes in housing consumption as households approach and enter retirement. During this stage of life, the accumulation of wealth encourages housing consumption, while from Tables 9.2 and 9.3 we can observe that the shrinking household sizes that accompany retirement can often lead households to downsize their consumption.

All of this suggests a short-term microeconomic picture of housing that is quite different from longer-term macroeconomic trends. The aggregate consumption of housing in the country as a whole changes only gradually over time, since national income, age, and household size evolve very slowly. This is evident in time series analysis. Beneath these slow macroeconomic trends, however, individual households and their housing consumption needs are changing far more rapidly, as shown by the cross-section data in Tables 9.1–9.3. Households whose demand for housing is growing purchase houses from those whose demand is declining. As a result, many of these individual changes are offset by one another, leading to a pattern of very gradual macroeconomic change.

HOUSEHOLD MOBILITY AND CHANGES IN HOUSING DEMAND

In Chapter 8, we learned that about 17 percent of American households move each year. By contrast, the number of households and the number of housing units has been increasing at a rate closer to 1.5 percent annually over the last decade. Since the mobility rate far outpaces the household growth rate, the vast majority of moves are by existing households who are changing their current house. Table 9.4 takes those households in the 1989 American Housing Survey who moved that year and identifies the reasons cited for the

TABLE 9.4 Reasons for Moving, 1989*

	% of Total Responses†		
	Total	Owner	Renter
Housing-related reasons	46.4	56.4	42.3
Job-related reasons	21.6	15.1	24.3
Family changes (marriage, divorce, etc.)	15.6	14.1	16.2
Miscellaneous other	11.3	11.4	11.3
Displacement by government or private sector	4.6	2.7	5.4
Disaster loss (fire, flood, etc.)	0.4	0.3	0.5

*Reasons for moving cited by households who had moved within the last 12 months.
†Respondents could cite more than one category.
Source: American Housing Survey 1989, Table 2–11; categories regrouped.

move. Included in "housing-related reasons" are responses such as needing a larger unit, changing tenure, and seeking a better neighborhood. While many moves occur from job relocations, marriage, and divorce, the single most important reason for moving is to adjust one's consumption of housing (46.4 percent). In fact, moving is the vehicle by which most households adjust their housing consumption to the changing needs accompanying either anticipated or unexpected changes in income or life cycle.

During a normal, or average, life cycle, a household might follow this typical path: starting with an initial apartment, followed by marriage and a larger apartment, then a first house, possibly moving to a trade-up home, and, finally, settling into a retirement house. Again relying on data from the American Housing Survey, Table 9.5 calculates the percentage of households who move each year, by housing tenure and age categories.

Table 9.5 clearly shows the influence of a household's life cycle on changes in housing consumption. The mobility of households is highest in the under-25 age bracket and declines steadily as households age. What is also clear from Table 9.5 is that housing tenure plays a crucial role in mobility. Moving rates are twice as high for young renters as opposed to owners, and in later years, older renters move five to six times more often than older owners. To explain these patterns, it is important to lay out carefully the various costs and benefits that households must consider in making a move.

As housing demand changes and a household contemplates moving, a number of costs must be weighed in the decision. First, a new (i.e., better) house must be found. While modern real estate brokerage services facilitate this process, searching for the best alternative to one's existing unit can still be a complex and time-consuming process. As each new house is inspected, the gains to be had from living in it as opposed to the existing house must be compared with the costs of making the change. The gains are represented by the increased flow of services or savings in expenditure from the adjustment in housing consumption. Since these gains will be ongoing over a number of years, households should calculate their present discounted value and compare this value to the value of staying in their current home. Let U_{old} stand for the annual utility, or willingness-to-pay, of a household to continue to live in its current (outmoded) house. Similarly, U_{new} represents the net flow of utility obtainable from a particular new house. Defining PDV as the

TABLE 9.5 Mobility Rates* by Age and Tenure, 1989

	Tenure %		
Age	Owner	Renter	All
Under 25	24.6	56.8	49.9
25–34	18.7	44.6	33.4
34–44	8.5	32.8	16.7
45–54	5.7	28.4	11.3
55–64	4.0	19.6	7.2
65+	2.2	12.2	4.6
All	7.6	35.7	17.8

*Number of household heads in each category who had moved within the last 12 months, as a percent of total households per category.
Source: Authors' tabulations of the American Housing Survey, 1989.

present discounted value, a household's net gain from a contemplated move is the difference in discounted utility flows minus moving and transaction costs.[2]

$$\text{Net Moving Gain} = \text{PDV}(U_{new}) - \text{PDV}(U_{old}) \\ - \text{Moving Expenses} - \text{Transaction Costs} \quad (9.1)$$

When the household finds a unit with a positive net gain, it must consider whether to continue searching for another unit that offers an even greater gain or to settle for the improved unit at hand. A household continues searching until it finds a unit whose net gain is at least as large as it expects to be able to find in the current market. Since younger households have a longer time horizon over which to discount the utility improvements from a new house, it has been argued that their net gains will be greater than that of older households when evaluating any given pair of houses. This may explain their greater propensity to move.

The fixed costs of moving can often be so significant that substantial utility gains are necessary before a move will be undertaken. The direct time and money expenses of moving, even within the same market, often amount to thousands of dollars. Even more important are the various transaction costs of changing units—costs that differ fundamentally by household tenure. For renters, the main transaction cost is the possible loss of security deposit and the payment of two monthly rents if the new and old leases must overlap. When a tenant has to move suddenly, there may be a long period during which the tenant pays two rents while searching for a new renter for the old unit.

With homeownership, moving entails much more significant transaction costs, involving not just closing expenditures, but resale risk. When an owner changes homes, normally there will be closing costs on the new house together with a realtor fee for selling the current home. Together, these can amount to between 6 and 9 percent of the value of the house. Even more important, however, there may be the cost of owning two homes over what is normally an uncertain period. Many owner transactions involve first the purchase of a new home and then bridge financing while the old home is sold. Each month of such dual ownership represents an additional transaction cost of almost one percentage point of the house value. Particularly in a soft real estate market, this can generate a substantial financial risk.

For homeowners in particular, then, the large transaction costs associated with moving to a different house suggest that the need for "better" housing must become quite strong before such a move is undertaken. This undoubtedly explains why rental mobility rates in Table 9.5 are so much higher, in every age bracket, than the corresponding rates for homeowners.

VACANCY, MOBILITY, AND HOUSING SALES

As households move between units, there is the accompanying risk of not being able to sell or lease the unit the household is moving from. The risk of resale is normally borne

---

[2]In fact, PDV(U_{old}) should incorporate the calculation that the household eventually may be forced to move again, so that it may not live forever in the old unit. Similarly, PDV(U_{new}) should consider the prospect that a new house will, at some point, become inappropriate and hence not provide that flow of services forever.

Chapter 9   The Market for Housing Services

by homeowners, while landlords generally undertake the risk of releasing. A softening real estate market will increase this risk, causing owners to become more desperate sellers. Households may even postpone their decision to move. The market factor that primarily determines this risk is the rate of vacancy. A house is defined as vacant if it is both physically unoccupied and for sale or rent. This definition excludes houses that are abandoned and ready for demolition, or second homes that are normally occupied only on a temporary or seasonal basis. Thus, *housing vacancy* is the period of time through which a house goes as it is being sold or rented. Houses that are sold quickly undergo only a brief spell of vacancy, while those that are difficult to sell may remain vacant for quite some time.

For a market as a whole, there is a simple relationship between the average length of time houses take to sell (or lease)—*sales time*—and the rate of housing vacancy. To complete the relationship, a third variable is needed—the *sales* (or leasing) *rate*. This is the flow of houses (units per year) that are sold or leased out of the vacant inventory. The relationship is:

$$\frac{\text{Vacant inventory (units)}}{\text{Sales (units / year)}} = \text{Average sale time (years)} \qquad (9.2)$$

In the U.S. single-family housing market, roughly 8 to 10 percent of the stock changes hands every year. This gives sales of roughly 5.5 million units. The single-family vacancy rate tends to be quite low, somewhere in the 2 percent range (giving an inventory of roughly 1.3 million units). This yields an average sales time of between two and three months (about 0.24 years). In the apartment market, the turnover or lease rate is much higher—closer to 30 percent of tenants change apartments each year. The vacancy rate among rental units, however, is also much higher, averaging around 8 percent. This yields an average lease up time of roughly three months.

The average sales (or lease) time within a market is an important barometer of market conditions. A long sales time results when the inventory of vacant units is unusually high and the sales rate is below average. The inventory will be high if there has been recent construction or some households decide to leave the market or both. The sales rate will depend mainly on how many households within the market desire to switch units, after searching over the inventory and weighing the net gains. High mobility generates a lot of sales activity; low mobility, the reverse. Table 9.6 examines the ratio of the vacancy rate to the household mobility rate in several major U.S. cities for the year 1989. In Minneapolis, the average sales time was 0.067 (years), or slightly less than one month (that is, a low vacancy rate of just 0.006 divided by a mobility rate of 0.089). In Dallas, it was 0.386 (years), or closer to five months.

Using somewhat different data at the regional level, it is possible to track over time the ratio of vacant units for sale to the number of units that were sold in the period. This ratio gives a similar measure of the expected sales time for single-family units. This is done in Figure 9.1, using data for the Northeast Census Region. The series shown with the dotted solid line is the number of single-family units vacant and for sale at the end of each year. This moves rather smoothly over the 17 years examined, but with a noticeable increase in the late 1980s, mainly because of rapid levels of new construction in this region during that time. The crossed-line series depicts the number of units sold each

TABLE 9.6 Homeowner Vacancy and Mobility Rates by Metropolitan Area, 1989

	Vacancy Rate	Annual Mobility Rate	Ratio (years to sale)
Minneapolis/St. Paul	0.6	8.9	0.067
Los Angeles	0.9	9.1	0.099
San Francisco	0.9	8.6	0.104
Detroit	1.0	6.9	0.145
Boston	1.0	5.5	0.181
Washington, D.C.	1.1	10.6	0.104
Philadelphia	1.2	5.8	0.208
Phoenix	2.8	12.0	0.234
Dallas	3.9	10.1	0.386

Source: Vacancy rates, "1989 Homeowner Vacancy Rates," Table 23, H111 Series, U.S. Bureau of Census; mobility rates, 1989 American Housing Survey.

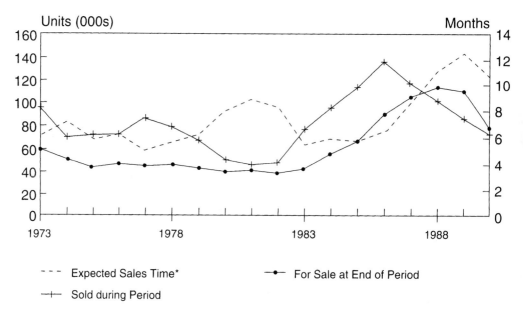

- - - Expected Sales Time*
—•— For Sale at End of Period
—+— Sold during Period

FIGURE 9.1 Northeast single-family vacancies, sales and expected sales time, 1973–1990.

*Ratio of houses for sale to houses sold, expressed as number of months' supply.
Source: C25 Series, Table 2, U.S. Bureau of the Census.

year. It tends to be more volatile, moving with the region's economy. It drops during the economic downturns of 1975, 1982, and 1990, and peaks with the strong recoveries of 1977 and 1986. The dashed line is the ratio of the two (vacant inventory to sales)—the expected sales time, or months of supply. This sales time moves almost exactly inversely to the sales series, peaking during recessions or at periods of low economic activity

(1975, 1982, 1990). The expected sales time never dropped to less than 5 months, and more recently climbed to higher than 12 months.

While higher expected sales times represent an unambiguous risk for property sellers, vacancy does perform a service of sorts for the market as a whole. The ideal vacancy rate is not zero, with an infinitely quick sales time. A market with only a few vacant units and an absurdly low sales time could occur only if frantic buyers selected the first unit that became available. That would mean that buyers would have virtually no choice. Without the ability to search and choose over a wide range of vacant units, buyers would not be able to find houses whose net utility gain was significantly better than their current unit. Just as excessive vacancy presents problems for sellers, too little vacancy tends to freeze a market and prevent buyers from improving their housing consumption. In between these extremes lies a market's normal, or *structural vacancy rate*, providing choice for buyers and sufficient incentive for sellers.

VACANCY, SALES TIME, PRICES, AND RENTS

Within a housing market, as the vacancy rate and average sales time rise, the situation for house sellers becomes increasingly precarious. Since most sellers are also buyers, they temporarily own two units and therefore are likely to be carrying an unusually large burden of mortgage debt. With longer expected sales times, sellers may decide to lower prices, preferring to trade sales proceeds for the carrying cost of this debt. House sellers who are not also buyers, such as the builders of new units, will be similarly inclined. Potential house buyers who already own a unit may shelve their purchase or mobility plans, fearing the difficulty of selling their old home. These arguments suggest a strong relationship between the average sales time in a market and movements in house prices. The empirical evidence of such a pattern is pervasive and convincing. Figure 9.2 follows the movements of a national house price index against the average national sales time for units. Again, sales time is calculated as the ratio of vacant units to current period sales. There is an overwhelming negative relationship: as the sales time rises, prices either fall or there is less price inflation.

The same logic yields a similar relationship in the rental housing market, this time between average lease time and movements in apartment rents. Unlike real estate sales, the annual number of rental or lease transactions is not recorded either nationally or at the local level. Thus, it is not possible to calculate directly the average lease time. There is good reason to expect, however, that rental leasing rates are more stable than sales rates and do not move as strongly with an area's economy. Switching apartments does not entail the kinds of risk and transactions costs that are associated with the purchase and then resale of a home. If leasing rates are generally stable, then variation in average leasing time should be determined largely by movements in apartment vacancy rates. Continuing this line of reasoning, we should expect to find that the rental vacancy rate itself is a strong determinant of changes in rents. To examine this, Figure 9.3 compares the movements in the rental index (in constant dollars) with the vacancy rate in Houston, Texas.

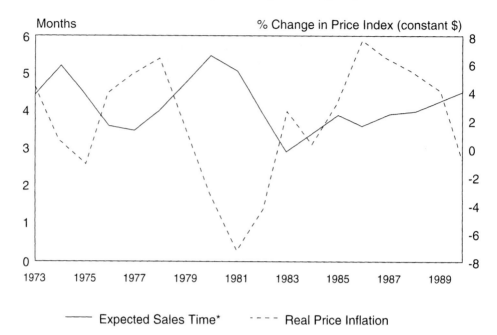

FIGURE 9.2 Single-family housing sales time and house price changes, 1973–1990.

*Ratio of houses for sale to houses sold, expressed as number of months' supply.

Source: Expected sales time, Series C25, U.S. Bureau of the Census; house price, *Freddie Mac Price Index of Existing One-Family Homes Sold.*

Figure 9.3 reveals a strong negative relationship between rental vacancy rates and the growth rate of apartment rents adjusted for inflation. When vacancy in Houston exceeds about 11 percent, rents rise at rates less than the overall CPI (i.e., real rents fall). This can be seen in 1983, when the dashed line depicting change in rent crosses zero. At vacancy levels of less than 11 percent, rents tend to rise faster than the CPI (i.e., real rents rise). Some authors have suggested that the structural level of vacancy for the market is that rate at which real rents are stable (in this case, 11 percent). At this vacancy rate, the needs of both sides of the market seem balanced. Buyers are provided with ample choice and sellers with rapid enough lease-up times so that rents continue to rise with inflation. Researchers have found such rent-vacancy relationships in almost every real estate market, but with noticeable differences in the structural rate between areas.[3]

[3] The statistical relationship that is estimated with the Houston data is between the vacancy rate (V_t) and the annual percentage change in constant dollar rents $(R_t - R_{t-1})/R_{t-1}$:

$$\frac{R_t - R_{t-1}}{R_{t-1}} = 9.16 - 0.77 V_{t-1} \qquad R^2 = .61, N = 9$$

The structural vacancy rate is estimated to be 11.9 percent, while rents adjust at an annual rate of 0.77 for every percentage point that vacancy exceeds or is less than the structural rate. The structural vacancy rate is calculated from the equation as that value of V at which rents will not change:

$$V = \frac{9.16}{0.77} = 11.9\%$$

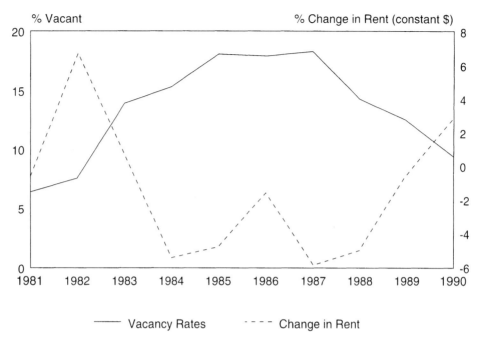

FIGURE 9.3 Apartment vacancies and real rent, Houston 1981–1990.
Source: Vacancy rates, Census H111 Series; rent, rent component of Consumer Price Index, U.S. Bureau of Labor Statistics.

VACANCY AND NEW CONSTRUCTION

The risk that vacancy imposes on homeowners seeking to move or landlords trying to fill their rental units is also felt by builders attempting to sell newly constructed housing. Chapter 8 showed that the price of housing, in relation to replacement costs, should be a major determinant of new construction. For a given level of prices and costs, however, the expected sales time for units should also play an important role in builder or developer decisions about whether to start new construction projects. Since we have seen in the previous section that the sales time of units influences the *change* in housing prices, there need not be a strong correlation between the *current level* of house prices and the sales time. Thus, sales time can have an additional impact on new construction, independent of the impact of house price levels.

Figure 9.4 tracks expected sales time and single-family home construction for the U.S. over the past three decades. As in Figure 9.1, *sales time* is defined as the ratio of the vacant inventory to sales. With a slight lag, the inverse relationship between the two is extraordinary. Within 12 months after the expected sales time peaks, construction bottoms out, and vice versa.

In some respects, it should come as no surprise that sales time has an effect on construction. Time is money, and so if new homes on average are selling within three months instead of six (the range observed in Figure 9.4), then, in principle, that means one-fourth of one year less in holding costs. If the short-term interest rate is 10 percent, the

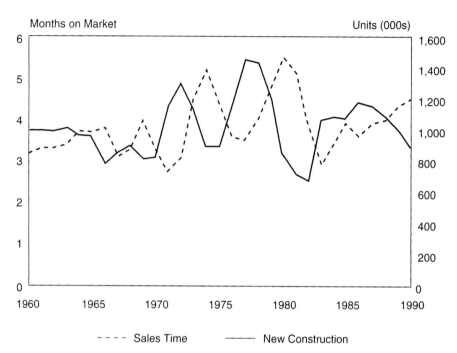

FIGURE 9.4 Single-family housing sales time vs. construction, 1960–1990.

Source: Sales time, Census C25 Series; new construction, *1991 Economic Report of the President,* February 1991.

three months saved are equivalent to receiving 2.5 percent more for the house in terms of a net price. In Figure 9.4, however, the sensitivity of construction to sales time is much stronger than could be accounted for purely from the increases or decreases in holding costs.

The strong relationship between sales time and construction has been found by several researchers to hold even when interest rates and house prices are controlled for. Since sales time predicts the *movement* in house prices (such as is shown in Figure 9.2), it may serve as a leading indicator of *future* house price levels. This could explain why it is such a powerful determinant of new construction. To see this, we can briefly reexamine the single-family price series in Figure 8.6. In that figure, the *level* of house prices in the U.S., in real terms, was roughly the same in 1977, 1980, and 1986. Returning to Figure 9.4, in 1977, the sales time was low, and construction high. Just after 1977, real house prices rose sharply. In 1980, the sales time was at an all-time high, construction was in a deep trough, and prices were falling. In 1986, the sales time was low, prices on the rise, and construction up. Thus at a given *level* of house prices, sales time is an excellent predictor of future price movements, and hence new construction.

VACANCY, SALES, AND PRICES: A SIMPLE MODEL

The data presented in the previous sections clearly show the central role that sales time plays in the residential real estate market. However, the strength of these relationships raises a number of questions about how and why vacancy and the rate of sales should be such important determinants of housing prices. We know that most sales represent turnover in the market rather than net movements in demand. How is it that the rate of household mobility or turnover can cause prices to change so significantly? What is it about gross movements that can alter prices, even if the net balance between unit demand and supply is fixed? Similarly, why are relatively small shifts in vacancy so important? If vacancy truly represents excess supply, why would seemingly small movements in total supply, say from the difference between a 2 percent and 6 percent vacancy rate, trigger very significant changes in price? In this section, we examine a number of economic arguments that have been developed to explain how vacancy, turnover, and sales together combine to determine the price level of houses.

In the modern economic theory of search and uncertainty, vacant units are not necessarily undesirable; rather, they are units that temporarily are in the process of being sold (or rented). Selling a unit takes time because units are different, buyers have preferences for particular types, and buyers must expend time and money searching for the right unit. It is the inability of this matching process to occur instantaneously that determines the duration of vacancy that any unit must undergo as it is sold and bought. To understand how important vacancy, sales, and sales time can be within this framework, we need to consider exactly how households move.

The process of housing mobility can be illustrated with the simplified flow diagram in Figure 9.5. Here, we assume that all households currently have a unit and that there are no new households being formed or households leaving the market. Later, we will discuss the role played by these entrants and exits from the market. We also assume that

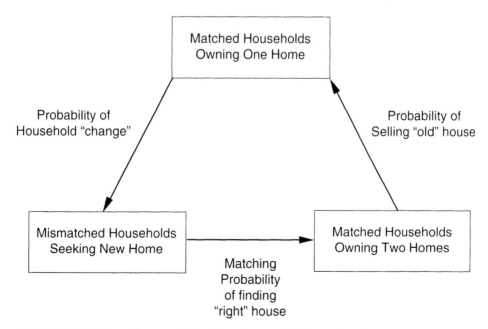

FIGURE 9.5 Flows in a model of housing mobility and sales.

households cannot be homeless or occupy some temporary lodging. As such, households must purchase a new unit before they sell their existing one.[4] There will be a fixed total number of housing units and households. Vacancy is simply the difference between the two (and is always positive). Households in this model differ by some unspecified characteristics such as size or income, which can change over time. Any household must be in one of three boxes in Figure 9.5. Those in the upper box own one unit, with which they are perfectly happy. Other households (those in the left box) have undergone some recent change in their economic or demographic status and now are dissatisfied with their unit. These households are searchers. A final group of households (in the right box) have found a new unit that is more suited to their changed status. They have purchased this unit, put their old unit up for sale, and temporarily own two houses. While the total number of households is fixed, the number in each state or box can vary with market conditions.

Let's consider how households move between the three boxes in the diagram. The movement between the upper and left boxes occurs, with some probability, when a household undergoes some form of economic or demographic change that makes it unhappy with its current unit. This change switches the household from the satisfied household group to the group who are searching for a new unit.

Searching households (in the left box) will change into households that have just purchased a unit (and own two) once they have found the right unit. This matching process again occurs with a probability that depends on the ease with which houses can be identified and inspected. Recent research has focused on the role of advertising, information systems, and real estate brokerage networks in facilitating this matching process (Yinger 1981, Read 1988, Anglin and Arnott 1991). When a searching household finds and purchases its desired unit, it then becomes a household that temporarily owns two houses.

The final step in the mobility process is the transition of households that own two units to those that are again satisfied households that own a single unit. This transition happens when they sell their old homes. The probability of this transition is simply the number of house sales per period divided by the number of vacant units or those for sale. The absolute number of house sales is equal to this matching probability times the number of searching households. Dividing this sales flow into the inventory of vacant units yields the inverse of the sale probability—the expected sales time. Thus, the relationship between sales probability and expected sales time is:

$$\text{Sales probability} = \frac{\text{House sales}}{\text{Vacant units}} = \frac{1}{\text{Expected sales time}} \quad (9.3)$$

Data about expected sales times was shown in Table 9.6 and graphed in Figure 9.1.

Since there are no entrants or exits from the market, the role of house prices is complicated in this model. House price does not represent the cost of buying a (first) house nor wealth that becomes liquid when the household leaves the market. Rather, price

---

[4] We preclude here the possibility of contingent contracts in which buyers promise to execute a purchase only after selling their existing home. In England, this practice leads to long chains of potential transactions that often wait years to occur (when a noncontingent buyer is finally found for some property in the chain).

serves only to regulate the flow of moves between boxes. At some high price, searching households may decide not to move, while at some low price, selling households might decide to hang onto two houses. In a market in which all sales simply represent turnover, prices are determined by bargaining between buyer and seller. When we better understand the role of housing prices, it will become clear why they are so sensitive to changes in the vacancy rate or flow of sales. Let's begin by considering the perspective of housing searchers or buyers.

Buyers

When a searching buyer finds the right unit, what role does price play? The price the searcher pays for his new unit will be recouped once the searcher becomes a seller and disposes of the old unit. In a market in which every buyer becomes a seller, why should price matter? If a household's new unit is more or less expensive to buy, its old unit will yield more or less value at sale. What Figure 9.5 illustrates is that moving entails a risk—the risk associated with being stuck with two units for the period it takes to sell the old unit. This risk can be substantial and its cost is proportional to the price of housing.

When the price level of housing is high, the financial exposure and risk of holding two houses may be great enough to discourage moving. In contrast, at a very low price level, there is little if any risk to holding two homes, even for an extended period. It is useful to consider the maximum price for housing that would leave a searching household indifferent between moving and continuing to live in a mismatched home. Earlier in this chapter, we described the net gains from a move as having two components: the present discounted value of the utility or willingness-to-pay for living in the "right" as opposed to "wrong" house, minus moving and transactions costs. Recalling Equation (9.1) we label this gain: Net Moving Gain. Here, we introduce a third component to the cost of moving: the financial exposure to owning two units. If the price of a house is P, the expected sales time L, and the interest rate i, the expected cost of holding the second home is expressed as iLP. The maximum price that buyers will offer for a new home (BMO) is a price that makes this expected holding cost high enough to exactly offset the net gain from moving:[5]

$$\text{Buyer Maximum Offer} = \text{BMO} = \frac{\text{Net Moving Gain}}{iL} \quad (9.4)$$

Sellers

At the other end of the bargaining table is the seller. When a buyer arrives (who finds the house to be "right"), the seller contemplates the minimum offer he would accept that would leave him indifferent between remaining a seller (hoping for another acceptable offer) and finally becoming a one-owner household. Since a seller already has the "right" house, his concern is simply whether to accept now, or wait. We can calculate the Seller

---

[5]The actual maximum buyer offer must consider a number of additional issues such as whether the buyer will remain in the "right" house forever. For a fuller, more complicated discussion, see (Wheaton 1990).

Minimum Accept (SMA) price as that *sure* price today that would leave it indifferent with an uncertain sale and price in the future. If the price to be actually received is P, the expected sales time L, and interest rate i, the seller's *sure* price today—the Seller Minimum Accept—is the (future) received price discounted by the expected sales time:[6]

$$\text{Seller Minimum Accept} = \text{SMA} = \frac{P}{1+iL} \tag{9.5}$$

In bargaining between parties, the market price P must lie somewhere between the Seller Minimum Accept price (SMA) and the Buyer Maximum Offer (BMO). In bargaining theory it is common to assume that market prices split the difference between minimum seller and maximum buyer reservations. If we solve for that value of P which lies halfway between the Buyer Maximum Offer and the Seller Minimum Accept, we get the following:[7]

$$P = \text{BMO} - \frac{1}{2}[\text{BMO} - \text{SMA}]$$

$$= \frac{\text{Net Moving Gain}}{iL} \frac{(1+iL)}{1+2iL} \tag{9.6}$$

The expression for market price above is extremely sensitive to the expected sales time. In fact, it is almost inverse to L. The expected sales time, in turn, simply equals the ratio of vacant units to total sales. Thus, prices should be roughly proportional to the flow of sales and inversely proportional to vacancy. Let's consider a numerical example in which the present discounted value of moving (net of transactions and moving costs) is, say, $10,000, and the interest rate 10 percent (0.10). With annual sales at three times the vacant inventory, L would be 0.33 years (4 months) and P would equal $293,649 (293,649 = 10,000/0.033 × 1.033/1.066). In a tight market, in which L might be equal to only 0.1 year (slightly more than one month), P would rise to $990,196. Conversely, in a slack market, with an expected sales time of one year, P would be only $91,666. The reason for this sensitivity is that buyers care very little about price when they are also sellers. In effect, demand is very inelastic because in our simple model of house trading, a buyer will get back what he pays only with a delay that depends on the expected sales time.

Like all theories, the economic insights from this trading model must be tempered by a dose of realism. In actual housing markets, new entrants and exits do occur. Earlier, we presented data that suggested that they might account for as many as 20 percent of all moves. For these players in the market, price has a much different meaning, and demand

---

[6] Denoting the Seller Minimum Accept as SMA, if the seller waits, he will receive the additional amount $(P - \text{SMA})$, but only with a sales probability, which in Equation (9.3) is equal to $1/L$. In the meantime, there will be the foregone interest income on the accept price $i\text{SMA}$. Equating $i\text{SMA}$ with $(P - \text{SMA})/L$ yields the expression above. For a fuller discussion of seller strategy, see (Wheaton 1990).

[7] We derive this by solving for P in the equation:

$$P = \frac{\text{Net Moving Gain}}{iL} - \frac{1}{2}\left(\frac{\text{Net Moving Gain}}{iL} - \frac{P}{1+iL}\right)$$

can be expected to be much more elastic with respect to price. Still, our model does outline why, for the majority of movers, demand might, in fact, be very inelastic. As a result, small differences in vacancy and the rate of sales can have large influences on market prices.

The theory in this section can also be used to understand why sales time has such a strong independent impact on new housing construction, given a fixed level of house prices. A builder is also a seller, and, as such, has a *reservation price* that is similar to Equation (9.5). In the long run, builders compare this reservation price to the costs of new construction. As the sales time increases, even if prices remain fixed, the Minimum Seller Accept falls, profit margins are reduced, and building activity slows.

NEW CONSTRUCTION AND THE EVOLUTION OF THE HOUSING STOCK

Every year, between 15 and 20 percent of U.S. households change homes. This market for house transactions plays an important role in determining the prices for units of different types. By contrast, the construction rate of new units each year varies between only 1 and 2 percent of the household population. The characteristics of these newly constructed units, however, are strongly influenced by the pattern of house prices that emerges in the transactions market. Developers construct those types of units with the highest return. From the model described above, this will be units with the greatest difference between expected price and replacement costs.

The new units that are easiest to sell are those types for which the expected sales time in the transaction market is shortest. Given the nation's demographic structure in the 1970s and 1980s (large numbers of young households), these tended to be middle-income, moderately priced units. With their ease of selling, such units had transaction prices that were close to replacement costs. In effect, there was not much difference between expected and transaction prices because the sales time was so short. The market for more expensive or unusual homes, on the other hand, often tends to be much thinner: the sales rate is low, and the expected time to sale is much greater. In this situation, developers need a price cushion to offset the longer expected sales time. Transaction prices in this case may far exceed replacement costs in order to cover the greater sales risk.

Are newly constructed units better than the average unit in the stock? A simple answer to this question can be had by comparing the characteristics or features of new and existing units. This is done in Table 9.7. In 1989, only 21 percent of all existing units had four or more bedrooms, while 27 percent had two or less. For units constructed that year, the same figures are 28 percent and 15 percent. With baths, the difference is far more dramatic: only 40 percent of existing units had two or more, while 86 percent of the new units did. The table shows that new units are more likely to be larger and to have a garage, air conditioning, and a fireplace. As a measure of how these differences add up, the median sales price for existing units in 1988, as reported by the National Association of Realtors, was $93,000, while the median price of new homes surveyed by the government in that year was $138,000. Thus, in 1988, the average new home might be said to be 48 percent better than the typical home in the existing stock. In fact, this calculation may *understate*

TABLE 9.7 Characteristics of New and Existing Housing Units, 1989

	% of Units	
	Existing Units*	New Construction
Bedrooms		
≤ 2	26.8	15.5
3	51.9	56.7
4+	21.3	27.7
Bathrooms		
0	1.0	0.0
1	39.9	8.3
1 1/2	18.2	5.9
2+	40.5	85.8
Size		
0–999 sq. ft.	12.3	3.8
1,000–1,999 sq. ft.	45.4	53.7
2,000–2,999 sq. ft.	23.8	30.2
3,000+ sq. ft.	11.5	12.3
Garage or carport	71.2	83.1
Central air conditioning	39.7	76.5
Fireplace(s)	41.4	64.8

*"Bathrooms" and "Size" for Existing Units may not add up to 100% because of missing or unreported data.
Source: Figures for Existing Units represent detached, single-family units, occupied and unoccupied, in 1989, from the 1989 American Housing Survey; figures for New Construction represent all privately owned, one-family houses completed in 1989, from *Characteristics of New Housing: 1990*, U.S. Bureau of the Census.

the structural differences between new and existing units. As discussed in Chapters 3 and 4, new units are largely constructed at the edges of cities in locations with less valuable land than existing houses. Thus, on average, new homes are in less desirable locations and therefore the structural characteristics may be greater than 48 percent better, all told.

Are new units becoming better over time? While some might feel that today's construction is not up to par with that of previous periods, the data suggest that new units do improve each year in what they offer the consumer. Figure 9.6 tracks the annual percentage increases in the average sales price of newly constructed units in the U.S., from 1964 through 1990. To determine what part of this increase is represented by price as opposed to quality improvements, we subtract the annual percentage increase in the price of an identical newly constructed unit (surveyed by the Commerce Department) from the percentage change in sales price.[8] This residual estimates the annual percentage increase in

---

[8]Remember from Chapter 8 that average sales price is average expenditures (E), which is price (P) times quantity (Q). Using the Commerce Department's constant quality price index as an estimate of P, we can estimate Q:

$$E = PQ, \quad \text{or,} \quad Q = \frac{E}{P}$$

Differentiating both sides in percentage terms, the changes over time (t) are:

$$\frac{\partial Q}{\partial t}\frac{1}{Q} = \frac{\partial E}{\partial t}\frac{1}{E} - \frac{\partial P}{\partial t}\frac{1}{P}$$

Chapter 9 The Market for Housing Services

FIGURE 9.6 Changes in the sales price and quality of new housing units, 1964–1990.

Average Sales Price of houses actually sold; Quality = Average Sales Price divided by indexed price of kinds of houses sold in 1987.

Source: C27 Series, Table 2, U.S. Bureau of the Census.

the quality and quantity of space offered in new units. For example, in 1987, the average new unit sales price (E) rose 14 percent, while the average price (P) of an identically constructed unit rose only 6 percent. Thus, of the 14 percent increase, 8 percent resulted because new houses were bigger and better. During the years 1977–1980, there were large increases in the price of housing, with no improvements in unit characteristics. By contrast, in 1983 and 1987, more than half of the sales price increase was explained by improvements in new housing, rather than by increases in pure price.

The fact that new units are much better than average and are also improving over time leads to an interesting calculation of how rapidly the overall housing stock is improving each year. In long-run equilibrium, we would expect that the quality improvement rate in the stock should roughly match the growth rate of real consumer income, at least if demand has an income elasticity of near to 1. Earlier in the chapter, we obtained an elasticity of 0.8 by examining individual data. Calculating the annual improvement in the stock requires knowing the average quality level of existing units, a similar value for new units, the construction rate (number of new units each year divided by the stock), and the rate of depreciation of existing units. The percentage change in average stock quality each year then equals:

$$\genfrac{}{}{0pt}{}{\% \text{ change in}}{\text{stock quality}} = \left(\genfrac{}{}{0pt}{}{\text{construction}}{\text{rate}} \times \frac{(\text{new unit quality})}{\text{stock quality}} \right) - \genfrac{}{}{0pt}{}{\text{depreciation}}{\text{rate}} \quad (9.7)$$

In the U.S. housing market, assuming a construction rate of 1.5 percent, a ratio of new unit quality to existing of 1.4, and a depreciation rate of around 0.5 percent annually would be quite reasonable. With these values for recent years, the U.S. housing stock has improved by about 1.6 percent annually. This is similar to the long-term growth rate in real household income, suggesting that the U.S. housing market is approximately keeping up with the housing needs of the country.

The market for housing services, then, can be studied either at a microeconomic or macroeconomic level. At the microeconomic level, individual households experience significant demographic and economic changes during their lifetimes—changes that alter their demand for housing. This leads to a huge number of housing transactions or moves each year, most of which involve existing households that are changing units. The ease with which this mobility occurs determines how well different households are matched with the nation's diverse inventory of units. Policies or institutions that facilitate mobility enable the existing stock of units to be better used. At the aggregate level, however, much of this change cancels out. The income or demographic growth of households at one stage of their lives is counterbalanced by income or demographic declines by other households at different stages. The economy as a whole, then, grows or changes only very slowly. Matching these aggregate movements, the overall housing stock also adjusts only very slowly as incremental new construction gradually shapes the characteristics of the nation's housing inventory.

SUMMARY

In this chapter, we examined the market for housing services, defined as the flow of utility or services that a housing unit provides to its users over time. Data on housing consumption suggest several general conclusions:

- Housing consumption increases with age and income. Housing demand is somewhat inelastic with respect to income, with estimates of the elasticity in the neighborhood of 0.8.
- Increases in household size do not seem to increase housing consumption.
- Desire to alter housing consumption is the largest single reason for moving, followed by job-related reasons. Renters are much more likely to move than homeowners, largely due to the high transaction costs of moving for homeowners.

As a result of demographic and income changes, the housing demand of individual households changes considerably over the life cycle, generating a large number of housing transactions every year. Vacancy and sales time are very important variables in the operation of the existing housing market.

- From the buyer's perspective, high vacancy means more choice, which in turn increases the probability of finding a unit that matches needs and desires. From

the seller's perspective, high vacancy means that sales time increases. The costs of holding a vacant unit can provide a substantial incentive for sellers to offer price concessions.
- The ideal vacancy rate is not zero. There is some structural vacancy rate that provides sufficient units for buyers but also sufficient incentive for sellers to enter the market.
- There is a negative relationship between sales time and construction. Sales time is a strong predictor of future trends in house prices. In aggregate, the characteristics of housing demand and the housing stock change very slowly over time.

REFERENCES AND ADDITIONAL READINGS

General

OLSEN, EDGAR. "The Demand and Supply of Housing Service: A Critical Survey of the Empirical Literature," chap. 25 in *Handbook of Regional and Urban Economics* (vol. 2), ed. Edwin S. Mills. New York: North-Holland, 1987.

QUIGLEY, JOHN M. "What Have We Learned About Urban Housing Markets?" in *Current Issues in Urban Economics*, ed. Peter Mieszkowski and Mahlon Straszheim, pp. 391–429. Baltimore: Johns Hopkins University Press, 1979.

Income and Housing Consumption: The Elasticity of Demand

CARLINER, GEOFFREY. "Income Elasticity of Housing Demand." *Review of Economics and Statistics* 55 (1973): 528–532.

DE LEEUW, FRANK. "The Demand for Housing: A Review of Cross-Section Evidence." *Review of Economics and Statistics* 53, 1 (1971): 1–10.

ELLWOOD, DAVID T., AND A. MITCHELL POLINSKY. "An Empirical Reconciliation of Micro and Grouped Estimates of the Demand for Housing." *Review of Economics and Statistics* 61, 2 (1979): 199–205.

MAYO, STEPHEN K. "Theory and Estimation in the Economics of Housing Demand." *Journal of Urban Economics* 10, 1 (1981): 95–116.

MUTH, RICHARD F. "The Demand for Non-Farm Housing," in *The Demand for Durable Goods*, ed. Arnold Harberger. Chicago: University of Chicago Press, 1960.

POLINSKY, MITCHELL A. "The Demand for Housing: A Study in Specification and Grouping." *Econometrica* 45, 2 (1977): 447–462.

Housing Consumption and Life Cycle

KAIN, JOHN F., AND JOHN M. QUIGLEY. *Housing Markets and Racial Discrimination: A Microeconomic Analysis.* New York: Columbia University Press, 1975.

KING, A. THOMAS. "The Demand for Housing: A Lancastrian Approach." *Southern Economic Journal* 43, 2 (1976): 1077–1087.

STRASZHEIM, MAHLON. *An Econometric Analysis of the Urban Housing Market.* New York: National Bureau of Economic Research, 1975.

Household Mobility and Changes in Housing Demand

HANUSHEK, ERIC, AND JOHN QUIGLEY. "The Dynamics of the Housing Market: A Stock Adjustment Model of Housing Consumption." *Journal of Urban Economics* 6 (1979): 90–111.

WEINBERG, DANIEL H., JOSEPH FRIEDMAN, AND STEPHEN K. MAYO. "Intraurban Residential Mobility: The Role of Transactions Costs, Market Imperfections, and Household Disequilibrium." *Journal of Urban Economics* 9, 3 (1981): 332–348.

Vacancy, Mobility, and Housing Sales

CHINLOY, PETER T. "An Empirical Model of the Market for Resale Homes." *Journal of Urban Economics* 7, 3 (1980): 279–292.

GUASCH, J. LUIS, AND ROBERT C. MARSHALL. "An Analysis of Vacancy Patterns in the Rental Housing Market." *Journal of Urban Economics* 17, 2 (1985): 208–229.

Vacancy, Sales Time, Prices, and Rents

GABRIEL, STUART A., AND FRANK E. NOTHAFT. "Rental Housing Markets and the Natural Vacancy Rate." *AREUEA Journal* 16, 4 (1988): 419–429.

ROSEN, KENNETH T., AND LAWRENCE B. SMITH. "The Price-Adjustment Process for Rental Housing and the Natural Vacancy Rate." *American Economic Review* 83, 4 (1983): 779–786.

STULL, WILLIAM. "The Landlord's Dilemma: Asking Rent Strategies in a Heterogenous Housing Market." *Journal of Urban Economics* 5, 1 (1978): 101–115.

Vacancy and New Construction

DIPASQUALE, DENISE, AND WILLIAM C. WHEATON. "Housing Market Dynamics and the Future of Housing Prices." *Journal of Urban Economics* 35, 1 (1994): 1–27.

TOPEL, ROBERT, AND SHERWIN ROSEN. "Housing Investment in the United States." *Journal of Political Economy* 96, 4 (1988): 718–740.

Vacancy, Sales, and Prices: A Simple Model

ANGLIN, PAUL, AND R. ARNOTT. "Residential Brokerage as a Principal-Agent Problem." *Journal of Real Estate Finance and Economics* 4 (1991): 99–125.

ARNOTT, RICHARD. "Housing Vacancies, Thin Markets and Idiosyncratic Tastes." *Journal of Real Estate Finance and Economics* 2, 1 (1989): 5–30.

READ, COLIN. "Advertising and Natural Vacancies in Rental Housing Markets." *AREUEA Journal* 16, 4 (1988): 354–363.

WHEATON, WILLIAM C. "Vacancy, Search and Prices in a Housing Market Matching Model." *Journal of Political Economy* 98, 6 (1990): 1270–1292.

YINGER, JOHN. "A Search Model of Real Estate Broker Behavior." *American Economic Review* 71 (September 1981): 591–605.

New Construction and the Evolution of the Housing Stock

HAURIN, DONALD. "The Duration of Marketing Time of Residential Housing." *AREUEA Journal* 16, 4 (1988): 396–410.

CHAPTER 10

THE CYCLICAL BEHAVIOR OF METROPOLITAN HOUSING MARKETS

Chapter 7 examined how regions undergo economic growth and decline within a static framework. For the sake of simplicity, we assumed immediate market adjustments and so the dimension of time was largely ignored. The focus instead was on comparing eventual economic outcomes or equilibria. For example, in response to an increase in demand for a region's products, the area's labor force will increase as will its stock of commercial and residential structures. Wages, house prices, and rents should eventually rise as well by amounts that depend on their elasticities. But what about the timing of these changes? Do factor supplies and prices increase smoothly or unevenly? Is it possible for supplies or prices to fall temporarily during the period of adjustment to growth? Can exogenous shocks to a region or market set off a repetitive cycle?

This chapter explores the dynamic operation of urban housing markets with a simple but realistic mathematical model. The model is based on the *stock-flow theory* of highly durable goods. The stock-flow approach holds that in the short run, house prices adjust quickly to equate housing demand to the existing stock of units. By contrast, adjustments to the stock of housing (such as new construction) occur only slowly over time, and often with lags. Such stock adjustments respond to the prices determined by the market's short-run equilibrium.

The stock-flow model of the housing market developed here will also incorporate the discussion in Chapters 8 and 9 about the various determinants of housing demand. For owner-occupied housing, demand depends not just on current population, income, and the level of house prices, but also on expectations about future prices. While high

Chapter 10   The Cyclical Behavior of Metropolitan Housing Markets

current house prices dampen demand, the anticipation of capital gains through rising prices stimulates demand. It turns out that the dynamic behavior of housing markets is keenly dependent on how important such anticipated capital gains are to consumers and how consumers form judgments or estimates about them.

We have two purposes for building this model. First, it allows us to learn about the operation of a market and the various economic forces that determine prices and output. Second, when combined with historical data, this modeling can form the basis for econometric forecasting. If done sensibly, such forecasting can provide insights that are absolutely necessary to making rational real estate decisions. This chapter pursues this approach by empirically estimating a stock-flow forecasting model for the single-family housing market in Boston, Massachusetts. Contingent forecasts made with this model are contrasted with more naive approaches to forecasting that use simple trend-line extrapolations that are often used by practitioners in the industry. Forecasts based on a stock-flow model are shown to provide a reasonable and inexpensive way to make educated judgments about the future.

A HOUSING MARKET STOCK-FLOW MODEL

Dynamic models differ from static models in that the dimension of time must be explicitly incorporated, and at least some of the variables of the model must be linked across time.[1] The stock-flow approach assumes that house prices in any period are determined only by current values of the model's other variables, while the stock of housing depends on the historic values of these variables. To make the model as simple as possible, the current demand for owner-occupied housing units, D_t, will be assumed proportional to the number of current households, H_t, and to an expression that depends linearly and negatively on the annual cost of owning a house, U_t (the owner cost of capital). The parameter, α_0, might be thought of as the fraction of households who would own homes if the annual cost were zero, while the parameter, α_1, is the responsiveness of this fraction to changes in the cost of owning.

$$D_t = H_t (\alpha_0 - \alpha_1 U_t) \tag{10.1}$$

The annual cost of owning a house, as discussed in Chapter 8, depends on the current price level, P_t, the current after-tax mortgage rate, M_t, and the expected rate of future house-price appreciation, I_t.[2] In the case of I_t, the time subscript represents the time period in which the judgment or estimate of future price appreciation is formed. The following expression is a restatement of Equation (8.7):

$$U_t = P_t (M_t - I_t) \tag{10.2}$$

---

[1] Throughout this chapter, therefore, variables such as the number of households, H, or the stock of housing, S, will be subscripted to denote the time at which the variable is being measured: H_t, S_t. The subscript t represents current time, while the subscript $t-1$ or $t+1$ represents one period back or forward from the current period. Variables without subscripts are assumed to be constant over time. Finally, capital letters refer to variables, while lower-case letters are used to represent model parameters.

[2] The after-tax mortgage rate, M_t, is equal to $(1 - t_y)i$, where t_y is the marginal income tax rate, and i is the nominal mortgage interest rate.

Stock-flow models assume that house prices today adjust so that the *ex ante* demand for owner-occupied units in Equation (10.1) equals the stock of these units that currently exists, S_t:

$$D_t = S_t \tag{10.3}$$

Solving Equation (10.3) for current house prices by successively substituting Equation (10.1) through Equation (10.3) yields the following:

$$P_t = \frac{(\alpha_0 - S_t/H_t)}{\alpha_1(M_t - I_t)} \tag{10.4}$$

The stock-flow approach assumes that Equation (10.4) holds during each and every period. Thus, the price level of housing today will be higher, all else being equal, when today's ratio of stock-to-households is smaller, mortgage rates lower, or expectations about future price appreciation more optimistic.

Because housing units are durable, the supply of housing involves a series of equations. The first is a dynamic relationship linking the change in the stock of units between periods to construction begun one period ago, C_{t-1}, minus a small fraction, δ, of the last period's stock that is lost to scrappage or demolition.[3]

$$S_t - S_{t-1} = C_{t-1} - \delta S_{t-1} \tag{10.5}$$

The relationship in Equation (10.5) states that the stock will increase as long as construction exceeds demolitions, and decrease if the opposite is true. When construction exactly equals replacement needs ($C_t = \delta S_t$), then the stock will not change ($S_t - S_{t-1} = 0$). In this case, the stock is said to be in a stable steady state. The reader may recall that in Chapter 1, we discussed this long-term steady-state relationship between construction and the stock in our four-quadrant diagram.

The amount of new construction clearly will depend on the current level of house prices but, as discussed in Chapter 3, it will also depend on the current stock of units. A high price for housing brings forth new construction into a market only until the stock expands to the point at which residual land prices at the edge of the city equal the opportunity cost of land. Let ES_t represent the long-run equilibrium stock of housing (and developed land) that would result using the static rent models of Chapters 3 and 4. This will be a direct function of housing prices, since land prices are a residual from those of housing. If the actual current stock equals ES_t, then no construction occurs, since, in this part of the model, we assume that no units are lost from the stock because of depreciation or scrappage. If the price of housing increases, potential land rents rise, ES_t increases, and development gradually expands until urban and rural rents are again equal. Current construction is a temporary flow that is needed only until the actual stock catches up to that

---

[3] We define C as housing starts rather than completions because data on units started are more common and available over a longer time period than data on units completed. It is necessary to lag starts in a stock equation if units are not completed within a single period. The assumption that it takes one period to complete newly constructed units is somewhat arbitrary. Longer lags do not alter any of the model's fundamental behavior.

long-run stock that is justified by land rent theory.[4] The two equations capturing this relationship are:

$$ES_t = -\beta_0 + \beta_1 P_t$$
$$C_t = \tau(ES_t - S_t) \geq 0 \tag{10.6}$$

In the first equation above, the parameter β_1 determines how rapidly increased prices bring forth new land for development. The ratio of the parameters (β_0/β_1) can be thought of as the minimal price of structures necessary to cover construction costs and, hence, generate any positive land rent. In the second equation, the parameter τ represents the speed with which construction occurs in response to some difference between the actual housing stock and the long-run equilibrium dictated by rent theory. Construction cannot be negative, even if prices are so low that ES_t falls below S_t. In a dynamic model where units are lost from the stock due to depreciation or scrappage, the stock, of course, will decrease if construction is zero. Thus, to keep the stock stable, ES_t must exceed the stock by enough to generate construction that exactly equals the depreciation of the stock.

Combining Equations (10.5) and (10.6), we get a relationship between the current price of housing and the growth (or decline) of the housing stock.

$$\begin{aligned} S_t - S_{t-1} &= \tau(-\beta_0 + \beta_1 P_{t-1} - S_{t-1}) - \delta S_{t-1}, & \text{if } -\beta_0 + \beta_1 P_{t-1} > S_{t-1} \\ S_t - S_{t-1} &= -\delta S_{t-1}, & \text{if } -\beta_0 + \beta_1 P_{t-1} < S_{t-1} \end{aligned} \tag{10.7}$$

The equations in (10.7) allow the stock to increase, if last period's price of housing is high enough so that the long-run equilibrium stock $(-\beta_0 + \beta_1 P_{t-1})$ exceeds the current stock by an amount that is sufficient so that construction will be greater than unit demolitions (δS_{t-1}). As the stock grows, the absolute amount of demolitions grows as well, until eventually the stock no longer increases. This is the steady-state level of the housing stock, S^*, that would eventually emerge if the price, P_{t-1}, held forever. Solving Equation (10.7) for $S_t = S_{t-1}$, the equation for S^* is as follows:

$$S^* = \frac{\tau(ES_t - S^*)}{\delta} = \frac{\tau(-\beta_0 + \beta_1 P_{t-1} - S^*)}{\delta} = \frac{\tau(-\beta_0 + \beta_1 P_{t-1})}{\delta + \tau} \tag{10.8}$$

If the current price is too low relative to the existing stock, then construction will be insufficient to replace the units lost through demolitions. Thus, the stock will start to fall. The smaller stock will need less construction for replacement, and, eventually, a new, lower steady-state S^* will be obtained. For any price, P_{t-1}, Equation (10.8) defines that stock that will eventually prevail if that price continues forever. Naturally, S^* will be higher (lower) with a higher (lower) price.

Equations (10.7) and (10.8) show how the stock moves as a function of the price. In contrast, Equation (10.4), states that the current price is a function of the current stock (and other exogenous variables such as households). If the stock initially is very low, then the price of housing from Equation (10.4) will be high enough so that new construction

---

[4] This approach to modeling housing supply is similar to the stock adjustment models used by macroeconomists to characterize aggregate investment (see Abel and Blanchard 1988).

exceeds replacement. In this case, the stock begins to increase. Alternatively, if for some reason the stock is initially too high, then the price of housing will be low enough so that construction is less than demolitions (possibly even zero). In this case, the stock will decline. Given fixed values for the exogenous variables in the model, there is always *one* value of the stock in between these extremes for which the resulting price for housing generates just enough new construction to sustain that value of the stock. We call this stock value and the associated value of housing price, P^*, the model's full *steady-state solution*. We determine this solution by solving Equations (10.4) and (10.7) together with the condition that the stock not change ($S_t = S_{t-1}$). Alternatively, we can solve Equations (10.4) and (10.8). This simultaneous system of two equations is reproduced in (10.9) below and must be solved for S^* and P^*.[5]

$$P^* = \frac{\alpha_0 - \dfrac{S^*}{H_t}}{\alpha_1(M_t - I_t)}$$

$$S^* = \frac{\tau(-\beta_0 + \beta_1 P^*)}{\delta + \tau}$$

(10.9)

The simultaneous solution to the equations in (10.9) gives the equilibrium price and stock that will prevail in the market if today's households, price expectations, mortgage rates, and model parameters ($\alpha_0, \alpha_1, \tau, \delta, \beta_0, \beta_1$) hold forever. This combined long-run, steady-state solution to the model will be different for various parameters and values of the exogenous variables. By inspecting the equations in (10.9), it can be seen that P^* increases with more households, higher expectations about future price inflation, or lower current mortgage rates. If P^* is higher, then S^* will be as well. We refer to these different P^* and S^* values as comparative steady-state solutions to the model. In effect, we are asking how the price (or stock) of housing will eventually change if, for example, the number of households undergoes a permanent increase and enough time elapses for the market to settle down to a new steady-state value. This is what we did with the four-quadrant diagram in Chapter 1.

The steady-state solution to the model is a hypothetical equilibrium that, in practice, is probably rarely, if ever, obtained in an actual market. The reason is that a market's exogenous variables are generally not constant for a period that is long enough for the full stabilization to occur. While H_t may remain fixed for a few years, once an area's economy begins to grow or decline, H_t does as well. National macroeconomic conditions lead to noticeable fluctuations in interest rates, and consumer expectations about the future also change, perhaps even in response to market movements. Each change in an exogenous variable means that the model variables all start to adjust—moving from the old solution of Equations (10.7–10.8) to a new one. Along the way, current prices always follow from

[5]Solving the system of equations yields the following solution for P^*.

$$P^* = \frac{\alpha_0 H_t(\tau + \delta) + \tau\beta_0}{H_t(\tau + \delta)\alpha_1(M_t - I_t) + \tau\beta_1}$$

Substituting this expression for P^* back into that for S^* in Equation (10.9) yields the final solution for S^*, a more complicated expression.

Chapter 10   The Cyclical Behavior of Metropolitan Housing Markets   247

Equation (10.4), and the stock evolves according to Equation (10.7). How these movements unfold constitutes the study of economic dynamics.

MARKET DYNAMICS WITH EXOGENOUS PRICE EXPECTATIONS

In order to complete our model of the housing market, we must specify a process by which consumers form expectations about future house price inflation, I_t. We begin our study of market dynamics with the simplest of assumptions about this process—that expectations are exogenous to the model and therefore formed independently of local housing market behavior. Such attitudes might exist if households believe that future prices grow with general economic inflation, or follow some long-run growth rate that is largely unaffected by short-run movements in the local housing market. The level of anticipated inflation is not important here; rather, the crucial assumption is that household beliefs, for whatever reason, are constant over time and not affected by recent price behavior in the local housing market. While such an extreme form of economic blindness might seem unrealistic, it is important to begin the dynamic analysis with this simplest of cases.

In the next three sections, we will work with a specific numerical example of our stock-flow model. The values of the parameters are selected to be representative for a medium-sized metropolitan area. Referring back to Equation (10.1), a realistic demand function would have the parameter α_0 equal to 1.0, which means that all households would own homes if the annual cost of owning a home was zero. The parameter α_1 is equal to 0.00003, if house prices are measured in dollars. If the after-tax mortgage interest rate were 10 percent (0.10) and no price inflation was expected, the annual cost of owning a home (Equation 10.2) would be $10,000 if house prices were $100,000. Given the assumed demand parameters, 70 percent of a market's households would desire single-family units at this price (Equation 10.1). At a price of $50,000, demand would rise to 85 percent, while at $200,000 it would drop to 40 percent. Moving to Equation (10.4), if the market has 1 million households and a stock of 700,000 units, Equation (10.4) dictates that the market requires a price of $100,000 to balance demand with supply.

On the supply side, a stock scrappage rate, δ, of 0.5 percent (.005) is assumed, in keeping with the estimates from Chapter 8. If the parameter β_0 equals 230,000 and β_1 equals 10, then a minimum price of $23,000 is necessary to generate the first dollar of residual land value. As house prices increase to $100,000, land rent increases to the point that the long-run equilibrium stock (ES_t in Equation 10.6) becomes 770,000 units—a reasonable size for a metropolitan area. If the actual stock is 700,000, at an adjustment rate of 5 percent, then new construction will be 3,500 units annually—just equal to scrappage. The reader can verify that $S^* = 700,000$, $P^* = 100,000$ are solutions to the equations in (10.9) when these parameters are used.

$$P^* = \frac{1.0 - S^*/1,000,000}{0.00003(0.1 - 0.0)}$$

$$S^* = \frac{0.05(-230,000 + 10\, P^*)}{0.005 + 0.05}$$

What happens to a market that is initially in the steady state above and then receives a positive demand shock? The easiest example of such a shock would be an increase in the number of households—by, say, 10 percent—from 1,000,000 to 1,100,000. Re-solving the equations above, there should eventually be a new equilibrium at which $P^* = \$105,650$ and $S^* = 751,357$. How will the market get to this new solution over time? Figure 10.1 traces the movements, period by period, in prices, construction, and the stock. The price for each period comes from Equation (10.4), while construction and the stock follow from the dynamic Equations (10.6) and (10.7).

With Equation (10.4), more households always means a higher price. The first result to notice is that price in the first few periods after the change in demand overshoots the ultimate long-run equilibrium value. This must always be true, because it takes time for supply to react to the demand shock. As new construction begins to occur, and the stock of units begins to rise, prices gradually decline, eventually reaching the new steady state. This is an inherent pattern with the stock-flow model because of the gradual and lagged adjustment in the stock. Construction exactly follows the movement in price. First, construction rises well above the replacement level then, gradually declines to that rate needed to sustain the new steady-state level of the stock. While the magnitude of the reactions depends on model parameters and the size of the shock, the market response to a one-time positive change almost always exhibits the patterns shown in Figure 10.1.

The reaction of the market to a negative demand shock is not the inverse of its response to a positive change. The reason is that supply behaves differently. With a positive change, higher rates of new construction occur, but negative change can only bring a slow decline in the stock through depreciation. Figure 10.2 portrays the period-by-period reaction of the market to a 10 percent decline in households, from 1,000,000 to 900,000. Prices drop initially, as the reduction in households cannot be matched by a decline in the stock. If the price drop is large enough, construction may cease altogether and the stock may decline at the scrappage rate. A gentler price drop will lead to only a decline in construction, with the stock declining at less than the scrappage rate. In either case, and after many periods, the stock erodes enough so that prices and construction begin to recover, eventually returning to a new steady state ($P^* = \$94,063$, $S^* = 646,029$).

The reactions portrayed in Figures 10.1 and 10.2 are largely generic to the model as specified. There is only one possible—and quite unlikely—response pattern other than that shown. In reaction to a one-time positive market shock, it is (remotely) possible that construction in *one* period could supply more than the needed stock. This would require an exceptionally elastic construction schedule. In such a case, the stock in the third period would exceed the new steady state ($S^* = 751,357$). This would cause third-period prices to drop below their steady-state value ($P^* = \$105,650$). After that, the reaction would resemble that in Figure 10.2: construction would drop below replacement levels, the excess stock would slowly erode, and prices would move upwards to the new steady state.

The general behavior of this model is one of stability and convergence. A positive (negative) market shock leads prices and construction to overshoot (undershoot) their new equilibrium values only once and then settle down. The stock of units never overshoots its new target, and there is no possibility of repeated oscillations or cycles. In fact, the downward rigidity of the stock (except for depreciation) results in a model that is

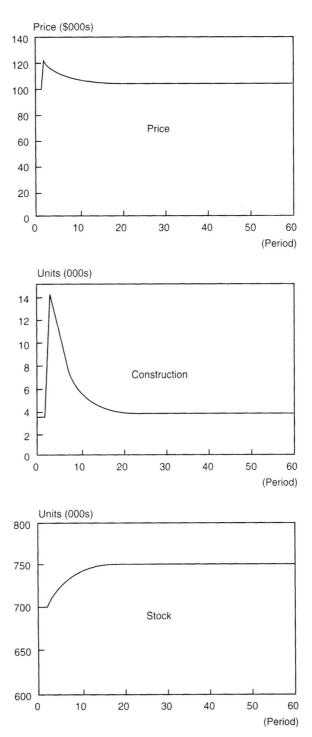

FIGURE 10.1 Market reaction to a positive demand shock: exogenous expectations.

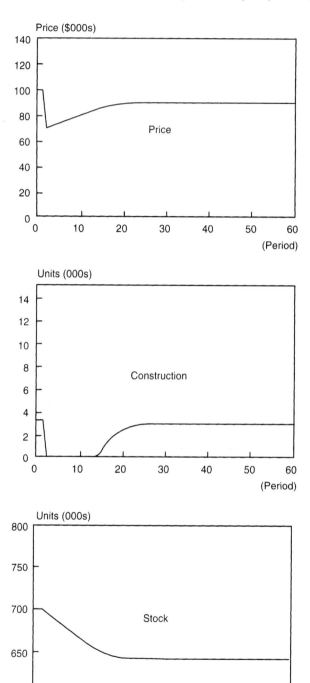

FIGURE 10.2 Market reaction to a negative demand shock: exogenous expectations.

generally *more stable* than comparable dynamic models for nondurable goods. For nondurables, where production each period must equal demand, elastic supply can cause wild oscillations in the market. The supply mechanism of the stock-flow model, with incremental upward stock additions and only very gradual downward adjustments, acts as a stabilizing force in the market.

These conclusions have important implications. The data in Chapters 8 and 9 certainly demonstrated that residential real estate is cyclical, in the sense that it exhibits movements in prices and construction that are repeated. The model above, however, clearly suggests that these movements are not inherent in the real estate market itself. The stability of the stock-flow model implies that any observed cyclical behavior in real estate must be due to cyclical behavior in the exogenous variables that drive the real estate market. In other words, there would appear to be no real estate cycle. Rather, it is instabilities in the U.S. macroeconomy and in the growth of particular regions that largely explain real estate movements. This strong conclusion, however, is highly dependent on the particular stock-flow model used above and its assumption of exogenous price expectations.

MARKET DYNAMICS WITH MYOPIC PRICE EXPECTATIONS

Are consumer expectations about future house prices really formed independently from actual behavior in the housing market? This assumption may form a useful intellectual exercise, but it does seem unrealistic. An alternative approach is to model directly the formation of expectations based on some pattern of current or past behavior in the market. Such *adaptive* or *backward-looking expectations* models are frequently criticized as being ad hoc, but there is evidence from consumer surveys that indicates that consumers frequently operate in this manner. When prices are rising, queried households will often respond that they expect future prices to rise similarly. Myopic foresight may turn out to be a bad forecasting tool, but there is evidence to suggest that consumers may in fact be bad forecasters.[6]

Even the simplest model with endogenous myopic expectations is considerably more complex than the model in the previous section. In effect, another equation must be added, in which the expected rate of price inflation in each period is somehow related to current or past price movements. To make this example simple, yet somewhat realistic, expected inflation in this section is assumed to equal an average of recent inflation:

$$I_t = \left(\frac{1}{n-1}\right)\frac{P_{t-1} - P_{t-n}}{P_{t-1}} \quad , \quad n > 1 \qquad (10.10)$$

In Equation (10.10), if $n = 2$, then consumers form their estimates of future price inflation only from that of the past period. This is myopia in the extreme. More realistically, expectations might be formed over several recent periods of price movements

---

[6]In a survey of homeowners in several markets, the respondents' attitudes about likely future house price appreciation were highly correlated with the recent price behavior in that market. See Case and Shiller (1988).

(for example, $n = 5$). Regardless of the period length, the implications of adding Equation (10.10) to the price determination Equation (10.4) are quite profound. No longer are current prices determined solely by the current value of exogenous variables. The role of history cannot be avoided. Two markets with the same current households, stock, and interest rates could have very different current prices. In a market experiencing a boom, expectations of future price appreciation would be high, and thus the anticipated total cost of ownership low. This would generate stronger demand, with resulting higher prices. A market experiencing a recent price slump would have lower prices, since the expectation of continued downward price movements would raise the cost of owning. In both cases, current and past price movements are positively related because of their connection through the formation of expectations.

Once past price inflation influences current price levels, the stock-flow model can easily exhibit oscillating behavior in reaction to a market shock or change in parameters. The explanation is straightforward. In the period in which the shock occurs, the model reacts as before—with a positive shock, prices rise to clear the market. In the next period, however, the initial price rise has created the expectation of future price inflation. Thus, even as new supply begins to arrive, prices may continue to increase, fueled by expected further price inflation. This continued rise in prices pushes up construction and makes it more likely that construction will be high enough so that the stock eventually overshoots its target. Once this happens, prices peak and then start to drop. This then creates the expectation of negative price inflation, which reduces demand and, thus, actual prices.

Why doesn't the initial shock create sufficiently strong inflationary expectations to keep demand and hence prices increasing forever? What ensures a turning point in the market? In most cases, the main factor generating a turning point is the arrival of new supply. As prices initially take off, it is only a matter of time until enough new supply arrives to begin exerting a strong downward force on prices. For the case of a negative shock, the absence of new construction and a gradual decline in the stock together help to turn around a sliding market.

To provide an example of such endemic cyclicality in the market, the stock-flow example from the previous section is enlarged to incorporate Equation (10.10). Expectations about future price inflation are assumed to be formed with a five-period moving average of past inflation. In all other respects, the model's parameters are identical to those used before. The market shock is also the same as before—a 10 percent increase in the number of households.

This expanded model has the same steady-state solution as the more simple model with exogenous expectations. If prices have been constant for some time, then expected price inflation is zero. If the market solution at which prices have stabilized is equal to $P^* = \$100,000$ and $S^* = 700,000$, then the market will not change from these initial values. With an increase in households to 1,100,000, the same new potential steady state also exists ($P^* = \$105,650$, $S^* = 751,357$). The question is, will the market be able to converge there over time as it did in the previous example? Figure 10.3 provides the time paths of prices, construction, and the stock in reaction to the market shock.

In Figure 10.3, the shock of a 10 percent increase in households sets off a large and recurrent cycle. The initial 21 percent rise in house prices alters household beliefs about

Chapter 10 The Cyclical Behavior of Metropolitan Housing Markets

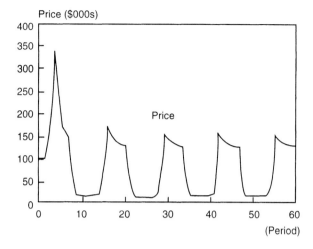

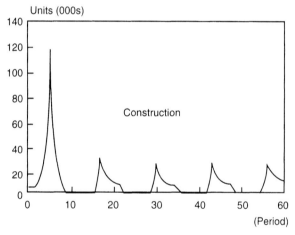

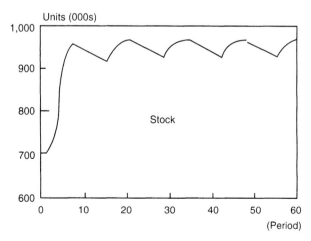

FIGURE 10.3 Market reaction to a positive demand shock: myopic expectations.

future price inflation. Averaging price movements over five years, households now expect prices to rise about 4 percent annually (as opposed to zero previously). This enormously reduces the annual cost of owning, boosts demand, and sends prices even higher. As the process continues, prices rise by three times their initial level. This, in turn, leads to an overbuilding of the stock, which then leads prices to peak and, finally, to start to fall. Falling prices lead to deflationary expectations, further price declines, and a period of no construction. The cycle in prices continues, and a parallel construction cycle emerges. Rather than constructing an even flow of new units each year to ensure the replacement of the stock, the price cycle leads to a replacement cycle. About every 13 years, 62,000 units are built. This averages to 4,800 units annually, or what is needed in the long run to sustain a stock that oscillates around 950,000 units. With a construction lag of only one year, the timing of the price, construction, and stock cycles is all quite close. The market is clearly unable to converge to its steady state, and appears to cycle indefinitely.

The combination of model parameters used in this example, together with the assumption of five-period price expectation formation, generates what seems to be a series of bubbles and bursts or a perpetual cycle. Different parameters or assumptions could yield a cycle that converges gradually to the steady state while oscillating significantly. Still other parameters could lead to a bubble that never bursts, causing infinite prices. Since price bubbles always seem to burst eventually in actual real estate markets, presumably such parameters are unrealistic. The point, however, is that backward-looking or myopic expectations about house price inflation are easily capable of creating a repetitive cycle in reaction to a single, one-time market shock. Such expectations generate a separate real estate cycle that can exist by itself without any cyclic movements in the market's exogenous variables.

The two models analyzed so far present something of a dilemma. In Chapter 8, the national movements of house prices and construction clearly have patterns that are related to macroeconomic movements in economic growth and interest rates. From these data, it would seem that the housing cycle is a reaction to current economic shocks rather than a repetitive oscillation from some event years ago. In this sense, the overt behavior of the market looks more like the first model (blind expectations), as opposed to the second (myopic expectations). On the other hand, the assumptions of the first model are more troublesome, since it is hard to imagine that well-informed consumers do not consider the operation of housing market or use its movements to make judgments about the future.

MARKET DYNAMICS WITH RATIONAL EXPECTATIONS

Macroeconomists have long looked for a theory of consumer expectations in which households use market information, yet their use of this information does not generate overwhelming market fluctuations. The current fashion is to assume that consumers are perfectly informed about the operation of the market. This does not mean that consumers can perfectly predict unforeseen changes or shocks to the market—it only means that once such shocks occur, informed consumers are able to predict correctly how the market will respond. In effect, once interest rates rise or it becomes widely known that changes in computer technology will spur economic growth in a particular region, consumers are able to predict correctly the impact of such changes on house prices and use these predictions as their forecast of future price appreciation.

The formal mathematics of incorporating rational expectations into the stock-flow model are quite complicated, but a simple explanation and example can be presented easily. *In rational expectations, the future path of prices that consumers expect to occur must actually occur, with the exception of the first-period price change following a shock.* Since the shock is unanticipated by definition, the first-period market reaction cannot be part of past consumer expectations. Future price movements in reaction to the shock, however, will be forecast perfectly and form the basis for expectations after the shock.

If the market is in the same initial steady state as the previous models ($P^* = \$100,000$, $S^* = 700,000$), then it is also in a rational-expectations steady state. Because nothing is expected to change, actual as well as expected price inflation is zero. Now suppose that the market is subjected to the same 10 percent increase in the number of households. Long after this shock has occurred, there exists a new steady-state equilibrium that is also the same as before ($P^* = \$105,650$, $S^* = 751,357$). Again, after the perfectly forecasted impact of the shock has worn off, both expected and actual price movements are zero. In between, the expected inflation rate at time t must equal the actual inflation rate that happens from time t to $t + 1$:[7]

$$I_t = \frac{(P_{t+1} - P_t)}{P_t} \tag{10.11}$$

Figure 10.4 traces the impact of a 10 percent increase in households on the market when rational expectations, as expressed in Equation (10.11), characterize the formation of consumer price forecasts. Relative to the first model (exogenous, or blind, expectations), the rational model has less of an initial price increase (12 percent versus 21 percent) and, hence, less decline in prices as the new steady state is approached. Otherwise, the market with sophisticated rational expectations behaves in exactly the same pattern as the more naive model. The explanation for this dampened behavior is simple. The initial price increase is less because consumers know that future supply will be forthcoming and that this eventually will lead to price decreases. The correct anticipation of these future price decreases leads to less demand and hence a lower initial price increase in reaction to the shock. If the shock is a negative one, such as that shown in Figure 10.2, the rational model will exhibit a similar dampened impact. The magnitude of the initial fall will be less because consumers correctly anticipate that eventually there will be rises in price as the stock declines.

With rational expectations, then, a market shock does not set off a recurrent cyclical pattern; there is only a single price overshoot and a single resulting construction boom. A fully informed, rational market will exhibit seemingly cyclical behavior only if the exogenous variables that affect the market have recurrent movements.

---

[7]Mathematically, Equation (10.11) requires that the model be solved backwards, from the future to the present. Prices today (given today's expected inflation rate) depend on prices tomorrow, and so on.

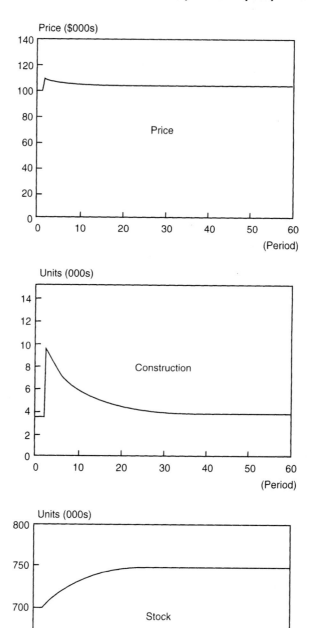

FIGURE 10.4 Market reaction to a positive demand shock: rational expectations.

FORECASTING BOSTON HOUSE PRICES: AN APPLICATION

To many real estate practitioners, the term *forecasting* denotes any simple technique for extrapolating the past movements in a data series into the future. Often this involves fitting trend lines. To economists, on the other hand, forecasting involves using *all* of the historical information available to them about how a market operates. In most cases, this results in attempts to estimate statistical versions of economic theories. How well do these theories work in practice? Which model of expectations seems to fit best with housing market data and experience? Do economic models make more reliable or useful forecasts than simpler extrapolative techniques? The stock-flow model developed in this chapter works very well in practice, can shed considerable insight into how individual markets work, and provides valuable estimates about future market behavior. To provide an example and demonstrate the model's applicability, we take a look at the single-family housing market in Boston, Massachusetts, from the vantage point of 1992.

In any econometric application, obtaining reliable data is half of the battle. In the housing market, the most difficult issue is obtaining a sufficiently long time series for a true house-price index as discussed in Chapter 8. A quality-controlled price series at the metropolitan level is not available for a sufficiently long time period.[8] The National Association of Realtors publishes the median price of houses sold through its Multiple Listing Service by metropolitan area, but this series is not quality-controlled and dates back only a decade or so for most areas. However, the Federal Housing Finance Board surveys the average price of existing housing units that are financed through the nation's mortgage institutions and publishes these figures for a number of metropolitan areas. While this series is not quality-controlled, it does date back to the early 1960s.[9] Figure 10.5 graphs this series for Boston, in constant 1990 dollars.

The Boston price data rise during the 1960s, decline somewhat through the mid-1970s, dip in 1981, skyrocket through 1988, and decrease sharply through 1991. While it can be argued that over the entire period there is a gradual upward trend, this overall observation clearly misses the sharp swings in the data. This pattern is a good example of the pitfalls likely to occur from undertaking simple trend or extrapolative forecasting. In *trend forecasting,* current values of a series, possibly in log form, are related statistically only to a time index, *t,* to allow for constant compounded growth rather than constant absolute growth. Examples of such equations using the Boston price data are shown following:

---

[8]Ideally, we would want a quality-controlled price series, but lack of a long data series prohibits us from using one. Two prominent sources for quality-controlled price indices are Freddie Mac and Case, Shiller, and Weiss, Inc. Freddie Mac produces metropolitan area indices that date back to the 1970s, but the indices in the early years are questionable due to small sample sizes. The Case, Shiller, and Weiss series in many cases date back only to 1980.

[9]Before 1989, this survey was conducted by the Federal Home Loan Bank Board. The series published by the Federal Housing Finance Board date back to 1974. The data in the years before 1974 are not publicly available, but we obtained them by request.

$$P_t = 85{,}587 + 2{,}984t, \quad R^2 = .55$$
$$(3.7) \quad (5.8) \quad N = 29$$

$$\log(P_t) = 11.42 + .021t, \quad R^2 = .60 \quad \quad (10.12)$$
$$(75.19)\ (6.3) \quad N = 29$$

What is missing from these equations is any economic logic or theory. They predict that as time goes forward, prices will simply continue to rise, either by $2,984 annually, as in the first equation, or by slightly more than 2 percent annually, as in the second (in constant dollars). By the year 2002, these equations predict that prices will be either $33,000, or 25 percent higher than in 1992. Surely the long-term magnitude of price growth in Boston must depend on the area's economic growth, as we discussed in the beginning of this chapter.

Trend equations also fail to predict the oscillation around the long-term trend. Why did the real growth in Boston prices during the 1960s stagnate and then reverse into declines during the 1970s? What accounts for the unprecedented growth in prices during the mid-1980s, again accompanied by the sharp reversal during 1988–91? The long-term trend and movements around it can be better understood by studying data on the area's economy and the construction of single-family units. In Figure 10.5, it is clear that the boom in house prices in the 1980s follows sharp growth in real income, and the decline in prices in the late 1980s and early 1990s follows declines in real income. In Figure 10.6, the three periods of real price increases in Boston (1966–69, 1976–79, and 1982–88) also correspond to periods when employment growth was in a strong expansionary phase. In terms of supply, construction was low during the middle period of price growth and was high during the first and last expansions. Thus, while construction and movements in

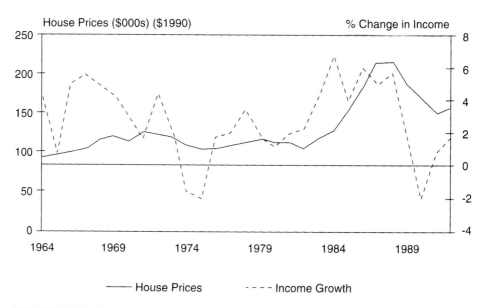

FIGURE 10.5 Boston house prices and income growth, 1964–1992.

Source: House prices, Federal Housing Finance Board; income, adjusted U.S. government figures courtesy of Regional Financial Associates, Bala-Cynwyd, PA.

Chapter 10   The Cyclical Behavior of Metropolitan Housing Markets

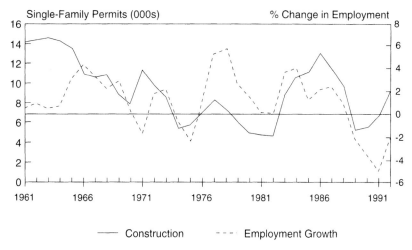

FIGURE 10.6 Boston employment and single-family construction, 1961–1992.

Source: Construction, special tabulations, U.S. Department of Commerce; employment, adjusted U.S. government figures courtesy of Regional Financial Associates, Bala-Cynwyd, PA.

Boston's economy explain some of the area's housing price fluctuations, other factors must also be influencing the market. As suggested in Chapter 8 and as illustrated in the first part of this chapter, the low costs of homeownership during the inflation of the late 1970s should be an important determinant as well. These various forces can best be disentangled with a statistical application of the type of stock-flow model discussed earlier in the chapter.

The first element of a stock-flow model is the *demand equation* and corresponding *price-determination equation*. Exactly following Equation (10.1), we can assume that the demand for single-family housing units is proportional to the estimated number of households in Boston, H_t. This proportion, which determines the homeownership rate, will be a linear function of the price of housing, P_t, the annual cost of purchasing $1 of housing, U_t, and the average income per household, Y_t.

Demand for single family housing units, D_t, is defined as follows:

$$D_t = H_t (\alpha_0 - \alpha_1 U_t - \alpha_2 P_t + \alpha_3 Y_t) \tag{10.13}$$

The term in parentheses represents the homeownership rate. Increases in P_t or U_t decrease the demand for homeownership, while increases in household income increase the demand for homeownership. In equilibrium,

$$D_t = S_t,$$

where S_t is the stock of housing. Setting demand equal to the stock and rearranging the equation, much as we did with Equation 10.4, we solve for the price that clears the market:

$$P_t = \frac{1}{\alpha_2}\left(\alpha_0 - \alpha_1 U_t + \alpha_3 Y_t - \frac{S_t}{H_t}\right) \tag{10.14}$$

Price is determined as a function of the exogenous demand variables and the ratio of households to the stock of housing. The signs in Equation (10.14) are the expected signs on the coefficients.

Since annual data on the numbers of households is not available by metropolitan area, we use employment, E_t, as an estimate of the number of households and then redefine Y_t as average income per worker.[10] As shown in Equation (8.7), the cost of capital to homeowners, U_t, must incorporate mortgage rates, tax rates, and the expected appreciation in housing. As discussed earlier in this chapter, there are three general approaches to measuring expected future appreciation in real estate prices. For the purposes of this exercise, we will use myopic, or backward-looking, expectations. Thus, at any time period, the expected price appreciation of housing over the next year will be a weighted average of price appreciation during recent past years.[11]

For the Boston metropolitan area, the statistical estimate of this equation is shown in Equation (10.15).[12]

$$P_t = \frac{1}{0.0000029} \left(0.069 - 0.0075 U_t + 0.0000174 Y_t - \frac{S_t}{E_t} \right), \quad \begin{matrix} R^2 = .95 \\ N = 29 \end{matrix} \quad (10.15)$$
$$\quad\quad (3.2) \quad\quad (3.1) \quad\quad (19.5) \quad\quad (-7.8)$$

Equation (10.15) suggests that in the Boston area, single-family housing demand is strongly affected by all three variables. How do we interpret the coefficients in Equation (10.15)? The estimates provided in Equation (10.15) are the demand parameters in (10.13).[13] Using these demand parameters, we can calculate the price and income elasticities of demand. The elasticity of single-family unit demand with respect to real

---

[10] This approximation contains some known bias because employment per household has grown somewhat in recent decades with the increased labor force participation of women.

[11] For our model of the Boston economy, we defined U_t as:

$$U_t = (1 - t_y) i - \frac{1}{2} \left(\frac{P_{t-1} - P_{t-2}}{P_{t-2}} + \frac{P_{t-2} - P_{t-3}}{P_{t-3}} \right)$$

We assumed that the average of price appreciation over the previous two years is used to determine future price growth. The variable i is the nominal Federal Home Loan Bank contract mortgage interest rate. The income tax rate, t_y, is defined as the marginal tax rate for first-time homebuyers defined in DiPasquale (1989). The definition of U_t defined in Equation (8.7) includes the after-income-tax property tax rate. We had no time series data on average property tax rates for the Boston metropolitan area and, therefore, we omitted property tax rate from our calculation of U_t.

[12] The numbers below each coefficient are the coefficient's t-statistics.

[13] The equation actually estimated was:

$$P_t = \frac{\alpha_0}{\alpha_2} - \frac{\alpha_1}{\alpha_2} U_t + \frac{\alpha_3}{\alpha_2} Y_t - \frac{1}{\alpha_2} \left(\frac{S_t}{E_t} \right)$$

$$P_t = 23818 - 2586 U_t + 6.01 Y_t - 345503 \left(\frac{S_t}{E_t} \right)$$
$$\quad\quad (3.1) \quad\quad (-7.8) \quad\quad (19.5) \quad\quad (-3.2)$$

The demand parameters in Equation (10.14) are obtained by multiplying each coefficient by α_2 ($\alpha_2 = 1/345{,}503 = 0.0000029$). For example, the demand parameter on Y_t is 0.0000174 ($\alpha_3 = 6.01 \times 0.0000029 = 0.0000174$).

income per worker is 1.78, while the elasticity of demand with respect to housing prices is −0.92.[14] A percentage point increase in the annual cost of owning housing (either through increased mortgage rates or decreased expected price appreciation) reduces the fraction of workers who demand single-family ownership by slightly less than 1 percentage point.

Using the estimated demand parameters (the α values) and Equation (10.13), we can calculate the impact of changes in U, P, and Y on the homeownership rate. Remember that the term in brackets in Equation (10.13) is the homeownership rate. For example, the baseline percentage of workers demanding single-family housing is about 37 percent when income per worker is $41,000, the annual cost of owning 5.0 percent, and the price of housing $130,000. Starting at this baseline, a price increase of $10,000 reduces the percentage to 34 percent, whereas a $10,000 increase in real income per worker would raise the percentage to 54 percent. A rise in mortgage interest rates that causes a 2 percentage-point increase in user costs reduces the baseline to 35 percent.

This simple demand equation fits the data quite well, as indicated by an $R^2 = 0.95$. Taking the actual data on our independent variables year by year, we can use Equation (10.15) to predict the price for each year in our sample. Figure 10.7 provides a graph of actual prices versus the predicted prices from our model. The model clearly does a very good job of predicting price.

On the supply side, the construction of new units can, in principle, be measured directly with an annual time series on building permits, C_t. In practice, it is not always easy to obtain a consistent long-term series on construction permits because the number of permit-issuing jurisdictions surveyed by the government has changed over time. There is some question whether early permit counts are comparable to more recent data.[15] The stock of single-family units is surveyed only every decade as part of the Census. Thus, an annual series for the stock must be estimated by taking the decennial census count and then successively adding permits for each new year. After every decade, this calculated stock can be compared with new Census figures. Normally, one would expect permits to slightly exceed the increase in Census stock counts—yielding a small scrappage rate. In the case of Boston, however, the calculated stock based on annual permits was slightly under the Census stock, suggesting that over much of the sample period, the count of permits understated true, new, single-family construction. To adjust, we scaled the permit series up slightly so that the calculated stocks matched the actual Census counts.[16] With this scaling, there was no scrappage, and Equation (10.16) is used as the stock-flow identity.

$$S_t - S_{t-1} = C_{t-1} \tag{10.16}$$

[14]The price elasticity is $-\alpha_2 P/(S/E) = -0.927$, where P and S/E are the average values over the period ($P = \$130,347$, $S/E = 0.408$). The income elasticity is $\alpha_3 Y/(S/E)$ equals 1.756 (average $Y = \$41,181$).

[15]The permit data used in this model represent an estimate made by the U.S. Commerce Department for a constant number of permit-issuing places (12,000 nationally).

[16]The scale factors applied to the permit series are small: −0.9 percent over the 1960–70 decade and +5 percent over the 1970–80 and 1980–90 decades. The benchmarks that we used in constructing the stock series were the 1960, 1970, and 1990 Census counts of single-family detached and attached units.

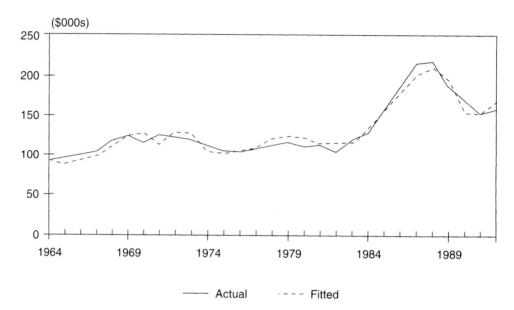

FIGURE 10.7 Actual versus predicted house prices, Boston 1964–1992.

Source: Actual prices, Federal Housing Finance Board; predicted values, authors' calculations.

The estimated construction equation is extremely simple and corresponds directly to Equation (10.6), incorporating only the price of housing and the lagged level of the Boston housing stock. Earlier in this chapter, it was argued that the lagged stock is necessary in a supply equation because greater construction does not continue indefinitely in reaction to higher prices. Eventually, as construction expands the stock and raises land prices (discussed in Chapter 3), the excess profits resulting from higher house prices are eroded. Construction will then slow. The data from the Boston market seems to support this contention; our estimated construction equation is:

$$C_t = 26069 + 0.0686\, P_t - .0405\, S_{t-1} \quad R^2 = .52 \quad (10.17)$$
$$(13.14)\ \ (4.3)\ \ \ \ \ (-5.3) \quad N = 29$$

In the equation above, the coefficient on price suggests that the immediate response of construction to higher prices occurs with an elasticity of 1.02.[17] In reaction to a doubling of prices, the flow of construction would roughly double as well. In the longer run, this higher flow of construction will not continue forever. As discussed earlier, a rise in house prices leads to an increase in long-run equilibrium stock, or *ES* defined in (10.6). The coefficient on stock in Equation (10.17) represents the rate at which the stock adjusts to this new equilibrium through construction. The coefficient suggests a slow stock adjustment process in which the stock adjusts 4 percent per year.

As the stock gradually increases, the rate of new construction declines and eventually ceases. Using the stock and price coefficients in Equation (10.17), we can calculate the long-run price elasticity of the desired stock. The equilibrium stock of housing

---

[17]The coefficient on price times the ratio of mean price to mean starts: $0.0686 \times (130{,}347/8732)$.

Chapter 10   The Cyclical Behavior of Metropolitan Housing Markets

expands with house prices at an elasticity of 0.35—as prices double, eventually the Boston stock increases by 35 percent.[18]

Our estimated construction equation is a very simple model. There are clearly other variables that influence construction, especially cost variables such as construction costs, the cost of short-term construction financing, and land costs. Still, the results of the model are consistent with the theory developed earlier in this chapter. The estimated supply equation ($R^2 = 0.52$) does not fit the data nearly as well as the demand equation ($R^2 = 0.95$). Again taking the actual data on our independent variables year by year, we can predict the level of construction. Figure 10.8 plots the actual construction versus predicted construction from our model. Actual construction is considerably more volatile than the construction predicted by our model.

Equations (10.15) through (10.17) constitute a full stock-flow model for the Boston single-family housing market. When combined, they will forecast prices, construction,

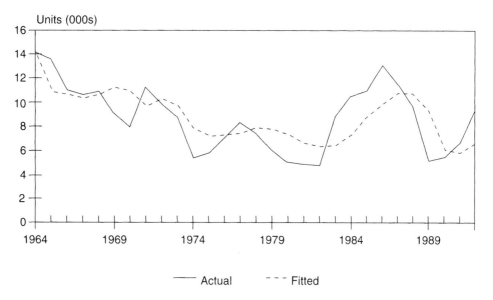

FIGURE 10.8 Actual versus predicted permits, Boston 1964–1992.

Source: Actual permits, special tabulations, U.S. Department of Commerce; predicted values, authors' calculations.

---

[18]From Equation (10.6), the parameters determining the long-run equilibrium stock of housing (β_0, β_1) will equal each coefficient in the statistical equation (10.17), divided by the coefficient estimated for the lagged stock ($\tau = .0405$). Combining this with the stock-flow identity in Equation (10.15), we get the stock-adjustment equation that is equivalent to Equation (10.7):

$$S_t - S_{t-1} = .0405 \, (643{,}679 + 1.69 P_t - S_{t-1})$$

These estimates are reasonable and consistent with theory, with one exception. The intercept is a significant positive number rather than the negative coefficient suggested by theory. Using this equation, price elasticity of the long-run equilibrium stock is $\beta_1 \, (P/S)$, where P is the average price (130,347) and S is the average stock (657,974). The calculation is $1.69 \times (130{,}347/657{,}974) = 0.33$.

and the stock of single-family units, given a forecast of the area's economy (employment and personal income) as well as U.S. macroeconomic conditions (tax and mortgage interest rates). The model operates recursively, starting in the first forecast year, 1993. The stock in that year is known from Equation (10.16) because 1992 construction and stock are both historical data. With the stock and the forecasts of the economic variables for 1993, Equation (10.15) then forecasts 1993 prices. With prices and the stock in 1993 known, Equation (10.17) then predicts 1993 construction, which, in turn, gives the 1994 stock. This, together with the 1994 economic outlook, then gives us 1994 prices. These calculations iterate recursively, in this example for 10 years.

Forecasting in this manner is called *contingent forecasting*. In macroeconomics, the term refers to a forecast of one sector (e.g., housing) given the economic outlook for the overall economy. Here, the term is used similarly: a metropolitan housing market forecast, given the area's expected economic growth and conditions in national financial markets.

Contingent real estate forecasts are useful for two reasons. First, they can provide a reasonable baseline outlook for an area's housing market. Commercial and government forecasts of the U.S. economy are regularly disaggregated to the metropolitan level, so the necessary economic data for contingent forecasting are available. Second, with a model such as that above, alternative optimistic and pessimistic forecasts can be made using somewhat different assumptions about the economic growth of the area being studied. This can provide considerable insight into the variance or risk associated with a particular real estate market.

As an example of this contingent approach, two forecasts of the Boston housing market are made using different economic outlooks. The first, the pessimistic, assumes that the Boston economy only gradually recovers from the recession of 1989–92. Employment begins to expand at only 0.5 percent annually and personal income increases 1.0 percent annually over the decade from 1993 to 2002. Inflation is set at 3.5 percent annually; mortgage interest rates are held constant at 8.11 percent. These rates of growth are considerably below both the long-run historic growth of the Boston metropolitan area, as well as economic forecasts made in 1993. The resulting outlook for construction and house prices is shown in Figure 10.9.

Figure 10.9 suggests that with very slow growth, real house prices in Boston should recover to beyond their previous peak level by 1996 and then begin a cycle downward with another recovery by the year 2002. By 2002, real house prices will be just 5 percentage points higher than the previous historic peak of the Boston market (1988). The future pattern of prices is a continued pronounced cycle around a long-term flat trend. In reaction to this price cycle, construction moves cyclically as well, but with a gradual, downward, long-term trend.

The optimistic forecast assumes that economic growth in the Boston area returns more to levels characteristic of historic expansionary periods. Job growth is assumed to be 2 percent annually, while personal income (per worker) grows at 3.5 percent annually throughout the 1990s. Inflation is again set at 3.5 percent annually and mortgage interest rates at 8.11 percent. This outlook has somewhat more growth occurring than economic forecasters were predicting in 1993. The resulting real estate forecast is shown in Figure 10.10.

Chapter 10 The Cyclical Behavior of Metropolitan Housing Markets   265

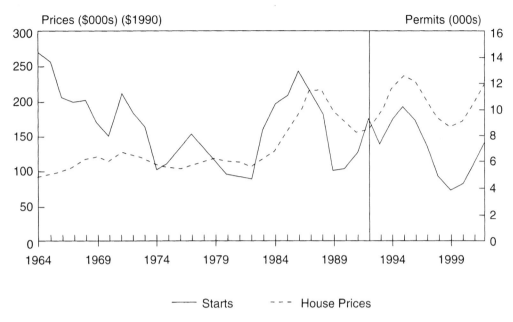

FIGURE 10.9 Pessimistic Boston construction and price forecasts, 1964–2002.

Source: Starts, *Current Construction Reports,* U.S. Census; prices, Federal Housing Finance Board; forecasts, authors' calculations.

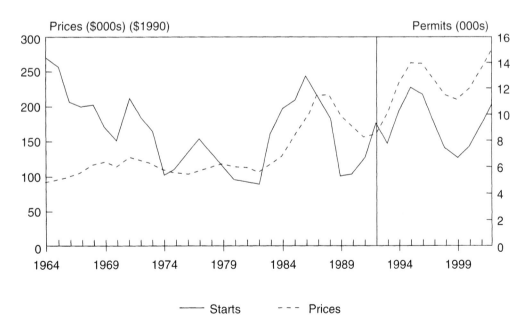

FIGURE 10.10 Optimistic Boston construction and price forecasts, 1964–2002.

Source: Starts, *Current Construction Reports,* U.S. Census; prices, Federal Housing Finance Board; forecasts, authors' calculations.

With the return of stronger growth to the Boston economy, prices in the single-family housing market experience a more pronounced upward long-term trend—rising 25 percent above the 1988 peak by the year 2002 (in constant dollars). With this increase in prices, the long-term trend in permits no longer is downward but rather seems flat. Like the pessimistic forecast, the optimistic forecast also has a strong cyclic movement around the longer-term trend. It is important to understand that these cycles occur without any cyclic fluctuation in economic growth. While the two economic outlooks differ in their long-term growth rates, both assume smooth growth, without any economic cycle. What is it about the housing market that generates cycles even with a smoothly growing economy?

Remember that this model of the Boston housing market uses myopic, or backward-looking, expectations in forecasting the future house prices used to calculate the annual cost of homeownership, U_t. In the first part of this chapter, we demonstrated that such expectations can generate an endogenous market cycle in reaction to some initial economic change or shock. Boston has had three positive economic shocks over this period: job growth was high during the late 1960s, late 1970s, and mid-1980s. During the first two expansions, income growth was only modest. During the last, however, real incomes soared. It was this combination of both income and job growth that set off the rapid rise in prices between 1983 and 1988. With this rapid rise, the investment returns on homeownership became extremely high, and the annual ownership cost fell. With the strong coefficient on U_t, housing demand soared, peaked, and then fell—just as in the simulations of Figure 10.3. Even with smooth economic growth after 1993, the ripple effect of this shock continues: prices recover in the mid-1990s and then turn temporarily downward in the late 1990s. While the cycle is not as severe as that in Figure 10.3, it is nevertheless quite pronounced. Thus, much of the cyclic movement in Boston house prices is not simply a reaction to current economic change, but rather an endogenous cycle wherein the market reacts to its own previous changes.

These structural forecasts with the stock-flow model differ dramatically from the extrapolative type of forecasts that would come from trend-line analysis. With structural economic forecasting, the long-term movements in house prices will depend on economic growth and the elasticity of housing construction. Further, we have seen that there may be strong cyclic movements in house prices, which would be completely missed with trend analysis. Structural models can also provide explanations for market movements by revealing just which economic variables the market seems to respond to most. The data series necessary to undertake this kind of forecasting is now becoming more available, and such time-series models can be estimated for the housing markets in a large number of areas.

SUMMARY

In this chapter, we explored the dynamic operation of urban housing markets using the stock-flow model for highly durable goods. The model assumes that:

- The current stock of housing is determined by the level of the stock in the previous period, plus the amount of new construction brought on the market, less any loss in the stock due to scrappage. In this model, new construction depends on both price levels as well as the stock of units.
- Demand for owner-occupied units is positively impacted by the number of households and household income, and is negatively impacted by the annual cost of owning a home. The annual cost of ownership is determined by the after-tax mortgage rate and the expected growth in house prices.

We considered three ways in which expectations about future house prices are formed, and each has different implications for market behavior:

- With exogenous expectations, households believe that future prices grow with the general economy and are unaffected by the local housing market. A positive demand shock causes prices and construction to rise, overshooting their new long-run equilibriums initially and then declining to the new equilibrium level. The stock rises gradually to its new equilibrium.
- With adaptive or backward-looking expectations, households estimate future house price behavior based on past trends in house prices. A positive demand shock causes prices to rise. Even with new construction, prices continue to rise since expectations are formed by past movements in prices. Prices peak when so much construction occurs that the stock overshoots its target; prices then decline. This process sets off a repeating cycle in prices, construction, and the stock.
- With rational expectations, households are perfectly informed about the operation of the market and are able to predict correctly how the market will respond to an unforeseen shock. The pattern of prices, construction, and the stock is similar to that with exogenous expectations. However, the initial overshooting in prices and construction is less than with exogenous expectations.

The stock-flow model of the Boston single-family housing market was estimated using adaptive expectations. This model fits the data quite well and provides reasonable forecasts of future changes in the housing market given assumptions about the future of Boston's economy.

REFERENCES AND ADDITIONAL READINGS

General

DiPasquale, Denise. "Homeowner Deductions and First Time Homebuyers." Joint Center for Housing Studies of Harvard University, Working Paper W89-2 (1989).

Housing Market Stock-Flow Models

ABEL, ANDREW, AND OLIVIER BLANCHARD. "Investment and Sales: Some Empirical Evidence," in *Dynamic Econometric Modeling,* William Barnett, Ernst Berndt, and Halbert White. New York: Cambridge University Press, 1988.

DIPASQUALE, DENISE, AND WILLIAM C. WHEATON. "The Cost of Capital, Tax Reform and the Future of the Rental Housing Market." *Journal of Urban Economics* 31, 3 (1992): 337–359.

DIPASQUALE, DENISE, AND WILLIAM C. WHEATON. "Housing Market Dynamics and the Future of Housing Prices." *Journal of Urban Economics* 35, 1 (1994): 1–27.

KEARL, J. R. "Inflation, Mortgages and Housing." *Journal of Political Economy* 87, 5 (1979): 1115–1138.

MAISEL, SHERMAN J. "A Theory of Fluctuations in Residential Construction Starts." *American Economic Review* 53, 3 (1963): 359–383.

SMITH, LAWRENCE B. "A Model of the Canadian Mortgage and Housing Markets." *Journal of Political Economy* 77, 5 (1969): 795–816.

Market Dynamics and Price Expectations

CASE, KARL E., AND ROBERT SHILLER. "The Behavior of Home Buyers in Boom and Post-Boom Markets." *New England Economic Review* (November/December 1988): 29–46.

CASE, KARL E., AND ROBERT J. SHILLER. "The Efficiency of the Market for Single Family Homes." *American Economic Review* 79, 1 (1989): 125–137.

HAMILTON, BRUCE W., AND ROBERT M. SCHWAB. "Expected Appreciation in Urban Housing Markets." *Journal of Urban Economics* 18, 1 (1985): 103–118.

POTERBA, JAMES M. "Tax Subsidies to Owner-Occupied Housing: An Asset-Market Approach." *Quarterly Journal of Economics* 99, 4 (1984): 729–752.

SHEFFRIN, STEVEN M. *Rational Expectations.* Cambridge: Cambridge University Press, 1983.

Section 3 Macroeconomic Analysis of Property Markets

CHAPTER

11

THE OPERATION OF NONRESIDENTIAL PROPERTY MARKETS

Chapters 5 and 6 examined industrial and commercial development from a microeconomic perspective. We discussed the factors that influence the location of such development and theories about the operation of the market for nonresidential urban land. In this chapter, the focus shifts to the aggregate behavior of the market for nonresidential property. Just as with housing, this macroeconomic approach allows us to provide perspective on how these markets operate, as well as permits us to study the short-run imbalances that occur between the aggregate demand and supply for such property. In this discussion, we develop explicit models of property demand and supply and use those models to forecast the nonresidential real estate markets.

The first section of the chapter takes an office project built on speculation and examines a typical pattern of development costs and rental income. We demonstrate that the long-term profitability of the project depends almost exclusively on how market conditions determine the building's initial rent and subsequent rental growth. How the building is financed and the structure of ownership can alter the pattern of net income over the project's length, but market conditions ultimately determine its long-term success or failure. This establishes the importance in any real estate venture of being able to make sound judgments about future market conditions.

The next section looks at the inventory of commercial and industrial buildings and at the growth and movements in the stock of space over the last several decades. In the markets for office and retail space, most new construction is by third-party developers, and a large fraction of the stock is rented to tenant-firms. In these markets, there also are long lags between development decisions and the actual completion of new space. Such lags create considerable risk for the developer and may be responsible for some of the cyclical behavior observed in these markets—particularly as judged by movements in vacancy rates. By contrast, in the industrial market a significant amount of space is built at the request of particular owners or tenants, and the lags associated with construction or planning are minimal. The vacancy data available for the industrial space seem to confirm less market volatility.

The next section studies the demand for nonresidential property and examines the types of firms that own and use it. Office space, at least that which is located in buildings that are exclusively used for offices, is occupied mainly by firms in either the services or FIRE (finance, insurance, and real estate) sectors. The space occupied by the headquarters of manufacturers, utilities, or trade industries constitutes a smaller share of the office market. Over the long term, the growth of office space seems to match reasonably closely with the growth of office employment. Industrial space is occupied mainly by firms in the manufacturing or wholesaling sectors. In the industrial market, the growth of industrial space has been noticeably greater than that of manufacturing and wholesale workers. Instead, it is more in line with the increases in industrial production and inventories.

Over the years, the financial needs of both firms and landlords have given rise to a reliance on long-term leasing in the markets for nonresidential rental space. In this chapter, we examine the structure of these leases because they are critical to understanding the cost of space to users in these property markets. These leases contain a number of interesting provisions that make the notion of a market rent much more complicated than in the case of rental housing.

Most of the discussion in this chapter centers on the markets for office and industrial space. When measured in square feet, these are the two largest categories of nonresidential property. As discussed in Chapter 1, however, the nation's retail space market may actually be the largest in dollar value. The absence of systematic data on retail square feet, vacancy, and rents limits our discussion of this important property type.

MARKET CONDITIONS AND THE INVESTMENT RETURNS TO REAL ESTATE

As will be discussed in the next section, most office and retail space and almost half of the nation's industrial space is rented. Historically, such space has been built speculatively, beginning with a development firm acquiring a site (or the option on the site), commissioning initial plans, and then securing whatever necessary permits are required. Land assembly, planning, and permitting can often take several years and involve considerable risk. Therefore, this stage of the process is normally funded by the development firm's own equity—with the possible addition of other equity partners.

Starting construction generally requires short-term financing (i.e., a construction loan from a commercial bank or thrift). Such financing is generally intended to cover only the cost of building the structure and possibly any site improvements. Upon completion of the structure, a period of leasing takes place—usually several years after the building was originally conceived. It is during this phase that market conditions begin to

Chapter 11 The Operation of Nonresidential Property Markets

establish firmly what the building's true income stream will be for the first decade of its operation. As this value is established, the development firm normally converts the short-term construction loan into a longer-term financing commitment.

Longer-term financing may be obtained generally in one of three ways. First, a large equity partner (e.g., a pension fund) or group of partners may purchase some or all of the building, possibly including the development firm's share. Second, a single investor or group of investors (e.g., an insurance company) may underwrite a long-term mortgage on the property, leaving the developer with a highly leveraged equity position. Third, if the property is having difficulty leasing or finding a buyer, the bank may convert its construction loan into a mid-term mortgage and possibly take some or all of the developer's equity. This is a so-called *work out* arrangement. Of course, some combination of these simple scenarios is also possible.

To understand the sources of profit and risk with speculative development, Figure 11.1 depicts a very simple yearly pro forma statement for a 100,000 square foot office building, from conception to final sale or financing. In year 0, land is purchased for $2 million. In years 1 and 2, initial site improvements and plan drawings lead to additional outlays of $2 million and $1 million, respectively. This $5 million constitutes the development firm's initial equity. In year 3, construction financing for $10 million is obtained at a 10 percent interest rate. The interest is initially deferred and accumulates as debt. In year 4, the construction is finished with an additional $5 million loan plus $1 million in deferred interest, and interest payments are again deferred and added to debt.

In the fifth year, the building is leased at a net rate (after operating expenses) of $20 per square foot. Assuming the entire 100,000 square feet is leased, net development income in that year is $240,000, given interest expenses of $1,760,000 (which are now paid rather than deferred). With anticipated inflation, both income and operating expenses are assumed to rise 5 percent annually beyond the fifth year. If net rents continue to grow forever at 5 percent annually and the building does not depreciate, then by year 10, the building generates $2,552,563 annually, or $792,563 after debt service. In year 10, the value of the building is determined by capitalizing its growing income stream. Assuming no debt and using a 10 percent interest rate and a 5 percent long-term income growth rate, current income should be capitalized at 10 percent minus 5 percent, or 5 percent. This yields a theoretical resale price for the building of $51,051,263. If a buyer could be found at this price, the developer's initial investment of $5,000,000 would yield $33,451,263 (after debt repayment) in the tenth year.

To determine the developer's profit, we must discount all receipts and outlays back to year 0. The net resale price yields $12,896,910 (in year 0 dollars), while income earned during years 5 through 10 yields $1,418,468. This is contrasted with the developer's initial investment of $5 million—actually, $4,644,628 in present value (year 0 dollars). Net profit is therefore $9,670,750. The *internal rate of return* (IRR) for the stream of payments is 22 percent—more than twice the discount rate used.[1] All in all, this is a handsome profit or return.

---

[1] The internal rate of return is the interest rate that would set the present discounted value of the developer's outlays minus the present discounted value of the income stream to zero.

Year	Total Equity	Total Debt* (Payments and Debt Service)	Net Operating Income† (Assume 5% Growth Rate)	Debt Service	Net Cash Flow	Contributions to Equity	Net Development Income
0	$2,000,000	$0	$0	$0	$0	$2,000,000	($2,000,000)
1	$4,000,000	$0	$0	$0	$0	$2,000,000	($2,000,000)
2	$5,000,000	$0	$0	$0	$0	$1,000,000	($1,000,000)
3	$5,000,000	$10,000,000	$0	$1,000,000 DEFERRED	$0	$0	$0
4	$5,000,000	$16,000,000	$0	$1,600,000 DEFERRED	$0	$0	$0
5	$5,000,000	$17,600,000	$2,000,000	$1,760,000	$240,000	$0	$240,000
6	$5,000,000	$17,600,000	$2,100,000	$1,760,000	$340,000	$0	$340,000
7	$5,000,000	$17,600,000	$2,205,000	$1,760,000	$445,000	$0	$445,000
8	$5,000,000	$17,600,000	$2,315,250	$1,760,000	$555,250	$0	$555,250
9	$5,000,000	$17,600,000	$2,431,013	$1,760,000	$671,013	$0	$671,013
10	$5,000,000	$17,600,000	$2,552,563	$1,760,000	$792,563	$0	$792,563
				PDV:	$1,418,468	$4,644,628	($3,226,160)

ASSUME BUILDING SOLD IN YEAR 10
WITH CONTINUED 5% GROWTH IN INCOME:

Value of Building in year 10 =	$2,552,583/(10% − 5%)
	= $51,051,263
Minus Debt in year 10:	− $17,600,000
	$33,451,263
Present Value =	$12,896,910
Minus Present Discounted Value of Equity:	− $4,644,628
	$8,252,282
Plus Present Discounted Value of Income:	+ $1,418,468
Profit:	$9,670,750
IRR: 0.22	

ASSUME BUILDING SOLD IN YEAR 10
WITH NO GROWTH IN INCOME:

Value of Building in year 10 =	$2,000,000/10%
	= $20,000,000
Minus Debt in year 10:	− $17,600,000
	$2,400,000
Present Value =	$925,304
Minus Present Discounted Value of Equity:	− $4,644,628
	($3,719,324)
Plus Present Discounted Value of Income:	+ $713,926
Profit:	($3,005,396)
IRR: −0.03	

FIGURE 11.1 Development pro forma for 100,000 square-foot office building.
*Assume 10% interest rate.
†Income of $20/SF.

The IRR or profit from the project can be altered to some extent by restructuring the manner in which the project is financed. If the developer were to borrow the outlays in years 2 and 3, then his net income and sales proceeds would be less because of greater debt service, but so would be his initial investment. Profits as a percent of initial investment can often be made to increase with greater leverage, but there are commensurate increases in project risk. As the project takes on more debt, its net income in years 5 through 10 may be negative. Without continued infusions of debt, there can be the risk of bankruptcy.

The combination of up-front costs from the construction loan and a five-year delay in income means that the developer's profit, or the project's internal rate of return, is extremely sensitive to both the level of rents in year 5, and their future growth. The lower-right-hand section in Figure 11.1 repeats the calculations above assuming that net rental income in year 5 is still $2,000,000—but does not increase beyond this level in the future. This has two impacts on the project's profitability. First, it reduces the present discounted value of the net (of debt service) income stream in years 5 through 10 by roughly 50 percent, to only $713,928. Second, and more importantly, prospective buyers in year 10 are looking at a building with little long-term income growth—and, hence, value the building at only $20 million instead of $51 million. After discounting these sales proceeds and repaying the debt, the project loses $3,000,000 in year 10, for a negative IRR. If rental income in year 5 is only $1,500,000 but growing at 2.5 percent annually, the project still loses money.

This simple example of a five-year speculative development highlights the important role played by expectations about future market rents. The eventual asset price of the building and the developer's rate of return depend crucially on estimates of future market conditions, which must be formed years before the completion of the development. The rest of this chapter and Chapter 12 are devoted to building an understanding of how nonresidential property markets operate and how this understanding can be used to assess and forecast future market conditions.

CONSTRUCTION CYCLES AND THE STOCK OF SPACE

To study the aggregate movements in the supply of nonresidential space, we proceed just as in Chapter 10. The flow of new commercial or industrial space is measured by a time series of the number of square feet completed or constructed each year. The total stock of space at any time can be ascertained either by annual surveys or by the summation of historic construction to date, as discussed in Chapter 1. If there is no scrappage of buildings, then these two methods should yield identical series for the stock of space. In the U.S., there are three general sources of data on building construction or completions that can be used to construct a series on the stock.

The first source of supply data is the federal government's building permit data. These data are published by metropolitan area and by type of building but contain only the dollar value of the proposed construction. This dollar value is frequently an estimate and, in any case, must be divided by some construction cost index to arrive at approximate square footage. Permit data is recorded at the time the permit is issued; so, given the lengthy development time frequently required for commercial space, the completion date of the structure must be estimated. The completion date is important because that is when the space enters the stock, becomes available to users, and begins to impact the market.

An alternative source of construction data can be purchased from the F. W. Dodge Company/McGraw-Hill, which maintains a data bank of known building contracts. These data contain both the dollar value and square footage of the contract and are also available by state and metropolitan area. However, as with permit data, the Dodge series is based on the date of contract signing, not building completion.

The final source of supply data are the inventories of buildings that are maintained by large commercial brokerage companies. Such inventories generally contain the completion date, square footage, number of stories, and other characteristics of each surveyed building. With the completion dates known, and assuming no building scrappage, a retrospective history of the stock can be reconstructed. The actual inventory figure provides base year numbers for the stock, which must be assumed or otherwise estimated with the other two sources. An issue often raised about such data, however, is the breadth of its coverage. In the case of the largest U.S. brokerage company, CB Commercial, the inventory covers all office or industrial buildings with more than 10,000 square feet, but only in major metropolitan areas. Office buildings likely to be overlooked in such surveys include city row houses converted to office use as well as the smaller suburban structures. Brokerage data can be tabulated by districts within metropolitan areas since it is collected by addresses.

Using brokerage data, Figure 11.2 tracks the total completions of space as a percentage of stock in 50 metropolitan areas of the U.S. This sample of areas represents that part of the U.S. covered by CB Commercial and is used throughout this chapter, for both industrial and office space (see Appendix 11-A). Completions of new office space seem to have a unique cyclic pattern not always linked to the U.S. macroeconomy. Completions dropped just after the recessions of 1975 and 1991, but continued to rise right through the downturns of 1970 and 1981. Figure 11.2 clearly shows that the building boom of the 1980s was not much greater than the earlier boom in the late 1960s to early 1970s when measured as a percentage of the existing stock. The strength of the cycle is evident by the observation that boom-period completion rates are about three times those in the trough.

In the industrial market, the cyclic pattern in construction is far less pronounced than with office space. Furthermore, the movements appear to be more closely timed to

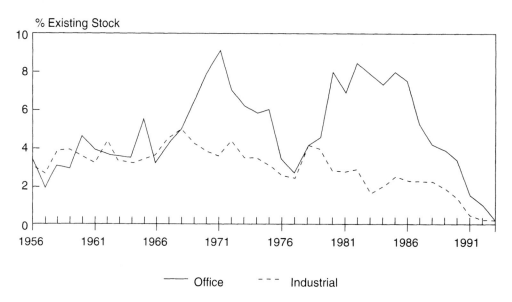

FIGURE 11.2 Metropolitan* office and industrial completions as a percentage of stock, 1956–1993.

*Aggregate data for 50 metropolitan areas.

Source: CB Commercial.

U.S. macroeconomic movements. Industrial completions drop during all recessions (1970, 1975, 1982, and 1991), but only by an average of about 25 percent. Over the last two decades, the figure suggests that there has been a gradual decline in the rate of new industrial completions. Even when measured in absolute square feet, the level of building activity in the 1980s was actually less than in the 1970s.

There are no national or metropolitan surveys of retail space undertaken by the brokerage industry, but it is possible to track the square feet of retail construction contracts signed each year with the F. W. Dodge data discussed previously. Figure 11.3 tracks these numbers for a series representing all retail space in the U.S. (rather than just that in the largest metropolitan areas). The movements in national retail construction seem to behave more like industrial than office space, moving in quite a pronounced manner with the U.S. macroeconomy—as evidenced by the close association between retail construction and aggregate retail sales. In Figure 11.3, retail contracts fall during each recession (1970, 1975, 1982, and 1991), reaching bottom just after sales do. In terms of volatility, retail construction lies somewhere between office and industrial space, with trough construction averaging about 60 percent of that during peaks.

Why does the supply of office space seems to have such a pronounced independent long-run cycle, while the supply of industrial and retail space fluctuates less and moves more closely with the national economy? We can only guess at this point, but one hypothesis is that most office space requires long lead times for planning and construction and is built by investors for eventual rental use. The argument is that this can generate market volatility since by the time space enters the stock, market conditions have changed. These issues are less important in the industrial market, in which properties

FIGURE 11.3 National retail construction and growth in retail sales, 1968–1991.

Source: Construction, F. W. Dodge; retail sales, U.S. Department of Commerce.

have far shorter development lead times and more often are built at the request of either an owner or a long-term tenant.

Space built by an owner may better be thought of as a form of investment rather than speculative development. When firms have space built for them, supply, by definition, is always equal to demand, and new capital construction is determined solely by its demand. Macroeconomic research has found that national aggregate investment demand depends on the growth prospects for firms, together with long-term real (after-tax) interest rates (Hall and Jorgenson 1967).

When space is constructed primarily for rental use, it need not be actually occupied. As we discussed in Chapter 9, vacancy plays the important role of distinguishing between the demand and supply for space. Particularly within the U.S., information about vacancy has become quite widespread and, in the case of office space, is quite long-standing. The Building Owners and Managers Association (BOMA) has surveyed office buildings in a number of major cities since the early 1920s. In recent years, the larger commercial brokerage companies have all undertaken systematic vacancy surveys, some beginning as far back as the mid-1970s. These broker surveys often cover industrial buildings as well as offices. As yet, there is no regular source of data on retail space vacancies. Figure 11.4 takes these vacancy surveys (the BOMA surveys prior to 1978 for offices, and CB Commercial surveys after 1978 for offices and industrial property) for 31 metropolitan areas

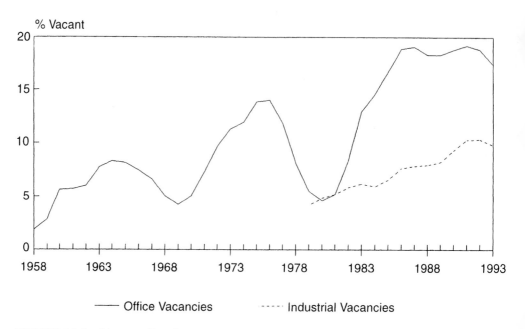

FIGURE 11.4 Metropolitan* vacancies, industrial versus office, 1958–1993.
*Aggregate data for 31 metropolitan areas.
Source: CB Commercial.

(out of the list of 50 in Appendix 11-A), and then weights them by the square footage in each area into an index that approximates the U.S. as a whole.[2]

Figure 11.4 again shows some important differences between the industrial and office property markets. Industrial vacancy is lower than office vacancy, and appears to be much less volatile—at least over the short time period for which we have comparable data. In many respects, this is in keeping with the suggested organizational difference between the two markets. In the office market, in which a larger percentage of buildings are speculatively constructed for rental use, it is much easier to imagine imbalances arising between space supply and demand.

Converting any series on space completions into a series on the total stock raises the important issue of building demolition or scrappage. Without demolitions, the stock at any time is simply the sum of completions prior to that date. With demolition, however, this relationship is more complicated. In the office markets of older cities such as Boston, New York, and San Francisco, demolitions sometimes have been a source of land for new inner city office developments. In these cities, however, there is little evidence that such demolitions represent a significant loss in square feet of office space. This is because older buildings tend to be much smaller and represent only a small fraction of the total stock. In newer cities, the demolition losses are likely to be even less. The completions series in Figure 11.2 suggests that without any scrappage, the stock of office space in the country's largest 50 MSAs should have increased 200 percent since 1972, from just over 1 billion square feet to 3.15 billion in 1993.

With industrial space, there also are few records of actual demolitions, but economic arguments suggest building scrappage might be more common. Industrial buildings are worth less (as compared to office structures) and often become functionally obsolete as production or distribution technology changes. As discussed in Chapter 5, the older industrial buildings in cities have become locationally obsolete, and, in some cases, have been demolished or converted to different uses. Again, assuming no scrappage, the completions series in Figure 11.2 implies that the industrial stock in the largest 50 MSAs increased 65 percent since 1972, from 5.5 billion to 9.1 billion square feet in 1993.

THE DEMAND FOR PROPERTY: OWNERSHIP AND OCCUPANCY

To study the demand for nonresidential property, we examine the types of firms that own and use such space and their growth over time. In the office market, we focus on the growth of employment in certain sectors of the economy, but in the industrial space market, it is industrial production and inventories that dictate the demand for space—more so than the number of workers in these sectors.

---

[2]Because single-tenant, owner-occupied space is a small part of the office market, the office vacancy data in Figure 11.4 takes space that is physically vacant and divides by the total stock of space in multi-tenant buildings. Because of the prevalence of single-tenant industrial space, the industrial vacancy data take space vacant and available for rent and divide by total space, whether owned or rented.

The use and ownership of nonresidential property varies greatly, depending on the category of property. Based on the same inventory of space that was used to track building completions (in 50 metropolitan areas of the U.S.), Figure 11.5 depicts the organization of both office and industrial space.[3] Unfortunately, a similar inventory of space does not exist for retail buildings. The 1991 data were collected by building but are presented in terms of square feet. Figure 11.5 highlights the important distinction between who owns space as opposed to who occupies it.

The inventory of office buildings in the 50 metropolitan areas represented 3.110 billion square feet of office space in 1991. In terms of ownership, the space in owner-occupied buildings accounted for 32 percent of the office space market; the other 68 percent was owned by someone other than an occupant. It is important to recognize, however, that not all of the space in an owner-occupied building needs to be used by the owner. In fact, there was more space in owner-occupied buildings that also have additional tenants than there was in single-tenant owner-occupied buildings (18 percent versus 14 percent). Remember that Figure 11.5 only categorizes *buildings* of each type. Figuring out how much actual *square feet of space* is used by each type of user is more difficult. If we were to assume that slightly more than half of the space in owner-occupied multitenant buildings was occupied by the owner, then using the numbers in Figure 11.5, about 25 percent of the office *space* in these 50 metropolitan markets was occupied by its owner, while around 75 percent was occupied by a tenant. Thus, at least in the office markets of America's large metropolitan areas, the vast majority of space is multitenanted rental space.

In the industrial market, the patterns of ownership are quite different. The inventory of industrial buildings in the 50 metropolitan areas represented just over 9.05 billion square feet of space in 1991. Of this space, 48 percent was in buildings that are owner-occupied, and, unlike the office market, virtually all of this space was in single-tenant buildings (43 percent versus 5 percent for multitenant buildings). It is also true that more than half of the space in rental buildings was composed of single-tenant structures. Thus, nearly three-fourths of all industrial space was in buildings with only one occupant. While rental tenure was still important in the industrial market, multitenant rental space accounted for only 22 percent of industrial space, at least in larger metropolitan areas.

There are two ways of thinking about the users of any kind of space: by occupation and by industry. In the office market, the first approach examines employment in those white collar occupations in which the worker is likely to conduct his or her business from a desk, table, or office. The second approach looks at firms that are likely to be housed in office buildings. All employees in these firms are assumed to occupy office space. The difference between these two is quite pronounced and can be illustrated by considering the office usage by the nation's manufacturing firms. According to the 1987 U.S. Census of Manufacturers, white-collar occupations (managerial, professional, clerical, sales)

---

[3]As discussed earlier in this chapter, this inventory of buildings comes from the data banks of the nation's largest commercial property brokerage company, CB Commercial. A list of the 50 metropolitan areas is in Appendix 11-A.

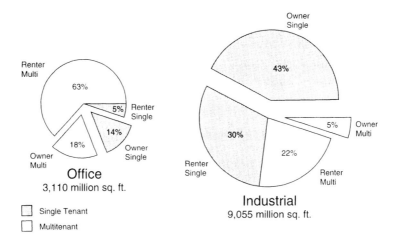

FIGURE 11.5 Metropolitan* tenancy by square feet, 1991.

*Aggregate data for 50 metropolitan areas.

Detached slices are owner-occupied. These data are based on detailed survey information obtained from about 80 percent of the buildings in CB Commercial's inventory of total office and industrial space.

Source: CB Commercial.

account for roughly 40 percent of employment in manufacturing firms. Many white-collar workers, such as technicians or salesmen, may actually not occupy office space, working perhaps instead mainly on the road or in laboratories. Alternatively, the office space occupied by such workers may not be in office buildings but instead may be located at sites of production or research. In fact, only about 10 percent of all manufacturing workers (or 25 percent of manufacturing white-collar workers) seem to reside in separate office buildings.

There are two problems with identifying office usage by occupation. First, periodic employment data by metropolitan area and occupation simply do not exist. Rather, periodic employment surveys tend to be of firms and record data by industry category (Standard Industrial Classification, or SIC). Second, it is difficult to match the notion of office usage by occupation to any measure of office-space supply. Doing so would require a count of office floor space in all kinds of structures, not just separate office buildings. While several measures of space in office buildings exist, data on office space in all buildings do not. Thus, while an occupation-defined measure of office demand is in principle more broadly based, realistically, it is infeasible to construct and track such a measure over time.

Turning to the industry approach, it *is* possible to determine which types of firms tend to occupy space in separate office buildings. Using this categorization, the number of workers employed by such firms can be followed over time and then compared with the supply of office buildings. Table 11.1 examines which types of firms use separate office building space in two metropolitan areas. These data are based on the U.S. Government's County Business Patterns survey of establishments. This survey records both total workers and workers in "separate administrative or auxiliary structures" within each industrial category. For firms in the SICs of manufacturing, mining, construction, trade, and transportation, communications, and utilities (TCU), it is assumed that only workers identified as being in separate office structures constitute office employment. In the FIRE sectors, it is assumed that all workers occupy office space. For the services sector, all workers in a set of quite detailed SIC categories (legal, advertising, accounting, consulting, etc.) are counted as occupying office space.

The numbers in Table 11.1 are quite representative of most larger metropolitan areas in the U.S. and suggest several conclusions. First, in 1989, roughly 25 percent of these cities' urban labor force worked in office buildings. Second, about three-fourths of these workers were in the FIRE and service sectors; the next-largest office building occupier was trade. Finally, the fraction of services that were office-occupying averaged about 30 percent. Of course, different cities have their own peculiar features. In Washington, D.C., for example, the government represented 30 percent of office employment, and the preponderance of lawyers raises the services' share of office workers to 52 percent. In Detroit, the service share was noticeably lower, while the manufacturing share was somewhat higher.

What Table 11.1 points to is a method for tracking an estimate of office workers over time. For the last 50 years, the U.S. Government's employment surveys have followed employment in most major metropolitan areas by the one-digit SIC categories shown in Table 11.1. Applying the ratio of office workers to total workers for each category yields an estimate of private-sector office employment each period. Figure 11.6 graphs the percentage change of this measure of office employment for the same 50

TABLE 11.1 Office Employment* in Dallas and Chicago, 1989

Standard Industrial Classification (SIC)	Dallas†		Chicago‡	
	Total (000s)	Office (000s)	Total (000s)	Office (000s)
Manufacturing	184.7	16.2	499.1	49.4
Mining	17.44	10.3	1.3	0.6
Construction	47.5	0.6	93.8	0.4
Transportation, Communication, and Utilities (TCU)	92.4	7.1	148.5	6.2
Trade	287.9	28.1	613.6	51.1
Finance, Insurance, and Real Estate (FIRE)	122.9	122.9	246.0	246.0
Services	314.8	105.8§	730.2	227.0
Total private	1067.6	291.0	2332.5	580.7

*Office Employment refers to those employees occupying separate office space from on-site manufacturing, retailing, or distribution activity.
†Dallas County.
‡Cook County.
§Services in office employment include advertising, computer and data processing, credit reporting, mailing and reproduction, legal and social services, membership organizations, and engineering and management services.
Source: U.S. Commerce Department, *County Business Patterns*, 1990, Washington, D.C.

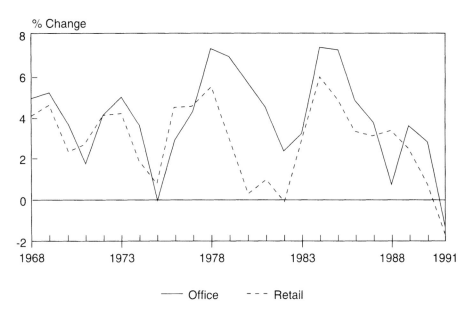

FIGURE 11.6 Changes in metropolitan employment, 1968–1991.

Source: Office employment figures, derived from 50 U.S. metropolitan areas, adjusted U.S. government figures courtesy of Regional Financial Associates, Bala-Cynwyd, PA; national retail employment, F. W. Dodge and Bureau of Labor Statistics, *Employment Situation* and *Employment and Earnings,* seasonally adjusted.

metropolitan areas used in the tenancy survey of Figure 11.5. Office employment, measured this way, is clearly cyclical. Growth rates approach zero during the recessions of 1970, 1975, 1982, and 1991, and tend to recover strongly in between. Over the last two decades, office employment in these major metropolitan areas has grown at an average annual rate of roughly 3.7 percent.

While there is virtually no data about the tenancy and ownership patterns for retail space in the U.S., it is very easy to identify those workers that occupy retail space by using employment numbers in the SIC retail categories.[4] Figure 11.6 also tracks the percentage growth in retail employment, again using a national series rather than data for the 50 metropolitan areas. Changes in retail employment follow a pattern that is quite similar to that for office employment.

In the industrial real estate sector, we turn again to inventories or surveys by private brokerage companies. According to Figure 11.5, the 50 metropolitan areas contained nearly 9.05 billion square feet of industrial space in 1991. This brokerage survey was able to identify both the SIC of the tenant and the building use for 6.2 billion of these square feet. These results are shown in Table 11.2.

Approximately 53 percent of the industrial space in the nation's major cities was occupied by firms with a manufacturing SIC. The next-biggest user was firms with a

---

[4] In government employment surveys, the direct retail outlets of a manufacturer (e.g., gas stations) are classified as retail rather than manufacturing employees.

TABLE 11.2 Industrial Tenants,* 1991

Industry of Occupant (SIC)	Building Use (millions of sq. ft.)				
	Manufacturing	Distribution	R & D	Other	Total
Manufacturing	2422.8	807.1	140.4	2.7	3,373.0
Transp/Commun/Utilities (TCU)	50.8	474.3	12.4	0.7	538.3
Wholesale Trade	260.1	1,047.0	43.8	2.5	1,353.4
Retail Trade	19.4	175.1	5.8	0.2	200.5
Services	90.6	202.2	129.8	1.8	424.4
Other†	73.0	190.4	21.6	31.1	316.1
Total	2,916.7	2,896.1	353.8	39.0	6,205.6‡

*Aggregate data for 50 metropolitan areas.
†Other represents Agriculture/Forestry/Fishing, Mining, Construction, Public Administration, and Nonclassifiable Establishments.
‡Profile based on detailed survey information from about 70 percent of industrial buildings in CB Commercial inventory.
Source: *The Industrial Outlook Report*, CB Commercial.

wholesaler SIC (22 percent), followed by TCU firms (9 percent) and then service firms (7 percent). When tallied by the *use* of the structure, almost 47 percent of this space was used for distribution. Of this distribution space, just over one-third was actually used by firms whose primary SIC category is wholesaling; the rest was used by manufacturers and firms in other SICs.

While Table 11.2 tells us what types of firms occupy industrial space, it is not easy to estimate the number of employees that use this space. The County Business Pattern data directly surveyed the number of workers (by SIC) that occupy office buildings. Brokerage surveys record only the fraction of space occupied by firms of various SICs. Thus, we do not know what fraction of workers (by SIC) use industrial buildings. It is reasonable to assume that most wholesale and manufacturing employees work out of industrial space, but we have little guidance for other SICs. Therefore, to judge industrial space demand in Figure 11.7, we track employment only for manufacturing and wholesaling, which, from Table 11.2, together use 75 percent of the nation's industrial space. When compared to Figure 11.6, this chart illustrates that employment among industrial space users is clearly more cyclic than for office or retail space users.

In trying to convert the employment of selected industries into an actual measure of potential space demand, it is useful to calculate how many square feet are occupied by employees in each property market. Using 1991 figures, and the definitions of office employment developed in Table 11.3, the office markets of 50 metropolitan areas had roughly 11.5 million office workers. Using the 3.11 billion square feet of office space in these 50 metropolitan areas (Figure 11.5) yields a space-consumption estimate of about 270 square feet per worker. In the industrial market, this calculation can be undertaken separately for manufacturing and wholesalers: Table 11.2 indicates that 53 percent of the industrial space was used by manufacturing workers and 22 percent by wholesale workers. Using the employment and total stock figures in Table 11.3 yields 619 square feet/manufacturing worker (9,050M SF × 0.53/7.752M) and 539 square feet/wholesale worker (9,050M SF × 0.22/3.693M). The absence of a retail space survey precludes estimating

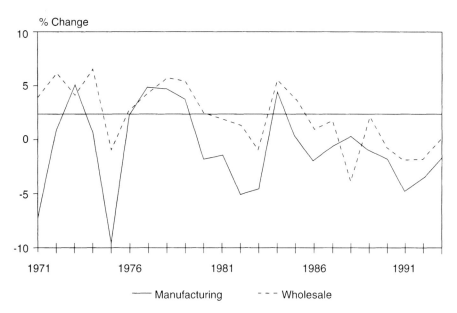

FIGURE 11.7 Changes in metropolitan employment, 1971–1993.

Aggregate data for 50 metropolitan areas.

Source: Adjusted U.S. government figures courtesy of Regional Financial Associates, Bala-Cynwyd, PA.

retail worker space occupancy. While such calculations are interesting, it is overly simplistic to assume that such consumption standards will remain constant over time as the industrial and occupational mix of workers changes and technology alters the amount of capital firms use per worker.

To test the long-term relationship between office or industrial employment and their respective stocks of space, we use the data presented so far in this chapter to create Table 11.3. This table compares the long-term growth of industrial and office space with that of industrial and office workers, together with several other measures of potential space demand, again in our 50 large metropolitan areas.

The long-term growth in manufacturing employment for these areas was slightly negative (–7.5 percent) over the last 19 years, while wholesale employment grew by 47.7 percent. Weighting these two growth rates by the levels of employment in Table 11.2 suggests that total industrial space employment has grown by only 8.5 percent over this period. In contrast, the stock of industrial space increased by 64 percent. How do we reconcile these differences?

Much of the discrepancy between the growth of industrial space and industrial employment can be explained by increases over this period in output and inventories per worker. Economists estimate that nationally about 50 percent of the growth in manufacturing output per worker comes from increases in capital or machinery, and such equipment requires space. In warehouse buildings, it would seem that the entire demand for space originates more from the volume of inventories stored, rather than from the

TABLE 11.3 Growth of Industrial Demand, Office Employment, and Stocks,* 1972–1991

Year	Manufacturing Employment	Output per Worker†	Wholesale Employment	Inventory per Worker‡	Industrial Stock	Office Employment§	Office Stock
1972	8385	0.0341	2500	0.223	5.52	5580	1.05
1991	7752	0.0581	3693	0.271	9.05	11500	3.11
% change	–7.5	70.4	47.7	21.5	63.9	106.1	196

*Aggregate data for 50 metropolitan areas: employment in thousands, stock in billions of square feet.
†Industrial production per manufacturing worker, national.
‡The real value of inventories carried per wholesale worker, national.
§Office employment includes all employment in FIRE and selected Services SICs.
Source: Output and inventory per worker, national data, *Survey of Current Business*, U.S. Department of Commerce, Bureau of Economic Analysis, Washington, D.C., monthly reports. Office employment and stock, *The Outlook Report*, CB Commercial.

workers used to move this material around. These ideas would be easy to test if we had direct data by metropolitan area on overall industrial production and inventories. In fact, however, actual data about inventories and industrial production are available only nationally. The federal government does provide some estimates of regional production, but these are created with a simple method, and are officially available only at the state level.[5]

To overcome these problems, we can examine national industrial output and inventory growth per worker and assume that any trends in these national variables also occurred in our 50 MSAs. In Table 11.3, we see that industrial output per worker grew a whopping 70.4 percent between 1972 and 1991. Together with the 7.5 percent decline in manufacturing workers, we can estimate that total industrial production in these cities increased by 63 percent. Similarly, on a national level, the value (not volume) of inventories held per wholesale worker grew 21.5 percent over our 19-year period. Extrapolating to our cities, where wholesale employment grew 48 percent, we conclude that total inventories might have increased 69 percent. These estimated increases in industrial production and inventory growth are consistent with the 64 percent increase in the stock of industrial space.

Of course, a 63 percent increase in industrial production does not mean that manufacturing space demands have increased at this rate. Some increases in productivity come simply from new ideas or work practices—rather than from more workers and machines, which clearly use space. Similarly, the estimated growth in the real value of inventories (69 percent) does not necessarily mean a comparable increase in the physical volume of inventories. Yet Table 11.3 clearly suggests that we must look beyond jobs to understand the demand for industrial space.

---

[5]As discussed in Chapter 7, data on product and income accounts at the state and local level are difficult to construct. The government takes national production-per-worker data at the detailed four-digit industry level and then weights this by each state's four-digit employment data. This is equivalent to assuming that within four-digit industry groupings all firms have equal productivity across all regions.

The comparison in Table 11.3 between the growth of the office stock and the increase in office employment leads to a similar issue: the growth of the office stock exceeds that of office workers—in this case by almost 100 percent. Since it is workers who occupy office space, this discrepancy must be a result of one of two factors: either the space per worker has increased enormously over the last two decades, or the data mismeasure the percentage growth of the office stock. In the next chapter, we argue that there are good economic reasons for the square foot per worker to change over time, although it seems unlikely that these reasons are sufficient to explain the large movements in Table 11.3. A more likely source of the discrepancy is the failure of most brokerage surveys to count small office buildings. Independent insurance agents, lawyers, architects, stockbrokers, and other office workers frequently occupy older townhouses in cities and converted houses or retail space along major roads in the suburbs. Such buildings normally have less than 10,000 square feet, which typically excludes them from brokerage surveys. Thus, while brokerage inventories likely track the completions of space in recent decades, they, as other sources, may also be off in estimating the total size of the complete office stock. The workers, however, are carefully counted in the government employment statistics. If the same amount of space was omitted from both the 1972 and 1991 surveys, the growth rate between these years would be overstated because the base used to calculate the rate was understated.

LEASES, RENTS, AND VACANCY: THE COST OF SPACE TO USERS

For commercial or industrial property that is rented, obtaining data about rent is quite central to understanding the historic fluctuations in the market. Rents not only influence investment returns and new construction but can also shape the amount of space (per worker) that tenant firms wish to occupy. Leasing arrangements negotiated between landlord and tenant are usually quite complicated. Unfortunately, and unlike property sales, leases are private contracts that are not publicly recorded. What we know about leases, therefore, tends to come from voluntary disclosure by tenants and landlords or from data gathered by the commercial brokers who often handle these transactions. The major provisions in leases are, for the most part, designed to accomplish two tasks: (1) to determine a pattern of payments over time, and (2) to distribute risk between the tenant and landlord. Each of these is discussed below as we examine the components of typical leases.

Lease term. This is simply the length of the lease. Figure 11.8 gives the distribution of lease lengths from a sample of 7,000 office leases that were brokered in 1989 through the nation's largest commercial realtor, CB Commercial. The extent to which this sample is representative of the overall market is unclear, but the mean lease length is 5 years, with distinct clusters at 3, 5, and 10 years. The sample includes no leases longer than 12 years. The longer the lease term, the more the effective ownership of the property is transferred to the tenant. This is because the tenant usually retains the right to sublet space and cannot nullify the lease commitment. With a very long term, the landlord has

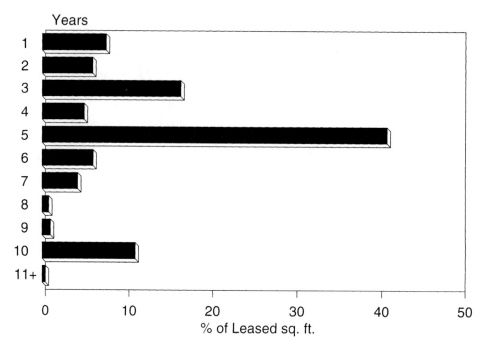

FIGURE 11.8 Frequency distribution of office lease lengths, 1989.
Source: CB Commercial.

implicitly sold the rights to an uncertain market income stream in exchange for the present discounted value of all lease payments.

Lease steps. Most leases specify either a uniform fixed rent or different specified rent levels over several subperiods within the lease term. The changes in rent (normally increases) that occur over these subperiods are referred to as *step increases.* Such steps are often designed to reflect what both parties believe will happen to the average market value of rents during the term of the lease.

Lease inflation indexation. In longer-term (5–10 year) leases, it is quite common to have the rent payments specified in real terms. This requires that the rent (including any step increases) rises annually with some agreed-upon price index that reflects overall economy-wide inflation. It is important to understand that inflation indexation introduces a pattern of uncertain increases in rent, since inflation is not known *ex ante.* It transfers the risk of inflation from the landlord to the tenant.

Gross/net rent. Some leases are specified in terms of gross dollars, others in net terms. In the former case, the landlord pays for utilities and property taxes. Unless otherwise specified, gross rent leases place the risk associated with operating expenses on the property owner. Leases specified in terms of net dollars usually make the tenant responsible for utilities and increases in property taxes. Here, the risk of changing operating expense is clearly born by the tenant.

Concessions. Concessions refer to additional adjustments in the rental lease—usually offered by the landlord as an enticement to potential tenants. The two most common concessions are (1) periods of free rent at the beginning of the lease, and (2) the landlord paying to remodel and renovate the interior of the tenant's space. In recent years, and especially in soft real estate markets, there has been a tendency for landlords to offer concessions to tenants rather than lowering the contract rent and charging the tenant for improvements.

Overage rent. In the market for retail space, rent is paid in two ways. First, there is *ground rent,* or *base rent,* which is just like that described above for the office or industrial markets. Second, however, there is also *overage rent* in which a tenant pays a percentage of his gross sales, usually after a minimum deductible amount. As discussed in Chapter 6, with overage rent, the landlord effectively becomes a partner in the tenant's business and has some stake in the growth of retail sales by the tenant. This provides the landlord with an incentive not to take actions which would be to the detriment of a tenant, such as admitting a strong competitor to the same shopping center. In the office and industrial markets, there seems to be less likelihood that such landlord decisions could be directly adverse to the operation of a tenant's business. Hence, overage rent is not a feature of leases for these types of properties.

Given all of the various provisions in most commercial leases, the notion of a single market rent is often difficult to define. Two common terms are used in practice: *total consideration,* and *net effective rent. Total consideration* refers to the sum of all gross payments made by the tenant over the lease term. Frequently, this figure is divided by the square footage of space and the lease term. This yields an average cost to the tenant per square foot per year over the length of the lease, undiscounted by the timing of those payments. Commercial and industrial brokerage commissions are frequently based on a lease's total consideration. *Net effective rent* takes this sum of all tenant payments over the lease term and then subtracts estimated total operating expenses, as well as the initial cost of tenant improvements. This, again, is divided by lease term and square footage to arrive at the actual rent received by the property owner.

Table 11.4 traces these different measures of market rent for a prototypical lease in the office or industrial markets. The sample 10-year term involves an initial year of free rent and then a base rent of $15 per square foot. In years 4 and 7 of the lease, a $5 step increase occurs, but there is no inflation indexation. Operating costs are initially $6 per square foot and are estimated to increase by $0.50 each year. The capital improvements required by the tenant in year 1 are $30 per square foot. Average consideration over the lease term is therefore $19, and net effective average rent is that figure minus average operating expenses and improvements, or $7.75. Notice that if the lease had the same figures but ran for only five years, net effective average rent would be only $1. This reflects

TABLE 11.4 Rent Determination per Square Foot

Year	Rent	Operating Costs	Improvements	Net Effective Rent
1	$0.00	$6.00	$30.00	$–36.00
2	15.00	6.50	0.00	8.50
3	15.00	7.00	0.00	8.00
4	20.00	7.50	0.00	12.50
5	20.00	8.00	0.00	12.00
6	20.00	8.50	0.00	11.50
7	25.00	9.00	0.00	16.00
8	25.00	9.50	0.00	15.50
9	25.00	10.00	0.00	15.00
10	25.00	10.50	0.00	14.50
Over 10 years:				
Average	19.00	8.25	3.00	7.75
PDV (10%)	105.77	48.31	27.27	30.18
Over 5 years:				
Average	14.00	7.00	6.00	1.00
PDV (10%)	49.75	26.18	27.27	–3.70

the important role that initial tenant improvements play on the cost side of the equation. The costs of tenant improvements provide landlords with a strong incentive to enter into longer-term leases.

It is often, and correctly, argued that the figures in Table 11.4 should be discounted to arrive at a total space cost for the term of the lease in present dollars. The present discounted value calculations (PDV), using a 10 percent discount rate, are provided in the table, assuming a 10-year lease and a 5-year lease. For the 10-year lease, this yields a present discounted value for total consideration rent of $105.77 per square foot, as opposed to an undiscounted cost of space for the 10 years of $190.00 (10 times average consideration). The present discounted value of net effective rent is only $30.18, as opposed to a 10-year space cost of $77.50. The present discounted value of net effective rent over only the first five years of the lease is negative. With discounting, the initial cost of free rent and any tenant improvements is more highly weighted, and the value of future rental step increases is likewise less.

The calculations above make it clear that any meaningful measure of market rent must be based on a careful analysis of individual leases. Given the proprietary nature of rental contracts, it is perhaps not surprising that there have been no standard surveys or indices, especially over time, about movements in either office or industrial space rents. An innovation in this regard is an office rental index recently prepared by CB Commercial, based on the brokerage fees received by its leasing agents. Leasing commissions are typically a variable percentage of each year's rent during the lease term. In calculating the commission, the brokerage company normally determines the total consideration of the lease, as described in the example of Table 11.4. The payroll records of CB Commercial date back to the late 1970s in a number of metropolitan areas, and these were used to retrospectively create a measure of consideration rent for each market.

Chapter 11 The Operation of Nonresidential Property Markets

A true rental index must compare the cost over time of identical space rented for similar lease terms. When the leases are from only one brokerage company, it raises the issue of whether that company's business is truly representative of the overall market. In addition, if the company's properties or the structure of its leases change from year to year, then movements in the average rent of the company's transactions might not represent true changes in market conditions. To allow for this possibility, the CB Commercial index statistically adjusts the data on consideration rent to estimate total consideration over time for space of constant quality. This can be done in one of the two ways discussed in Chapter 8 for determining a house price index. Either leases for the same space can be repeatedly surveyed, or a statistical (hedonic) model can be estimated that predicts how consideration rent varies by factors in addition to the year it was signed, such as the type and location of the building or the lease term and square footage. The CB Commercial index uses the hedonic approach.[6]

In Figure 11.9, the solid line represents the average actual consideration rent each year in San Francisco, based on 2,193 leases brokered by CB Commercial since 1979. The dashed line is the predicted rent from the hedonic model. Both rental measures have been adjusted for inflation and are expressed in constant 1990 dollars. While the long-term trend in the two is the same, the year-to-year movements are sometimes different. Between 1987 and 1988, for example, the simple average consideration rises by $0.91 from $19.73 to $20.64 (adjusted for inflation), while the predicted index falls by $0.70

---

[6]The statistical model used for the CB Commercial Index uses leases signed in up to 15 zip codes within each metropolitan area, for the years 1979 to 1993. With this equation, the rent index is calculated for a 10,000-square-foot lease, with gross rent over five years in an existing building located in a zip code whose coefficient is average for that metropolitan area. Varying the time dummy variables (D_i), the index determines how the consideration for this lease and property has varied over time. The model is as follows:

$$\log(R) = \alpha_0 + \alpha_1 SQFT + \alpha_2 TERM + \alpha_3 HIGH + \alpha_4 NEW + \alpha_5 GROSS$$

$$+ \sum_{i=1980}^{1993} \beta_i D_i + \sum_{j=1}^{15} \delta_j Z_j$$

where:

R = Total consideration/square foot/year
$SQFT$ = Square feet of lease
$TERM$ = Length of lease (year)
$HIGH$ = (= 1 if 5+ stories, = 0 otherwise)
NEW = (= 1 if new building, = 0 if existing)
$GROSS$ = (= 1 if lease in gross rent, = 0 if net)
D_i = Dummy variable for each year (i = 1980 to 1993)
Z_j = Dummy variable for each zip code (j = 1 to 15)
α, β, δ = estimated statistical parameters

The model predicts what the consideration should be for leases with certain characteristics in certain locations during specified years. The estimated coefficient α_3, for example, determines how much greater, on average, consideration is in buildings five stories or higher. The dummy variable D_i reveals how much greater (or less) consideration is in that year relative to the base year of 1979. The dummy variable Z_j determines how much of a location premium (or discount) there is for leases in that zip code versus others. A separate equation is estimated for each metropolitan area.

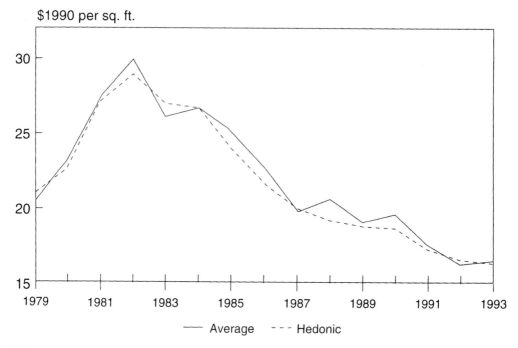

FIGURE 11.9 Average office rents versus hedonic index, San Francisco 1979–1993.
Source: CB Commercial.

from $19.90 to $19.20 (or a 3.5 percent decline). This suggests that the buildings in the 1988 sample of leases were of higher quality than those in the 1987 sample.

While the CB index of consideration rent is a promising improvement, its usefulness is limited, for it goes back just a decade and only for a small number of market areas. As of this date, the longer-run movements of commercial or industrial rents are largely unknown.

While it is clear that there is less systematic data on key variables for non-residential property markets than for residental markets, the data series in this chapter indicate that quantitative time-series forecasting of nonresidential real estate markets should still be feasible. The next chapter pursues this notion further, with several examples that are not only useful as forecasting tools but also provide some insights into the causes and consequences of market cyclicality.

SUMMARY

In this chapter, we began our analysis of the operation of the nonresidential property markets, particularly the markets for office and industrial space. The available data indicates that there are fundamental differences between the commercial and industrial markets:

- The majority of office space is rented; a large portion of owner-occupied office buildings also rent space to other tenants. In the past four decades, there have been two major office building booms in the U.S. The first was in the late 1960s to early 1970s and the second was in the early to mid-1980s.

- The vast majority of industrial buildings have a single occupant. Close to half of the industrial space is owner-occupied. Industrial construction is less volatile than office construction and is more likely to follow trends in the national economy.

Historically, conditions in the economy clearly have a profound impact on the market for office and industrial space.

- The demand for industrial space grows with increases in industrial employment, inventories, and industrial production. The demand for office space grows with office employment and changes in the amount of space per worker.
- The relationship between tenant and landlord for commercial and industrial space is generally governed by long-term leases. The 5-year lease seems to be the most common with 3- and 10-year leases also quite prevalent. Leases determine the structure of payments over time as well as the distribution of risk between the tenant and the landlord.

Analyzing the nonresidential property market is hampered by the lack of systematic long-term data on key variables. While private firms do provide some data on amount a space (square feet) and vacancy, the lack of a consistent time series on quality-controlled rents and prices has limited research.

APPENDIX 11-A

50 U.S. Metropolitan Areas Used in This Chapter

Albuquerque	Jacksonville
Atlanta	Kansas City
Austin	Las Vegas
Baltimore	Long Island
Boston	Los Angeles
Charlotte	Miami
Chicago	Minneapolis
Cincinnati	Nashville
Cleveland	New York
Columbus, OH	Northern New Jersey
Dallas	Oakland
Denver	Oklahoma City
Detroit	Orange County
Fort Lauderdale	Orlando
Fort Worth	Oxnard
Fresno	Philadelphia
Hartford	Phoenix
Houston	Portland, OR
Indianapolis	Riverside

Sacramento
Salt Lake City
San Diego
San Francisco
San Jose
Seattle

Stamford
St. Louis
Tampa
Tucson
Washington, D.C.
West Palm Beach

REFERENCES AND ADDITIONAL READINGS

General

WURTZEBACH, CHARLES H., AND MIKE E. MILES. *Modern Real Estate.* New York: Wiley, 1991.

The Demand for Property: Ownership and Occupancy

WHEATON, WILLIAM C. "The Cyclic Behavior of the National Office Market." *AREUEA Journal* 15, 4 (1987): 281–299.

WHEATON, WILLIAM C., AND RAYMOND G. TORTO. "An Investment Model of the Demand and Supply for Industrial Real Estate." *AREUEA Journal* 18, 4 (1990): 530–547.

Construction Cycles and the Stock of Space

F. W. DODGE COMPANY. *Building Contracts.* New York: McGraw-Hill, 1960–92.

GREBLER, LEO, AND LELAND S. BURNS. "Construction Cycles in the United States Since World War II." *AREUEA Journal* 10, 2 (1982): 123–151.

HALL, ROBERT, AND DALE JORGENSON. "Tax Policy and Investment Balance." *American Economic Review* 57 (1967): 391–414.

SOLOW, ROBERT M. "Technical Progress, Capital Formation and Economic Growth." *American Economic Review* 52, 2 (1962): 76–86.

Leases, Rents, and Vacancy: The Cost of Space to Users

BENJAMIN, JOHN D., GLENN W. BOYLE, AND C. F. SIRMANS. "Retail Leasing: The Determinants of Shopping Center Rents." *AREUEA Journal* 18, 3 (1990): 302–312.

BRENNAN, THOMAS P., ROGER E. CANNADY, AND PETER F. COLWELL. "Office Rent in the Chicago CBD." *AREUEA Journal* 12, 3 (1984): 243–260.

BUILDING OWNERS AND MANAGERS ASSOCIATION. *Experience Exchange Report.* Washington, DC: 1931–1984.

CB COMMERCIAL. *Office Vacancy Index.* Los Angeles, 1979–92, quarterly.

CB COMMERCIAL. *Industrial Availability Index.* Los Angeles, 1979–92, quarterly.

WHEATON, WILLIAM C., AND RAYMOND G. TORTO. "Office Rent Indices and Their Behavior Over Time." *Journal of Urban Economics* 35 (1994): 112–139.

CHAPTER 12

ECONOMETRIC ANALYSIS OF METROPOLITAN OFFICE AND INDUSTRIAL MARKETS

The historic behavior of commercial real estate and the future outlook for a property market are closely connected to an area's economy. The historic movements in economic growth and the future of certain sectors in an area's economy always act as the driving force for a local real estate market. At the same time, each metropolitan area and type of property can react to economic change with a different pattern of response. The demand for property, for example, does not always increase immediately after economic growth, nor does it do so in a directly proportional relationship. In this respect, commercial markets can be quite different from the housing market models of Chapter 10. Supply, likewise, responds with different timing and magnitudes, depending on the organization of the building industry and local development regulations. In this chapter, we build on the data and discussion presented in Chapter 11 by developing several time series models of the demand for and supply of nonresidential property. The models are estimated statistically for the San Francisco office market and for industrial property in the Philadelphia metropolitan area. In both cases, contingent forecasts are developed based on different scenarios for the long-term economic growth of each area, just as we did with the Boston housing market in Chapter 10.

Contingent econometric forecasting of local real estate markets offers important advantages over more intuitive analysis. The systematic collection and analysis of historical data, for example, frequently reveals which economic factors drive both the demand for property as well as new building activity. Often this can yield new insights into the operation of local property markets. Contingent forecasting also provides a range of outcomes that can depict the future degree of risk or uncertainty that is likely in a particular market. The general approach of applying time series analysis to nonresidential property also suggests that we should be able to forecast the systematic movements in these markets. More widespread use of such analysis would probably help to stabilize some of the cyclic fluctuations that occur with nonresidential property.

THE MARKET FOR OFFICE SPACE IN SAN FRANCISCO

Office space has the most detailed and reliable information available of all the nonresidential property markets. Using the data discussed in Chapter 11, it is possible to study systematically the longer-run movements in office building construction, the stock of space, rents, and vacancy rates. Such data can be tracked for several decades in many metropolitan areas. San Francisco is used here simply as an example. With proper modeling and interpretation, these data can shed considerable light on the behavior of a local office market.

Our approach to studying the market for office space in San Francisco will involve quite different assumptions from the models developed in Chapter 10 for the housing market. These differences mainly concern the behavior of the demand side of the market. With housing, our stock-flow model was based on the assumption that prices or rents adjusted within one period to clear the market, equating housing demand with the stock of available units. Since housing vacancy rates tend to be both low and relatively stable over time, this somewhat simple approach seems reasonable. In the commercial market, however, movements or fluctuations in vacancy are far more pronounced and persist for many periods. This suggests that rents or prices are not clearing the market, and that demand must be measured distinct from supply—*demand* is measured as the amount of occupied space, whereas *supply* is the sum of occupied and vacant space.

In tracking movements in the amount of occupied space, we notice that this measure of property demand rarely changes in direct proportion with changes in the number of office workers. The discussion in Chapter 11 suggests that this may be due to the complicated leasing arrangements that characterize the use of commercial space. Firms may wait until their leases expire before adjusting their space consumption, even if their workforce is growing or declining. The measurement of occupied space and its gradual adjustment over time will form the basis for the demand side of our office market model.

Our approach to modeling commercial space begins with three accounting identities. First, the stock of total space in each period, S_t, is updated from that of the previous period with new space deliveries or completions, C_t, minus any space lost to scrappage or demolition, δ. This stock-flow equation, Equation (12.1), is no different from that of our housing models in Chapter 10. Next, the demand for office space at any time can be measured *ex post* as the portion of office stock that is actually consumed or occupied, OC_t. This involves defining the vacancy rate, V_t, as the percentage difference between the total stock and the occupied stock, Equation (12.2). Finally, the net absorption of office space, AB_t, is defined as the change in the amount of occupied office space from period to period. Thus, in Equation (12.3) the current amount of occupied space, OC_t, equals that

Chapter 12   Econometric Analysis

of the previous period plus the net space absorption, AB_t.[1] Net absorption is positive when existing vacant space is leased, or when newly built office space is leased without increasing the vacancy of existing buildings. These three relationships are accounting identities, rather than behavioral economic theories.

$$S_t = (1 - \delta)S_{t-1} + C_t \tag{12.1}$$

$$V_t = \frac{(S_t - OC_t)}{S_t} \tag{12.2}$$

$$OC_t = OC_{t-1} + AB_t \tag{12.3}$$

These three identities form the basis for modeling commercial property markets. Given the total stock of space in the previous period (S_{t-1}), the current period's total stock (S_t) can be determined with a forecast of this period's completions, C_t. This forecast of completions will involve a behavioral model similar to that for housing. It is the demand side of the market that is different. If all office tenants could adjust their space consumption instantaneously we could forecast the current amount of occupied space (OC_t) directly. Instead, we make a forecast of space absorption (AB_t) and then let the occupied stock gradually adjust from its value in the previous period (OC_{t-1}) by using the identity, Equation (12.3). From the combined forecast of the total and occupied stock, we can then calculate the present vacancy rate, V_t. To complete the model we will have vacancy determine the movement in rents, and then allow rents to affect both absorption and new completions. Let's take the model one step at a time, beginning with the forecast for absorption.

Forecasting Office Space Demand

Using the SIC employment data described in Chapter 11, we can calculate a measure of office employment and trace its growth in the San Francisco metropolitan area (Figure 12.1).[2] Office employment in San Francisco experienced significant downturns near the national recessions in 1971, 1982, and 1991, but was not hit as hard by the recession of 1975. The long-term growth of the area's office sectors was noticeably lower in the 1980s than during the 1970s, running somewhat contrary to national patterns.

If every office worker in San Francisco used the same amount of office space, then the growth of office employment would lead to proportionate increases in the amount of occupied or leased office space. To see if this relationship holds, Figure 12.1 compares annual office employment growth with the annual net absorption of office space in the San Francisco area.

Figure 12.1 suggests that although there is a strong relationship between office employment growth and net space absorption, the relationship is far from perfect. During the late 1980s, absorption was at least as strong as that which occurred throughout the 1970s. Employment growth in the 1980s, however, was noticeably less than during the

---

[1] Net absorption must be distinguished from gross absorption. Gross absorption measures primarily the amount of movement by tenants, or space turnover, and not necessarily the increase in space demand.

[2] The San Francisco metropolitan area includes San Francisco, Marin, and San Mateo counties.

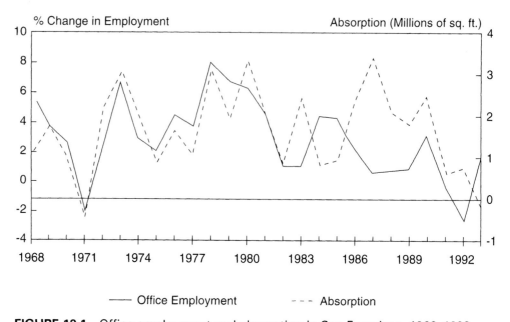

FIGURE 12.1 Office employment and absorption in San Francisco, 1968–1993.

Source: Employment, adjusted U.S. government figures courtesy of Regional Financial Associates, Bala-Cynwyd, PA; absorption, CB Commercial.

1970s. When employment growth and absorption diverge, the amount of space per office worker must be changing.

Why would space per worker change over time? One explanation is that space use per worker varies across occupations, and the area's occupational mix may change over time. Clerks, for example, use less space than managers. If automation is eliminating clerical positions, then the space per (remaining) office worker would be expected to rise. It is difficult to test this notion since time series data by occupation do not exist at the metropolitan level. Since occupations vary by industry, it also is possible that space usage might vary across types of firms. To identify these differences, we would need survey data from individual establishments that contain information about square feet per worker. Again, these data do not exist. Clearly, though, longer-term changes in occupation and industry mixes do potentially affect the demand for office space per worker.

A second explanation for variations in space use per worker recognizes that office space is a factor of production, like labor or equipment. As such, its use should depend on its price. In the case at hand, the amount of space per worker should vary with the cost of space or the level of office rents. To test if a demand elasticity really exists, Figure 12.2 compares the average rent for office space in 12 of the largest metropolitan areas with estimates of overall office space per worker. The rent data is based on the index developed in the previous chapter and illustrated in Figure 11.9. The use rates are obtained by dividing the known inventory of occupied space in office buildings by office employment figures such as developed in Table 11.1.

The line in Figure 12.2 is the statistical regression of rent on square feet per worker. The relationship is significant and negative, yielding a rent elasticity of space demand of

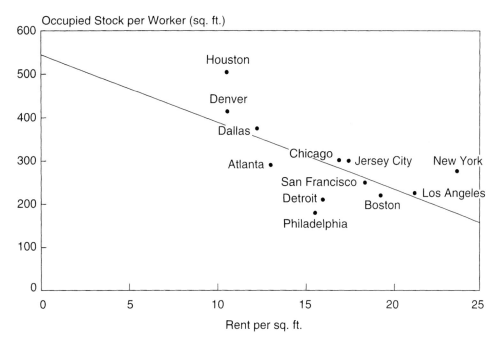

FIGURE 12.2 1990 rent and office space usage in twelve of the largest U.S. cities.

Source: Rent, occupancy and stock, CB Commercial; employment, adjusted U.S. government figures courtesy of Regional Financial Associates, Bala-Cynwyd, PA.

–0.85; rent explains 45 percent of the variation in space use across markets.[3] Anecdotal evidence from leasing agents also suggests that this demand elasticity is observable within markets across time. During periods when office vacancy is high and rents low, firms often increase their space use per worker. Conversely, usage frequently contracts when space is scarce and rents high. Leasing agents also suggest that firms often "bank" space in a growing economy by leasing more than they need initially in anticipation of expanding into the space later. This gives them the option of having contiguous space, rather than later having to lease space elsewhere to accommodate their growing needs.

To model net absorption, or the change in occupied space, let OC^* represent the amount of space that all firms in the market would in principle demand if there were no leases, moving, or adjustment costs to obtaining such space. This represents potential office space demand, or demand *ex ante*. From the discussion above, market demand should be the product of the number of office workers, E_t, multiplied by the amount of

---

[3] The data displayed in Figure 12.2 yields the following regression equation between rent, R, and square feet per worker:

$$\text{square feet per worker} = 545.2 - 15.4\,R \qquad R^2 = .45,\ N = 12$$
$$\qquad\qquad\qquad\quad (7.4)\quad\ (2.8)$$

The rent coefficient of –15.4 yields a rental elasticity of space demand that is around –0.85 when evaluated at the sample average values of $R = \$16.20$ and square feet per worker = 295. The elasticity calculation is $(-15.4 \times 16.2/295)$.

office space per worker that firms would in the long run like to occupy. The desired amount of space per worker should depend on the current rent for space, R_t, and possibly the current or expected growth rate of the firm $[(E_t - E_{t-1})/E_t]$—as in the "space banking" argument described above. In Equation (12.4), the term within brackets represents the office space demanded per worker. The coefficient α_1 determines a baseline amount of square feet per worker, while α_2 and α_3 determine how much this space use increases with greater employment growth and decreases with higher rent.

$$OC_t^* = \alpha_0 + E_t[\alpha_1 + \alpha_2 \frac{(E_t - E_{t-1})}{E_t} - \alpha_3 R_t] \tag{12.4}$$

The actual consumption of space, OC_t, does not equal OC_t^*, because firms cannot immediately adjust their consumption in response to changes in demand (caused either by employment growth or rent movements). Suppose that all firms whose leases are up for renewal in a given time period adjust their actual space consumption to long-run demand, while other firms wait for their leases to expire. Using the identity in Equation (12.3), if some fraction of leased space, τ_1, expires each period, we have adjustment Equation (12.5).

$$OC_t - OC_{t-1} = AB_t = \tau_1[OC_t^* - OC_{t-1}] \tag{12.5}$$

Equation (12.5) says that each period, a portion, τ_1, of office-space occupiers changes the amount of space they occupy, from what prevailed in the market previously, to what is now desired. After some number of periods, then (depending on the speed of adjustment, τ_1), actual occupied space in the market as a whole (OC_t) will equal that which is desired (OC_t^*). Equation (12.4) says that what is now desired depends on current office employment, its growth rate, and market rent levels. Combining the two yields a linear equation in which absorption and the occupied stock gradually adjust to a target defined by office employment and rents.

$$AB_t = \tau_1[\alpha_0 + E_t[\alpha_1 + \alpha_2 \frac{(E_t - E_{t-1})}{E_t} - \alpha_3 R_t]] - \tau_1 OC_{t-1} \tag{12.6}$$

With Equation (12.6), absorption will adjust the amount of occupied space until it eventually reaches a stable value (OC_t^*) that depends on office employment and office rents. If we compare this amount of occupied space with the total space in the market (S_t), the identity in Equation (12.2) yields a vacancy rate. Thus, the level of office rents, by determining the amount of occupied space per worker, eventually leads to a specific vacancy rate. To determine rents as well as vacancy, we need another relationship between these two variables that reflects economic behavior. As tenants and landlords bargain over space, the question is whether the vacancy rate that results from a rent level in the office space demand model, in turn, leads landlords to adjust or change those rents.

Vacancy and the Movement in Office Rents

Vacancy plays the same role in commercial real estate markets that it does in housing markets. Vacancy is a period through which parcels of space within buildings pass either as they wait to be rented for the first time or become available after a tenant moves. Just as households may change their housing choices during their life cycle, firms likewise experience change and periodically seek to relocate. If the average lease length were, say, five years, then 20 percent of all leases would expire each year, creating quite a large pool of tenants who potentially might move. As discussed in Chapter 9, the ratio of the amount of vacant space to the total space needed by the pool of moving tenants represents a measure of the expected time it will take a landlord to rent his space. The inverse of this ratio is the probability that space is rented over an interval of time.

As with housing, the search by tenants for appropriate office space can be an extensive process. Space not only varies by location and building, but parcels of space come in widely different sizes and configurations, especially within existing buildings. When appropriate space has been found by a tenant, the stage is set for a round of bargaining between tenant and landlord over both the rent and the other terms of the lease.

In a rental market, the risk of vacancy lies mainly with the landlord. When a potential tenant arrives, the landlord has to consider the cost of not accepting the tenant's offer—the prospect of the property remaining vacant. A landlord establishes a reservation or minimum rent that would make him indifferent between renting the space or keeping it vacant. The longer the expected lease-up time for vacant space, the lower will be the landlord's reservation rent: a bird in the hand is worth two in the bush. Greater vacancy and fewer relocating tenants raise the expected leasing time, and hence lower the minimum rent that landlords are willing to accept.

On the tenant's side of the negotiation, when there are few other searching tenants and much vacant space, it becomes easier to find appropriate new space. This reduces the cost to the tenant of not closing any particular deal, since the search for some other suitable space will be less difficult. Thus, the maximum rent the tenant is willing to offer will be less when vacant space is plentiful and there are few competing tenants. The eventual contract rent that emerges in the bargaining process must lie between the tenant's maximum offer and the landlord's minimum reservation. Both of these move inversely with vacancy and positively with the number of tenants in the market.

In Chapter 9, the impact of residential vacancy rates on house rents and prices was clearly demonstrated. Many researchers have found that similar relationships exist in commercial markets as well. Figure 12.3 takes the office rent index for San Francisco developed in Chapter 11 and compares its annual change (in real dollars) to the area's office vacancy rate series. Clearly, there appears to be some form of a simple negative relationship between the level of vacancy and the change in rents.[4]

While simple relationships between vacancy and rents are intuitively appealing, if the theory of tenant search and bargaining is correct, the relationship is more complicated. Some measure of tenant mobility or market growth should also influence rental movements. It is the combination of the amount of vacant space and the level of tenant

[4] With the two San Francisco series, the relationship between the change in real rents and vacancy, V_{t-1}, is:

$$R_t - R_{t-1} = 1.36 - 0.14 V_{t-1} \qquad R^2 = .35$$
$$(2.85)\ (-3.68) \qquad N = 27 \text{ (semiannual periods)}$$

In this equation, the *structural vacancy rate* for this market is around 10 percent (the 1.36 coefficient for the constant divided by the 0.14 coefficient for vacancy). At vacancy rates higher than this, real rents fall; below this level, they will rise.

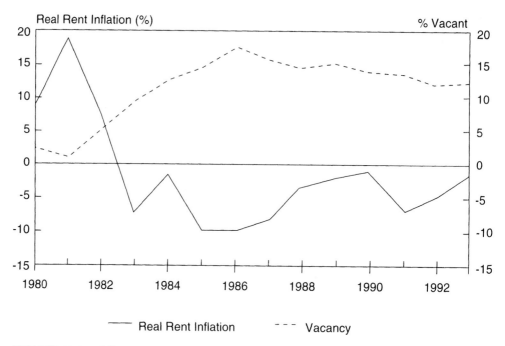

FIGURE 12.3 Office vacancy and rent inflation in San Francisco, 1980–1993.
Source: CB Commercial.

activity that determines the expected leasing time for vacant space. While direct estimates of tenant leasing activity or mobility are largely unknown, net space absorption should serve as a close approximation. Thus, an equation predicting rental inflation might include the recent rate of office space absorption (AB_{t-1}/S_{t-1}) as well as the rate of vacancy, V_{t-1}.

The theory of tenant search and landlord bargaining also suggests that for given levels of vacancy and absorption, there eventually emerges a stable *level* of market rent. Rents do not fall (rise) continuously in response to overly high (low) vacancy. This also is suggested by Figure 12.3. From 1982 through 1988, rental growth was noticeably less than inflation—a reaction to the rise in vacancy in the early 1980s. By 1990, however, this decline in real rents had somewhat stabilized, despite continued high vacancy. The return of negative real rental growth in 1991 was a temporary reaction to the economic recession and sharp slowdown in absorption. A rental adjustment model that incorporates these features is developed in Equation (12.7).

$$R^* = \mu_0 - \mu_1 V_{t-1} + \mu_2 \frac{AB_{t-1}}{S_{t-1}}$$

$$R_t - R_{t-1} = \mu_3 (R^* - R_{t-1}) \qquad (12.7)$$

$$= \mu_3 (\mu_0 - \mu_1 V_{t-1} + \mu_2 \frac{AB_{t-1}}{S_{t-1}}) - \mu_3 R_{t-1}$$

In Equation (12.7) above, R^* represents the equilibrium rent that eventually emerges in the market, determined as a linear function of absorption and vacancy rates. Market rents move toward that rent at a rate of μ_3 per period. When Equation (12.7) is estimated with the San Francisco data, the results are:[5]

$$R_t - R_{t-1} = 0.15 \, (30.2 - 1.187 \, V_{t-1} + 3.42 \, \frac{AB_{t-1}}{S_{t-1}}) - 0.15 \, R_{t-1}$$
$$\phantom{R_t - R_{t-1} = 0.15\,(}(3.8) (-5.16) (3.8) \phantom{\frac{AB_{t-1}}{S_{t-1}}}(-4.24) \quad (12.8)$$

$$R^2 = .73, \quad N = 27 \text{ (semiannual periods)}$$

In Equation (12.8), both vacancy and absorption are measured as a percent of the stock. Remember that the term in brackets represents the equilibrium or target rent, R^*. Using historic average values for San Francisco ($V = 11.8$ percent, $AB = 1.7$ percent), the equation implies that real rents will head toward $22 per square foot in 1993 dollars (30.2 − (1.187 × 11.8) + (3.42 × 1.7) = 22). With vacancy near 17 percent (such as in 1986) and with only 1 percent absorption, rents in constant dollars would move toward a level of only $13 (30.2 − (1.187 × 17) + 3.42 = 13). In each of these examples, the rate (per six-month period) at which rents adjust toward these targets is 15 percent ($\mu_3 = 0.15$). Thus, if current rents were $18 while average vacancy and absorption created a target rent of $22, rents would rise by $0.60 (15 percent of 22 − 18) during the first six months, and progressively less thereafter, until the target level is reached.

The model to this point captures how rents determine absorption, absorption determines vacancy, and then how vacancy determines the changes in rent. Given a fixed stock of space, Equation (12.6) takes current rents and projects future absorption. The identities in Equations (12.1) through (12.3) use absorption to adjust the occupied stock, which then yields a vacancy rate for the next period. Equation (12.7) then takes absorption and vacancy and determines future rent levels. Thus, given a stock of space and level of office employment, these combined equations depict how rents eventually adjust to equate office demand to a given stock of office space. They work as follows:

1. Given a level of office employment and total stock of space, Equations (12.6) and (12.2) eventually yield a stable (zero absorption) occupied stock and hence

---

[5]In order to estimate Equation (12.7), we made the following transformation:

$$R_t - R_{t-1} = \mu_3\mu_0 - \mu_3\mu_1 V_{t-1} + \mu_3\mu_2 \frac{AB_{t-1}}{S_{t-1}} - \mu_3 R_{t-1}$$

Our regression estimate of this equation produced:

$$R_t - R_{t-1} = 4.53 - 0.178 V_{t-1} + 0.513 \frac{AB_{t-1}}{S_{t-1}} - 0.15 R_{t-1}$$
$$\phantom{R_t - R_{t-1} = }(3.78) (-5.16) (3.78) \phantom{\frac{AB_{t-1}}{S_{t-1}}}(-4.24)$$

$$R^2 = .73, \quad N = 27$$

The t-statistics are in parentheses beneath the estimated coefficients. In order to calculate the structural parameters, the μs, in Equation (12.7), we divide each of the estimated coefficients by μ_3, the coefficient on rent (0.15). For example, the structural parameter on lagged vacancy is $\mu_1 = -0.178/0.15 = -1.187$.

vacancy rate. Equation (12.7) takes this vacancy rate and adjusts rents until they are stable. When rents and vacancy rates are the same in Equation (12.7) as they are in Equation (12.6), then the market is at equilibrium. In this equilibrium, rents lead tenants, on average, to demand an amount of space that yields a vacancy rate, which, in turn, leads to the same stable value of rents.

2. If office employment increases, absorption turns positive, and, with the given stock, vacancy falls; see Equations (12.2) and (12.6). The drop in vacancy causes rents to increase (Equation 12.7). As rents rise, the level of absorption is at least partially reduced. Eventually, a new stable equilibrium is reached with a higher level of real rents, zero absorption, and a lower vacancy rate. The amount of occupied space in the market will have increased, but the space per worker will be less.

3. If the stock of space increases, vacancy rises, and this causes rents to fall (in real terms). Falling rents generate positive absorption, which in turn helps to bring down the vacancy rate. Eventually, at the new stable equilibrium, real rents are lower, absorption is zero, and the vacancy rate is at a higher level. The amount of occupied space has increased (from the new supply) and lower rents have led to greater space per worker.

Thus, the system of Equations (12.1) through (12.7) has all of the intuitive properties of a logically consistent market mechanism in which rents adjust to bring demand in balance with supply. Its distinctive (and complicating) feature involves the gradual response of office space demand to rents and employment, the continual presence of vacant space, as well as the gradual response of rents to changes in vacant space. This mirrors the behavior of the market, behavior that comes from the market's use of longer-term leases and the bargaining that occurs over lease terms.

While we have already statistically estimated the rent equation in Equation (12.8), we still need to estimate the equation for space absorption in the San Francisco metropolitan area. Returning to Figure 12.1, we see that net absorption moves closely, but not perfectly, with the growth in office workers. Like office employment, absorption drops during the economic downturns of 1971 and 1982 and reaches peaks just after periods of strong growth, such as 1973, 1980, and 1987. On the other hand, it is hard to explain why absorption during the 1978–81 period was actually less than during 1986–89, even though employment growth was much stronger during the earlier period.

At least a partial answer to the absorption puzzle in San Francisco can be seen by examining the city's vacancy rate and the history of office rents. Figure 12.3 suggests that the high rates of office absorption during the modest economic growth of 1986–89 were likely a response to the decline in rents (in real dollars) that occurred from 1982 through 1988. Conversely, in 1978–82, vacancy was at record lows, while by 1982, real rents were at a record high. Thus, the movements of office space absorption in San Francisco do provide some evidence of a rental elasticity of space demand.

Since rental data is available only from 1980, it is difficult to statistically estimate the equation for absorption (12.6), unless the sample is trimmed to only 13 years. This is a very short period to capture the long-run movements of office space demand. An alternative approach is to use lagged values of office vacancy as an approximation for current levels of office rent. The rent-vacancy relationship in Equation (12.7) suggests that current vacancy influences the movement in rents, so current rent levels are largely the product of past vacancy rates. Since the coefficient on rent is negative in the absorption equation, a lagged vacancy variable would be expected to have a positive impact on current absorption. When estimated for the period 1968–93, the absorption equation (12.6) estimated for San Francisco is:[6]

$$AB_t = 0.20\,[-530 + E_{t-2}\,[218.5 + 110.5\,\frac{(E_t - E_{t-2})}{E_{t-2}} + 1.77V_{t-8}]] - 0.20OC_{t-2} \quad (12.9)$$
$$(-0.3)\phantom{+ E_{t-2}\,[}(6.9)(2.2)\phantom{\frac{(E_t - E_{t-2})}{E_{t-2}}}(5.7)\phantom{V_{t-8}]]}(-7.3)$$

$R^2 = .64, \quad N = 43$ (semiannual periods)

In Equation (12.9), the parameters tell a plausible and interesting story. The amount of office space demanded per office worker is the term within the inner brackets that is multiplied by E_{t-2}. At a market average vacancy rate of 10 percent and no employment growth, the amount of space demanded per worker is 236.2 square feet (218.5 + 1.77 × 10). If the vacancy rate six periods previous was zero (and the market quite tight), this would drop to 218.5 square feet, whereas in a typically soft market with 18 percent vacancy, lower rents would raise space demand to 250 square feet per worker (218.5 + 1.77 × 18). During periods of rapid employment growth (e.g., 4 percent annually), space demand would increase by another 4.4 square feet per worker (110.5 × 0.04). The coefficient on the occupied stock, OC, is the rate at which the occupied stock adjusts to changes in the demand for space. Given the target square footage of space demanded by the market, OC^*, the occupied stock will adjust 20 percent in each (six-month) period from its current level to that target.

Now that we are using lagged vacancy in place of office rents, the reader may question how our overall model will operate. In Equation (12.9), lagged vacancy will determine current absorption, which, together with the identity in Equation (12.2), will determine an occupied stock and hence current vacancy. Given a fixed stock of space and stable office employment, lagged and current vacancy eventually converge to the same value. Turning to the supply side, we will also use vacancy as a proxy for rents, and ask what levels of construction and the stock will emerge from a given vacancy rate. With both supply and demand adjusting to vacancy (instead of rents) we have a consistent market model.

---

[6]As with Equation (12.7), the actual equation that is statistically estimated in order to obtain Equation (12.9) is a transformation of Equation (12.6):

$$AB_t = \tau_1\alpha_0 + \tau_1\alpha_1 E_{t-2} + \tau_1\alpha_2(E_t - E_{t-2}) + \tau_1\alpha_3 E_{t-2}V_{t-8} - \tau_1 OC_{t-2}$$

Remember that we are substituting lagged vacancy as an approximation of rent. The coefficients actually estimated are the product of τ_1 and the structural parameters, the α values. As a result, the parameters presented in Equation (12.9) are the statistical coefficients divided by τ_1. We use a two-period, rather than one-period, lag on E and OC because the data series are semi-annual, while absorption is annual. An eight-period lag on vacancy produces the best statistical results.

Forecasting Office-Space Supply

Figure 12.4 tracks the completions of space in the San Francisco market since 1967. It clearly shows that the building boom of the 1980s was noticeably greater than the earlier boom in the 1970s, at least when measured in square feet of completions. If completions are taken as a percentage of the stock, the level of building activity during 1972–76 averaged about as high as that during 1982–89.

In the example of speculative development presented in Chapter 11, we saw that the eventual asset price of the building and the developer's rate of return depend crucially on estimates of future market conditions, which must be formed years prior to the completion of the development. As discussed in Chapter 10, the expectations by market participants about the future can be characterized in three general ways: exogenous, myopic, or rational. The history of systematic movements in vacancy and rent suggests that market participants would indeed be foolish to operate with exogenous expectations.

Myopic expectations, which developers have when they expect current conditions to prevail in the future, can lead to severe and repeated market oscillations. On the other hand, even rational expectations will generate a single market cycle in the presence of long construction lags. If there is a sudden change in office demand (e.g., increase in employment), rationally based construction eventually will build just the right amount of additional

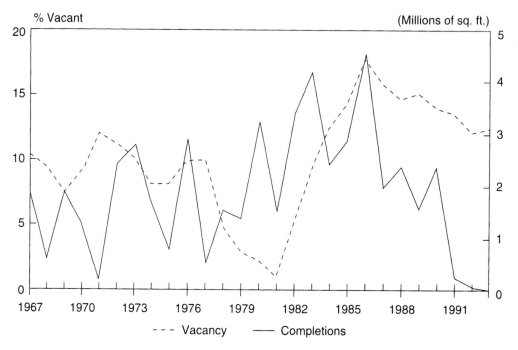

FIGURE 12.4 Office vacancy and completions in San Francisco, 1967–1993.
Source: CB Commercial.

space. Even though fully anticipated, the lagged timing of this new supply cannot be avoided. It is this lag that leads to a rise and then fall of rents (fall and then rise in vacancy).

Given that office rents, absorption, and vacancy all adjust slowly, even rational, forward-looking suppliers who use all available information must consider the current values of these market conditions as part of their decision making.[7] This link can be clearly seen by returning to Figure 12.4, in which completions of new office space in San Francisco are compared to the current vacancy rate. The construction boom of 1972–74 seems to be a response to lower vacancy during 1968–69, just as the boom during 1980-86 seems a reaction to low vacancy in 1978–81. Lagged space absorption (see Figure 12.1) may also play a role, because it also helps determine the future movement of rents. Strong absorption during 1978–81 helps to explain the large size of the 1980–86 boom, whereas weak absorption during 1969–71 explains the more modest size of the 1972–74 boom.

A simple equation for predicting new completions can be developed along the lines of that used for absorption. It seems reasonable to suppose that the desired *rate* of new completions (as a percent of stock) that developers would like to bring to the market depends on their estimate of the level of rents at the time of delivery. Thus, the absolute level of new completions (in square feet) will depend on the estimated future level of rents together with the current stock of space. The stock must be incorporated, since a given rent level in a market with 40 million square feet leads to very different building activity than when that same market has 100 million square feet. From Equation (12.7), it is clear that future rents will depend on the rate of rental growth, which, in turn, depends on lagged absorption and vacancy rates. When the rate of absorption and vacancy is multiplied by the stock, we have desired construction as a function of the stock of space, vacant space, and absorption in square feet.[8]

We define C_t^* as the level of desired completions and assume that it is a linear function of these variables, appropriately lagged. For purposes of illustration, this lag is assumed to be four years (eight six-month periods). To account for a gradual response by construction, actual completions at t are assumed to move proportionally (at the rate τ_2) to the difference between desired completions and those just undertaken.

$$C_t^* = \beta_0 + \beta_1 S_{t-8} + \beta_2 S_{t-8} V_{t-8} + \beta_3 AB_{t-8}$$
$$C_t - C_{t-1} = \tau_2(C_t^* - C_{t-1}) \qquad (12.10)$$
$$C_t = \tau_2(\beta_0 + \beta_1 S_{t-8} + \beta_2 S_{t-8} V_{t-8} + \beta_3 AB_{t-8}) + (1-\tau_2)C_{t-1}$$

---

[7]The slow adjustment of rents in Equation (12.7) and occupied space in Equation (12.5) means that any forecast made at time t about future rents and vacancy must include the level of rent and vacancy at time t as variables used to make the forecast.

[8]If the desired construction *rate* at time t depends on estimates (made last period) about rents at time t, then the *level* of construction depends on those estimated rents together with the stock of space:

$$\frac{C_t}{S_{t-1}} = \beta_1 + \beta_2 R_t, \text{ implies } C_t = \beta_1 S_{t-1} + \beta_2 R_t S_{t-1}$$

If the estimate of R_t depends linearly on past vacancy and absorption rates, V_{t-1}, AB_{t-1}/S_{t-1}, then substituting yields: $C = \beta_1 S_{t-1} + \beta_2 (V_{t-1} S_{t-1} + AB_{t-1})$.

When the parameters of Equation (12.10) are estimated with the San Francisco data, the results are:[9]

$$C_t = 0.51 \ [196 + 0.035 S_{t-8} - 0.27(V_{t-8} S_{t-8}) + 0.62 AB_{t-5}] + 0.49 C_{t-1}$$
$$(0.5) \quad (2.12) \qquad (-3.4) \qquad\quad (2.4) \qquad\quad (4.4) \tag{12.11}$$

$R^2 = .61$, $N = 51$ (semiannual periods)

The implications of this model are reasonable and easy to interpret. There is a fairly rapid adjustment of construction to changes in market conditions: the adjustment rate parameter τ_2 is estimated to be 0.51. This indicates that more than half of the difference between desired and actual construction will be made up in only six months. In contrast, there is a long four-year (eight six-month periods) lag between the completion of space and the market conditions that influenced the construction decision. The lag is slightly less on absorption, but the reported difficulty in acquiring building permits in the Bay Area is clearly reflected in these results.

Let's consider some other implications of the model presented in Equation (12.11). If the market is depressed with no growth, how much excess inventory (vacancy) would have to develop to bring long-term desired completions, C^*, to zero? Remember that C^* is the term in brackets in Equation (12.11). With zero absorption and the stock at the average historic value ($S_t = 57,000$), a vacancy rate of 14 percent would bring C^* to zero.[10] In contrast, a strong market with vacancy and absorption rates both at 5 percent would drive long-term desired completions, C^*, to 3.2 million square feet.[11] This completion level represents 5.6 percent of the average level of the stock. Finally, in the long run, if demand is growing smoothly with absorption at 1.7 percent of the stock (the historic average), this model will supply space exactly equal to absorption when the vacancy rate

---

[9]The parameters reported in Equation (12.11) are the structural parameters described in Equation (12.10). The statistical coefficients that are actually estimated are the product of τ_2 and the β parameters. The parameter τ_2 is equal to 1 minus the coefficient on lagged completions (0.49).

As was the case in Equations (12.8) and (12.9), the four-year (eight-period) lag on vacancy and the 2.5-year (five-period) lag on absorption were chosen as those that yield the highest R^2 with coefficients of the appropriate sign.

[10]Assuming absorption is 0,

$$C^* = 196 + 0.035 S_{t-8} - 0.27(V_{t-8} S_{t-8})$$

Setting C^* equal to zero, substituting in the average value of the stock (57,000 in thousands of square feet), and solving for V_{t-8} yields

$$V_{t-8} = \frac{196 + 1,995}{15390} = 0.14$$

[11]An absorption rate of 5 percent and a mean value of stock of 57,000, means the amount of space being absorbed is 2,850 (2.85 million square feet). At these values and a vacancy rate of 5 percent, we have:

$$C^* = 196 + 0.035 S_{t-8} - 0.27(V_{t-8} S_{t-8}) + 0.62 AB_{t-5}$$
$$= 196 + (0.035 \times 57000) - (0.27 \times .05 \times 57000) + (0.62 \times 2850)$$
$$= 3189$$

Chapter 12 Econometric Analysis

is at 11.8 percent.[12] The market cycle is caused by the fact that the growth in demand (absorption) is never smooth and by the fact that it takes four years for supply to respond to changes in demand.

Contingent Forecasts of the San Francisco Office Market

When the econometric equations predicting absorption, Equation (12.9), and new space completions, Equation (12.11), are combined with the identities in Equations (12.1) through (12.3), a complete forecasting model is obtained. Given a prediction about future office employment, the equations will forecast future space absorption, completions, vacancy, and the stock of space. Figure 12.5 takes the history of office employment in San Francisco and examines two alternative outlooks for the future. The relatively optimistic outlook projects job growth to average 3 percent per year throughout the next decade, whereas the relatively pessimistic view projects employment growth to average only 1.4 percent per year.[13] Also included in Figure 12.5 are the corresponding forecasts of net office space absorption.

Figure 12.6 portrays the history of space completions and vacancy in San Francisco, again with two alternative forecasts. In the optimistic forecast, stronger job growth generates absorption rates equal to those in the mid-1980s. This economic scenario causes vacancy to drop relatively rapidly, reaching around 3 percent by 1999. This recovery begins to set the stage for a new construction boom, but the traditionally long lags in the San Francisco area mean that this surge in new construction will not occur until after the year 1999.

In the pessimistic forecast (low employment growth), the recovery in office vacancy (from its 18 percent peak in 1986) occurs only moderately, eventually reaching 9 percent by the end of the 1990s. The low levels of completions in 1992, 1993, and 1994 are a reaction to the combination of high vacancy rates and slowing absorption that began four years earlier. Given the long lags in the San Francisco market, the slow recovery of office vacancy means that little or no construction will occur over the forecast horizon.

In the San Francisco office market, the source of the market's cyclical behavior is the combination of very long lags in the delivery of new buildings, together with systematic fluctuations in economic growth and the demand for office space. With the optimistic forecast, the stronger growth in the 1990s, after the economic downturn of 1988–92, eventually drives vacancy below the equilibrium level, implying rising rents and a new round of construction after the year 2000. Because of the long delay, this new development will likely overshoot demand, leading to another overbuilt market. Ironically, it is in

---

[12]When the absorption rate is 1.7 percent, the amount of space absorbed is $.017 \times 57,000 = 969$ thousand square feet (at the average stock level). Setting $C^* = 969$ and solving for vacancy yields:

$$V_{t-8} = \frac{196 + 1,995 + 600}{15390} = .118$$

[13]The employment forecasts include a small cyclic component to reflect the effects of the 1992 recession and subsequent recovery. These employment forecasts are based on forecasts by Regional Financial Associates, Inc.

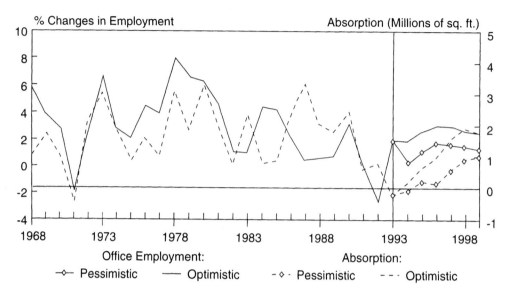

FIGURE 12.5 Office employment and absorption projections for San Francisco, 1968–1999.

Source: Employment, adjusted U.S. government figures courtesy of Regional Financial Associates, Bala-Cynwyd, PA; absorption, CB Commercial.

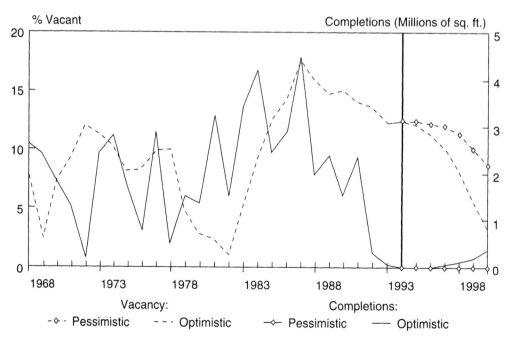

FIGURE 12.6 Office vacancy and completion projections for San Francisco, 1967–1999.

Source: CB Commercial.

the pessimistic forecast, with slow but steady economic growth, where the market eventually stabilizes at a vacancy rate of around 8 percent. Without the fluctuation in demand, just enough construction occurs (after the year 2000) to balance the slower growth in jobs. Without economic shocks, the model is dynamically stable.

THE MARKET FOR INDUSTRIAL SPACE IN PHILADELPHIA

The discussion in Chapter 11 raised a number of important differences between the office space market and that for industrial property. First, the occupants of industrial buildings use that space for very different activities, from large volume storage, to laboratory research, to high technology manufacturing. Thus, we should expect very different space usage levels (per worker) depending on the SIC of the occupant. At a minimum, we should at least distinguish between demand that originates in the distribution as opposed to manufacturing sectors. Second, we questioned whether industrial property demand is determined by employment, output, or inventories. As a practical matter, at the metropolitan level, employment data are much more readily available than series on output or inventories. Finally, a large portion of the industrial market is owner-occupied, and separate time series data by tenure are not available. Thus, it is not clear whether the models developed for the office market will work as well in the case of industrial space. For example, should vacancy or rents be included in the absorption equation, or even in the completions equation, if much space is directly built for the occupant?

Our approach will be to adapt the same models developed for office space to the industrial market, using, of course, different variables and data series. We will see that with some minor changes, this approach seems to work. What this suggests is that there is less of a distinction between owner and rental industrial space than might have been expected. If excess space is developed for the rental portion of the market, falling rents will not only curtail speculative construction but also attract potential owners into renting space. This, in turn, reduces the construction of owner-occupied space. If the mode of tenure is highly discretionary, then conditions in one sector of the market will influence the other.

Modeling Industrial Space Demand

In the industrial property market, the demand for distribution space is directly derived from the level of inventories that manufacturers in the area decide to hold. In addition to inventories held by manufacturers, certain areas also can act as broader distribution "hubs" within the nation's transportation system. Firms that are in the wholesaling SIC category thus provide another important source of demand for warehouses. While data on employment in manufacturing and wholesale SICs are widely available, information on inventories is gathered by the federal government only at the national level. Employment is simply the only available series that can be used to estimate the demand for warehouse space.

In a similar manner, the demand for manufacturing space depends on the production of goods within a metropolitan area. Here again, there is no direct data on industrial production at the metropolitan area. The federal government does *estimate* industrial production at the state level. It does this by taking national output per worker at the detailed four-digit SIC level and then weighting this by each state's distribution of workers (at the four-digit level). These estimates effectively assume that, at a four-digit level of detail, there is little difference between regions in the productivity of similar industries. This procedure also has been adapted by several regional forecasting firms to estimate industrial production at the metropolitan level.[14]

In Figure 12.7, we trace manufacturing employment, wholesale employment, and industrial output per worker in the Philadelphia metropolitan area from 1978 through 1993. These series are quite typical of many older metropolitan areas. Manufacturing employment during this period severely declined (decreased 30 percent). During this time, wholesale employment grew by 12 percent, while the estimated industrial output per worker grew by 93 percent. Thus, estimated total industrial production would have grown by 63 percent at the same time that industrial employment sharply declined. The stock of occupied industrial space increased by 14 percent in the Philadelphia market over this time, while production was growing rapidly and employment was declining sharply.

With the three data series, we can develop a model just like that for the office market. The net absorption of space, AB_t, will be an adjustment between the desired amount of occupied space, OC_t^*, and that used last period, OC_{t-1}. The desired amount of space will be a linear function of current or lagged employment in the wholesale and manufacturing sectors (EW_t, EM_t), together with the level of industrial output per worker (Q_t). We use manufacturing employment and output per worker as separate variables (instead of using total industrial production), recognizing that the space demand which originates from more workers can be quite different from that arising when firms use more capital and knowledge to generate additional output.

Our time series on vacancy rates for industrial property is also noticeably shorter than that for office space. Prior to the early 1980s, there were no systematic surveys of industrial vacancy rates; as a result, we have only a decade or more of such data from CB Commercial. This means that the calculation of absorption (and the occupied stock of industrial space) can be done only over a short period of time, and this limits the sample of observations we can use.

Information on industrial rental rates is available for at least as long as the data series on vacancy. Using a sample of 507 leases signed in the Philadelphia market between 1981 and 1993, we adopt a similar approach to that used for the office market (Chapter 11) and construct an index of industrial rents.[15] Since this index is available for the same limited time period as the vacancy data, there is no advantage to using lagged vacancy as an approximation for industrial rents. Hence, to estimate an industrial rental elasticity of space demand, the rental rate for industrial space (R_t) is entered directly into the equation for the desired stock of space.

---

[14]Regional Forecasting Associates, Inc., and Regional Econometric Modeling, Incorporated, are two sources of such estimated production data.

[15]For a description of the CB Commercial rental index for San Francisco, see footnote 6 in Chapter 11.

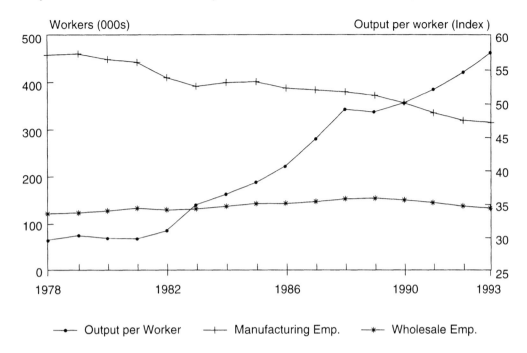

FIGURE 12.7 Industrial growth in Philadelphia, 1978–1993.
Source: Adjusted U.S. government figures courtesy of Regional Financial Associates, Bala-Cynwyd, PA.

Following Equations (12.5) and (12.6), our model of industrial space absorption is:

$$AB_t = \tau_1(OC_t^* - OC_{t-1})$$
$$= \tau_1(\alpha_0 + \alpha_1 EM_t + \alpha_2 EW_t + \alpha_3 Q_t - \alpha_4 R_{t-2}) - \tau_1 OC_{t-2} \quad (12.12)$$

When estimated with 24 (semiannual) observations for the period 1981–93, we obtain the following parameter values:

$$AB_t = 0.37\ (28303 + 383 EM_t + 846 EW_t + 1600 Q_t - 5854 R_{t-2}) - 0.37 OC_{t-2}$$
$$\quad\quad (0.38)\quad (3.05)\quad (1.9)\quad\ (3.6)\quad\ (-2.2)\quad\ (-3.4) \quad (12.13)$$

$R^2 = .87$, $N = 24$ (semiannual periods)

Although estimated over a shorter time interval than the office space absorption model, the statistical results of this equation are quite plausible. The term within brackets equals the long-run desired amount of occupied industrial space (OC_t^*). This amount of space will increase with manufacturing and wholesale workers at rates estimated to be 383 and 846 square feet per worker, respectively.[16] The absence of lags on the

---

[16] The long-term square feet demanded per manufacturing and wholesale workers are the parameters α_1, α_2 in Equation (12.12). The actual estimated statistical coefficients on manufacturing and wholesale employment are these parameters multiplied by the estimated parameter on the lagged occupied stock ($\tau_1 = 0.37$).

employment variables imply that both types of firms expand their space at the same time they hire new workers. The coefficient on manufacturing output per worker, Q_t, implies that a 4 percent increase in productivity (roughly the annual growth over this period) will generate demand for 2.86 million more square feet of industrial space when evaluated at the sample mean output per worker of 44.7 (1600 × 0.04 × 44.7 = 2860). This increased demand represents only 0.8 percent of the average occupied space over the period (337 million). Thus, space demand seems to increase much less than proportionately with output per worker—at least when employment remains fixed.

The coefficient on rent implies that a 20 percent increase in rent (over the mean rent of $4.60 per square foot) would decrease space demand by 5.39 million square feet (−5854 × 0.2 × 4.60 = −5386). This reduction represents a 1.6 percent decline in the average amount of occupied space (337 million square feet). This yields a relatively low rental elasticity of space demand, in the range of −0.08 (−5854 × 4.6/337,000). Finally, the large value for the adjustment parameter, τ_1, (0.37) suggests that more than one-third of the adjustment in demand to employment or output growth occurs in the first (six-month) period following the increase in economic activity. Figure 12.8 shows that the absorption of industrial space in Philadelphia is indeed closely related to both the growth in wholesale employment and to annual increases in overall industrial production.

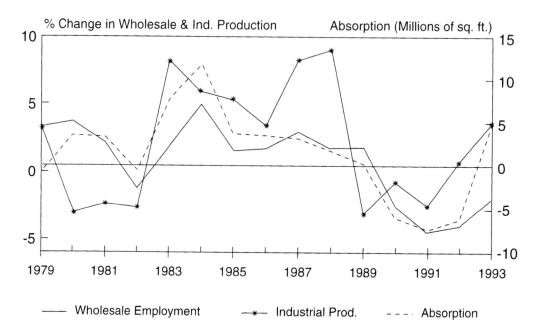

FIGURE 12.8 Growth in industrial production, wholesale employment, and absorption in Philadelphia, 1979–1993.

Source: Employment and production, adjusted U.S. government figures courtesy of Regional Financial Associates, Bala-Cynwyd, PA.

Industrial Rents and Vacancy

Using the industrial rental index, available from 1981 onward, we can estimate a rental adjustment equation, similar to that used for office space in Equation (12.8). Our results for the Philadelphia market are:

$$R_t - R_{t-1} = 0.69 \ (5.9 - 0.162 V_{t-4} + 27.6 \ \frac{AB_t}{S_t}) - 0.69 R_{t-1}$$
$$(6.3) \ (-5.2) \quad\quad (5.3) \quad\quad (-6.3)$$

$$R^2 = .70, \quad N = 25 \text{ (semiannual periods)} \tag{12.14}$$

In the equation above, industrial rents in Philadelphia will converge toward $5.70 a square foot (in constant dollars) if the market is tight, with vacancy at 5 percent and historically strong absorption of 1.7 percent ($R^* = 5.9 - (0.16 \times 5) + (39.6 \times 0.015) = 5.70$). Alternatively, if the market is weak with 12 percent vacancy and zero absorption, rents will converge toward $4.00 ($R^* = 5.9 - (0.16 \times 12) = \$3.98$). The rate of convergence or adjustment for rents in this model is considerably faster than for the office market in Equation (12.8). Each six month period, rents move 69 percent toward their target level.

Construction and Investment in Industrial Space

Having estimated absorption and rental adjustment equation, we can also develop a construction or new supply equation with the same type of model used to predict office space completions. Of course, this assumes that the economic forces driving the construction of owner-occupied space are the same as those influencing rental space construction. In Equation (12.10), office completions depended on vacancy rates, the stock of space, and recent absorption. It was argued that these three variables together can be used to make forecasts of future rental levels, which, with a construction lag, should be what determines new building activity. Using the shorter time series on Philadelphia's industrial market, the equivalent equation to Equation (12.11) is:[17]

$$C_t = 0.27 \ (-369 + 0.012 S_{t-2} - 0.096 S_{t-2} V_{t-2} + 0.31 AB_t) + 0.73 C_{t-1}$$
$$(-0.027) \ (0.31) \quad (-2.0) \quad\quad (1.8) \quad\quad (5.9) \tag{12.15}$$

$$R^2 = .83, \quad N = 27 \text{ (semiannual periods)}$$

---

[17]Since a series on industrial rents is available for a period as long as vacancy rates, we might also try using recent rents instead of vacancy as a determinant of new industrial space construction. The results, in the equation below, are roughly equivalent to those with the vacancy data in Equation (12.15).

$$C_t = 0.22 \ (-13271 + 2909 R_{t-3} + 0.64 AB_t) + 0.78 C_{t-1}$$
$$(-1.7) \quad (1.7) \quad\quad (2.8) \quad\quad (7.3)$$

$$R^2 = .82, \quad N = 25 \text{ (semiannual periods)}$$

In this equation, with no absorption, long-run equilibrium construction, C^*, falls to zero when real rents fall below $4.56 ($C^* = 0 = -13271 + 2909 R_{t-3}$; $R_{t-3} = \$4.56$).

Equation (12.15) implies that at about 11.5 percent vacancy, and with no market absorption, industrial construction will cease. At zero vacancy and with 2 percent absorption, long-run construction will reach about 1.7 percent of the stock.[18]

Unlike the office market in San Francisco, new industrial space is supplied rather quickly in response to market changes in Philadelphia. There is no lag on absorption, and the lags on vacancy or rent are only two periods (12 months). This is consistent with the shorter construction time for industrial space and the observation that much of this space tends to be constructed directly for the occupant (Chapter 11).

Contingent Forecasts of the Philadelphia Industrial Market

The statistical equations predicting absorption, rents, and new space completions—Equations (12.13), (12.14), and (12.15), respectively—can be combined with the identities in Equations (12.1) through (12.3) into a complete forecasting model. The exogenous (forecasted) variables necessary for the model are estimates of future employment in the manufacturing and wholesaling sectors, together with estimates of industrial output per worker. The econometric estimates of absorption in a future period are based on these exogenous variables, together with current rents and the previous period's occupied stock. Completions in a future period use the absorption forecast plus data on past vacancy or rents. Using the identities, the stock of space, total occupied space, and the vacancy rate can be calculated. The vacancy rate and level of absorption also determine the movement in rents. The new values for rents, vacancy, and occupied stock then go back into the equations for predicting absorption and completions in later periods.

Figure 12.9 takes the history of wholesale employment and overall industrial production (output per worker times manufacturing workers) in Philadelphia and examines two different outlooks for the future. The first is an optimistic view which has wholesale employment growth recovering strongly from the economic recession of 1991 and growing at an average rate of 2.2 percent per year; industrial production is assumed to grow at an annual average rate of 5 percent. With a forecast of a 0.2 percent decrease in manufacturing employment per year, the increase in industrial production comes exclusively from increased output per worker. The second outlook is more pessimistic. Wholesale employment is projected to increase by an average of only 0.2 percent per year during the decade, and industrial production increases average only 3 percent per year; manufacturing employment declines by 0.6 percent per year.[19]

Figure 12.10 combines the history of industrial space completions and absorption in Philadelphia and gives the forecast of each based on the two economic outlooks from

---

[18]With no absorption, $C^* = -369 + 0.012 S_{t-2} - 0.096 S_{t-2} V_{t-2}$; at the mean value of stock (369,300), solving for $C^* = 0$ yields $V_{t-2} = 0.115$. Absorption at a rate of 2 percent implies demand of 7.386 million additional square feet. In a market with no vacancy, $C^* = -369 + (369,300 \times 0.012) + (0.31 \times 7386) = 6352$. This level of C^* represents 1.7 percent of the mean value of the stock.

[19]The employment and output forecasts include a cyclic component to reflect the strong impact of the 1992 recession and subsequent recovery. The reported growth rates are averaged over this cyclic component. These forecasts are based on forecasts by Regional Financial Associates, Inc.

Chapter 12 Econometric Analysis 315

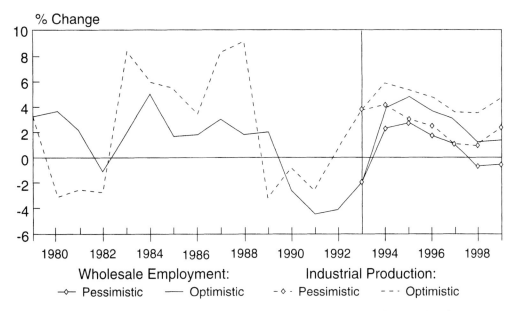

FIGURE 12.9 Forecasts of wholesale employment and industrial production growth for Philadelphia, 1979–1999.

Source: Adjusted U.S. government figures courtesy of Regional Financial Associates, Bala-Cynwyd, PA; forecasts, authors' calculations.

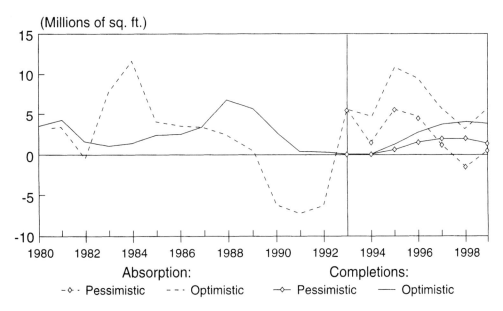

FIGURE 12.10 Forecasts of industrial absorption and completions for Philadelphia, 1980–1999.

Source: Adjusted U.S. government figures courtesy of Regional Financial Associates, Bala-Cynwyd, PA; forecasts, authors' calculations.

Figure 12.9. In the optimistic forecast, which assumed strong growth in employment and production, absorption recovers quickly from the recession of 1991 and then fluctuates at levels characteristic of the mid-1980s. After just a short lag of a year or two, the completions of new industrial space do likewise and both seem in close balance from 1996 to 1999. In the pessimistic outlook, with much slower growth in employment and industrial output, the recovery in absorption is much less and is short-lived. By 1996, construction has caught up to absorption and begins to exceed it slightly from 1996 to 1999.

Finally, Figure 12.11 shows the impact that these two scenarios have on vacancy and rents. In the optimistic forecast, vacancy drops from its 1992 peak of 13.6 percent to 6 percent in 1996 and then stabilizes thereafter. At this lower vacancy rate, industrial rents begin to grow in real terms again, at about 3 percent annually. These conditions are sufficient to generate new completions, which, in Figure 12.10, are seen to match the growth in industrial demand. In the pessimistic forecast, vacancy recovers to only 10 percent by 1996 and then also stabilizes. At this higher vacancy rate, rents still increase just slightly in real terms, which accounts for the market's willingness to undertake a lower but still positive level of industrial completions, roughly matching the much lower growth in demand.

This behavior of the Philadelphia industrial market is quite different from that of the San Francisco office market. With short building lags and much industrial space constructed for its occupant, the market appears to be not as volatile. Fluctuations in economic activity do generate some swings in industrial market demand, but the response of supply is more immediate and balanced than was the case with San Francisco office

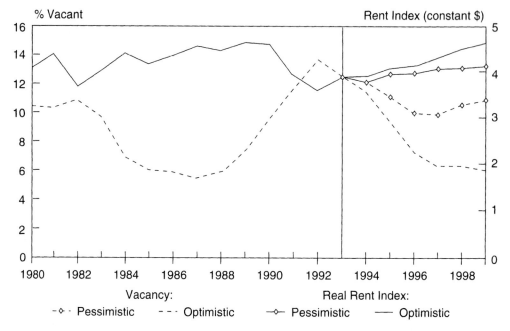

FIGURE 12.11 Forecasts of industrial vacancy and rents in Philadelphia, 1980–1999.
Source: CB Commercial.

space. This prevents Philadelphia's industrial market from becoming seriously overbuilt or undersupplied for extensive periods of time.

This chapter has demonstrated that, with careful econometric analysis, the response patterns of an area's real estate market can be forecast with some degree of confidence, conditional on having a forecast of economic growth. As for predictions about economic growth in different areas of the country, econometric analysis can also be useful, as discussed in Chapter 7. Forecasting the economy of a metropolitan area involves a more complicated analysis than that undertaken here, because the economic outlook for one area is crucially linked to the nation's overall macroeconomic outlook, as well as to forecasts of economic activity in all other metropolitan areas. Thus, while real estate markets in different areas are not directly linked and can be forecast independently, given an economic outlook, they are indirectly linked through regional economic competition.

SUMMARY

In this chapter we demonstrate that by combining information on an area's economy with real estate data on vacancy, rents, and construction, it is possible to develop econometric models of a local commercial property market. This kind of analysis yields useful insights into the operation of such markets, as well as provides a tool for making market forecasts.

- In the market for office space, the use of long-term leases leads the market to react gradually to economic changes. The consumption of office space responds gradually to changes in office employment; rental rates adjust slowly to changes in vacancy. And, with longer construction lags, deliveries of new space react slowly to changes in vacancy and rents.

- Using data for the San Francisco office market, we find that these long lags and slow rates of adjustment have helped generate a noticeable long-term cycle in the market over the last 25 years.

- With a predominance of single-tenant and owner-occupied space, the industrial market exhibits a number of different properties. Construction lags are shorter, and so new space responds more immediately to market rents. Rents, in turn, move more quickly in reaction to industrial vacancy.

- Data on the industrial space market in Philadelphia illustrate that with shorter lags and more rapid response, the market cycle appears to be less volatile. In the Philadelphia data, the demand for industrial space is inelastic with respect to rental rates.

REFERENCES AND ADDITIONAL READINGS

The Market for Office Space in San Francisco

HEKMAN, JOHN S. "Rental Price Adjustment and Investment in the Office Market." *AREUEA Journal* 13, 1 (1985): 32–47.

KING, JOHN L., AND THOMAS E. MCCUE. "Office Building Investment and the Macroeconomy: Empirical Evidence 1973–85." *AREUEA Journal* 15, 3 (1987): 234–255.

ROSEN, KENNETH T. "Toward a Model of the Office Building Sector." *AREUEA Journal* 12, 3 (1984): 261–269.

SHILLING, JAMES D., C. F. SIRMANS, AND JOHN B. CORGEL. "Price Adjustment Process for Rental Office Space." *Journal of Urban Economics* 22, 1 (1987): 90–100.

VOITH, RICHARD, AND THEODORE CRONE. "National Vacancy Rates and the Persistence of Shocks in U.S. Office Markets." *AREUEA Journal* 16, 4 (1988): 437–458.

WHEATON, WILLIAM C. "The Cyclic Behavior of the National Office Market." *AREUEA Journal* 15, 4 (1987): 281–299.

WHEATON, WILLIAM C., AND RAYMOND G. TORTO. "Office Rent Indices and Their Behavior Over Time." *Journal of Urban Economics* 35 (1994): 112–139.

The Market for Industrial Space in Philadelphia

ABEL, ANDREW B., AND OLIVIER J. BLANCHARD. "The Present Value of Profits and Cyclic Movements in Investment." *Econometrica*, 54, 2 (1986): 249–273.

FELDSTEIN, MARTIN, ed. *The Effects of Taxation on Capital Accumulation*. Chicago: University of Chicago Press, 1987.

KING, JOHN L., AND THOMAS MCCUE. "Stylized Facts about Industrial Property Construction." *Journal of Real Estate Research* 6, 3 (1991): 293–304.

WHEATON, WILLIAM C., AND RAYMOND G. TORTO. "An Investment Model of the Demand and Supply for Industrial Real Estate." *AREUEA Journal* 18, 4 (1990): 530–547.

Section 4 The Impact of Local Governments on Real Estate Markets

CHAPTER 13

LOCAL GOVERNMENTS, PROPERTY TAXES, AND REAL ESTATE MARKETS

In most countries, local governments are the primary authorities that directly regulate how land is developed. Local governments control the pattern of development through type-of-use zoning, the character of buildings through subdivision regulations, and the location of development through the provision of infrastructure, roads, and utilities. Local governments are also the major providers of public services to residents and local government taxation of real estate assets is the dominant source of revenue for funding these services. In this chapter, we examine the provision of and payment for local public goods and services. In Chapter 14, we analyze the impact of local land use regulations on the pattern of development and the market for land.

In the United States in particular, a wide range of local jurisdictions holds the legal power to tax (mostly real estate) and the responsibility to provide certain public services. Municipalities or towns, counties, and school and special districts all operate with property taxes as their major source of tax revenue. In turn, these governments provide a range of public services that includes education, police and fire protection, water, sewage, and other infrastructure. In many instances, federal and state governments will financially assist local governments with funding for these services. While many government services, such as highway construction and welfare, are administered by state and local governments, often the federal government transfers money for these services and sometimes regulates their administration. In the U.S., federal and state governments are the direct providers of only a small number of services, most notably defense, national infrastructure, and social insurance programs such as social security.

The relationship between local governments and real estate markets is one of mutual interdependence. Since each local government may provide a very different package of services and taxes, household and firm location decisions are strongly influenced by local government behavior and the spatial distribution of local jurisdictions within a metropolitan area. Households, for example, will often commute extraordinary distances to live in a community with an acclaimed school system. Likewise, real estate values can be profoundly affected by a neighborhood's level of crime or its tax rate. In short, the system of local governments that exists within a metropolitan area exerts a major impact on the location of firms and households as well as the resulting pattern of prices for real estate assets.

The impact of local governments on property rents or real estate prices can be so strong that it dominates many other factors. Consider, for example, the simple land-price gradient in Chapter 3 that emerged as a result of commuting. This is shown as the dashed line in Figure 13.1. In many metropolitan areas, however, the actual pattern of land prices may resemble that of the solid line. As a result of deteriorating services, crime, and high taxes, many inner cities have depressed land prices. Frequently, there are established affluent communities adjacent to central cities, incorporated many years ago to provide their own services and escape the financial burdens of the city. Within literally a few blocks, land prices can change dramatically. Moving further out, there are numerous other suburbs for which land prices also vary in response to zoning regulations, taxes, and the quality of services. The net result is that better services are frequently found in communities located at greater distances from the city center, and this can override the effect

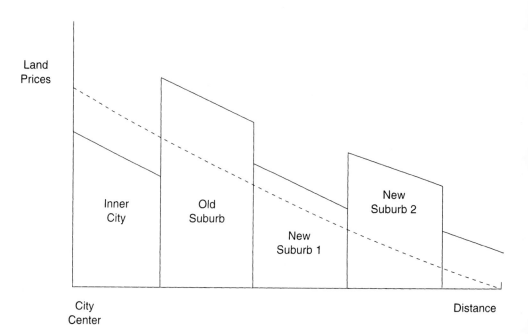

FIGURE 13.1 Land-price gradient with local jurisdictions.

Chapter 13 Local Governments, Property Taxes, and Real Estate Markets

of commuting, leading to a price or rent gradient that resembles the solid line rather than the dashed line in Figure 13.1.

While the services that local governments provide influence the real estate market, the opposite is also true: the real estate market can determine the character of communities and their financial ability to provide services. The link operates both ways. The composition of a town can change over time, altering the real estate tax base that is needed to raise the town's revenue. Often, different towns can wind up competing with each other over land use developments that provide (or are perceived to provide) more tax revenue than they use in services. Through zoning or other mechanisms, towns can try to block real estate developments that will use more services than they yield in new tax receipts.

In this chapter, we explore the different links that exist between the real estate market and the system of local governments that provides many of our services. We begin by documenting how local governments operate in the U.S. and describe the patterns of service responsibility and taxation between the federal, state, and local level. This is followed by a careful examination of different town budgets within a metropolitan area to explore the role that real estate markets play as a town's resource base. In the next section, we look at how property taxation creates a number of financial incentives for towns to regulate development and to exclude certain uses. The final sections of the chapter tackle the question of how firms and households select a town in which to reside or set up business. This leads to a theory of *fiscal capitalization* in which the value of services received and taxes paid across different local governments may be reflected exactly in the real estate values of those communities.

GOVERNMENTS AND PUBLIC SERVICES

In the United States, three levels of government provide public services: federal, state, and local. The Statistical Abstract of the United States recorded the following numbers for the five types of legal local jurisdictions in 1992: 3,043 counties, 19,296 municipalities, 16,666 townships or towns, 14,556 school districts, and 33,131 special districts. County governments cover almost all the land in the U.S., while municipalities, townships, and school and special districts cover only a small fraction of the nation's land area. Furthermore, counties, towns, and districts are rarely mutually exclusive. Thus, in the urban portions of California, for example, it is quite common for a household to pay a share of property taxes to a county (for roads and social services), to a town (for police, fire, and sanitation services), to a special district (for water and power), and to a school district. In Massachusetts, on the other hand, districts rarely exist and counties have virtually no responsibilities. Almost all local public services are provided by a system of municipalities or towns that covers the state completely. The most common arrangement in other states is for rural residents to be served by county governments only, whereas urban residents are most commonly served by some mix of towns and districts.

In Table 13.1, we group the expenditures made by all local governments and districts into a single category and compare those figures to expenditures made by the federal and state governments for FY 1990–1991. The first column, "Federal, Direct,"

TABLE 13.1 Government Expenditures,* 1990–1991

Expenditure	Federal Direct	Federal Transfer†	State Direct	State Transfer	Local Direct	Local Transfer	All Governments Expenditure‡	All Governments Transfer
Defense and international relations	366,112	—	—	—	—	—	366,112	—
Health, welfare and social insurance§	523,071	101,472	207,986	32,781	94,301	3,111	825,358	137,364
Education	20,192	24,537	80,468	116,180	228,834	429	329,494	141,146
Infrastructure and natural resources**	54,801	18,382	52,808	11,985	51,107	779	158,716	31,146
Law enforcement and fire protection††	8,111	736	22,592	2,154	51,332	103	82,035	2,993
Sewage, solid waste management and utilities	0	0	8,050	761	99,802	96	107,852	857
Other‡‡	347,077	15,018	70,391	22,679	92,133	883	509,601	38,580
Total	1,319,364	160,145	442,295	186,540	617,509	5,401	2,379,168	352,086

*In millions of 1991 dollars.
†Transfer columns represent intergovernmental transfers to all other levels of government. Total expenditure per category for each level of government is the sum of Direct and Transfer columns.
‡Excludes duplicative intergovernmental transactions.
§Includes social services and income maintenance, insurance trust expenditure, housing, and community development.
**Includes natural resources, parks and recreation, highways, air transportation/airports, and other transportation.
††Includes police protection, fire protection, and correction.
‡‡Includes other general expenditures such as space research and technology, postal service, and libraries; government administration; and interest on debts.
Source: Government Finances: *1990–91, U.S. Census of Governments,* U.S. Bureau of the Census, Washington, D.C., vol. 4, no. 5.

gives the direct expenditure outlay for each budgetary category made by the federal government. The next column to the right, "Federal, Transfer," gives the federal expenditure that was disbursed in the form of grants to lower levels of government. The sum of the two is the total federal outlay for each Expenditure category. For example, the federal government takes full responsibility for defense and international relations and spent $366 billion in this category in 1990–1991. Under infrastructure and natural resources, the federal government spent $73 billion, of which $18 billion was in the form of grants to state and local governments. The remaining $55 billion was in the form of direct federal purchases for the interstate highway system, national parks, and so on. State governments spent nearly $65 billion within this category, roughly $53 billion directly, and $12 billion in the form of intergovernmental transfers. Local governments, in turn, spent $52 billion. Total spending for all governments on infrastructure and natural resources was $159 billion, excluding the $31 billion of duplicative intergovernmental transfers.

Table 13.1 has some limitations. Of the $52 billion that local governments spent on infrastructure and natural resources, for example, we don't know how much of that derived from their own funds and how much derived from grants from states and federal government. The Census of Governments data does not specify the different recipients of federal aid expenditures—all intergovernmental transactions are lumped together.

Therefore, we can't be certain what portion of the total $18 billion in federal aid for infrastructure eventually went to local governments as opposed to states. What we can be certain of, however, is the portion of total expenditures each level of government directly controlled.

The categories of expenditure that are used in Table 13.1 are chosen to illustrate the different responsibilities of each level of government. The largest category of federal expenditure (accounting for 42 percent of the federal budget) covers all transfer payments: health, welfare, and social insurance. The major items in this category are social security payments and health insurance. Other items include direct welfare payments, unemployment insurance, veterans benefits, and housing assistance. Total state expenditure (direct and transfer) in this category is much smaller than that made by the federal government, but it accounts for a similar share of total state expenditure (about 38 percent). State expenditure on transfer programs reflects mainly the state share of federally mandated programs (Aid to Families with Dependent Children, Unemployment Insurance, Medicare); local governments spend only 16 percent of their budget on this category. Some local governments operate their own hospitals and health clinics. Overall, the federal government is responsible for more than three-fourths of spending on health, welfare, and social insurance.

The category of infrastructure and natural resources is more evenly split between the three levels of government. The federal government gives only a fraction (25 percent) of what it spends to lower levels of government; the states transfer 18 percent of their expenditures in this category to local governments. As a share of each level's budget, infrastructure represents between 5 percent and 10 percent of total expenditure.

The "Education" category covers higher education as well as primary and secondary schools. Federal government expenditure is mainly for scholarship support with a small amount for primary education programs such as school lunches. State governments spend directly on their systems of public colleges and universities, but the largest item of state expenditure is financial aid to school districts for primary and secondary schools. In the U.S., local governments are responsible for primary and secondary education, spending almost 70 percent of the education budget for all governments. However, nearly two-thirds of local government expenditures on education may come from higher level government funds.

The final two categories of services are all primarily local functions: law enforcement, fire protection, and sanitation and utilities (water, solid waste management). There is virtually no federal role in any of these services.

The differences between the three levels of governments in the U.S. are reflected in revenue sources as well. Table 13.2 divides up the revenue of each level of government by several common categories that distinguish between types of taxes, user fees, and grants.[1] At one extreme, the federal government collects 79 percent of its revenue from personal and corporate income taxes and only 14 percent from direct charges or user fees. At the other extreme, local governments receive 20 percent of their revenue from

---

[1]Excise taxes cover both general sales taxes as well as specific sales taxes such as that on cigarettes, lodging, and gasoline. Fees include any charge for a service and cover such items as postal service revenue, water and sewer fees, publicly operated utility charges, and license or registration fees.

TABLE 13.2 Government Receipts,* 1990–1991

Revenue Source	Federal	State	Local	All Governments
Personal income and wages†	856,170	201,031	26,229	1,083,430
Corporate income	98,086	20,357	1,886	120,329
Excise‡	58,495	160,009	86,299	304,803
Property	0	6,228	161,772	168,000
Fees§	167,123	97,627	125,126	389,876
Other taxes	17,574	31,163	9,039	57,776
Receipts from intergovernmental transactions	3,234	143,534	201,833	348,601
Total revenue	1,200,682	659,949	612,184	2,124,214**
Employment (000s)	3,091††	4,115	10,076	17,281

*In millions of 1991 dollars.
†Includes individual income, and insurance trust revenue.
‡Includes sales, gross receipts and customs, and utility and liquor store revenue.
§Includes charges and miscellaneous general revenue.
**Excludes receipts from intergovernmental transactions.
††Civilian. Includes employees outside the United States.
Source: Revenues, 1990–1991 U.S. Census of Governments, U.S. Bureau of the Census. Washington, D.C., vol. 4, no. 5; employment, *Statistical Abstract of the United States,* Washington, D.C., 1991.

user fees and another third from federal and state grants. Only 47 percent of local government income is accounted for by all forms of taxation. This breaks down to 5 percent from personal or corporate income taxes, 14 percent from excise taxes, and 26 percent from taxes on property (the remainder comes from miscellaneous other taxes). State governments lie between these two extremes, with the most diversified revenue sources: 34 percent from income taxes, 24 percent from excise taxes, 15 percent from fees, and 22 percent from intergovernmental transfers.

Several conclusions emerge from Tables 13.1 and 13.2 about the structure of government in the U.S. Local governments collect the least revenue from their constituents but use that money to provide services directly. Thus, local governments employ more than 10 million workers, far more than either state or federal governments. The main civilian role of the federal and state governments is to provide a system of health, welfare, and social insurance with transfer payments to individuals and to contract with the private sector for infrastructure. Grants from state and federal governments provide one-third of the funding for direct services provided by local governments. The largest local revenue source is a tax on property or real estate assets.

Economists have developed a number of theories about the advantages and consequences of assigning public services to different levels of government. In this literature, for example, it is argued that income redistribution and social transfer payments belong at the federal level. If local governments were responsible for welfare programs, not only would there be uneven benefits across local jurisdictions, but governments that provided higher-than-average benefits would attract eligible recipients. The possibility of attracting program recipients from other jurisdictions could lead local governments to provide less of such a public service than the country as a whole might find desirable. In addition, if local governments were responsible for funding social transfer programs, wealthy citizens might move from jurisdictions with poor citizens to avoid paying the higher local taxes needed to provide such programs. Federal funding of transfer programs makes it difficult for wealthy citizens to avoid paying for these services (Ladd and Doolittle 1982).

In the case of services such as air quality and interstate highways, there is a different argument for federal provision that involves the benefits that the national population receives from locally produced services. Without assistance, local governments might ignore these external benefits, and again would underprovide services relative to what the nation as a whole would deem appropriate.

The primary economic argument favoring local service provision is that it introduces variety and competition into government, and this allows the quality and breadth of services to be custom-tailored to the demands of local constituents. Matching the provision of services to differences in the preferences of local residents can enhance efficiency. For example, national systems of primary and secondary schooling (such as exist in Japan or France) typically have a more uniform educational program throughout the country. By contrast, it is argued that a system of locally run schools can better tailor curricula to the needs and demands of local residents. This efficiency argument assumes that there are widespread differences within a nation in the kinds and degree of services that local residents need or desire. Since the level of education, law enforcement, fire protection, and sanitation services often vary widely across localities, perhaps there are substantial differences in the service demands of local residents.

LOCAL GOVERNMENTS AND PROPERTY TAXES IN METROPOLITAN AREAS

Within metropolitan areas, significant differences in the patterns of both expenditure and revenue exist between central cities and the numerous smaller suburban communities that normally surround them. These differences are particularly important because they may influence the location of resources across towns within a metropolitan area. That is, the movement of firms and households between communities can put strong competitive pressures on local governments. To illustrate these differences, we examine local expenditure in 1990 for a sample of towns in the Boston metropolitan area, where municipalities are virtually the sole form of local government. With a single system of local governments we avoid the problem of trying to add up budgets over different layers of local governments whose boundaries often overlap.[2] In Table 13.3, the city of Boston is compared with an affluent suburb (Concord), two middle-class growing suburbs (Burlington and Needham), and an older working-class suburb (Quincy). These communities are reasonably representative of the different types of towns found within the broader metropolitan area.

---

[2] While Boston's single system of local governments makes it ideal to examine local variation of public services, the state government has imposed a uniform maximum limit on the property tax rate of local jurisdictions. Although not always binding, this provision can limit some of the variation that might occur across towns in revenue collection and spending.

TABLE 13.3 Profiles of Selected Massachusetts Cities, 1990*

Item	Boston	Burlington	Concord	Needham	Quincy
1989 Median HH income	30,757	58,975	73,695	63,618	37,795
Households	250,683	8,054	4,764	10,405	37,732
Population	574,283	23,302	17,076	27,557	84,985
Unemployment rate	5.5%	5.0%	2.7%	3.2%	5.8%
Expenditures[†]					
Education/pupil	6,679	5,501	7,179	6,053	5,836
Education/HH	1,438	2,340	3,156	1,876	992
General government/HH	280	244	339	214	136
Police & fire/HH	836	773	641	544	590
Other public safety/HH	224	36	41	62	39
Public works/HH	284	577	300	416	313
Health & welfare/HH	704	76	64	56	19
Culture and recreation/HH	138	165	234	101	67
Debt service/HH	328	233	256	370	205
Other expenditures/HH[‡]	955	816	553	855	902
Total expenditures/HH	5,184	5,260	5,584	4,495	3,263
Revenues					
State aid/HH	1,846	707	554	360	942
Local receipts/HH[§]	1,425	993	434	954	461
Total property tax levy/HH	2,071	3,768	4,535	3,167	1,749
Other revenue/HH**	45	362	349	314	415
Total revenue/HH	5,389	5,830	5,872	4,795	3,567
Residential tax rate	0.85%	0.88%	0.97%	1.00%	1.02%
Percent of total levy	30.1%	36.0%	81.7%	73.0%	60.0%
Commercial & industrial tax rate	2.39%	1.73%	1.08%	1.22%	2.29%
Percent of total levy	64.3%	61.9%	16.5%	25.3%	37.4%
Assessed residential value ($ billion)	20.6	1.2	1.8	2.4	3.9
Total assessed value ($ billion)	35.8	2.4	2.2	3.1	5
Residential taxes/HH	623	1,358	3,706	2,313	1,050
Estimated total payments/HH[††]	1,052	1,716	4,061	3,010	1,327
Avg. single-family property tax bill[‡‡]	1,377	1,577	3,535	2,647	1,608

HH, Household.
*In 1990 dollars.
[†]Expenditures are from general fund only; special revenues, enterprise capital projects, and trust funds are not included.
[‡]Other Expenditures includes court judgments, municipal employees' health insurance and retirement plans, medicaid, liability insurance, payments to school, water, and fire districts; and expenditures not otherwise classified.
[§]Local Receipts includes excise taxes, interest on investments, fines, permits, rentals, forfeits, and water and sewer funds surpluses.
**Other Revenue includes capitalization and stabilization funds and municipal light surpluses.
[††]Total Payments/HH are estimated by multiplying the percent of tax levy from residential property by local receipts/HH and adding residential taxes/HH.
[‡‡]Average single-family property tax bill is computed by multiplying the single-family assessed value by the residential property tax rate and dividing by the number of single-family parcels.
Source: All data from Massachusetts Department of Revenue Data Bank/Online Service, except Median HH income; Median HH income, U.S. Bureau of the Census.

Chapter 13   Local Governments, Property Taxes, and Real Estate Markets

The first row in Table 13.3 shows the wide differences that exist in the average income of their residents. Median annual household income ranges from $31,000 in Boston to $74,000 in Concord, with Burlington and the other towns in between. The next few rows illustrate some of the demographic differences between the towns. In Boston, households have only an average of two persons, whereas in Concord and Burlington, the average is closer to four. Turning to "Expenditures," when measured on a per-pupil basis, educational expenditure is only weakly related to town income: Concord spends more than Needham, which spends more than Burlington or Quincy, but Boston (the community with the lowest median household income) has the second-highest per-pupil spending. When the comparison is made on a per-household basis, however, the Boston anomaly vanishes. Because Boston has fewer pupils per household than its surrounding bedroom suburbs, it is able to match their pupil expenditure with a lower cost per taxpayer or household. When measured per household, the 140 percent difference in income between Boston and Concord results in a 119 percent difference in educational expenditure. This suggests (as many studies have found) that spending on educational services is somewhat income inelastic.

The next several rows show that expenditures on services besides education also do not seem related to a town's income level. Police and fire outlays are again highest in Boston, whereas among the suburban communities, these expenditures show little relationship to town income. The wealthiest and poorest suburbs (Concord and Quincy) spend almost the same, while Burlington spends the most. A similar pattern among the suburbs emerges with public works expenditures, whereas the city of Boston spends noticeably less per household. In the health and welfare category, the social problems of inner cities have hit hard in Boston, resulting in a high level of expenditure there, whereas each of the suburbs spends virtually nothing.

The net result of these expenditure patterns is that the city of Boston spends nearly as much or more per household in the aggregate than all but the wealthiest suburb, despite having only half of the income per household of many of these towns. The 95 percent income difference between Concord and Quincy leads to only 71 percent greater per household expenditure.

Two explanations have been offered for why the simple link between town expenditure and average town income appears to be so weak. The first is that there are other important demand factors that generate public expenditure besides a town's resources. For example, when a town has a needy, low-income constituency or a land-use pattern comprised of dense, wood-frame houses, it may simply need to spend more on social services or fire protection. A second explanation emphasizes that a town's resources, at least as viewed by its decision makers, often consist of far more than its residents' income. Additional resources include the grants that are made available to local governments and the ability to tax business, tourists, and other uses or activities.

The row that depicts state aid suggests that at least some of the spending paradox may be explained by the grants that each town receives from the state government. Such grants make up more than 34 percent of Boston's per-household revenue but between only 7.5 and 12 percent for the wealthier towns of Concord, Needham, and Burlington. The poorer suburb of Quincy receives slightly more than 26 percent of its budget in state aid. Thus, public spending with only local resources is more strongly related to income than is total spending. Would the city of Boston spend as much as it currently does if those grants were withdrawn? In many situations, towns have the flexibility to use grants in one of two ways. They can either augment services (spending) and leave their own tax effort fixed, or they can reduce local taxes and leave service levels the same.[3]

The next row, labeled "Local Receipts," gives the amount of revenue per household that each town receives from fees (e.g., water and sewer), permits, excise taxes, and other sources. While some of this revenue comes from town households, firms and businesses make significant payments as well. This explains why this entry is so large for the city of Boston and also suggests that firms can represent an important potential source of revenue for a community.

If we take total expenditure per household and subtract state aid and other receipts, we are left with tax revenue. In Massachusetts, cities and towns can only tax property. Thus, total property tax revenue in Boston is $2,071 per household, and in Concord $4,535. In Boston's case, however, only 30 percent of this amount is raised from property taxes on households, whereas 64 percent ($1,325) is raised from property taxes on business. In Concord, property taxes on businesses are only 16.5 percent of the levy. To the extent that the owners of this business property do not live in the town in which their business is located, taxes on this property represent a potential source of revenue that does not come from town or city residents. In fact, property tax payments from residential property (houses and apartments) only account for $623 per household in Boston, a small share of local revenue. In Concord, residential taxes per household are $3,706.

If we assume that the same share of the category "Local Recipts/HH" comes from businesses as does property tax revenue, then in Boston, households pay an average of only $1,052 annually—for $5,184 worth of services! A full 80 percent of Boston's expenditures are financed from state aid and taxes or fees on businesses. In Concord, households pay $4,060 for $5,584 worth of services, so only 27 percent comes from sources other than town residents. In Quincy, 60 percent of expenditure is financed from nonresidents, while in Needham the share is 33 percent. Thus, there is a strong negative correlation between town income and the share of a town's budget that is financed from nonresidents. The exception is Burlington, a middle-income suburb that has undergone an explosive growth of suburban office and retail development over the last two decades. Here, two-thirds of total expenditures are from sources other than town residents.

If we take the average estimated total payments made by town households (next to last row) and divide it by the town's median household income (top row), we get some

---

[3]An economic argument can be made that the effect of grants on a town's budget depends very much on the terms of the grant. *Matching grants* reimburse a town for some fraction of its own expenditure (on certain budget items). Since the dollar value of the grant depends on how much the town spends, this form of aid tends to encourage higher spending, and the grant mostly augments services. *Block grants* are given in a fixed amount per capita or per pupil. Since block grants are not tied to local expenditures, they do not encourage increased local spending. Local governments may use block grants more as a substitute for local taxes.

Different state or federal programs use different grant formulas, but most grant programs are targeted toward cities or towns with fewer resources, and/or many needy constituents. Thus, the choice by Massachusetts to give more aid to Boston than to Concord is clearly one of social policy.

idea of the tax burden paid by residents. The residents of Boston wind up with taxes and fees that are about 3.4 percent of their income, even though total expenditure per household is close to 17 percent of income. In Concord and Needham, residents contribute 5.5 percent and 4.7 percent of their incomes, respectively, but without the extra nonresidential resources of Boston, this yields lower service percentages (7.6 and 7.1 percent of income, respectively). Thus, when measured as a percentage of town income, public expenditure is far less in wealthier towns. On the other hand, tax payments as a percentage of income rise slightly with town income. Of course, all of this would look quite different if the pattern of state aid or the distribution of nonresidential property were different across towns.

The last row in Table 13.3 gives the average tax payment made per single-family house, as opposed to a household. Comparing this number to average residential property taxes per household provides an indication of the pattern of housing in each town. In Boston, the average residential payment is almost half of the average single-family tax bill. This confirms that the city has many apartments and that their average unit value is far less than the city's typical single-family home. A similar story occurs in Quincy. However, in the middle- and upper-income suburbs, where single-family housing predominates, the two numbers are much closer. If the single-family tax bill is divided by the residential tax rate, the result is an average assessed value for the town's single-family housing.[4] Average assessed housing values—$162,000 in Boston, $265,000 in Needham, and $364,000 in Concord—tend to be roughly proportional to average town household income.

The data in Table 13.3, together with numerous studies, suggest a series of conclusions about the comparative fiscal behavior of cities and towns within metropolitan areas:

1. The demand for services is quite inelastic with respect to town income. In part, this results because education, police, and fire protection are viewed as necessities, rather than luxuries. It also results because expenditure on some services is generated by need (crime, poverty), rather than by demand.
2. Since the demand for housing has an income elasticity near to one, residential property value tends to be roughly proportional to town income. With no other resources, this would potentially lead to much lower property tax rates in higher income communities.
3. Nonresidential property provides an important tax resource for many communities, tending to be concentrated in inner cities or in selected moderate income suburban towns. This helps to offset the tax burden of providing services in these communities and makes property tax rates more equal across communities.

[4]The town's statutory residential tax rate, t_s, multiplied by the average assessed value of single-family property, AV, equals the average single-family tax bill, T, or $T = t_s AV$. The town *effective rate* t is the tax bill divided by the true "market" value of homes, P, or:

$$t = \frac{T}{P} = t_s \frac{AV}{P}$$

4. The progressive distribution of state and federal aid also is crucial in helping lower-income communities to provide comparable levels of public services without unusually high property tax rates.

The conclusions about how a town's residential property tax rate is determined and how this rate tends to vary across towns with different household income can be illustrated with a simplified town budget as shown in Equation (13.1).

$$t = \frac{(G - A - N)s}{P} \tag{13.1}$$

Where: t = town residential effective tax rate
G = total town expenditure/household
A = state aid received/household
N = nonproperty tax revenue
P = average market value of houses in the town
s = share of property value that is residential

Using Equation (13.1) and the figures provided in Table 13.3, we can calculate the effective residential tax rate for Boston and Concord. For these calculations, we take total expenditures per household and subtract revenues per household from state aid and nonproperty tax revenue per household. We then take that sum times the portion of the tax base that is residential and divide by the average market value of housing units in the town. The average market value of housing units is determined by taking assessed residential value of houses and apartments in Table 13.3 and dividing by the total number of households.[5] Boston's average unit value, P, is $82,175, whereas Concord's average unit value is $377,834. For Boston, Equation (13.1) would yield an effective residential tax rate of:

$$t = \frac{(5184 - 1846 - 1470)0.301}{82175}$$

$$= 0.68 \text{ percent}$$

This calculated effective tax rate is reasonably close to the actual residential tax rate given in Table 13.3 of 0.85 percent. Using Equation (13.1), we calculate an effective residential tax rate for Concord of 0.92 percent. While Concord's household income is 140 percent that of Boston, Concord's per household expenditures are only 7.7 percent higher than Boston's. However, Concord's effective residential tax rate is 35 percent higher than Boston's.

How does Boston spend close to what Concord spends per household given its lower income and effective residential property tax rate? The answer lies in the large amount of state aid that Boston receives relative to Concord, Boston's large nonresidential property tax base, and the city's nonproperty tax sources of revenue. To illustrate the point, let's assume that the level of state aid, the nonresidential property tax base, and nonproperty tax revenues were equal across towns. For example, assume that Boston continued to spend $5,184 per household but now had the same state aid, nonproperty tax

---

[5]For these calculations, we are assuming that average assessed value is equal to average market value.

revenues, and residential portion of its property tax base as Concord. Assuming that Boston's average house value would be the same, the city's effective residential property tax rate would skyrocket to 3.8 percent, or 4.1 times Concord's effective tax rate.

The balance that seems to exist between cities and towns within a metropolitan area raises several questions about how resources are distributed across these communities. Why is there so much variation in town income? Why is it that nonresidential real estate tends to be located in communities that have lower incomes and thus are most pressed for tax resources? Why is it important for tax rates not to differ widely across communities? To answer these, we need first to consider the motives and incentives that households face when selecting a community to live in. It is equally important to examine the fiscal incentives that towns face when regulating their residential development. Finally, we look at the fiscal and environmental benefits to towns of nonresidential development.

HOUSEHOLD LOCATION AND COMMUNITY STRATIFICATION

The observation that communities vary widely in terms of average household income can be at least partially explained by extending the models developed in Chapter 3. In that chapter, we determined how, in equilibrium, the price of housing would vary across locations with commuting costs so as to leave households indifferent between living at each location. We also determined that if there were different types of households, those whose time was more valuable would be willing to pay relatively more for housing nearer to work. This is a location pattern that represents a competitive market equilibrium. As we discussed in Chapter 3, this approach assumes that there is perfect mobility, so that a form of price arbitrage exists across locations. In this chapter, we adapt this model to consider how households select a home from among a continuum of towns. In effect, "town" replaces a location's commuting cost as the determinant of price. We then ask what different households are willing to pay for a house (assumed uniform) in towns with different levels of expenditures and tax rates. Following Tiebout (1956), we seek to ascertain how, in equilibrium, a competitive housing market will allocate households to towns. To be complete, we also must incorporate the fact that the prices households are willing to pay for houses ultimately will determine town property values and hence tax rates.

In Figure 13.2, the horizontal axis depicts the level of town expenditure on public services, G. Towns to the left spend less, while towns to the right spend more. Consider for the moment three types of households, subscripted $j = L, M, H$, for low-, middle-, and high-income levels. Each line in Figure 13.2 depicts the price of housing, P_j, that would make that type of household equally well off across towns with different public expenditure levels. There are two considerations that go into determining these house price indifference lines. First, there is the willingness-to-pay for public services. This locational rent is the product of the annual dollar value that the household places on a unit of town public services (R_j) multiplied by the level of service (G). Second, there is the cost that a household faces for these public services, which is measured by the taxes that the household will pay if it lives in the town. If the town tax rate is t, then the household's annual tax payment will be tP_j. With a discount or interest rate of i, the house price that makes

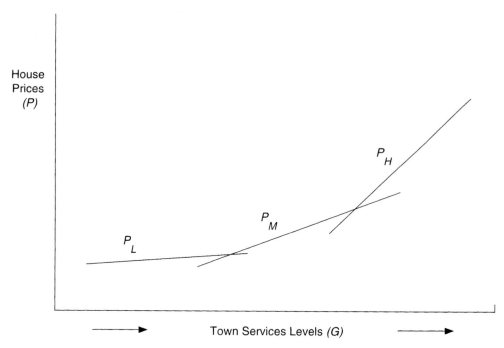

FIGURE 13.2 House prices and town service levels.

each household indifferent should be the present value of the household's valuation of services minus tax payments:

$$P_j = \frac{R_j G - t P_j}{i}, \quad j = L, M, H, \text{ or, on solving for } P_j:$$

$$= \frac{R_j G}{(i + t)} \tag{13.2}$$

As long as households with a greater income have a greater willingness-to-pay for public services (i.e., $R_H > R_M > R_L$), then the P_j lines will be as depicted in Figure 13.2.[6] At the right-hand extreme, high-income households will outbid those with moderate or lower incomes for the right to occupy housing in towns with high levels of public services. This conclusion holds even when such households consider that by bidding more, their taxes will also be (relatively) greater. Moving from right to left, middle-income households will likewise outbid lower-income households for units in middle-service towns, and so on through any number of household-income categories. If towns with higher levels of public services are those with greater incomes (which, all else being equal, they should be), then households will self-sort by income and maintain a pattern of income stratification. The importance of this simple argument cannot be overemphasized. In a competitive

---

[6]If the annual willingness-to-pay for services is ordered by income, then the derivative of P_j with respect to G, $R_j/(i + t)$, will also be ordered by income: P_H rises with greater services, G, more than P_M does, and so on. This ensures that the P_j are as depicted in Figure 13.2 and that stratification by income prevails.

Chapter 13 Local Governments, Property Taxes, and Real Estate Markets

housing market, income stratification across towns by public service levels would seem to be a natural outcome of market locational forces.[7]

In the real world, the housing market that exists across towns is not uniform, as assumed in this simple model. Larger homes, for example, which are often preferred by high-income households, tend to be located in wealthier, high-service towns. This only increases the tendency for wealthier households to segregate into their own communities, outbidding lower-income households for units in these communities. If the housing in each town has been built primarily for the existing residents, then those residents are more likely be the highest bidders for such units. Self-sorting by income is only reinforced in this situation.

The picture changes quite dramatically when we consider the development of new land: how do the offered prices made for land by different income groups vary across towns with different service levels? This is crucial for determining how a town's housing pattern changes over time. A wealthy community will be able to maintain its character only if wealthy residents are willing to pay more (per acre) than other moderate- or lower-income households for the right to develop raw land in the town. We again return to Chapters 4 and 5 to examine how household bids for unimproved land are determined. We continue to assume that houses are identical except for lot size and denote C as the capital cost of constructing this identical unit. If q_j represents the size of lot demanded by households of each income level, then we can define an equation for that price of raw land, p_j, that makes each type of household indifferent across towns with different service levels. Land prices again will be a residual value per acre from house prices minus construction costs.

$$p_j = \frac{P_j - C}{q_j} = \frac{R_j G}{q_j(i+t)} - \frac{C}{q_j}, \quad j = L, M, H \quad (13.3)$$

The pattern of raw land prices across towns, p_j, need not resemble at all the pattern shown in Figure 13.2. It will certainly be true that the lot sizes demanded by households are ordered with income ($q_L < q_M < q_H$), as will be their values for government services. In this case, it is not clear that high-income households will be willing to offer more per acre for raw land in their town than will households with less income. If low-income households are willing to live on much smaller lots than wealthier residents, then they may be

---

[7]The reader may notice that in this model of income stratification, the tax rate in each town is assumed to be independent of the town's level of expenditure and its property values. It ignores how tax rates will eventually depend on expenditures and house prices. This simultaneous relationship is easily incorporated into the model, with no change in the model's conclusions. With no federal or state aid or nonresidential property, the town's budget relationship between services (measured in dollars), house prices, and the tax rate is simply:

$$t = \frac{G}{P}$$

Incorporating this into Equation (13.2), we get the revised house price equations:

$$P_j = \frac{G(R_j - 1)}{i}, \quad j = L, M, H$$

As long as the annual willingness to pay for services, R_j, is ordered by income, then the house price lines above will still resemble those in Figure 13.2.

willing to pay more *per acre* than their wealthier competitors. The price *per acre* for raw land depends not only on the value of the community services obtained by living there, but also is based on how many households per acre are experiencing these advantages.[8]

If lower-income households are able to offer more for raw land in higher-income communities, then these communities will not remain high-income for very long. In effect, income stratification across towns might not be sustainable by a private market. Yet, there are strong incentives that encourage middle- and higher-income communities to try and maintain themselves, even when the market would not sustain them. Given these incentives, communities have developed a system of regulating land use through *zoning.* Zoning laws allow towns to set minimum lot sizes that are equal to or often greater than those that already exist in the community. This effectively prevents lower-income residents from consuming the smaller quantities of land which, in turn, would allow them to compete with higher-income residents for town land at offered prices. By requiring equal or minimum land consumption, towns are able to ensure that offered land prices resemble the house prices in Figure 13.2. Thus, income stratification across towns is maintained. But why are towns so interested in maintaining such stratification?

ZONING AND THE FISCAL IMPACTS OF RESIDENTIAL DEVELOPMENT

The determination of a town's property tax rate through Equation (13.1) provides some powerful incentives for communities to regulate the development of new land. Under current state enabling legislation, zoning laws permit towns to control several aspects of development, primarily density and land use. Since local governments are generally directly elected, the presumption is that such land-use regulations will be designed to achieve the maximum fiscal benefit or fiscal surplus for a town's current residents.

As a city or town grows, development inevitably requires the expansion of services, particularly in the long run. Studies suggest that police, fire, and school services often exhibit roughly constant returns to scale. Thus, as long as the character of a community does not change, long-term growth tends to require a proportional expansion of municipal budgets.[9] New development, however, can often affect the character of a

---

[8]In order for income stratification to occur across communities, it must be the case that p_H increases more than p_M and p_L as one moves from left to right in Figure 13.2. This will occur only if the derivative of p_j with respect to town services, G, is ordered by income. This derivative is equal to $R_j/q_j(i + t)$, so stratification happens only if:

$$\frac{R_L}{q_L} < \frac{R_M}{q_M} < \frac{R_H}{q_H}$$

In effect, if high-income households value public services only slightly more than lower-income households, while the latter are willing to live on much smaller lots, then low-income households will outbid high-income residents for raw land in high-income (high-service) towns.

[9]Numerous statistical studies have examined the issue of returns to scale in municipal services. The most common approach analyzes how local public expenditure on a particular sector (e.g., schools) varies with the size of the population (e.g., children), holding other factors that might influence costs (e.g., salaries) or demand (e.g., town income) constant. There is some evidence of scale economies in fire protection, but little in education or law enforcement.

community and always adds to the community's base of taxable property. In Equation (13.1), new development can alter a town's tax rate in three possible ways. It can change the level of public expenditure per household, G, the average value of houses, P, or the percentage of residential property, s. If the net effect of these changes leads to a lower tax rate, then existing residents will benefit from the development's fiscal surplus. A higher tax rate means that residents must pay more for the same services, since the new development creates a fiscal deficit.

The citizens of a community are the primary users of public services. The quality of services that residents receive depends on how much is spent per household (G) relative to how much "need" there is per household. "Need" is a tricky concept and is best illustrated with some examples. Two communities will have very different school systems if they spend the same per household but the average number of children per household (i.e., need) is quite different. Likewise, two communities that spend the same amount on police and fire services per household can have quite different risks depending on their density levels, building types, or underlying social problems (i.e., need). If a new residential development in a community adds an average number of new school children per housing unit and requires average per unit servicing by the police and fire departments, then in Equation (13.1), G does not have to change to keep service quality at existing levels. On the other hand, if community growth occurs with developments that are safer than average or that contain households with fewer children, average town expenditure on services can fall, while service quality remains intact.[10] Thus, the character of new residential development can alter the public expenditure that existing inhabitants must pay to maintain their current level of services.

On the revenue side, the character of new residential development also alters a town's tax rate by directly affecting the average value of houses (P). New development that adds houses which are above average in value causes the tax rate to fall, while the opposite will be true for development that is below average in value. The fiscal surplus of a development is its net effect on town finances considering both its expenditure and revenue impacts. A large mansion inhabited by a widow normally will generate a significant fiscal surplus, while a small apartment occupied by a family with four children should create a fiscal deficit.

As communities attempt to encourage residential development which generates a fiscal surplus, they have a limited number of policies at their disposal. The major one is the requirement that land be developed with a minimum lot size (MLS) or at a maximum density. Such zoning, if enforced, is almost always able to ensure that new development is of a minimum taxable value. While this may not directly prohibit someone from buying a 2-acre, $150,000 lot and then parking a $10,000 trailer on it, those with $160,000 to spend on housing generally prefer a better balance between land and capital. If binding, MLS zoning requires that a development use more land than it otherwise would and makes it more likely that the houses developed will be of higher value. This yields greater tax revenue (per new household).

---

[10]Alternatively, the existing citizenry can keep expenditure the same and achieve a fiscal surplus through an improved level of service quality.

While MLS zoning encourages higher value houses, it can also reduce the value (per acre) of unimproved land. This effect can be seen by referring back to the model of development density used in Chapter 4. In the top frame of Figure 13.3, the downward-sloping willingness-to-pay schedule (P) gives the market price (per square foot of house floor area) as a function of that house's FAR (floor-to-land area ratio). It slopes downward because, all else equal, households prefer a larger yard area or lower residential density. The construction cost schedule for the house, C, may rise slightly, as more dense development tends to have higher costs (per square foot of floor area). The profit per square foot of house floor area is simply the difference between the P and C schedules. Beyond the FAR level labeled d, construction costs exceed house prices and development is no longer profitable. In the lower frame, the hump-shaped p schedule represents the profit per square foot of land area. Recalling Chapter 4, we derive this by multiplying the FAR level (F) by the profit per square foot of house floor area in the upper frame: $p = F[P - C]$. At the FAR level of F^*, development yields the maximum profit per square foot of land area, p^*. With no regulation, F^* would be the FAR or density level privately chosen by developers, and p^* would be the competitive market price for land.

With MLS zoning, the FAR allowed for development is constrained to be F^0. If the zoning limit is binding, then $F^0 < F^*$. At F^0, land profit (and, hence, land price) is only p^0, which must be less than p^* since p^* is the maximum land price achievable. Moving back to the upper frame, the greater required lot area yields a finished house price (per square foot) that is higher: $P^0 > P^*$.

What minimum lot size should a town choose in its zoning laws? If the community is interested only in the fiscal surplus of new development, the larger the required lot size, the greater will be the fiscal surplus (per developed housing unit). The problem with requiring FAR values that are near to the origin in Figure 13.3 is that they diminish the value of raw land. While the existing residents of the town obtain a fiscal surplus, the owners of unimproved land suffer losses in value. The legal tradition in the United States is that regulations in the public interest are allowed within reason until they deny property owners so much of their value as to be considered an effective seizing of property by the government. In practice, courts have upheld the right of towns to enact minimum lot sizes that are somewhat but not too much larger than the existing patterns of land use.[11]

The widespread use of minimum lot size zoning provides a compelling explanation for how income stratification across towns is maintained over time. Each town is effectively able to exclude residents whose income is significantly lower than the town's average from developing land. When forced to compete over a common-sized lot, lower-income households simply cannot match the offers of higher-income residents. When applied to towns at each level of income or public services, town stratification by income results.

---

[11] In some states like Massachusetts and New Jersey, state government has intervened to restrict the local application of MLS zoning. This is done to encourage the development of more affordable, higher-density housing.

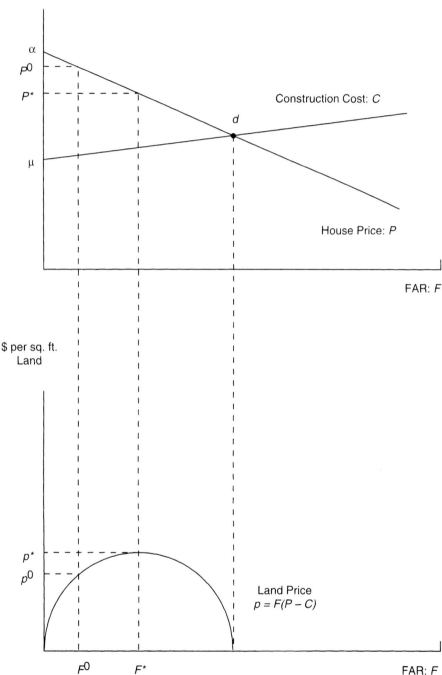

FIGURE 13.3 FAR model with zoning.

THE FISCAL COSTS AND BENEFITS OF NONRESIDENTIAL DEVELOPMENT

The zoning laws that enable communities to regulate the density of residential development also provide considerable power over the nonresidential use of land. Towns that wish to encourage commercial or industrial development designate large tracts of land for that use and then provide the access to infrastructure necessary to service such development. Communities that wish to remain residential need only refrain from these policies. There is little precedent in the law that prevents a town from excluding commercial development—even if such uses have existed historically in the community. As communities decide on their local zoning plans, a common issue of concern is the fiscal surplus or deficit that arises from nonresidential development.

The net fiscal impact of commercial or industrial uses involves three considerations. As with residential developments, a town must assess the likely impact of the commercial use on service demand as well as the likely tax payments to be made by the development. In the case of nonresidential uses, however, a third concern also arises frequently—the environment. The term *environment* here covers not only the obvious problems of noise and pollution, but also a range of more broadly defined issues such as congestion, changing town character, or the visual impact of the development. Let's examine these three fiscal impacts in turn.

It is now generally agreed that commercial and industrial uses generate very little demand on public services. The children of those workers employed in a town or of those shoppers using a store in a town do not attend the town's schools unless they are town residents. It is the children of *residents* who are educated in a town. In a similar manner, residential neighborhoods normally place greater demand on police and fire services than commercial and industrial areas. As for sanitation, most communities require that firms privately dispose of refuse—only residents are provided with free municipal collection. Businesses can use large quantities of water and produce commensurate waste, but in most cases they pay directly for these with a combination of hook-up and usage fees.

The primary public service demand that firms impose on towns is for infrastructure. The demand for transportation infrastructure by commercial or industrial development can create large service burdens that must be publicly financed. New industrial parks, shopping centers, and office buildings all act as traffic "attractors." When undertaken at large scale, such development can easily overwhelm existing roads or highways. The costs of adaptation can range from installing a small intersection to a major arterial or highway expansion. While commercial development can strain a town's transportation system, aggregate outlays on such infrastructure usually represents between only 5 and 10 percent of a community's budget. Furthermore, only a fraction of these outlays is generally attributable to commercial development. Thus, while a particular development may necessitate significant infrastructure upgrades, on average, the cost of infrastructure that is attributable to such development is only a small share of most municipal budgets.

On the revenue side, some forms of nonresidential development provide lucrative tax resources. A 3-acre site with a 40-story office building can easily be appraised at

$200 million and generate $4 million annually in tax revenue. The same size site with a warehouse in the suburbs, on the other hand, might yield only $50,000 in taxes. In most cases, the present discounted value of such revenue streams significantly exceeds the infrastructure or other tax-based service costs that such developments impose.[12]

The final consideration for towns in their zoning deliberation concerns the broadly defined environmental costs of nonresidential development. Does the development add to congestion, pollution, or noise? Does it create a visual blight on an otherwise peaceful country landscape? How important are such considerations to the town's residents? What dollar value do the residents of the community place on the loss of such amenities, if they are to be sacrificed? A town must compare the value of such losses against the net fiscal surplus of the development. This involves the following comparison of development impacts:

$$\begin{matrix}\text{Development} \\ \text{Environmental Loss}\end{matrix} \times \begin{matrix}\text{Community Value} \\ \text{of Environment}\end{matrix} + \begin{matrix}\text{Development} \\ \text{Service Usage}\end{matrix} > \text{or} < \begin{matrix}\text{Development} \\ \text{Tax Revenue}\end{matrix} \quad (13.4)$$

It is important to realize that the outcome of the comparison in Equation (13.4) will depend not just on the specific features of the development being proposed, but also on the community making the decision. It is the community's current tax rate that helps to determine the likely revenue from the development and the community's residents that value any environmental impacts. Two communities can evaluate the same development quite differently.

In Equation (13.4) it is clear that communities with low tax rates and where residents value the environment most highly will be those least likely to approve of nonresidential development. Conversely, those towns that place a lower dollar value on the environment and who have higher tax rates will often find the tradeoff worthwhile. The notion of valuing the environment is an economic concept exactly like that discussed in Chapter 4 for valuing a feature or an attribute of a house. It depends partly on an individual's own utility for or from the environment, but it also depends on an individual's income. All else equal, households with greater income are willing or able to sacrifice more of that income to purchase something.

The discussion in the previous section illustrated how wealthier towns tend to have at least modestly lower tax rates than poorer communities. When combined with the observation that wealthier communities may also be willing to sacrifice more to preserve the environment, the implication of Equation (13.4) is that such towns will opt to exclude commercial development. On the other hand, poorer communities with higher tax rates and lower environmental valuation will tend to embrace commercial development. Since central cities frequently have long histories of industrial development, it is perhaps not fair to compare their industrial land-use policies with those of newer suburbs. To avoid

---

[12]As with other examples in this book, a real discount rate, r, should be used in this present value calculation. Let i be the nominal interest rate, and g the likely rate of growth of the town's expenditure per household. The latter should at least equal the CPI inflation rate and reflects the speed with which property tax collections will rise. Adding in the rate of physical decay or obsolescence in the structure, δ, the appropriate discount rate would be $r = i - g + \delta$.

this bias, Table 13.4 examines some of those suburban towns within the Boston metropolitan area that adjoin Route 128, the region's major circumferential highway. Such communities have roughly comparable transportation access, which Chapters 5 and 6 showed was of importance for commercial and industrial firms. The table shows town income and the number of employees in the town relative to the town's resident population. Also depicted is the percent of the appraised property tax base that comes from nonresidential uses. There is at least a partial inverse relationship between town income and commercial-industrial activity. With the exception of Burlington (a more affluent community with a high ratio of jobs to population), the suburbs with higher incomes tend to have around 20 percent or less of their tax base in the nonresidential category (Concord, Lexington, Needham, Reading). These towns also have job-household ratios that are between 0.8 and 2.4. The three lower-income towns (Braintree, Peabody, Waltham) have nonresidential tax base shares that range from 27 to 39 percent, and the job-population ratios for Braintree and Waltham are between 2.5 and 3.0.

Table 13.4 shows that there can be systematic patterns in the way communities respond to the choice of whether to allow or encourage nonresidential development. It is interesting that there is also a relationship across industries or types of development between the magnitude of taxes paid and the general severity of environmental impacts created. With property as the tax base, the local taxes received from a development are determined largely by the value of the capital improvements placed on the land. A petrochemical complex, steel factory, or electric power plant can involve billions of dollars of capital investment. If appraised at such values, these facilities can generate tens of millions of dollars annually in tax revenue. This is equivalent to the entire budget of many smaller-sized suburbs. At the same time, such uses often expose a community to environmental risks and costs.

At the other extreme, suburban office parks and light industrial facilities normally pose little environmental risks and, if properly designed and located, create few environmental costs. The value of capital improvements from such development, however, is normally only a fraction of that from heavier industries. Thus, commercial uses tend to

TABLE 13.4 Distribution of Employment in Boston-Area Communities, 1989

	Braintree	Burlington	Concord	Lexington	Needham	Peabody	Reading	Waltham
Households	11,978	8,054	4,764	10,515	10,405	17,556	7,932	20,728
Employment	29,610	33,103	11,643	18,527	18,449	21,692	6,060	63,087
Jobs/HH	2.5	4.1	2.4	1.8	1.8	1.2	0.8	3.0
1989 Median HH income	47,151	58,975	73,695	71,030	63,618	41,950	55,635	40,595
Nonresidential tax base ($ billion)*	0.7	1.1	0.3	0.8	0.7	0.9	0.2	1.9
Nonresidential share of total tax base	31.70%	45.90%	15.10%	21.20%	21.80%	26.80%	10.80%	39.30%
Nonresidential tax rate	1.7%	1.57%	1.08%	1.59%	1.22%	1.38%	1.18%	1.46%

HH, Household.
*Nonresidential properties include assessed commercial and industrial values.
Source: Employment, Massachusetts Department of Employment & Training; Households, income, 1990 U.S. Bureau of the Census; Tax information, Massachusetts Department of Revenue.

provide tax revenues that are commensurate with their lower social costs. But what of a light industrial facility that processes hazardous waste and generates little tax revenue? Even more problematic, consider a public prison that yields no tax revenue at all. At the other end of the scale, a complicated telephone switching center may contain hundreds of millions of dollars worth of equipment, generate lucrative tax revenue, and be virtually invisible to the community. None of these uses is likely to generate tax revenue that in any way match the social costs of these uses.

Many economists have argued that the siting of major commercial or institutional uses should be determined according to a process of bargaining or bidding. Consider the hazardous waste facility mentioned above. The proposal is to require such a facility to pay communities whatever amount is necessary until some community accepts the compensation payment in exchange for allowing the facility to locate there. The community willing to accept the facility with the least compensation payment would presumably be that town where environmental issues were of less concern and where the facility would not create much inherent risk (because of topographical or locational factors). A facility that was viewed as an economic blessing might *receive* payments from communities and thereby wind up in the community that offered to *make* the largest payment. In either case, the siting decision would seem to occur at an efficient location where its harm is minimized or its advantages maximized.[13]

The argument to allow facilities and towns to bargain over the rights of firms to locate there has considerable merit. The payment of property taxes is based on the capital improvements that the facility requires, not the true economic costs or benefits that the development imposes on its host community. At the same time, it may be overly simple to assume that the impacts of a large facility are limited only to its host town. A hazardous waste plant may well impose risks on adjoining communities. These communities would not receive any tax revenue from the facility under current law, nor any compensation payments under the bargaining proposal above. The bargaining proposal works only if the boundaries of towns happen to reflect the boundaries of the impacts of a facility siting.

---

[13]An alternative to requiring facilities to pay towns for the right to locate would be to require towns to pay for the right to exclude facilities. The argument, according to Ronald Coase, is that the facility winds up at the same location with either scheme. To see this, consider the following table, in which a firm contemplates locating in either town A or town B. With no tax payment or compensation, the site minimizing production costs is in town B. Production plus environmental costs, however, are lowest in town A. If firms must pay for the right to locate, towns will require a compensation payment at least equal to the environmental costs imposed by the firm. The firm's total production plus compensation payment cost is minimized by locating in town A. Alternatively, towns could make a payment to the firm not to locate there, which would not exceed the environmental cost caused by the firm. If the firm locates in town A, it gets an *exclusionary* payment from town B of $20; if the firm locates in town B, it gets a $10 payment from town A. With exclusionary payments, locating in town A would also yield the lowest total production cost (net of exclusionary payment).

	Town A	Town B
Firm production costs:	$15	$10
Town environmental costs:	$10	$20
Prod. costs + "compensation":	$25	$30
Prod. costs − "exclusionary":	−$5	$0

CAPITALIZATION AND THE INCIDENCE OF LOCAL TAXES AND SERVICES

In the discussion about how households select communities, we adopted the approach of Chapter 3 in which we assume that house prices fully reflect both the value of services received and taxes paid at different locations. This approach assumes perfect capitalization, and it hinges on an assumed high degree of mobility by households. But what if households, particularly over a shorter time period, are not free to move for some reason? In Chapter 9, for example, we discussed how the high transaction costs of buying a home might limit mobility. Will house prices still reflect the value of services and taxes in this case?

In the sections above, the households or firms who reside in a town benefit from the community's public services. We have assumed that these town residents also pay for the services they enjoy through their property taxes. With rental real estate, the legal liability for property taxes rests with the owner and not its occupant. This is true whether the occupant is residential or nonresidential. For rental real estate, there arises the complicated question of whether the beneficiary of town services (the tenant) is actually paying the taxes for what is consumed. Imagine a town composed exclusively of tenants (residents) who live in buildings owned exclusively by absentee owners. Since only town residents have the power of voting, why wouldn't the tenants decide to greatly expand public services, at the expense of landlords? Under what conditions could (or would) the property owners be able to raise tenant rents by the amount of the taxes necessary to finance the expansion of services?

The economic issue of who pays for taxes on property when the owner and occupant are different is referred to as the question of *tax incidence*. Figure 13.4 explores tax incidence for the property market in a particular town. On the horizontal axis is the stock of space or housing in the community, and the level of rent is on the vertical axis. The downward-sloping demand curve, D, represents how many households (or firms) would choose to live in the community, depending on the town's average rent. The assumption earlier in this chapter, and in Chapters 3 and 4, was that mobility is sufficient so that this demand curve should be very elastic (nearly horizontal). With many communities to choose from, higher (lower) rents in one town should lead to sharp reductions (increases) in demanded space.

The supply schedule, S, represents how much space property owners would choose to develop at given rent levels. Alternatively, the schedule depicts the cost of supplying a given amount of space to the market. In Chapter 10, however, we demonstrated that space supply is inherently a dynamic concept. In the short run, the supply of space is largely fixed, as the number of units or buildings in any market declines only very slowly through depreciation or scrappage. Even the upward expansion of space takes time and is limited by the scarcity of land and its rising cost as the market grows. Thus, the notion in Figure 13.4 of a single supply schedule is perhaps overly simplistic. We might better think of a short-run supply schedule that is quite vertical (inelastic), as the stock is largely fixed and has trouble expanding quickly. In the longer run, the schedule is sometimes assumed to be more horizontal as the stock of space can expand or contract more elastically in response to changes in rent.

Chapter 13   Local Governments, Property Taxes, and Real Estate Markets   343

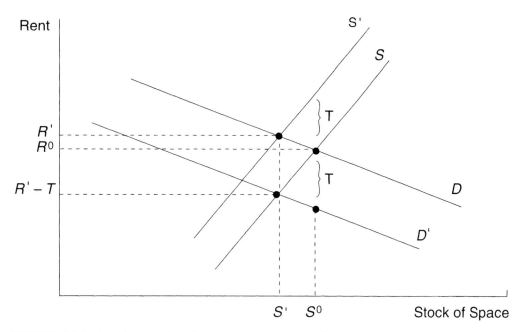

FIGURE 13.4 Incidence of real estate taxes on rental property.

Initially, the rental property market in this town can be assumed to be in long-run equilibrium at the point (S^0, R^0). This means that at the rent level R^0, and given the level of services in the town, S^0 amount of space is demanded. We now imagine that state aid suddenly contracts (for this town alone) by an amount equal to T per unit of space. The town can either raise property taxes by this amount (and leave services intact), or cut services by T and leave taxes unchanged.

If services remain fixed while taxes rise, then the cost of supplying space has risen by the amount of the tax increase, T. This shifts the space cost or supply schedule up to S', with a new equilibrium rent at R'. The rent actually received by the landlord moves from R^0 to $R' - T$, and this eventually causes a decline in the operational stock from S^0 to S'. The share of the tax increase that is accounted for by the upward movement of tenant rents, $(R' - R^0)/T$, is called the *incidence* of the tax that is paid for by tenants. Clearly this share will be small when demand is horizontal (elastic with respect to rents) while supply is inelastic (a vertical schedule). As a result, the tax is capitalized into the value of the property, which means that the owner pays the tax. This is the capitalization assumption that was made in earlier chapters. If supply is elastic, however, while demand is for some reason captive or inelastic, then capitalization will be incomplete and the owner can pass a significant portion of the tax to the tenant.

If taxes remain fixed while services fall (by an amount T), then the demand schedule must shift down by the tenant valuation of this loss in services. Assuming that services are valued at their cost, the demand schedule would shift down to D' by the amount T. In this case, however, the difference between gross and net rents has not been disturbed—both are lower by T. If supply is inelastic, however, and eventually contracts from S^0 to S', there is a partial recovery in rents. The ultimate equilibrium in either case is the same, as long as services are valued by tenants at their cost of provision.

The reader might reasonably question why in the very long run the supply schedule for space is not close to horizontal (perfectly elastic). Why would any landlord supply space at a lower rent than was obtainable elsewhere in other towns? Were this to be the case, the full long-run incidence of the tax would always be carried by tenants. The complete answer to the issue of long-run tax incidence involves a more complicated model that separately considers the capital and land inputs that are necessary to provide housing or commercial space. In the long run, the supply of capital is highly mobile (between towns), whereas the supply of land is almost, by definition, fixed. Thus, if higher taxes cause landlords to abandon (and not replace) their structures, the demand for land shifts and its price falls. With lower land prices, development can then profitably resume.

With this theory, the long-run incidence of the tax increase always lies with landowners, not tenants. This is consistent with the view in Chapter 3 that eventually the land market fully capitalizes locational advantage. With a highly elastic long-run demand curve, the rent for space in one community will always reflect only the valuation (by tenants) of the services they receive. It is the price of land that will eventually absorb the cost of providing those services. If the cost of provision and the value of the benefits received move with each other dollar for dollar, then tenants will pay for the services they receive. It is when cost and value move differently that landlords may receive a windfall gain or loss. If two towns have identical public services, but one receives significantly more state aid or has a sizeable base of taxable commercial property, then its lower taxes will be reflected in higher land prices. Rents, however, will be the same in the two communities. If the "fortunate" town opts to spend more on services, leaving taxes the same, then rents will be higher, and this (rather than lower taxes) will generate greater land prices.

SUBURBAN COMPETITION, TAXES, AND THE PLIGHT OF CENTRAL CITIES

The information in Table 13.3 illustrates a common problem that has plagued all major metropolitan areas of the U.S. during the last half-century. Sparked by a decaying housing stock and zoning constraints in adjoining suburban communities, lower-income households have been able to afford housing only in inner cities. Once concentrated there, the "need" for public services becomes especially acute. Greater crime, the need for special education programs, and social services all place great strains on central-city budgets. City governments find themselves "between a rock and a hard place." To meet these services in a manner that is even partially comparable to that of the suburbs will require greater expense, and, hence, higher taxes. These taxes, in turn, will lower property values. The alternative is to leave taxes at competitive levels, but allow services to decay. This will also lead to lower property values and also possibly exacerbate the city's difficult social problems.

The dilemma creates a vicious cycle. A declining real estate market only serves to attract or maintain the city's lower-income population and its resulting demands on public services. There is no way to strengthen the real estate market and attract a greater mix of households into an inner city without simultaneously lowering taxes, improving services, and solving city social problems. Two sources of assistance to cities have been discussed in this chapter: grants from state or federal governments and the tax subsidies that come from the city's commercial land uses.

Chapters 5 and 6 suggest that central cities may be in danger of losing the commercial land uses that for so long have helped finance their necessary services. Many manufacturers have already left for cheaper suburban land, while retailers are moving out to be nearer the greater purchasing power of suburban households. In the last decade, there has been a tendency for service firms, once centralized in inner city CBDs, also to cluster in newer suburban subcenters. Unless this loss of employment and the resulting erosion of inner-city tax bases is reversed, America's central cities increasingly will be forced to depend on higher-level governments for their financial viability.

SUMMARY

In this chapter, we examined several important connections between the real estate market of a metropolitan area and local governments. Not only do the taxes and services of local governments influence the locational choice of firms and households, but the impact this has on property prices greatly affects the financial resources of local governments.

- In the U.S., local governments provide most of our direct public services. In addition to assistance from states and the federal government, the property tax is the major source of local revenue to provide these services.

- Within metropolitan areas, suburbs, with their wealthier residents, tend to have similar total expenditure budgets as inner cities with poorer households. Greater assistance from state and federal governments, together with an extensive non-residential property tax base, are additional resources that enable inner cities to provide similar service expenditures with property tax rates comparable to the suburbs. The greater density and social problems of inner cities dictate a different mix of services and impact the quality of services obtained from comparable spending.

- Local governments face strong financial incentives to regulate new development so that the combination of a project's environmental impact and its use of public services is more than offset by its tax payments. Zoning laws are used by local governments to achieve this kind of fiscal surplus.

- In a market equilibrium, the housing market tends to sort households by income level. Thus, the existence of communities with different income levels is a natural outcome of a competitive housing market. In the long run, however, this pattern often would not be sustainable without imposing zoning restrictions. Minimum lot size zoning, for examine, can block the development of higher density housing that would enable lower income households to live in more affluent towns.

REFERENCES AND ADDITIONAL READINGS

General

MUSGRAVE, PEGGY B., AND RICHARD A. MUSGRAVE. *Public Finance in Theory and Practice*. New York: McGraw-Hill, 1989.

Governments and Public Services

LADD, HELEN, AND FRED DOOLITTLE. "Who Should Take Care of Poor People?" *National Tax Journal* 35, 3 (September 1982): 323–336.

OATES, WALLACE E. *Fiscal Federalism*. New York: Harcourt, Brace, Jovanovich, 1972.

U.S. DEPARTMENT OF COMMERCE. *Census of Governments*. Washington, DC: U.S. Department of Commerce, 1982, 1987, 1992.

Local Governments and Property Taxes in Metropolitan Areas

FELDSTEIN, MARTIN S. "Wealth Neutrality and Local Choice in Public Education." *American Economic Review* 65, 1 (March, 1975): 75–89.

GRAMLICH, EDWARD M. "Intergovernmental Grants: A Review of the Empirical Evidence." pp. 219–239, in *Political Economy of Fiscal Federalism,* ed. Wallace E. Oates. Lexington: 1977.

GRAMLICH, EDWARD M., AND DANIEL L. RUBINFELD. "Micro Estimates of Public Spending Demand Functions and Tests of the Tiebout and Median-Voter Hypotheses." *Journal of Political Economy* 90, 3 (1982): 536–560.

LADD, HELEN F. "Local Education Expenditures, Fiscal Capacity, and the Composition of the Property Tax Base." *National Tax Journal* 28, 2 (June 1975): 145–158.

MUELLER, DENNIS C. "Public Choice: A Survey." *Journal of Economic Literature* 14, 2 (June 1976): 395–433.

Household Location and Community Stratification

TIEBOUT, C. "A Pure Theory of Local Public Expenditure." *Journal of Political Economy* 64 (October 1956): 416–424.

WHEATON, WILLIAM C. "Land Capitalization, Tiebout Mobility and the Role of Zoning Regulations." *Journal of Urban Economics,* 34 2 (1993).

YINGER, JOHN. "Capitalization and the Theory of Local Public Finance." *Journal of Political Economy* 90, 5 (1982): 917–943.

Zoning and the Fiscal Impacts of Residential Development

HANUSHEK, ERIC A. "The Economics of Schooling: Production and Efficiency in the Public Schools." *Journal of Economic Literature* 24, 3 (1986): 1141–1177.

KEMPER, P., AND J. QUIGLEY. *The Economics of Refuse Collection.* Cambridge, MA: Ballinger Press, 1976.

SCHWAB, ROBERT M., AND ERNEST M. ZAMPELLI. "Disentangling the Demand Function from the Production Function for Local Public Services: The Case of Public Safety." *Journal of Public Economics* 33, 2 (1987): 245–260.

WHITE, M. "Fiscal Zoning in Fragmented Metropolitan Areas," in *Fiscal Zoning and Land Use Controls,* ed. Mills and Oates. Lexington, MA: D. C. Heath, 1975.

The Fiscal Costs and Benefits of Nonresidential Development

COASE, RONALD H. "The Problem of Social Cost." *The Journal of Law and Economics* (October 1960).

FISCHEL, W. "Fiscal and Environmental Considerations in the Location of Firms," in *Fiscal Zoning and Land Use Controls,* ed. Mills and Oates. Lexington, MA: D. C. Heath, 1975.

Capitalization and the Incidence of Local Taxes and Services

DUSANSKY, RICHARD, MELVIN INGBER, AND NICHOLAS KARATJAS. "The Impact of Property Taxation on Housing Values and Rents." *Journal of Urban Economics* 10, 2 (1981): 240–255.

MIESZKOWSKI, PETER. "The Property Tax: An Excise Tax or a Profits Tax?" *Journal of Public Economics* 1 (1972): 73–96.

OATES, WALLACE E. "The Effects of Property Taxes and Local Public Spending on Property Values: An Empirical Study of Tax Capitalization and the Tiebout Hypothesis." *Journal of Political Economy* 77, 6 (1969): 957–971.

WHEATON, WILLIAM C. "The Incidence of Inter-Jurisdictional Differences in Commercial Property Taxes." *National Tax Journal* 37, 4 (1984): 515–527.

Suburban Competition, Taxes, and the Plight of Central Cities

BRADFORD, DAVID F., AND HARRY H. KELEJIAN. "An Econometric Model of the Flight to the Suburbs." *Journal of Political Economy* 81, 3 (1973): 566–589.

CHAPTER 14

PUBLIC GOODS, EXTERNALITIES, AND DEVELOPMENT REGULATION

The quality of the urban environment often is more than simply the sum of the qualities of each individual parcel of land that makes up that environment. The quality of urban life is influenced by the overall aesthetics of the physical environment including the architectural compatibility of buildings in the community and the use and design of public spaces. Environmental conditions such as air and water quality and the treatment and disposal of waste are also important determinants of the livability of cities. Why do some communities provide a high quality of life while others do not?

In this chapter, we argue that quality of life depends on two important economic issues which must be acknowledged and appropriately managed. First, there exists a wide range of public goods which create collective enjoyment for all property owners. Being collectively enjoyed rather than individually consumed, these public goods are difficult to provide when individual property owners act independently. Thus, the individual decision making that characterizes private land markets does not work well for such goods. Institutional mechanisms are often necessary for owners to act cooperatively in determining what public goods ought to be provided and how they should be financed.

A second distinctive feature of real estate is that the independent actions of nearby property owners can have a dramatic impact on the value of a specific property. In other words, the real estate fortunes of one property owner are critically linked to the actions of others. This is a classic example of what economists call externalities—the action of one individual results in external costs or benefits to another individual. This interdependence between real estate sites can lead to fundamental coordination problems among owners:

all owners might be better off by acting in a certain way, but none has an individual incentive to do so. In an attempt to remedy this coordination problem, local governments have developed mechanisms for interfering with private property decisions. The most common of these is zoning laws. The land market, however, has also evolved at least some partial remedies for externalities. Privately written and enforced restrictive contracts or covenants often can coordinate the actions of individual property owners. Furthermore, when land is owned and developed simply at a larger scale, certain problems of coordination become better internalized or controlled.

In this chapter, we present a number of simple economic models that illustrate this class of problems and suggest a number of alternative solutions. Many of these remedies can involve governmental interference in the land market, suggesting that public planning has an important role to play in securing private interests. To illustrate the influence of public goods and external effects on the land market, we begin by illustrating some examples of how important these can be in determining property values.

PROPERTY VALUES AND PUBLIC AMENITIES

In Chapters 3 to 5, we demonstrated that market equilibrium and the indifference principle can help to uncover the value that consumers place on housing attributes, location, and commuting. In Chapter 4, we presented hedonic pricing models that provided estimates of the value placed on specific attributes of a house, including location. This same approach has been used often in recent years to obtain estimates of the value that consumers place on public goods or amenities. The fundamental principle is the same: if markets are in equilibrium, the value of otherwise identical housing or land in a location that offers more amenities should be priced just high enough to make buyers indifferent; lower prices in areas with poor amenities should just compensate buyers. Let's look at some specific examples.

Certain uses of land such as airports and heavy industrial plants are known to produce noise and air pollution as part of their normal operation. Since the early 1970s, economists have studied the impact that such facilities have on nearby property values (e.g., Mieszkowski and Saper 1978, Nelson 1978, and Smith 1978). In general, this research suggests that poor air quality can reduce residential property values by roughly 15 percent. Similarly, moderate noise under flight paths has been shown to reduce housing values by 5 to 10 percent, whereas more severe noise nearer to airports has a 20 to 30 percent negative impact. Grether and Mieszkowski (1980) found that residential property values increase with greater distance from disruptive land uses.

The siting of waste facilities often presents a problem because residents fear health risks and a potential negative impact on their property values. Kohlhase (1991) examined the impact on property values when the Environmental Protection Agency (EPA) places a toxic waste site on the Superfund list, meaning that the site becomes a federal priority for clean up efforts. Using data from Houston, she estimated that property values within a 6.2 mile radius of the site were decreased by as much as $3,310 for each mile closer to the site following the EPA announcement.

Publicly provided land uses, such as highways and open space, can also create external effects on nearby sites. Highways, for example, impact the land market in two ways. As part of a transportation network, highways increase property values by providing accessibility. At the same time, sites in close proximity to highways are exposed to greater noise and air pollution, which, according to Waddell, Berry, and Hoch (1993), can depress adjacent property values by 5 to 10 percent. Households want access to highways, but they don't want to be so close that they notice the noise and poor air quality when they are at home. The public preservation of land as open space likewise has two impacts. By reducing the supply of developable land, open space can raise surrounding land prices, as discussed in Chapter 3. Proximity to open space, however, also is a distinct public benefit to nearby private landowners. Frech and Lafferty (1984) found both of these effects in analyzing the impact of the California Coastal Commission on property values near the coast. The California Coastal Commission could veto any development within 1,000 yards of the high tide line as part of a policy to keep the land open for public use. Frech and Lafferty estimated that the Commission's control over development increased property values on the coast by 4 percent as a result of the reduced land supply and an additional 4 to 9 percent from increasing amenities.

On a more local level, there is growing evidence that the design of buildings and overall manner in which land is developed can significantly impact property value. There is clear evidence that households are willing to pay price premiums for houses of different architectural styles (Asabere, Hachey, and Grubaugh 1989). Vandell and Lane (1989) indicate that firms also seem willing to pay higher rents to occupy buildings with good architectural design as judged by professional panels. The design of one's building, however, is not only a private good to the occupant, but also a public good to the immediate environment. Are consumers willing to pay more to have *other* houses designed or laid out in a particular manner? Here, the results are new, but quite suggestive. Asabere (1990) found that a winding street/cul-de-sac layout in subdivisions, which creates visual diversity and green space, increases property prices by 25 percent over a simple grid layout. Several studies of house prices in historic districts where facades are strictly regulated also indicate that consumers value architectural compatibility and are willing to pay a price premium for it in their neighborhoods (Ford 1989).

Thus, there is substantial empirical evidence that the value of each particular site depends not just on its own intrinsic characteristics, but is also strongly influenced by the uses that occur on other nearby sites, the overall design of the neighborhood, and by the way streets, infrastructure, and open space are provided throughout the community.

PUBLIC AMENITIES AND FREE RIDERS

The problems associated with providing public amenities can be seen by considering the following simple example. Suppose a neighborhood has n individual property owners with identical lots that are already developed and one centrally located lot that is undeveloped. Each owner contemplates the development of the one remaining lot and decides that leaving the lot undeveloped as open space would increase the value of their property

Chapter 14   Public Goods, Externalities, and Development Regulation   351

by $MV (the marginal value of having the open lot). In effect, MV represents the increase in house value to each of the n property owners that comes from having adjacent open space. The market value of the lot if it were sold for private development is $p. To preserve the land for open space will require that it be purchased. We will assume that the price of the land exceeds its private value as open space to any one individual ($p > MV$), but that the aggregate or collective value of having the land remain open might justify its purchase ($p < nMV$). Two conclusions can be drawn from the facts in this example:

1. No individual owner will unilaterally purchase the lot for use as open space.
2. If the group were to agree to purchase the lot jointly, with individual owners contributing p/n, each owner would seek to abandon the group, allowing the others to purchase and split the cost (as long as $p > MV$).

Thus, there is a fundamental divergence between short-run individual interest and the longer-run collective good. This divergence results from three features of this simple example. First, we have assumed that the benefit of preserving the remaining lot is *nonexcludable*—none of the n property owners can be denied the advantage of the open space. Second, the benefit to each property owner of leaving the land open is *nonexhaustible*—it does not depend on how many owners share in the expense of acquisition. Finally, we have not introduced any contractual, legal, or institutional mechanism that *enforces participation* by all n property owners in the decision.

Consider the following illustration of this last point. Suppose all owners of the n lots were part of a majority-rule government that could propose only a "take it or leave it" vote with *all* owners required to pay p/n if the acquisition passed. Given the values of MV and p ($p > MV$) and the homogeneity of open space valuations, the vote would be unanimous in favor of acquisition. Of course, this would not work if owners could be individually excluded from the acquisition decision and cost. The nature of this public amenity problem is that each owner hopes to *free ride* on others. Without mandatory participation, it is difficult, if not impossible, to get the n members to participate in the common effort.

It is important to point out that this decision about open space would be made very differently if done prior to the sale of the n lots to individual owners. Consider the decision faced originally by a single owner-developer of $n + 1$ lots. If only n lots are developed and one left open, then the value of the n lots will increase by nMV, assuming the market would have valued open space the same then as the current owners do now; the proceeds lost from not developing the remaining lot are only p. Since $p < nMV$, the single developer-owner would clearly decide to keep the lot vacant. This example raises the broader question of exactly how much open space should be included in a development.

Consider a slightly more complicated example in which some agent has the power to require property owners to participate. We will again assume that there are n owners of existing developed 1-acre lots, who now face the possibility of acquiring any amount of adjacent land for open space. Let's further assume that the owners are divided into two groups with quite different views about open space. Suppose $n_1 < n$ owners value open space highly and feel that each acre of open space acquired (A) is worth $MV_1(A)$ to them.

With the law of diminishing marginal utility, we will expect that MV_1 declines with more A, which means that the value of additional open space is less as the amount of open space in the development increases. The remaining owners $n_2 = n - n_1$ have open space valuations of $MV_2(A)$, which are lower than those of the first group. Thus, $MV_2(A) < MV_1(A)$ for all ranges of A. Finally, the market value of a lot for private development, again, is p, which is the price that will have to be paid to acquire the adjacent land.

What is in the collective interest of all n owners? For each additional acre of open space purchased, the total benefit to all is simply the aggregate benefit to both types of owners: $n_1 MV_1(A) + n_2 MV_2(A)$. This total marginal benefit declines as more A is acquired. The collective interest of all is highest when the total marginal benefit of additional acreage just equals the marginal cost of acquisition (p).[1] Thus, the net value to all owners will be maximized with a purchase of open space acreage (A^*) such that:

$$n_1 MV_1(A^*) + n_2 MV_2(A^*) = p, \text{ or, } \left(\frac{n_1}{n}\right) MV_1(A^*) + \left(\frac{n_2}{n}\right) MV_2(A^*) = \frac{p}{n} \quad (14.1)$$

The second part of Equation (14.1) defines the optimal purchase of open space as occurring where the *weighted average* valuation of additional open space by the two types of households equals the per-household share of the cost of acquiring additional land.

While this ideal solution to the acquisition of open space is easy to define in principle, it is difficult to imagine a process by which it can be realized. To begin with, each individual property owner (of either type) would still like to free-ride or opt out of the group acquisition, thereby saving the cost (p/n) while still reaping the benefits of the nonexcludable, nonexhaustible open space. If we could enforce participation, we would have the additional problem of *social choice*—getting the two groups to agree on what action to take.

Suppose that all of the n property owners are required to participate in a collective decision and that all will be required to pay an even share of the amount of open space the group decides to acquire. In effect, we are requiring complete participation by all in a social choice process with the power to enforce the group's decision. Within this institutional mechanism, we ask what level of open space acquisition would each type of household like the group as a whole to undertake. With a unit acquisition cost to each household of (p/n), the level of open space that each household would prefer that the group select (A_1^*, A_2^*) will be such that its own marginal benefit equals its cost share:

$$MV_1(A_1^*) = \frac{p}{n}, \quad MV_2(A_2^*) = \frac{p}{n} \quad (14.2)$$

In Figure 14.1, we depict the three solutions (A^*, A_1^*, A_2^*). Each occurs at a level of open space (A) at which the marginal benefit schedule intersects the horizontal unit cost line. Of course, since the first household type values open space more than the second, its marginal benefit curve, $MV_1(A)$, is to the right of the second household type's

---

[1] Rational owners would seek to acquire that level of open space at which the total value to them net of acquisition cost is maximized. As discussed in Chapter 4, this occurs at that level of open space at which marginal benefits (the MV functions) equal marginal costs (p). At open space levels less than this, marginal benefits exceed costs, so further purchases are warranted. With more open space, the net gains are negative.

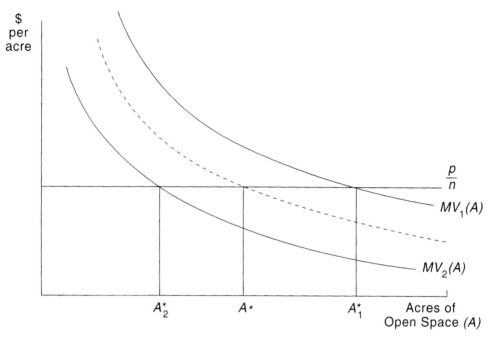

FIGURE 14.1 Social choice with two household types.

The dashed line represents the weighted average of open space valuations $MV_1(A)$ and $MV_2(A)$.

curve, $MV_2(A)$. Hence, the preferred outcome for group 1, A_1^*, is greater than A_2^*. We have defined the optimal amount of open space as A^*, a point at which the weighted average of the benefit curves for the two household types (the dashed line in Figure 14.1) intersects the cost line (p/n).

It is important to note that if the collectively optimal level of open space is somehow selected, each group of households would still prefer a different outcome: the 2s would want less and the 1s more. Such conflict is inherent in collective choice problems in which the "best" solution may not be preferred by anyone.

While having determined what each type of household would prefer to select, we still need to specify a process for arriving at a group decision. The most common mechanism used in such collective choice problems is voting. If a majority rule vote is adopted, then the group would select either A_1^* or A_2^*, depending on which group has the most members (whether n_1 is greater or less than n_2). Thus, direct voting normally will not yield the open space policy that is in the best collective interest of the group.[2]

---

[2]Other social choice processes have often been suggested by economists. For example, consider a binding mechanism that requires unanimous support but in which votes can be bought and sold. To see how this would work, imagine the group as a whole considering the point A^* as opposed to A_2^*. Only the 1s favor this change (since their preferred level is greater than A_2^*). The n_1 households of type 1 could all contribute funds equal to their incremental gain and then give $1/n_2$ of this amount to each of the type 2 households. Since A^* is defined as the point at which the weighted average gains are maximized, each group would be better off. In effect, the 1s have bought the support of the 2s.

It is important to point out that in most cases, any level of open space acquisition between A_1^* and A_2^* makes the property owners as a whole better off than having no open space at all. In this sense, even an imperfectly operating group decision process is likely to be better than simply leaving the n property owners alone to try and bargain in private. With the free-rider problem present, voluntary cooperation becomes more difficult, and private decision making will often fail to provide any level of public amenities, particularly when the number of property owners is large.

We should point out again that the problem of open space acquisition would, in principle, be far easier to handle by an original single developer-owner of the lots. In that case, we might assume that the overall market values adjacent open space at the average valuation of the two groups that will eventually purchase the lots, and that the owner knows this market value. As long as the aggregate value of the n lots owned by the developer can be increased by more than the cost of acquiring and preserving adjacent land, then the acquisition is in the developer's self-interest. This criteria is simply the same as Equation (14.1) for the optimal amount of open space (A^*).[3]

The kinds of public goods and amenities that we have illustrated in this section involve the creation of collective value on third-party land. Open space or parks, waterways, or sidewalks all occur on land outside of each owner's individual parcel. Often, individual actions on one's own property enhance or diminish the value of others' property.

EXTERNAL EFFECTS ACROSS PROPERTIES

Property owners are often interested in the actions of other property owners in their communities because those actions may directly impact their own properties or quality of life. For example, a homeowner may be justifiably concerned when an adjacent property is abandoned or permitted to deteriorate, because it is aesthetically unappealing and this may negatively impact the value of his property.

In Chapter 4, we argued that the density of development is an important attribute of a property to its occupant, and that, all else equal, households desire to live in structures of lower densities. With a demonstrated willingness-to-pay for lower-density development, profitable land development involves trading this off against the ability to put more houses on each parcel of land. Particularly in large urban areas, density takes on an additional dimension and becomes an important quality of life variable. In this setting, the density of a particular parcel not only affects its own value, but impacts the value of surrounding properties as well. When a neighborhood is dense, light is reduced, wind tunnels are created, and there is little public space. Older historic neighborhoods with four-story townhouses, such as the Back Bay area of Boston discussed in Chapter 4 and found in other cities as well, are often preferred to neighborhoods with rows of apartment

---

[3]If the buyers are representative of the market, the market average increase in lot value for an acre of adjacent open space would be $(n_1/n)MV_1 + (n_2/n)MV_2$. The owner would acquire open space until the aggregate value of his developed land net of acquisition cost for the adjacent land was maximized. This would occur when n times the market valuation equals the acquisition cost, as in Equation (14.1).

Chapter 14   Public Goods, Externalities, and Development Regulation

towers. This preference has as much to do with the atmosphere of the neighborhood (e.g., its openness and human scale) as it does with the private value of townhouses as opposed to apartment buildings. Current residents of these historic areas often band together and fight politically to oppose newer, denser development in order to preserve the character of the neighborhood. Surely this indicates that the neighborhood density of surrounding buildings has an "external" impact on each individual property. It also means that individual decisions about density can have broader ramifications that the developer may ignore. The conflict between the individual and the neighborhood can be resolved either cooperatively or individually, with quite different results.

To illustrate the distinction between individual and cooperative choices, let's return to the example of the Back Bay area of Boston presented in Chapter 4. Remember that this area of Boston is dominated by four-story townhouses with an occasional 8-to-12 story building. We defined the price per square foot of housing as $P = \alpha - \beta F$, where α is the collective value of all other locational and housing attributes that can affect the price per square foot of a house and β is the marginal reduction in value that occurs when the FAR of the building, F, increases. At what FAR will an individual owner develop his site? As we showed in Chapter 4, the developer will choose the FAR that maximizes the residual profit per square foot of land, defined as $p = F(P - C)$, where C is per-square-foot construction cost. Our innovation to the model here is to incorporate the loss in value to each property that results from denser development of the neighborhood. Let's define f as the FAR of the neighborhood (as distinct from individual property FAR, F) and γ as the incremental loss in value to each house with increased neighborhood density. The developer of any individual property, then, takes the neighborhood density as given and chooses that FAR, F, that maximizes p:[4]

$$p = (\alpha - \beta F - C - \gamma f)F$$

$$F = \frac{(\alpha - C - \gamma f)}{2\beta} \qquad (14.3)$$

Over time, as all developers act this way, the neighborhood FAR will begin to evolve towards that chosen by each developer. As each parcel is developed at F, neighborhood density, f, moves towards F. Thus, in the long run, $f = F$. Using $f = F$, we can define the long-run equilibrium level of density that will prevail when all property owners act individually (F^m):

$$F^m = \frac{\alpha - C}{2\beta + \gamma} \qquad (14.4)$$

---

[4]The residual profit per square foot of land development (p) equals the floor area profit multiplied by the development's FAR: $p = (\alpha - \beta F - C - \gamma f)F$. We find the F that maximizes p by setting the derivative $\partial p/\partial F$ equal to 0:

$$\partial p/\partial F = \alpha - 2\beta F - C - \gamma f = 0$$

Solving for F, we obtain:

$$F = \frac{\alpha - C - \gamma f}{2\beta}$$

At this level of density, we can also determine the value of land (p^m).[5]

$$p^m = \beta \left(\frac{\alpha - C}{2\beta + \gamma} \right)^2 \tag{14.5}$$

In Chapter 4, we estimated α at $222 per square foot and β at 1.48. To continue this numerical example, we assume for simplicity that construction costs are constant at $120 per square foot. If we assume a value of γ of $4 per square foot (the incremental loss in value for each house in the neighborhood as the neighborhood FAR increases), $F^m = 14.7$, considerably higher than the four-story brownstones in the area. When neighborhood concern over density is lower (i.e., lower γ), the neighborhood FAR and land prices will be higher. For example, in our Chapter 4 exercise, γ equalled 0, F^m was 17.5, and p^m was $1,068. With $\gamma = 4$, $F^m = 14.7$ and $p^m = \$318$ per square foot.

It should be clear in the example so far that while each property owner considers the external cost imposed on him by other property owners, each property owner is ignoring his external impact on others. What happens if, rather than having individual owners make density choices independently, these choices are made collectively? Suppose owners cooperate to choose a common FAR for their entire neighborhood, considering all of the costs incurred. In this case, they jointly select the density they want *both* for the neighborhood *and* for their individual properties. Assume that landowners are constructing a new neighborhood on vacant land and must decide on the density of all development. With cooperation, the neighborhood FAR gets defined in advance as equal to that of each property, $f = F$. As a result, the collectively optimal FAR, F^*, is that which maximizes:[6]

---

[5]We can determine land value, p^m, by using Equation (14.3):

$$p^m = (\alpha - \beta F - C - \gamma f)F$$

Substituting $f = F$ yields:

$$p^m = (\alpha - C)F - (\beta + \gamma)F^2$$

Substituting $F = F^m = \dfrac{\alpha - C}{2\beta + \gamma}$:

$$p^m = \frac{(2\beta + \gamma)(\alpha - C)^2 - (\beta + \gamma)(\alpha - C)^2}{(2\beta + \gamma)^2}$$

$$= \beta \left(\frac{\alpha - C}{2\beta + \gamma} \right)^2 = \beta (F^m)^2$$

[6]Here, cooperation means that we begin with $F = f$, so we maximize:

$$p = (\alpha - \beta F - C - \gamma F)F$$

Following footnote 4: $\partial p / \partial F = \alpha - 2\beta F - C - 2\gamma F = 0$

$$F^* = \frac{\alpha - C}{2(\beta + \gamma)}$$

Chapter 14 Public Goods, Externalities, and Development Regulation

$$p = (\alpha - \beta F - C - \gamma F)F$$

$$F^* = \frac{\alpha - C}{2(\beta + \gamma)} < F^m \qquad (14.6)$$

Clearly, cooperation leads to a lower density of development. Using the parameter values outlined above, $F^* = 9.3$. What is the impact on the value of land? Our expression for land value, p^*, becomes:[7]

$$p^* = \frac{(\alpha - C)^2}{4(\beta + \gamma)} > p^m \qquad (14.7)$$

Cooperation winds up yielding a higher value for land. Again using the parameter values outlined above, p^* equals $475 per square foot, considerably higher than the p^m value of $318 when there was no cooperation. In the long run, cooperative behavior will yield higher property values and is in the best interest of all parties.

As a practical matter, how are cooperative decisions made? There may be neighborhood or community associations that exert influence over certain aspects of development such as density. But more often, these issues are dealt with by local governments through land-use controls such as height restrictions, minimum setbacks, and open space requirements. Under the assumptions used in this model, there can be a lot gained from such regulations.

CONTRACTS, COOPERATION, AND GOVERNMENT REGULATION

How can we encourage individual lot owners to develop their parcels at densities and use architectural designs that are compatible with the community? How can we best prevent individual property owners from introducing an adverse use into an otherwise harmonious neighborhood? In seeking to remedy the externality problem discussed above, economists and lawyers have developed three general approaches. None is foolproof and the usefulness of each depends on the situation.

Private Bargaining with Contracts

Particularly when the number of participants is small, it has been argued that private agreements among property owners sometimes will work. While each owner may have

---

[7]Following footnote 5, we now determine land value, p^*, by substituting $F = F^* = \frac{\alpha - C}{2(\beta + \gamma)}$ into the equation for p in Equation (14.6):

$$p = (\alpha - C)\left(\frac{\alpha - C}{2(\beta + \gamma)}\right) - (\beta + \gamma)\left(\frac{\alpha - C}{2(\beta + \gamma)}\right)^2$$

$$= \frac{(\beta + \gamma)(\alpha - C)^2}{4(\beta + \gamma)^2}$$

$$= \frac{(\alpha - C)^2}{4(\beta + \gamma)}$$

an incentive to shirk, through education and enlightenment, owners may agree to act in the group's interest *if* the others do so as well. To ensure this, the group can attempt to agree on a contract or accept a common deed restriction on their properties. Either will provide both the initial commitment and the ongoing enforcement that is necessary to ensure the cooperative outcome. This voluntary approach to the externality problem is frequently attributed to the University of Chicago School of Economics.

Private contracts or deed restrictions are quite common in a few American cities, generally those with little or no government land-use regulations. Such deed restrictions frequently require minimal home maintenance, prevent obtrusive activities, and limit any change in land use. Any individual owner might find such restrictions privately undesirable but recognizes that all will be better off with them. For example, Speyer (1989) found that Houston subdivisions containing such restrictions have higher property values than those with no controls, providing evidence that cooperative solutions can indeed be superior.

The problem with private contracts is that when the number of participants is large, they rarely work. In Houston, for example, deed covenants most frequently are placed on properties at the time of development when there is only a single owner-developer. To continue to remain valid, courts often require that deed covenants be resigned by the current occupants after a number of years. Researchers have documented the difficulty of getting a large number of property owners to recommit to the original agreement that was imposed by a single-minded developer (see Siegan 1972).

Larger Scale Developments

The problem with public goods is caused by having multiple owners of a common resource. With externalities, the problem is getting multiple owners to acknowledge the economic links among their properties. Both of these problems cease to exist when a single owner is making decisions. This suggests that when land is developed at a larger scale, it is more likely that compatible design, landscaping, infrastructure, or other public goods will be provided, assuming that these features really do add to the net collective value of the property being developed.

There are two problems with relying on a larger scale of development. First, there are limits to this solution. It is sometimes difficult both to assemble large tracts of land and to acquire the capital resources necessary for such large-scale development. Second, this solution works only to internalize externalities and provide initial public goods at the time of development. What about subsequent changes in market demand? How is the ongoing management of these problems to be handled after the land is subdivided, developed, and sold to many individual owners?

Government Policy

Many economists and planners argue that public goods and the management of external effects among properties rightly belong in the domain of the public sector through local

Chapter 14 Public Goods, Externalities, and Development Regulation

governments. Two types of public policies are often advocated: regulation and economic incentives.

One solution to the public good–externality problem would be for some public entity simply to require that individual property owners or developers behave in the collective interest. In principle, the cooperative solution in the examples discussed above could become dictated by law. Thus, subdivision regulations frequently require certain levels of infrastructure, landscaping, density, and house layout, and zoning laws limit the range of uses allowed initially on property as well as future alterations. Such laws can be viewed as trying to ensure that minimum public goods are provided and that negative use externalities among property owners do not occur. Of course, this view of regulation assumes that the regulating authority has the information necessary (e.g., about individual or market valuations) to make a reasonable estimate of the collective solution. It is not at all clear that such information is widely known, particularly about the value of many types of externalities and public goods.

A second form of government intervention is to have some public authority tax undesirable activity and financially assist or subsidize behavior that is in the collective interest. Thus, in the externality example above, the private individual developer might be taxed for a FAR level above the level chosen by the neighborhood. In principle, there is a tax rate which will be sufficient to induce individuals to build at the cooperative FAR level even if individuals act in their own self-interest.[8] In practice, during the 1980s some U.S. cities created linkage programs under which developers were permitted to build above the FAR limits set by the city if they paid a surcharge. Often, the revenues from the surcharge were earmarked for affordable housing or other community development projects. Alternatively, tax credits have been used widely to encourage development that creates a positive externality, such as restoring properties of historic importance. Of course, determining the proper tax or credit again requires that a public agency be able to determine how much individuals value such public amenities.

In the U.S., the regulatory approach is far more prevalent than the use of financial incentives. Even here, the government limits its regulations primarily to restricting use and requiring infrastructure provision. There is virtually no public design review power like that found in some European countries. It has been argued that in the U.S. there is little consensus about which public goods should be provided or which externalities should be addressed by intervention. As a result, it may be reasonable for a representative government to take a more cautious approach and intervene only with minimal (and hence more widely accepted) regulations.

---

[8]The tax on FAR would be equal to the social impact of the higher FAR ($-\gamma F$). Thus, individuals would not develop their parcels to the point where private benefits equal cost, but rather to where private benefits equal cost plus the tax.

HISTORY, EXTERNALITIES, AND LAND-USE PATTERNS

Sometimes external economic impacts occur not only across properties within neighborhoods, but between development at one location in a city and land throughout the remainder of the metropolitan area. When these broader impacts are not fully internalized by the private land market, then private development decisions may need to be planned, guided, or regulated in order to yield outcomes that are in the collective interest. The incompatibility between major land uses is a widespread issue that can affect not only local property values but may also lead a private land market into a regional development pattern that is distinctly suboptimal and determined more by history than by current economic forces.

To illustrate this problem, let's again return to a simple, single-centered city with two uses, residential and industrial, much like the model discussed at the beginning of Chapter 5. To keep matters simple, we assume that both uses occupy 1 acre of land per household or industrial firm. Further, both uses incur travel costs to the city center—residents for commuting and firms to acquire materials and ship products. Annual commuting costs reduce the residential land rent gradient by $-k_H$ per mile, whereas shipping costs reduce the industrial rent gradient by $-k_I$ per mile. The central land rents for each use are r_H, r_I.

Our innovation to this model is to assume that industrial noise and pollution create an annual cost for residents that decreases with greater distance between households and industrial firms. Thus, residential land rents depend not only negatively on distance to the urban center but also positively on the distance between a residence and the nearest industrial use. The annual value that households place on each mile of separation will be γ, and, for the moment, we may assume that the two uses occupy separate areas of the city with a boundary between them occurring at a distance of m from the city center. The two gradients for land rent, therefore, are:

$$\begin{aligned} r_I(d) &= r_I - k_I d \\ r_H(d) &= r_H - k_H d + |m - d|\gamma \end{aligned} \quad (14.8)$$

In Equation (14.8), it is important to note that residential land rents depend on the absolute value of the difference $m - d$. When residents live closer to the center than industries, their rents decrease with distance from the center due to two forces: commuting to the center and proximity to industries. The farther from the center a resident is located, the closer she comes to the nearest offending industry. In this case, the slope of residential land rents (with respect to d) is $-[k_H + \gamma]$. On the other hand, when residents live beyond industries, these two forces act in opposite directions; greater distance reduces land rents because of commuting and increases them as distance generates greater separation. In this case, the residential land rent gradient has a slope of $-[k_H - \gamma]$.

To make this model more realistic, we may assume that residential commuting costs are more important than firm shipping costs ($k_H > k_I$), as Chapter 5 demonstrated was likely to be the case in modern cities. We also assume that the incremental externality cost is large relative to commuting costs, so much so that $\gamma > [k_H - k_I]$. With these parameters, our city has *two* land market equilibria as shown in Figure 14.2.

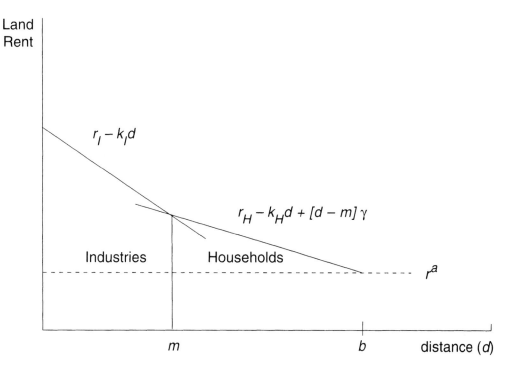

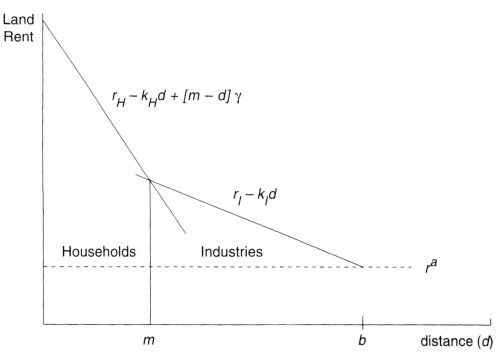

FIGURE 14.2 Alternative locational equilibria with residential and industrial uses.

Two market equilibria exist because being separate from each other is more important to the two uses than the absolute location pattern by which that separation occurs (center versus periphery locations). Even though residents prefer central locations more than industries do, their *net* preference for centrality *given that industries are already located there* is less. As a result, a location pattern in which industries occupy central sites becomes a stable, sustainable market equilibrium. Of course, if industries are already located in the more peripheral locations, then residents will clearly outbid them for central sites, since centrality now offers not only less commuting, but freedom from noise and pollution as well.

One of these market solutions is clearly preferred to the other. From the point of view of separating land uses due to the externality placed on residents by firms, either equilibrium is equally satisfactory. However, firms do not value centrality as much as residents do, which means that the second solution in Figure 14.2 is preferred. In fact, if we were to calculate the aggregate value of land rent in the two solutions, we would also find that it is larger in the second equilibrium.[9] This difference in the aggregate value of rent is illustrated in Figure 14.2, in which the total area under the rent gradients is greater in the second graph than in the first.

When markets have more than one equilibrium, we need to explain which one actually occurs and why. In many cases, history provides the answer. In Chapter 5, we argued that in the nineteenth century, industrial uses might well have valued access to some central transportation terminal more than residents, leading to the initial development of a central industrial district in many cities. In the twentieth century, however, industrial needs changed along with their rent gradients. In many cities, however, central waterfront locations are still occupied by industrial enterprises even though denser residential uses might offer higher rents than industries for such locations *if there were no other industries already there*. It is the externality that prevents residents *individually* from offering enough rent to begin the transition of central sites from industrial to residential use. In effect, the land market is, at least for a while, locked into the first solution in Figure 14.2 because of historical precedent. Economically, it would be more efficient and profitable to reverse the location pattern. However, rents are based on individuals and firms acting *unilaterally*. Thus, no market participant finds it individually advantageous to make the switch in location.

The existence of multiple market solutions also raises the broad issue of whether public sector intervention is needed. In the example above, market participants in the aggregate would be better off with the second solution even though no individual participant wishes to be the first to make the change. Several public policies could accomplish the transition from the first to the second equilibrium. A government or planning agency

---

[9] In the outer ring of development, the slope of industrial rents in the second equilibrium $(-k_I)$ is greater than the slope of residential rents in the first equilibrium solution $(-k_H + \gamma)$ because of our assumption about the magnitude of the externality. Therefore, at the boundary m, rents are higher in the second solution, whereas they are equal at the urban border, b. From the boundary inward, the slope of residential rents in the second solution $(-k_H - \gamma)$ is greater than industrial rents in the first $(-k_I)$, since $k_H > k_I$. As a result, land rent also is higher over the inner ring in the second solution.

Chapter 14   Public Goods, Externalities, and Development Regulation   363

might initially subsidize those residents that agreed to make the first move into the industrial areas or those firms that agreed to move outward. Alternatively, industries and households that remained in the inefficient pattern could be taxed or fined. Rezoning each part of the city for the alternative use might also accomplish the change. Once existing industrial plants or houses deteriorated, owners could only rebuild by relocating. Given the long life of structures, this approach could take a long time to accomplish the goal.

It is important to remember that public intervention in this example has not been necessary to ensure the separation of the two uses. Given the model's parameters, this will occur automatically in the private market. The public role here is to bring about a more efficient location pattern. The possibility that some form of central planning may be essential to proper market functioning can be further illustrated with the issue of traffic congestion.

CONGESTION EXTERNALITIES, REGIONAL PLANNING, AND THE LAND MARKET

Throughout this book, we have argued that the accessibility of the site is an important determinant of the value of a development. But suppose as the development occurs, the traffic generated dramatically decreases that original accessibility? More importantly, what if the development decreases (through greater congestion) the accessibility of other land in the area that was already developed or adjacent land that has yet to be developed? Should the development still occur at this location? Since increased traffic congestion commonly accompanies larger scale development, let's examine this important problem in more detail.

We begin with the most simple of our single-centered cities developed in Chapters 3 through 5. Let's make the city linear with some width, meaning that the city is developed on a long, narrow strip of land, and note location along this strip as distance d. The city is composed of identical households who work in the center (distance d_0) and live at a constant residential density $1/q$, where q represents the acres of land consumed per household. Our innovation to this model will be to assume that residents of the east side of the city (at distances $d > d_0$) use cars and a road network for commuting to the center, whereas residents on the west side (at distances $d < d_0$) use a rapid transit subway system.

The subway system on the west side has considerable excess capacity, as is frequently the case with transit systems. As a result, any number of commuters can travel at a fixed cost of k_w per mile per year. For households to be in locational equilibrium, land on the west side of the city will have a rent gradient that declines over distance with a slope of $-k_w/q$. Development on the west extends to d_w miles. On the east side, drivers using the road system experience some degree of congestion. The level of congestion increases with the number of road users, which depends directly on how far the city extends to the east (distance d_e). Thus, for those on the east side, the cost per mile of travel will not be constant. Transportation costs per mile will depend on the amount of development there, which means that k_e is a function of d_e, that is, $k_e(d_e)$. For locational equilibrium in the east, land rents must decrease from the center with a slope of $-k_e(d_e)/q$.

Given the difference in transportation technologies on the east and west sides and the resulting differences in commuting costs per mile, we expect that the land rent gradient on the east will have a different slope than the land rent gradient to the west. Let's explore further the east and west land rent gradients.

Beyond the development borders d_e and d_w, land is devoted to agricultural use that yields a land rent, r^a. The land rent gradients to the east, r_e, and the west, r_w, are:

$$r_e(d) = r^a + k_e(d_e)\left[\frac{d_e - d}{q}\right]$$

$$r_w(d) = r^a + k_w\left[\frac{d - d_w}{q}\right] \quad (14.9)$$

From Equations (14.9), we know that land rents at the east and west borders of the city, $r_e(d_e)$ and $r_w(d_w)$, are equal. At the borders where $d = d_e$ or $d = d_w$, the second term of both equations in (14.9) vanish and rents at both borders equal the agricultural land rent, r^a.

What do we know about land rents at the center of the city? In order for the land market to be in spatial equilibrium, land rents at the center must be equal $[r_e(d_0) = r_w(d_0)]$. The equality of rents at the center is a key condition. If land rents at the center were not equal, then a household or firm could be better off by making a slight move to the east or west where rents are lower. In Equations (14.9), land rents are equal at the center (d_0) only if total commuting expenses on the east and the west sides are equal. If the per-mile commuting costs vary because of the differences in transportation systems on the two sides of the city, total transportation expenses can only be the same if east and west borders of the city are at different distances from the center. This distance difference must offset the per-mile commuting costs variations between the east and the west. Figure 14.3 illustrates this asymmetric land market in which rents are equal at the center, and the eastern border is a greater distance from the center than the western border, yielding a flatter gradient in the east.

How do the east and west land rent gradients change as more development occurs? If the city is small, and, hence, the distance to both borders (d_w, d_e) is short, the slope of the east-side rent gradient would be quite flat since use of the road system would not be sufficient to cause congestion. In this case, the city would extend to the east much farther than to the west. As the city expands from population growth, the west-side rent gradient shifts proportionately outward and d_w increases, just as with the cities in Chapter 3. In the east, however, more development increases road use, congestion sets in, travel speeds fall, and the slope of the land rent gradient begins to steepen as auto commuting costs rise. As a result, the expansion of the east side of the city begins to slow.[10]

As d_e expands and extra vehicles are added to the road system, the expense of commuting at any given closer location, $k_e(d_e)[d_e - d]$, increases. As one more person develops land to the east, the commuting cost per mile for all other east-side residents is made

---

[10] For simplicity, we assume that the subway system to the west and the road to the east extend beyond the borders.

Chapter 14   Public Goods, Externalities, and Development Regulation

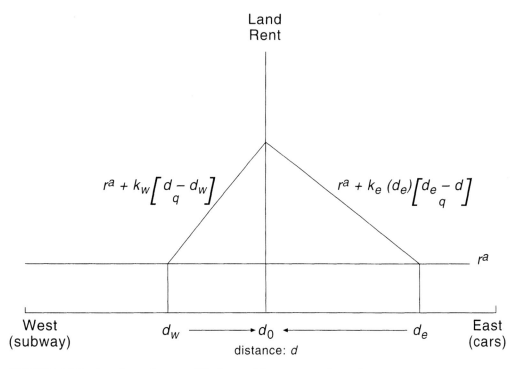

FIGURE 14.3 Land market equilibrium with two travel modes.

worse. On the west side, where k_w is fixed, this is not the case. Growth on the west side imposes no costs on existing west-side residents.

Consider the city to be in equilibrium as illustrated in Figure 14.3. Suppose that there is enough development on the east side so that there is some road congestion. The spatial equilibrium means that no individual can improve his situation by moving. However, suppose such a move would make others better off. In this model, the overall welfare of the city is determined by aggregate commuting expenditures. A city planner examining this situation could reduce aggregate commuting expenses and improve the city's welfare beyond that resulting from the equilibrium in Figure 14.3. The planner contemplates somehow moving a household from the east to the west, slightly expanding d_w and reducing d_e. The aggregate commuting expense incurred by the city's population will rise by $k_w d_w$ from the added trip on the west. In the east, one less trip will reduce aggregate commuting by $k_e(d_e)d_e$ *plus the savings to all the other east-side commuters who now have one less car to contend with on the roads*. The reduction in aggregate commuting expenses on the east is greater than the increase in the west, and thus this exchange would be in the interest of all. The household making the move is indifferent to living at either border as implied by the original spatial equilibrium. However, all the other residents of the east side will be better off.

Suppose the planner continues to make this exchange, moving residents from the east to the west, expanding d_w and contracting d_e. As these changes are made, the expense of commuting from the western edge grows, while that from the eastern fringe shrinks. Residents making the move are now personally worse off even though the remaining east-side residents are made better off. From the city's perspective, the moves should continue as long as the benefits to the remaining east-side residents exceed the costs to the individual making the move. When should the planner stop moving residents from the east to the west? Eventually, the west edge grows so much and the east contracts so much, that *the incremental resident making the move incurs losses that are greater than the gain for all the east-side residents that remain. At this point, the planner should stop making the switch since the city as a whole can be made no better off.*

In this example, the initial spatial equilibrium is reached with individual commuters considering only their own commuting costs, not the costs that they impose on other commuters by being on the road. What the city planner is doing by moving residents is considering the costs to all commuters. The problem with the city planner's solution is that it is not a market equilibrium. What we mean by this can be most easily seen by turning to Figure 14.4. If development of the west end is extended out beyond the market solution d_w to d_w^*, then for west-side households to be in locational equilibrium, land rents

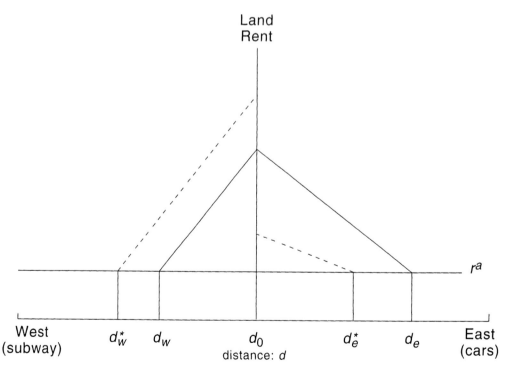

FIGURE 14.4 Market disequilibrium at planner's development solution.

will have to rise to the dashed line on the west side in the figure. On the other hand, with development on the east end curtailed, locational equilibrium among its residents will require both a lower and flatter land rent gradient. The gradient will be flatter because with less development on the east side, congestion will be less and the cost per mile of travel will be lower. With these land rents, eastern residents at the center pay far less than do western residents at the center. All residents on the east side therefore are better off than their west-side counterparts who therefore will want to move. Land rents which are set in the private market cannot maintain the city planner's more efficient development pattern.

In this example, the city planner correctly perceives that the overall welfare of the city is improved by minimizing transportation expenses. But how can this increase in efficiency be sustained in the private land market? Suppose that instead of the planner forcing households to move from east to west, commuters on the east side considered not only their commuting costs but the external costs that they impose on other drivers by being on the road. This could be done by having the city impose a congestion toll on each user of the road that exactly equals the costs that a commuter's use of the road imposes

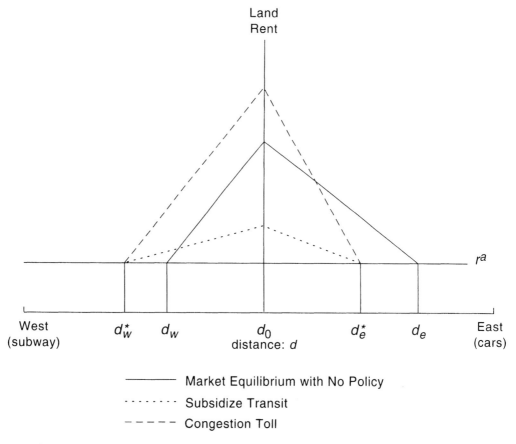

FIGURE 14.5 Policies to achieve market equilibrium at planner's development solution.

on other commuters. The toll revenues would be rebated to all residents. The congestion toll would force east-side commuters to pay the full costs of their travel by internalizing the externality that arises from their commuting.

What's the impact of this toll on the land rents that commuters are willing to pay? As shown in Figure 14.5, the increase in commuting costs as a result of the toll would increase the slope of the land rent gradient on the east side to the point at which east-side rents equaled west-side rents at the center. In the long run, there would be less growth on the east side with the toll in place than there would be without the toll, so the east boundary would be closer. The important point here is that with the toll, the land market would move to a new spatial equilibrium, with the same boundaries as the planner's solution.

There are alternative public interventions that also would lead to a land market equilibrium in which the borders match the planner's solution. For example, on the west side, the city could subsidize the public transit system, reducing transit costs for commuters. With this reduction in commuting costs, the land rent gradient on the west side will become flatter. With sufficient subsidy, it can be flattened to the point where west-side rents at the center are identical to those from the east. This transit subsidy solution is also illustrated in Figure 14.5. The reduction in transit costs could take the form of either a fare subsidy and/or an expansion of the system to provide uneconomically fast service. The gains to city residents from this policy of less expensive transit for west-side residents and less congestion for east-side residents could exceed the cost of the taxes needed to finance it.

Economists have long supported the implementation of congestion tolls over other approaches to solving congestion because this mechanism solves the problem by correctly pricing road use. Other policies can be less precise in correcting the problem. In our example, if the city instead subsidizes transit on the west side rather than charging the congestion toll on the east, then both the roads on the east and the subway on the west are incorrectly priced with the possible effect of encouraging more travel. Fuel taxes are often proposed as a method of dealing with congestion problems. But these taxes are blunt instruments since they tax fuel whether the travel occurs on a congested urban road or a rural uncongested road. The tax is also the same if the travel takes place during peak congestion times or at off-peak times. Congestion tolls that vary by time and location would force the private market to price correctly commuting by car.

The creation of congested transportation facilities is one of the most common problems in land development. The lesson of this simple example is that this congestion can require significant public intervention. The intervention not only alters the transportation system but can also redirect the entire pattern of development. Such government intervention, if appropriately done, can lead to significant improvements in the quality of urban life over that which results from an unregulated private market.

SUMMARY

In this chapter we discussed how certain economic goods and services are collectively enjoyed by a wider community of adjacent property owners. Public goods like open space and environmental quality can be highly valued by property owners, but must be provided collectively. Individual owners also contribute to the community environment through their own design and development decisions, creating additional economic externalities.

- Individual decisions about the provision of public goods can lead to a misallocation of resources. Providing the "right" level of public services often requires contractual arrangements, larger scale developments, or the formation of government or quasi-governmental organizations. Unregulated private markets generally fail to adequately account for public goods.

- In a similar manner, decisions about individual property development, such as density, can often be detrimental or beneficial to adjacent properties. Coordinated decisions made by a number of property owners often can lead to a better development plan. Such coordination, however, again requires some form of organization or institutional assistance outside of private market behavior.

- At the metropolitan level, longer-term land-use patterns also can lead to externalities which the private market ignores. The noise and environmental impact of large industrial districts or the congestion that follows new development are just two examples. Public planning offers the potential of controlling these externalities through, for example, the use of metropolitan-wide land-use regulations or infrastructure fees. In principle, such policies could lead to land-use configurations that improve urban living.

REFERENCES AND ADDITIONAL READINGS

ARNOTT, RICHARD, A. DE PALMA, AND R. LINDSEY. "A Structural Model of Peak Period Congestion." *American Economic Review* 83, 1 (1993): 161–178.

ASABERE, PAUL K. "The Value of a Neighborhood Street with Reference to the Cul-de-Sac." *Journal of Real Estate Finance and Economics* 3 (1990): 185–193.

ASABERE, PAUL K., GEORGE HACHEY, AND STEVEN GRUBAUGH. "Architecture, Historic Zoning, and the Value of Homes." *Journal of Real Estate Finance and Economics* 2 (1989): 181–195.

DOWNS, ANTHONY. *An Economic Theory of Democracy.* New York: Harper & Row, 1957.

FORD, DEBORAH ANN. "The Effect of Historic District Designation on Single-Family Home Prices." *AREUEA Journal* 17 (1989): 353–362.

FRECH III, H. E., AND RONALD N. LAFFERTY. "The Effect of the California Coastal Commission on Housing Prices." *Journal of Urban Economics* 16 (1984): 105–123.

GRETHER, DAVID M., AND PETER MIESZKOWSKI. "The Effects of Nonresidential Land Uses on the Prices of Adjacent Housing: Some Estimates of Proximity Effects." *Journal of Urban Economics* 8 (1980): 1–15.

KOHLHASE, JANET E. "The Impact of Toxic Waste Sites on Housing Values." *Journal of Urban Economics* 30 (1991): 1–26.

MIESZKOWSKI, PETER, AND ARTHUR M. SAPER. "An Estimate of the Effects of Airport Noise on Property Values." *Journal of Urban Economics* 5 (1978): 425–440.

NELSON, JON P. "Residential Choice, Hedonic Prices, and the Demand for Urban Air Quality." *Journal of Urban Economics* 5 (1978): 357–369.

SIEGAN, BERNARD. *Land Use Without Zoning.* Lexington, MA: Lexington Books, 1972.

SMITH, BARTON A. "Measuring the Value of Urban Amenities." *Journal of Urban Economics* 5 (1978): 370–387.

SPEYER, JANET. "Effects of Land Use Restrictions on Single Family Housing in Houston." *Journal of Real Estate Finance and Economics* 2 (1989): 117–230.

VANDELL, KERRY D., AND JONATHAN S. LANE. "The Economics of Architecture and Urban Design: Some Preliminary Findings." *AREUEA Journal.* 17 (1989): 235–260.

WADDELL, PAUL, BRIAN J. L. BERRY, AND IRVING HOCH. "Residential Property Values in a Multinodal Urban Area: New Evidence on the Implicit Price of Location." *Journal of Real Estate Finance and Economics* 7 (1993): 117–141.

INDEX

A

Adjustable rate mortgage (ARM), 198
Age
  home ownership *vs.* renting and, 186–88
  household formation and, 183–84
  housing consumption patterns and, 217–22
Agglomeration
  benefits, 109–11
  defined, 170*n*
Agricultural value of land, 50
Air quality, property values and, 349
Alonso, William, 36
American Housing Survey (AHS), 4, 68–69, 217
Anchor stores, 139
Anglin, Paul, 232
Annual costs of homeownership, 202–6
Apartment rents, measurement of, 191–93
Archer, Wayne, 109
Arnott, R., 232
Asabere, Paul K., 350
Asset markets, 2, 6–10. *See also* Property markets
  long-term interest rates and, 13–15
Asset price of space, 2
  as determinant of construction levels, 7
Assets. *See* Real estate assets

B

Backward-looking expectations
  future house price estimates and, 251–54
  homeownership costs and, 204–5
Barro, Robert J., 177
Bartik, Timothy J., 173*n*
Benjamin, J., 139
Berenson, Stephen C., 192*n*
Berndt, Ernst R., 67*n*

Berry, B., 131
Berry, Brian J.L., 350
Boston
  central
    density/profitability in, 77–79
    redevelopment in, 86
  metropolitan area
    employment density in, 92–96
    forecasting shopping behavior in, 143–46
    forecasting single-family house prices in, 257–66
    hedonic price technique applied to, 68–70
    industrial decentralization in, 100–102
    local expenditure in 1990, 325–31
    office decentralization in, 102–5
    population density of, 61–65, 66
    redevelopment patterns in, 83–86
    retail census data for, 129–30
    retail location patterns in, 125–28
    subcenters/rents in, 118–20
Boyle, G., 139
Brokerage companies, construction data and, 273–74
Brueckner, Jan, 139
Building design, property values and, 350
Building Owners and Managers Association (BOMA), 276
Building permit data, 272
Bureau of Economic Analysis (BEA), 4
Bureau of Labor Statistics (BLS) rent indices, 192
Business cycle, national, 165–66
Business density gradient, 99

C

Capitalization, incidence of local taxes/services and, 342–44
Capital markets, 2, 6–10. *See also* Property markets
Capozza, Dennis R., 46*n*

Carlton, Dennis W., 172n, 175
Cawley, John H., Jr., 193
CB Commercial, 274, 285
 index, 288–89
Census of Retail Trade, 128
Central business districts (CBDs), 30
 origins of, 97–99
Central cities, declining financial viability of, 344–45
Clapp, John, 109
Commodity markets, 26, 35
Community stratification, income levels and, 331–34
Commuting. *See also* Employment decentralization, firm site selection and
 land-price gradient and, 320–21, 331
 rents and, 36–40, 360
Comparative static analysis, 11
Competition, Ricardian rents and, 42–46
Competitive effect, 167
Concessions, in leases, 287
Congestion externalities, 363–69
Construction. *See also* Development; Redevelopment
 asset prices and, 6–10
 cycles, stock of space and, 273–77
  data sources for, 273–74
 new
  evolution of housing stock and, 235–38
  financing, 270–71
  housing attributes and, 72–73
  housing vacancy and, 229–30
  of office and retail space, 269
  shift in supply schedule for, 15–18
  value of, in 1990, 3–4
Consumer Price Index (CPI), 192
Consumption, defined, 189
Contingent forecasting, 264, 293–94
 of Philadelphia industrial market, 314–17
 of San Francisco office market, 307–9
Continuous time discounting, 58–59
Cost of capital, homeownership costs and, 205
Counties, 319, 321
County Business Patterns survey, 279–80
Court, Andrew T., 67
Current location value, 50

D

Decentralization. *See* Employment decentralization, firm site selection and
Default risk, mortgages and, 201
Delivered price, 134
Demand equation, 259
Demand-induced regional growth, 159–62
Demolitions, 277
Density
 employment, 92–96
 urban
  changes in, 64–65
  development/redevelopment and, 81–86
  individual *vs.* cooperative decisions about, 354–57
  land-use succession and, 87–89
  location and, 79–81
  profitability and, 73–81
  variation in, 61–64
Density gradient, 63
Department of Housing and Urban Development (HUD), 200
Department stores, price coordination and, 139–40

Development
 externalities and. *See* Externalities
 of new land, 333–34
  zoning and, 334–41
 nonresidential, fiscal costs/benefits of, 338–41
 patterns of, 81–86
 profitability of, 73–81
 public amenities and
  free riders, 350–54
  property values, 349–50
 residential, fiscal impacts of, 334–37
 speculative, 270–73
Development regulation, 120–22, 359
 zoning, 334–41
Diminishing marginal utility, law of, 67, 70, 72
DiPasquale, Denise, 69n, 185, 193, 204n
Discounted value of depreciation deduction, 209
Discrete choice analysis, 140
Doeringer, Peter B., 169
Doolittle, Fred, 325
Dougherty, Ann, 205

E

Eberts, R.W., 108
Econometric analysis
 of industrial-space market in Philadelphia, 309–17
 of office space market in San Francisco, 294–309
Economic growth. *See* Regional economic growth
Economic Recovery Tax Act of 1981 (ERTA), 204, 208
Economies of scale, defined, 170n
Elasticity of housing demand, 217–19
Employee Retirement Income Security Act (ERISA), 1974, 20
Employment decentralization, firm site selection and
 central business district origins, 97–99
 industrial firms, 100–102
  production and storage technology, 100
  transportation technology, 100
 limitations/impediments of decentralization, 108, 109–22
  land-use regulation, 120–22
  subcenters, 109–21
 office firms, 102–8
 spatial distribution of jobs, 92–96
Employment density, 92
Endogenous variables, 2
Environment
 nonresidential development and, 338, 339–41
 quality of, 349–50
Environmental Protection Agency (EPA), 349
Epple, Dennis, 190
Equilibrium compensation theory, 36
Equilibrium rent gradient, 38, 39
Equilibrium rents, 38, 43
Exogenous forces, 2. *See also* National economy, real estate and
 labor supply and, 176
Exogenous price expectations, 247–51
Expenditures, defined, 189
Externalities
 congestion, 363–69
 defined, 348
 density, individual *vs.* cooperative decisions about, 354–57
 land-use patterns and, 360–63
 partial remedies for
  government incentives, 359
  government regulation, 358–59

Index

larger scale developments, 358
private bargaining with contracts, 357–58
property values and, 349–50
public amenities/free riders and, 350–54

F

Fabozzi, Frank J., 201
Factor substitution, 61
Federal government
    expenditures, 321–25
    real estate taxation and, 19
    regional economies and, 152–53
    revenue sources, 323–24
Federal Home Loan Mortgage Corporation (Freddie Mac), 200, 201
Federal Housing Administration (FHA), 200
Federal National Mortgage Association (Fannie Mae), 200, 201
Federal Reserve Board, 4, 5
Federal tax policy
    homeownership and, 202–6
    rental housing and, 206–11
Financial Institutions Reform, Recovery and Enforcement Act (FIRREA), 1989, 20
Financing homeownership. *See* Homeownership financing
FIRE (finance, insurance, real state) sector, 103, 270, 280
Firms, location decisions of, 91–122
    industrial firms, 91–102
    office-using firms, 102–8
    retail firms, 124–47
    spatial distribution of employment and, 92–96
    subcenters and, 109–22
Fiscal capitalization, theory of, 321, 342–44
Fixed-payment mortgage (FPM), 194–95
    ARM compared to, 198
    PLAM compared to, 195–98
Floor area ratio (FAR)
    redevelopment and, 83–86
    as residential density measure, 74–79
    residential zoning and, 336
Florida, regional economic accounts for, 151–54
Flow variables, 3
Follain, James R., 208
Ford, Deborah Ann, 350
Forecasting
    contingent, 264, 293–94
    of Philadelphia industrial market, 314–17
    of San Francisco office market, 294–309
    with stock-flow model, 257–66
    trend, 257
Forward-looking (rational) expectations
    homeownership costs and, 204
    of house prices, 254–56
Four-quadrant model, 6–10
    national economy and, 11–18
    owner-occupied model for, 10–11
Frech, H.E., III, 350
Free riders, public amenities and, 350–54
F.W. Dodge Company/McGraw-Hill, 273

G

Goddard, John B., 109
Gordon, P., 108
Government National Mortgage Association (Ginnie Mae), 200, 201
Greenwood, Michael J., 175

Grether, David M., 349
Gross domestic product (GDP)
    fluctuations in, 165
    real estate as percentage of, 1, 5
Gross rent, 286–87
Ground rent, 139
Grubaugh, Steven, 350

H

Hachey, George, 350
Harrison, David, 73
Haurin, Donald R., 190
Hazardous waste facilities
    impact on property values, 349
    siting decisions and, 341
Hedonic price
    equation, 67, 189
    indices, 189–90
Helseley, R., 111
Helsley, Robert W., 46n
Hendershott, Patric H., 190, 208, 209, 214
Henderson, J. Vernon, 169
History, land-use patterns and, 362
Hoch, Irving, 350
Homeowner's equity
    defined, 196
    FPM/PLAM and, 196–97
Homeownership financing
    annual costs and, 202–6
    federal tax policy and, 202–6
    inflation and, 197–98
    mortgage instruments and, 193–99
    U.S. mortgage market and, 199–202
Homeownership *vs.* renting. *See* Tenure choice
Household. *See also* Housing services, market for
    defined, 183
    formation, demand for housing units and, 183–86
    location, community stratification and, 331–34
    mobility rates, renting *vs.* owning and, 186
    preferences, housing attributes and, 65–72
Housing
    attributes, household preferences and, 65–72
    buyers, 233
    consumption
        income and, 217–19
        life cycle and, 220–22
    as heterogeneous good, 65–66
    market. *See* Urban housing markets
    mobility. *See* Housing mobility
    prices
        empirical evidence on, 56–57
        housing attributes and, 65–72, 189–90
        population growth and, 46
        sales time and, 227
        true price measurement, 189–93
    publicly assisted, 18–19
    rent, 39–40
        urban commuting and, 36–40
    sellers, 233–35
    units. *See* Housing units
    urban density and, 61–65
    vacancy. *See* Housing vacancy
Housing mobility
    housing demand and, 222–24
    process of, 230–35
    rates, renting/owning and, 186

Household mobility (*continued*)
  sales and, 224–27
  vacancy rates and, 224–27
Housing services market, 182–83, 216–38
  household consumption patterns
    age and, 217–22
    household mobility and, 222–24
    household size and, 221, 222
    income and, 217–19
    life cycle and, 220–22
    vacancy rate and, 224–35
Housing units. *See also* Homeownership financing
  household formation and demand for, 183–86
  market for, 182–211
  measuring prices of, 189–93
    hedonic price indices, 189–90
    repeat sales price indices, 191–93
  tenure choice and, 186–88
Housing vacancy
  benefit of, 227
  housing sales and, 224–27
  mobility and, 224–27
  model, for sales and prices, 230–35
  new construction and, 229–30
  sales time and, 225, 227–29
    house prices, 227
    rents, 227–29

I

Ihlanfeldt, K.R., 108
Income
  home ownership and, 186, 188
  housing consumption and, 217–19
Industrial mix, regional growth and, 166–69
Industrial property markets
  construction cycles and, 274–75
  employment decentralization and
    central business district origins, 97–99
    production and storage technology, 100–102
    subcenters, 109–22
    transportation technology, 100
  ownership of space in, 278
  in Philadelphia, 309–17
  space-consumption estimate, per worker, 282
  space users, by type of firm, 281–82
  spatial distribution of employment and, 92–96
  stock of space, industrial employment and, 283–84
  vacancies and, 277
Industrial technology, employment decentralization and, 100–102
Industry mix effect, 167
Inflation, homeownership financing and, 197–98
Infrastructure, 319, 323
  commercial development demands and, 338
Interdependent product demand, 138
Interest rates
  long-term, 13–15, 46
  lower, rents and, 11
Internal rate of return (IRR), 271–72
International Council of Shopping Centers, 4
Interregional migration, labor supply and, 175–76
IREM Foundation study (1991), 4–5

J

Joint purchase trips, 138

K

Kain, John, 73
Kohlhase, Janet E., 349
Krugman, Paul, 170
Kumar, A., 108

L

Labor market
  metropolitan economic growth and, 155, 156–58
  office-firm decentralization and, 104–8
  regional economic growth and. *See* Regional economic growth
  supply-induced regional growth and, 162–65
Labor-mobility definition, of local economy, 24–25
Ladd, Helen F., 325
Lafferty, Ronald N., 350
Land, 1, 3
  market, regional planning and, 363–69
  prices, urban, 46–56
  rent, urban, 36–40
  supply, Ricardian rents and, 40–42
  value, residential density and, 73–79
Land-price gradient, commuting and, 320–21
Land-use succession, 87–89
Lane, Jonathan S., 350
Lane, Walter F., 192*n*
Lease inflation indexation, 286
Lease steps, 286
Lease term, 285–86
Life cycle, housing consumption patterns and, 220–22
Ling, David C., 208, 209, 214
Linneman, Peter, 203, 214
Local governments
  central cities and, 344–45
  development regulation by, 19
    nonresidential, 338–41
    residential, 334–37
  expenditures by
    in metropolitan areas, 325–31
    in 1991, 321–25
  incidence of local taxes/services, capitalization and, 342–44
  property taxes and, 19–20, 324, 325–31
  public services and, 321–25
  real estate market and, 319–45
  revenue sources for, 323–24
  stratification by income levels and, 331–34
  subcenters and, 120–22
Localization economy, 170
Location
  decisions
    households. *See* Urban housing markets; Urban land market
    industrial firms, 97–102
    office-using firms, 102–8
    retail firms, 124–47
  theory. *See* Urban land and location theory
Long-term interest rates
  conversion of income into value and, 46
  demand for real estate assets and, 13–15

M

Macroeconomics, defined, 22. *See also* Real estate macroeconomics
Madden, J.F., 108

Index

Malls. *See* Shopping centers
Marginal tax rate, homeownership and, 203–4
Market competition. *See* Retail property markets
Metropolitan housing markets. *See also* Local governments; Urban housing markets
  behavior of individual parcels in, 26
  cyclical behavior of, 242–66
  economic growth and. *See* Regional economic growth
  50 largest U.S. metropolitan areas, 291
  principles governing behavior of, 33–34
  property taxes in, 325–31
  relative price shifts in, 29–30
  relative price stability in, 26, 28–29
  stock-flow model of, 243–46
    exogenous price expectations and, 247–51
    myopic price expectations and, 251–54
    rational price expectations and, 254–57
  urban land and location theory, 25–30
Metropolitan statistical areas (MSAs), property markets and, 24–25
Microeconomics, defined, 22. *See also* Real estate microeconomics
Mieszkowski, Peter, 349
Miles, Mike E., 4, 5*n*, 21
Mills, Edwin S., 36, 65
Minimum lot sizes (MLS), 334, 335–36
Mobility. *See* Housing mobility
Modigliani, Franco, 201
Monopolistic competition, defined, 170*n*
Mortgage-backed securities (MBS), 200–202
Mortgage default, 198
Mortgage market, 199–202
  primary, 199
  secondary, 199–202
Mortgages, 193–99
  adjustable rate (ARM), 198
  fixed-payment (FPM), 194–95
  guidelines for granting of, 194–95, 199–200
  price-level-adjusted (PLAM), 195–98
  risk and, 197–98, 201–2
  self-amortizing, 194
Mortgage tilt, 195
Moses, L.N., 104–5
Multicentered cities. *See* Subcenters, firm decentralization and
Multiplier models, 154–55
Municipalities, 319, 321
Muth, Richard F., 36
Myopic price expectations, 251–54

N

National business cycle, 165–66
National economy, real estate and, 11–18
  credit/costs/new space supply, 15–18
  economic growth, 11–13
  long-term interest rates, 13–15
Nations, distinguished from regions, 149, 150–51
Nelson, Jon P., 349
Neoclassical retailing
  department stores and price coordination, 139–40
  interdependent product demand, 138
  joint purchase trips, 137–38
  retail mix and center leases, 138–39
Net effective rent, 287
Net operating income, rental housing and, 207
Net proceeds from sale of building, 210

Net rent, 287
Net rental income, 209
New land development
  community stratification and, 333–34
  zoning and
    nonresidential, 338–41
    residential, 334–37
Noise pollution, property values and, 349. *See also* Externalities
Nominal wages, 175, 177
Nonresidential property markets
  construction cycles and stock of space, 273–77
  cost of space to users, 285–90, 287–88
    concessions, 287
    gross/net rent, 286–87
    lease inflation indexation, 286
    lease steps, 286
    lease terms, 285–86
    overage rent, 287
  location decisions. *See* Firms, location decisions of
  at macroeconomic level, 23, 269–90
  market conditions and real estate investment returns, 270–73
  at microeconomic level, 23–24
  nonresidential tax rates and, 329
  property demands in, 270
    ownership/occupancy and, 277–85
  zoning and, 338–41
Norton, R.D., 169

O

Office property markets, 102–8
  ownership of space in, 277–78
  in San Francisco, 294–309
  space-consumption estimate, per worker, 282
  space supply, cyclic nature of, 275–77
  space users
    by occupation, 278–79
    by type of industry, 278, 279–81
  spatial distribution of employment and, 92–96
  stock of space, office employment and, 285
  subcenters and, 109–22
  vacancies and, 276–77
  wages/office decentralization and, 102–8
Open space, property values and, 350. *See also* Development
Opportunity cost, homeownership costs and, 205
Output market, 155–56
Overage rent, 139, 287
Owner-occupied real estate, 10–11

P

Palmquist, Raymond B., 190
Pennsylvania, regional economic accounts for, 151–54
Permanent income, as predictor of housing consumption, 219
Philadelphia, market for industrial space in, 309–17
  construction/investment in industrial space, 313–14
  contingent forecasts of, 314–17
  industrial rents/vacancy, 313
  modeling space demand, 309–12
Pindyck, Robert S., 70*n*, 71*n*
Population
  density. *See* Urban housing markets
  growth, housing/land prices and, 46–56
  Ricardian rents and, 40–42
Prepayment risk, mortgages and, 201
Present discounted value (PDV) 49
Price, defined, 189

Price-determination equation, 259
Price elastic demand, 29, 35
Price inelastic supply, 35
Price-level-adjusted mortgage (PLAM), 195–98
Prices
 asset, construction and, 6–10
 housing, 46, 56–57, 65–72, 189–93, 227, 254–56
  exogenous expectations of, 247–51
  myopic expectations of, 251–54
  rational expectations of, 254–56
 property
  relative stability of, 26, 28–29
  sources of shifts in, 29–30
 transaction, 235
 urban land, 46–56
Primary mortgage market, 199
Private real estate, 2
Product cycle theory, regional growth and, 169–74
Product-differentiated markets, 25, 35
 patterns of behavior in, 26
Production technologies, firm site selection and, 91–92, 100
Profitability of development, residential density and, 73–81
Property markets, 2, 6–10. *See also* specific markets
 geographical areas and, 24–25
 macroeconomics and, 22, 23, 31–34
 microeconomics and, 22–23, 25–30, 34
 property types and, 23–24
Property prices
 relative stability of, 26, 28–29
 sources of shifts in, 29–30
Property taxes, 324–31
 nonresidential, 329
 nonresidential development and, 338–41
 residential rate of, determining, 330
 residential zoning and, 334–37
Property values, public amenities and, 349–50
Public amenities
 free riders and, 350–54
 property values and, 349–50
Public goods
 environmental quality and, 349–50
 externalities and, 348–49
 open space acquisition and, 350
Publicly assisted housing, 18–20
Public policy, real estate markets and, 18–20
 local government development regulations, 19, 334–41
 publicly assisted housing, 18–19
 real estate financial institutions/regulations, 20
 tax policy, 19–20
Public real estate, 2. *See also* Public policy, real estate markets and
Public services, 319
 federal/state/local
  expenditures, 321–25
  revenue sources, 323–25
 nonresidential demand on, 338
 residential development and, 335

Q

Quality-controlled house price, 189, 192–93
Quality of life, economic issues in, 348–49
Quigley, John M., 219

R

Randolph, William C., 192n
Rational price expectations, 254–56

Read, Colin, 232
Real estate
 cost of living and, 179
 defined, 1
 flow, 3
 GDP and, 1
 investment returns to, 270–73
 markets, 2, 6–10, 155, 156, 157–58. *See also* specific markets
  local governments and, 319–45
  public policy and, 18–20
 national economy and, 11–18
 owner-occupied, 10–11
 ownership of, 5, 6
 size/character of, 2–5
 space, 1, 2
 taxation of, 19–20
 use, economic growth and, 11–13
 valuing, difficulties in, 4–5
Real estate assets, 1, 2
 long-term interest rates and, 13
 lower interest rates and, 11
 markets for, 6–10
Real estate macroeconomics, 22, 23
 cyclical aspects, 242–66
 econometric analyses, 293–317
 economic growth, 149–79
 housing services market, 216–38
 housing units market, 182–212
 market growth and dynamics, 31–34
 nonresidential property markets, 269–90
 objective of, 32
Real estate microeconomics, 22–23
 firm site selection, 91–122
 retail location/market competition, 124–47
 urban housing markets, 60–89
 urban land and location theory, 25–30
  behavior of individual parcels, 26
  metropolitan areas, 24–25
  relative price shifts, 29–30
  relative property price stability, 28–29
 urban land markets, 35–57
Real estate use
 economic growth and demand for, 11–13
 markets for, 6–10
Redevelopment
 occupancy/land-use succession and, 87–89
 patterns of, 83–86
Rees, J., 169
Regional economic growth, 175
 demand-induced, 159–62
 labor supply and, 175–77
 regional competition and, 177–78
 regional economies, 150–55
 regional exports and product demand shifts, 165–75
  industrial mix, 166–69
  national business cycle, 165–66
  product cycle, 169–74
  regional demand, government and, 175
 supply-induced regional growth, 162–65
 three-sector model, 155–59
Regional exports, product demand shifts and, 165–75
Regional planning, congestion externalities and, 363–69
Regions, nations distinguished from, 149, 150–51
Regulation. *See* Development regulation
Relative effective wage, 175, 177
Rental housing, federal tax policy and, 206–11

Index

Rental property capitalization rate, 209
Renting vs. home ownership, 186–88
Rents
  apartment, measurement of, 191–93
  base, 287
  as determinant of asset demand, 6–10
  equilibrium, 38, 43
  in greater Boston, 118–20
  gross, 286–87
  ground, 139, 287
  leases and, 285–90
  location, 61, 331
  net, 287
  net effective, 287
  overage, 139, 287
  quality-controlled, 192–93
  Ricardian. *See* Ricardian rents
  sales time and, 227–29
  total consideration, 287
  urban housing and, 36–38
  urban land, 38–39
Repeat sales price indices, 191–93
Reservation price, 235
Residential property markets. *See also* Metropolitan housing markets; Nonresidential property markets; Urban housing markets
  at macroeconomic level, 23
  at microeconomic level, 23–24
Residential real estate. *See also* specific markets
  development, fiscal impacts of, 334–37
  value of, 4–5
Restrictive covenants, 349
Retail competition
  classical theory, 133–37
    delivered price, 134
    entry and store density, 136–37
    market area boundary, 135
    objective of, 133
    price determination, 135–36
  computer models for, 140–43
  neoclassical retailing, 137–40
    department stores and price coordination, 139–40
    interdependent product demand, 138
    joint purchase trips, 137–38
    retail mix and center leases, 138–39
Retail property markets, 124–47
  classical retail competition theory, 133–37
  construction movements, 275
  goods and shopping frequency, 132–33
  location decisions in
    store frequency and consumer shopping behavior, 128–31
  location patterns, 125–28
  markets and retail sales, 146–47
  neoclassical retailing, 137–40
  shopping behavior forecasts and, 143–46
  shopping center attraction, computer models for, 140–43
  tenancy/ownership patterns, 281
Ricardian rents, 36
  competition/spatial separation and, 42–46
  housing/land prices and, 46–56
  population/land supply and, 40–42
  urban commuting and, 36–40
Ricardo, David, 36
Richardson, H., 108

Risk
  housing sales and, 224–25
  mortgages and, 197–98, 201–2
  in nonresidential property markets, 269–70
Rosen, Harvey S., 188
Rosen, Kenneth T., 188
Rubinfeld, Daniel L., 70, 71n

S

Sala-i-Martin, Xavier, 177
Sales rate, 225
Sales time, 225, 227–29
  house prices and, 227
  new construction and, 229–30
  rents and, 227–29
San Francisco, market for office space in, 294–309
  contingent forecasts of, 307–9
  forecasting demand, 295–98
  forecasting supply, 304–7
  vacancy and movement in office rents, 298–303
Saper, Arthur M., 349
Schmenner, Roger W., 175
School districts, 321
Scrappage, 277
Secondary mortgage market, 199–201
Self-amortizing mortgage, 194
Shift-share analysis, 167
Shopping centers
  retail competition and, 137–40
    computer models for, 140–43
    department stores and price coordination, 139–40
    interdependent product demand, 138
    joint purchase trips, 137–38
    retail mix and center leases, 138–39
Shopping frequency, goods and, 132–33
Siegan, Bernard, 358
Sirmans, C.F., 139
Sivitanidou, Rena, 121
Smith, Barton A., 349
Social choice, free riders and, 352
Somerville, C. Tsuriel, 69n, 193
Spatial distribution of employment, 92–96
  retail firms, 125–28
Spatial separation, Ricardian rents and, 42–46
Special districts, 319, 321
Speculative development, 270–73
Speyer, Janet, 358
Stahl, K., 138
Standard Industrial Classification (SIC), 125, 128, 167, 279
State governments
  expenditures by, 321–25
  revenue sources, 323–24
Step increases, leases and, 286
Stock-flow model of housing market
  forecasting with, 257–66
  market dynamics and
    with exogenous price expectations, 247–51
    with myopic price expectations, 251–54
    with rational price expectations, 254–56
Stock variables, 3
Storage technology, job decentralization and, 100
Store frequency, consumer shopping behavior and, 128–31
Straight-line method, for depreciation deduction, 207
Structural vacancy rate, 227

Subcenters, firm decentralization and
  agglomeration benefits, 109–11
  land-use regulation, 120–22
  rents in greater Boston, 118–20
  wages/land market, 111–18
Sullivan, A., 111
Supply-induced regional growth, 162–65
Surveys, of retail establishments, 128–31

T

Taxes. *See* Local governments; Property taxes
Tax incidence question, 342–44
Tax life of buildings, 207
Tax Reform Act (1986), 204, 208, 211
Technology
  retailing and, 147
  storage, 100
  telecommunication, 92
  transportation, 100
Tenure choice, 186–88
  age and, 186–88
  federal tax policy and
    homeownership costs, 202–6
    rental housing, 206–11
  homeownership financing and, 193–202
  household mobility rates and, 186
  income and, 186, 188
  price of housing and, 189–93
    hedonic price indices, 189–90
    repeat sales price indices, 191–93
Terkla, David G., 169
Thorngren, B., 109
Three-sector model, of metropolitan economic growth, 155–59
Total consideration, lease terms and, 287
Total patronage, 142–43
Towns/townships, 319, 321
Transaction costs, 235
  renting *vs.* homeownership and, 186, 224
Transfer programs, 322, 323
Transportation system
  creation of CBDs and, 97–99
  evolution of, 100
Trend forecasting, 257
Truck transportation, 92
True market price, 66, 189–93

U

Urban housing markets, 60–89. *See also* Housing mobility; Housing services market; Housing units; Metropolitan housing markets
  density, 61–65
    highest/best use and, 73–79
    location and, 79–81
  development/redevelopment, 81–86
    occupancy/land use succession and, 87–89
  housing attributes
    household preferences and, 65–72
    new construction and, 72–73
Urbanization economy, defined, 170n
Urban land and location theory, 25–30
Urban land market, 35–57
  with central business district, 97–99
  Ricardian rents
    competition/spatial separation and, 42–46
    growth/rents/prices and, 46–56
    population/land supply and, 40–42
    urban commuting and, 36–40
U.S. Census Bureau, 24

V

Vacancy. *See* Housing vacancy
Valuation process for housing, household preferences in, 65–72
Van Order, Robert, 205
Vandell, Kerry D., 350

W

Wachter, Susan M., 203, 214
Waddell, Paul, 350
Wages
  cost of living and, 179
  nominal, 175
  office-firm decentralization and, 104–8
  regional competition and, 177–80
Wasylenko, M., 121, 123
Wheaton, William C., 46n, 59, 185
White, Michele, 108
Wolinsky, A., 139, 148
Work out arrangement, 271

Y

Yinger, John, 232

Z

Zoning
  nonresidential, 338–41
  residential, 334–38